THE BALKAN RECONQUISTA AND TURKEY'S FORGOTTEN REFUGEE CRISIS

THE BALKAN RECONQUISTA *and* TURKEY'S FORGOTTEN REFUGEE CRISIS

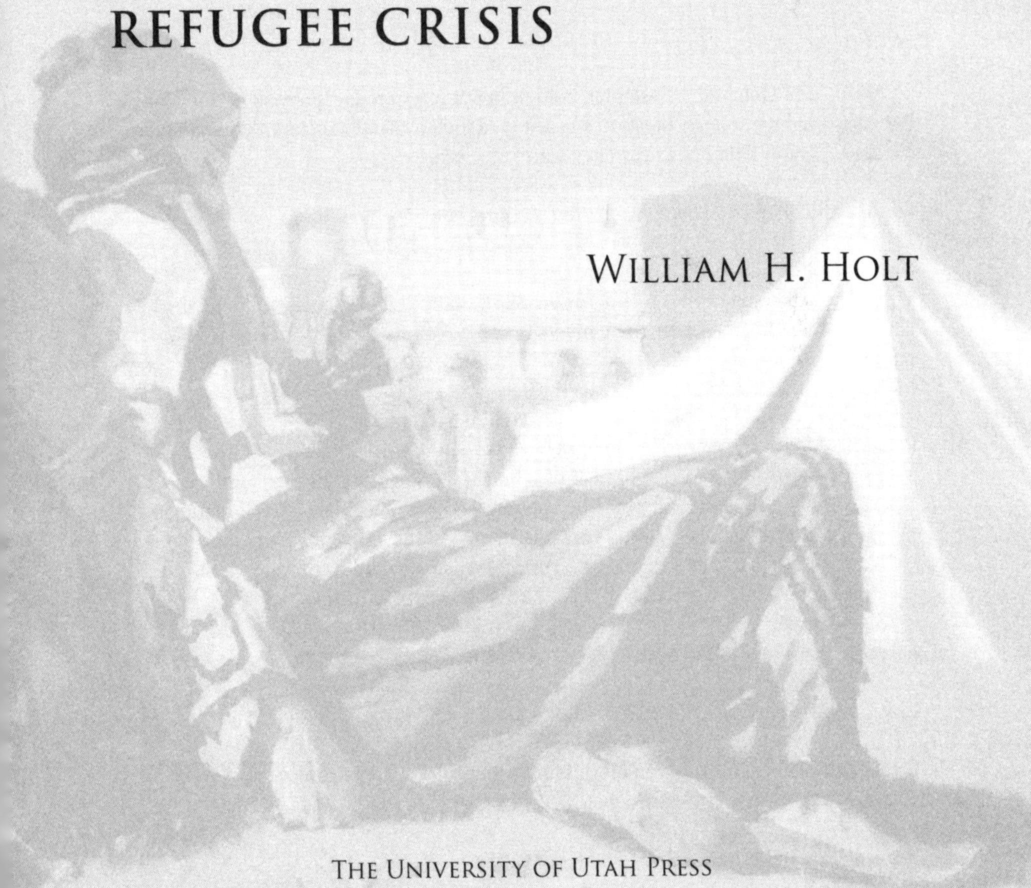

WILLIAM H. HOLT

THE UNIVERSITY OF UTAH PRESS
Salt Lake City

The Defiance House Man colophon is a registered trademark of The University of Utah Press. It is based on a four-foot-tall Ancient Puebloan pictograph (late PIII) near Glen Canyon, Utah.

Library of Congress Cataloging-in-Publication Data

Names: Holt, William H., 1979- author.
Title: The Balkan reconquista and Turkey's Forgotten Refugee Crisis/William H. Holt.
Description: Salt Lake City : The University of Utah Press, [2019] | Includes bibliographical references index.
Identifiers: LCCN 2018051870 (print) | LCCN 2018053846 (ebook) | ISBN 9781607816966 () | ISBN 9781607816959 (cloth : alk. paper)
Subjects: LCSH: Russo-Turkish War, 1877-1878—Atrocities. | Muslims—Crimes against—Balkan Peninsula. | Muslims—Balkan Peninsula—History—19th century. | Muslims—Turkey—History—19th century. | Balkan Peninsula—Emigration and immigration—History—19th century. | Turkey—Emigration and immigration—History—19th century. | Refugees—Turkey—History—19th century.
Classification: LCC DR573 (ebook) | LCC DR573 .H73 2019 (print) | DDC 949.6 /0387—dc23
LC record available at https://lccn.loc.gov/2018051870

Cover image courtesy Damien Peronnet / Art Digital Studio © Sotheby's.

Errata and further information on this and other titles available online at UofUpress.com.

Printed and bound in the United States of America.

for ADRIAN C. S. SAUNDERS (1958–2017)

CONTENTS

FIGURES

ACKNOWLEDGMENTS

The process of creating this work turned out to be fascinating, frustrating, and ultimately very rewarding. Many people throughout this project have assisted me. I must acknowledge the special help and direction offered by Dr. M. Hakan Yavuz, who gave me the initial nudge in the direction of ethnic violence in the Balkans at the end of the Ottoman Empire for a research topic. Throughout the research I have met with several individuals who demonstrated by their generous willingness to share information and sources that for them scholarship is more than a profession: it is a vocation. I specifically would like to thank Sinan Kuneralp, Rossitsa Gradeva, and Hakan Yavuz, whose willingness to put me in contact with the right people, to help me obtain documents, and to offer suggestions and critiques was an indispensable part of the project. I am grateful to Alexandre Toumarkine and Nedim İpek for granting me interviews and suggesting directions for research. I would also like to thank Erika Daines, Peter Daniels, John Francis, Gary Gillespie, Kathy Lewis, Robert Lorimer, Carolina Orphanidou, Tetsuya Sahara, Pam Sezgin, Peter von Sivers, Kaye Summers, Fabio Vicini, and David Wilson for their suggestions, proofreading, and encouragement and Erika Daines again for her help with German texts. All translations from foreign-language sources are mine unless otherwise noted. Finally, I am very grateful for the financial support offered to me by the Turkish Coalition of America through its generous grant to the Turkish Studies Project at the University of Utah. As with any such work, ultimate responsibility lies with me.

INTRODUCTION

While only a small portion of Turkey today lies in Europe, this small piece of land is like the tip of an iceberg—a visible Muslim tip with a much bigger part submerged in the waters of Lethe. Turkey has roots in Europe that stretch deep in the Balkan Peninsula. Muslims in their multifarious Balkan forms herded their flocks through Balkan hills, planted rice on the banks of the blue Danube, and fished the waters of the western Black Sea. Centuries passed, and those hills, mountains, rivers, and sea were as much a part of the Ottoman Empire as the plateaus, hills, and rivulets of Anatolia.

But suddenly it ended. It ended with Muslims at the bottom of mass graves and immolated in mosques. It ended with tearful masses slowly moving through thick snow or exposed to fatal cold and tightly packed in open-air train cattle wagons destined for Istanbul. It ended with homeless Balkan Muslims huddled in Istanbul's celebrated mosques. And it ended with oblivion and forgetting: today we might lament, "If only those walls could speak!" Sorrow and suffering were followed by an abrupt amnesia. In addition to the hows and whys that would lead us to understand the causes and events of the massacres and migrations of Muslims from Bulgaria to Turkey in 1877–1878, it is no less important to ask why such events have been broadly dismissed from public memory. Many other societies seemingly hold fast to their memories, nurture them, and publicize them, even to the point of becoming in thrall to them, nurtured by them, and known for them.

One gray autumn day in Paris I was walking along a street in the Île de la Cité when a banal plaque on the wall of a building crossed my line of vision and caught my attention:

> Upon the occasion of the 60th anniversary of the liberation of Paris,
> Monsieur Jacques Chirac
> President of the Republic
> Unveiled this commemorative plaque
> August 25, 2004

The names of the prime minister, minister of the interior, mayor of Paris, and prefect of the police followed. What I found so curious about the plaque, which was for the most part rather unobtrusive, was that that it was a commemoration of a commemoration. Another city marker had already been standing just below it to explain the importance of that particular spot on that Parisian street. It was bumptious and redundant—absurdly redundant, in fact. Yet Paris is a city heavy with history, and this is literally true: all the bronze cast and marble chiseled for the numerous plaques, statues, and monuments throughout the city that unflinchingly remind passersby of events and figures from the city's past must certainly weigh tons!

It is almost impossible to go anywhere in the City of Lights without coming across some immortalization of a historic event or person. Commemorating a commemoration seemed superfluous to me, but the plaque also offers a good illustration of a state engaged in its own history making, even to the point of excess. A physical monument's primary function is more than aesthetic—it is mnemonic.[1] And the state is more often than not involved in either paying for or approving whatever monument sprouts up in its jurisdiction. Robert Musil may well be correct in writing, "The most striking thing about monuments is how little they are noticed. Nothing in the world is as invisible as a monument. Although they are erected to be seen, to draw attention to themselves, some substance seems to render them attention-proof."[2] Nonetheless, the effort to monumentalize, to memorialize, and to commemorate, whether successful or not, at the very least is revealing in regard to the wishes and choices of a community, a nation, or a state to portray itself through its past.

0.1. 2004 plaque commemorating the commemoration of the liberation of Paris in 1944. Photo by author.

But something else about the plaque was telling when I compared the ubiquity of such monuments in Paris to their relative scarcity in Istanbul—a city of no short historical pedigree. Co-capital of the Roman Empire, capital of the Byzantine Empire, its successor in the east, and the Ottoman Empire, its eventual usurper, Istanbul (formerly known as Constantinople) has witnessed more than its fair share of momentous yet unmonumentalized events.[3] Despite all the old edifices, someone not knowing any better and focusing solely on commemorative monuments might get the impression that the city is somehow young, with few of the heroes and events that so abound and redound in the French capital. Sure, statues of Mustafa Kemal Atatürk are in no short supply, but, besides that, the best bet for anyone really wanting to see the human form in bronze or marble would be to buy a ticket to the Istanbul Archaeology Museum tucked away in the grounds near Topkapı Palace, where Hellenic antiquaries proliferate. Otherwise, plaques and monuments, which tell passersby lapidarily and unabashedly what moment from the past they were built to echo, are not nearly as ubiquitous as in Paris.

An observant eye, however, will find fountains and mosques whose initial purpose was to commemorate. Yet their abstract design, coupled with an indecipherable Ottoman script, leaves their intended commemorative purpose unfulfilled in the present. They have, it appears, lost their mnemonic function and now serve only as ornaments to an already handsome city. We can imagine Turkish children playing by an Ottoman fountain who are as oblivious to the meaning of the Ottoman calligraphy adorning it as Arab Egyptian children are of the hieroglyphs chiseled into pharaonic ruins in the midst of their cities. Traditionally, sultans would seek to celebrate their reigns through the construction of imperial mosques, which would then bear their names. The mosque most famous to the world as the Blue Mosque is known to the Turks as Sultan Ahmet Camii, in honor of Ahmet I (1590–1617). The skyline of Istanbul is further punctuated by the minarets from Fatih Camii (named for Mehmet II, the Conqueror, 1432–1481), Süleymaniye Camii (for Suleiman the Magnificent, 1494–1566), Beyazıt Camii (for Beyazıt II, 1447–1512), and so on. Fortunate members of the royal family also might get their names adorned as mosque eponyms, whereas lesser grandees would hope to prolong the memory of their existence through the construction of elaborate domed tombs known as *türbe*s, found throughout Istanbul. But the Ottoman state, for the most part, was much less conscious of creating spaces of memory in its capital city than its European counterparts.

In Yeşilköy, which was once on the outskirts of Istanbul but has since been swallowed up in the megacity's urban sprawl and is now just another suburb, there once stood a hastily erected monument to the dead soldiers of the 1877–1878 Russo-Turkish War. Here Russia and the Ottoman Empire signed a peace treaty that initiated the end of Ottoman rule in the Balkans. With Russian troops within eyeshot of the city, the sultan lacked the courage to hold out for better terms, and the resulting Treaty of San Stefano was a humiliation for the Ottomans. The Russians wanted to build a monument to their victory straight away, but only in 1893 did they finally ask for and receive permission to erect an edifice to the Russian war dead. The remains of five thousand Russian soldiers buried in small, scattered cemeteries in the area were assembled in one location and the Russian monument at San Stefano was built. Three platforms with columns and arches, a tower topped by a Russian onion dome, and a finely decorated door underneath the figures of saints gave the monument a Byzantine feel. But today the monument is no more. Thirteen days after the proclamation of the First World War, the Ottoman government had the monument destroyed by explosives. This act was filmed and is now considered the first attempt at Turkish filmmaking.[4]

The Ottomans had seen the power of immortalizing events and individuals through statues. Sultan Abdülaziz II commissioned a sculpture of himself after viewing statues of rulers during his trip to Europe in 1867, although the final product was never shown to the Ottoman public. Ottoman diplomats and other important persons attended unveiling ceremonies for statues and plaques dedicated to Russian tsars in the Balkans, including the large statue in Sofia, Bulgaria, dedicated to Aleksandr II, the Liberator.[5] Although these representations had powerful effects on the Ottoman elites, they did not attempt to imitate them in their own public spaces.[6] The Ottoman Empire boasted virtually no figural representations as public monuments. Abdülhamid II had many public monuments built to glorify his reign, but these usually also served a dual utilitarian function such as fountain or clock tower. After the Young Turk revolution, a proposal to rehabilitate the important Ottoman reformer Mithat Paşa with a statue was objected to on the religious grounds that Islam shuns representation of humans in art and was thus rejected.[7] Only after

0.2. Russian monument at San Stefano. Public domain: Wikimedia Commons.

0.3. Bombing of San Stefano Russian monument. Public domain: Wikimedia Commons.

0.4. Destroyed San Stefano Russian monument. Public domain: Wikimedia Commons.

the First World War and the Turkish War of Independence did human statues and large monumental projects enter the urban landscape, with the aim of defining a new history in the minds of the people and thereby legitimizing the Republic.

The poses that statues throughout Paris strike make a clear appeal to pathos. Triumphant or sorrowful, theirs is a direct connection with passersby. Moreover, they seem to more fully integrate the width and breadth of the country's history, with the glaring exception that precious few statues of Napoleon Bonaparte exist in the French hexagon, outside of his only large memorial at Les Invalides—his tomb.[8] Coincidentally, most Ottoman sultans are memorialized in ornate domed tombs as well. Muslims may be disinclined to monumentalize historical events and personages using statuary and the human form, resulting in a tendency toward more abstract monumentalizing, which raises the question about Muslim memory: does it somehow differ from Western memory? Although this study does not attempt to answer that question directly, I do wish to point out that many of the Turks with whom I have discussed the topic refer to culture as an explanation for the way in which their society deals with the past. I will ultimately seek, and find, answers elsewhere, but it may be beneficial to keep in mind the ways in which our various societies promote memories.

The purpose of this study is to find the reasons not for remembering but rather for forgetting. I may be using the word "forgetting" a bit loosely. Normally one forgets something that one once knew or experienced. But what if one does not remember that which was not personally experienced? The idea that societies can remember moments from history may strike some as being self-evident, but that they choose to remember certain historical events at the expense of others may be less obvious. The whys reveal a great deal about those societies and the bonds that hold them together.

In the following pages I examine the expulsion of Muslims from Bulgaria during the Russo-Turkish War of 1877–1878 from three perspectives: ideas, action, and memory. Before the Muslims of southeastern Europe were expelled, an idea of ridding Europe of the Turks was imagined and discussed. Discourses justified it and encouraged action that would accomplish it. In western Europe, Russia, and the Balkans these discourses all evolved within their own contexts. But the frenzy that resulted from the reports about the Bulgarian Horrors was buttressed by these very ideas of Muslim expulsion that had been simmering for centuries.

The actual practice of expelling Muslims from Europe had a real human impact. After Russia crossed the Danube in the summer of 1877 on the pretext of liberating Slavic kin from the Ottoman yoke, a torrent of violence followed. As word spread about the violence committed by Russian troops, Cossacks, and Bulgarians, the Muslims were faced with the difficult choice of abandoning the only home they had ever known in search of safety from imminent danger. The road to Istanbul became littered with Muslim corpses and smoldering villages as the Turks fell victim to a cold winter and the cruelty inspired by hatred and greed. The peril was not yet behind the refugees upon their arrival in the empire's capital, as hunger, cold, and disease menaced and took a heavy toll.

The memory of these events, though, did not much survive the first generation. This study poses the question of why this episode of Turkish history has been forgotten, given that other societies not only do not forget their sufferings but craft from them the very centerpiece of their identity.

The region and its history and peoples might not be altogether familiar to readers. Moreover, we are in essence dropping in, as it were, midway through a fairly complex chess match. In chapter 1 I identify not only who the pieces on the board are but how and why they got there. History is never static, though nationalist narratives would have us believe in the timelessness of nations. Migration, however, is a fact of human existence, albeit with changed impetus and means in the modern world. The Ottoman Empire was diverse, and it is important to explore that diversity before undertaking an examination of the big changes that would eventually occur. I also examine how all of these varied communities existed under one authority and how they related to one another.

The Muslims have tended to get short shrift in Balkan histories, usually dismissed as despotic administrators or summed up as shallow-rooted and small in number. I demonstrate here that the Muslim presence in the Bulgarian provinces was not only real but large and deeply rooted. Moreover, it was far from monolithic. My discussion also brings to light some of the ways in which Muslims in Ottoman Bulgaria were heterogeneous as a community. I attempt to understand the relationship, for good and for bad, that existed between the Muslims and the Christians in Ottoman Bulgaria. Finally, I show the path that Bulgarian nationalism took toward independence.

In chapter 2 I describe the events that led to the declaration of war, more specifically the April Uprising of Bulgarians, the suppression of the revolt by the Ottomans, dubbed the "Bulgarian Horrors," and the debates that raged across Europe as a result. I frame these debates within the development of European discourses about the Ottoman Turks. These discourses, which can be filed under the categories of Orientalism and Turkophobia, had special meaning in a Russian context, where the emerging Russian superpower was increasingly disgruntled by its relationship with Europe. Russia became enamored with the idea of controlling the gateway from the Black Sea to the Mediterranean with its jewel, Constantinople, a city loftily fixed in the firmament of Russian imagination. I also examine how the European discourses of Orientalism and Turkophobia were translated to a Balkan context, where the development of a "Catastrophe Theory" meant that Balkan elites had come to blame all negative aspects of life on Turkish rule. When this filtered to the masses, vengeance and greed paved the road for the expulsion of the Muslims from Europe.

In chapter 3 I document the violence against Muslims committed by Bulgarians, Russians, and Cossacks that accompanied the Russian crossing of the Danube and how these events precipitated massive flight by the Muslim population. The incidences of violence greatly resembled the type of actions that would later fall under the rubric of "ethnic cleansing." I provide evidence to apportion blame, in terms of willful negligence, incompetence, and intermittent participation on the part of the Russians as well as incitement and direct involvement of the Cossacks and Bulgarians. Moreover, I show that the violence was systematic, repetitive, and on a colossal scale. I conclude with a brief reflection on the meaning and relationship of nationalism and violence, especially in a post Ottoman context.

In chapter 4 I examine the refugee crisis that resulted from the violence and deeply affected Istanbul as well as other parts of the empire. Flight was perilous and deadly in unforgiving winter conditions. After the refugees arrived in Constantinople, disease raged, a coup threatened, and their presence brought the totality of the defeat to the empire's attention. The city's public and religious buildings were turned into makeshift refugee shelters. I show how the state coped with the refugee crisis and how it ultimately settled and assimilated the erstwhile Muslims of the Danube and Rumelia into the newly designated homeland of the Turks—Anatolia.

In chapter 5 I analyze the factors that affected the memory of society vis-à-vis the suffering of these Muslims. The title of the book may sound curious to some. However, the expulsion of Muslims from the Balkans summons a Spanish ghost: a memory of the expulsion of Muslims from Iberia. I entertain their semblances from one peninsula to the other and how both fit into a larger narrative of Islam's relations with Europe. My discussion also includes comparisons of trauma and memory from the Jewish, Armenian, and Palestinian experiences. Each of these groups has developed a strong identity and memory based on its respective tragedy. Through an investigation of pertinent sociopolitical factors, I offer conclusions about the fate of memory and forgetting in this particular case. I also delve into how memory is changing in Turkey today. As a result, we should expect to see an increasing awareness of the suffering of Muslims in the Ottoman Balkans, a change that may be a harbinger of a revanchist-type of foreign policy in the future.

Over the course of my research I have been made aware of how much this subject can excite the passions of nationals from the Balkans or indeed in many parts of the former Ottoman Empire. Much of the scholarship is classified as being pro-Turk or anti-Turk. However, it has become clear to me that the label "pro-Turk" is not intended as a euphemism in an academic context; rather, it is meant as a warning label. Works deemed to be "pro-Turk" should be, for some reason, studied with a massive dose of suspicion.

While nationalist passions can easily be an obstacle to good scholarship, sympathy for the researchers' subject should not necessarily be seen negatively as long as one presents the information to the best of one's ability. Objectivity should of course be the goal, but it is always more of an ideal than an attainable reality. The very choice of a subject for research is subjective, so my decision to investigate the plight and memory of Muslim refugees from Bulgaria inevitably influences which sources I avail myself of, which questions I ask, and which avenues I travel. I have sympathies for Turkey, Russia, and Bulgaria. I have spent significant time in each country and have made good friends in each as well. I have tried to write a narrative that will be accessible to a general readership, with information that should also be new and important for specialists. The subject matter is not a happy one, but I hope to add something to a conversation about Islamophobia and Turkophobia, ethnic violence, and memory in the Balkans, Turkey, and beyond.

A note on place-names: as boundaries have shifted over time, a number of names have accrued to certain locations. As I searched for these places on maps myself, I have come to the conclusion that the most convenient option is to use the place-name that is officially used in the country where it is found today, although some villages mentioned cannot be found and are left in the names from the documents. A chart of the other pertinent options is included in the appendix. The only exception is Istanbul, which is a city too grand for one name alone.

In citations of translations, the author's name is spelled as it is spelled in that particular edition.

One

TWILIGHT IN TURKEY-IN-EUROPE

> I asked her, why across your cheeks,
> So disordered roam your tresses?
> It is Rumeli, she replied,
> Where high starred heroes gallop.
>
> Mehmet the Conqueror (quoted in David Nicolle, *Cross and Crescent in the Balkans*)

> If there is a river in the soul of a Turk, it is the Danube;
> if there is a mountain, it is the Balkan mountain.
>
> Yahya Kemal (quoted in Ebru Boyar, *Ottomans, Turks and the Balkans*)

Rudyard Kipling is famous for his exploration in prose and poetry of the frontier of East and West. For Kipling, the frontier was fixed, unbridgeable: "never the twain shall meet," as he famously wrote.[1] But using terms such as "Occident" and "Orient" begs us to trace their boundaries. Just where do the ends of West and East meet? Where exactly do Orient and Occident begin? This is still an unsettled matter among intellectuals, politicians, and the mass media. To complicate matters further, we might consider the "when" when asking the question. That is to say, shifting frontiers and movements of people have meant that this question cannot be answered with a straightforward reply. For example, we might be surprised to read in Bram Stoker's *Dracula* the mention of an indelible boundary, "the Great River into Turkeyland," marking the end of European civilization as then known and the beginning of a dark and menacing elsewhere.[2] This line that for centuries had marked Europe's margin was the Danube River, and the elsewhere was the Turkish-ruled Ottoman Empire. In the preceding millennium that same boundary, the Danube River, also demarcated the civilized Roman world from the barbarian other. However, civilized Europe and the barbarian other switched banks—a paradox that proves the point: borders are social as much as physical constructs.

The Ottoman border developed with the push-and-pull of time. The Turks' failure to capture Vienna and their eventual defeat at Hungarian hands eventually pushed them back to a more natural frontier, the Danube, which became an established boundary marker. As soon as the Turks reached the Danube in the fourteenth century, they built fortifications on its southern bank and created a fleet to defend against threats from the north, which was followed by Muslim settlement.

The Danube was the Ottomans' northern border, the very same "Blue Danube" celebrated by Johann Strauss (1866):

> Danube so blue
> so bright and blue . . .
> you merry the heart
> with your beautiful shores . . .
> the mermaids from the riverbed
> whisper as you flow by
> and heard by all
> under the blue sky.[3]

This waltz nurtured the idea of a thoroughly European river in the Western mind. Yet, had Strauss sailed downstream (past the mermaids), he might very well have seen Turkish farmers cultivating rice on its right bank.

Ottoman rule straddled three continents. Its great rivers, like arteries that pulsed through the empire's limbs, illustrated that fact—the Nile in Africa, the Tigris and Euphrates in Asia, and the Danube in Europe. The Turks had a deep attachment to the Danube. It was symbolic of a Turkey-in-Europe and was the Ottoman waterway in the north, bringing together the empire's territories in southeastern Europe. A border, but not a barrier, the Danube facilitated the flow of people up, down, and across, resulting in religiously and ethnically diverse settlements downstream.[4]

The European realms of the Ottoman Empire were something of a mystery for contemporary Europeans—laden with forests and pleated with formidable mountain ranges, populated by diverse peoples of varied religions and languages, who were often seen as savage and uncivilized by Europeans. The Balkans were unquestionably foreign lands, albeit situated in Europe. But Ottoman Europe, perhaps more than any other place (despite Kipling's dictum), was the point where East and West did meet and mingle. Muslims, Christians, and Jews shared this territory, where churches, mosques, and synagogues were commonplace. Monks and dervishes promoted Christian and Islamic mysticism, and shrines of both religions welcomed pilgrims. Goods passed through the Balkan corridor from the Silk Road to Europe as Muslim, Jewish, and Christian traders engaged in commerce.

Multitudinous languages were spoken throughout the provinces. Centuries of an amalgamated existence led not only to vocabulary borrowings but even to common grammatical patterns labeled as the Balkansprachbund.[5] Melodies traversed ethnic boundaries: today's opposing national claims to Balkan songs are Ottoman echoes of deeper commonalities that could only have come about through exchange and sharing.[6]

While large swaths of this region had been part of the same polity in previous centuries—under the Roman Empire, the Byzantine Empire, the First Bulgarian Empire, and the Serbian Empire—the Ottoman Turks held sway last and longest. From the fourteenth century to the nineteenth century, the Turks were the sultans of southeast Europe.

Just as the Ottoman sun was rising on the eastern horizon of Europe, the Andalusian sun was setting in the west, over the previous melting pot of Islamo-Judeo-Christian civilizations, Moorish Spain. Toledo was lost in 1085, Córdoba fell in 1236, and Seville followed in 1248. By 1252 only Granada remained as a weak vestige of a once-formidable and refined Islamo-Iberian empire. In the East the Ottomans took Bursa in 1324 and Salonika (Thessaloniki) in 1387. They defeated the Serbs in Kosovo in 1389 and smashed the last crusade in the Battle of Nicopolis (Nikopol) in 1396. Constantinople, the second Rome and one of the five holy cities of Christendom,[7] and a few outlying provinces were all that remained of the Byzantine Empire. In the fifteenth century Byzantium and Andalusia would both be laid to rest. The Ottomans took Constantinople in 1453, and the Spanish took Granada in 1492. Chapter 5 returns to the fate of Andalusia, which foreshadowed the demise of the Muslims in the Balkans.

The subdued Christians of the Balkans were to become an indispensable part of the Ottoman Empire, especially in its early years. The conquering Turks developed systems of autonomy and rule that allowed for the coexistence of the varied religions of the empire. In contrast, the burgeoning Spanish Empire on the other side of Europe chose, for the most part, a different path to deal with its non-Christian subjects: a concatenation of forced conversions, the Inquisition, rejection of the conversions as authentic, and ultimately expulsion of the remaining Muslims. The Muslims of the Balkans would later face similar coercions as the shrinking Ottoman Empire left its former Muslim citizens vulnerable to violence at the hands of the new overlords. The fate of the Ottoman Muslims of the Balkans is not widely known, even among Muslims today. To understand what happened, we need a better appreciation of the edifice that existed before the collapse.

THE LAST MINARET OF SOFIA

Western travelers in the cities of Bulgaria before 1877 often noted (and not without a bit of scorn) their "oriental" qualities. Narrow winding streets with delicate wooden homes, public fountains, camels, caravansaries, bazaars, hammams, and solitary cemeteries topped with turbaned tombstones were all part of the topography typical of Bulgaria before its independence. And yes, mosques too: loads of them. The seemingly numberless minarets pointing heavenward were a prominent feature of Balkan skylines. In 1877 Russian imperial commissar Aleksandr Mikhailovich Dondukov-Korsakov described Sofia as a "forest of minarets."[8] The area that is now Bulgaria had over 2,300 mosques, and its present-day capital Sofia alone contained forty-five mosques on the eve of the birth of the Bulgarian nation-state. The Rose Mosque and the Black Mosque mingled in the city skyline with the Great Mosque, Siyavuş Mosque, Kafenebaşı Mosque, and many others to endow the city with a Muslim character.

All of these architectural components testified to the presence of a Muslim community and the attendant Muslim quotidian life extending backward for centuries. The fountains, engraved with the stylized Arabic script of the Quran, provided water to the population; the markets buzzed with chatter in a cacophony of languages; and the minarets marked the passing of time as the call to prayer was issued in the singsong Azan five times each day.

The Ottomans ruled Bulgaria from the late fourteenth century on, but (and this requires emphasis) their rule was characterized by much more than just administrators collecting tribute. There ordinary people, as Muslims, developed a certain way of life over the centuries. These customs set deep roots in the Balkan soil. Weddings, births, and funerals; prayers, Ramadan fasting, Bayram (Eid) feasting, and Iftar fast breaking; circumcisions; harvests, feasts, and celebrations all marked the passing of days, months, and generations. Yet all this would abruptly be uprooted.

One night during a thunderstorm in December 1878 the Russian commissar called an assistant and directed him, "Go immediately to the city with six electricians from the engineering regiment. They are waiting for you. Make sure that lightning strikes the minarets. The pioneers have already taken the dynamite.... Understood?"[9] That night seven mosques were detonated under the cover of bellowing thunder. The destruction of mosques was widespread throughout the country. In Sofia some mosques were converted or reconverted into churches, while others became museums, granaries, hospitals, and printing presses, but most were reduced to rubble or demolished under the convenient guise of "city planning."[10] Of all the mosques that once adorned the Bulgarian capital, today only the Banyabaşı Mosque still functions as such—its one minaret the sole survivor from an entire forest. The final minaret of a formerly sylvan Sofia evokes some lines from a Nazim Hikmet poem:

> With a gallop from distant Asia,
> Like a mare's head stretching towards the Mediterranean,
> This land is our homeland . . .
>
> . . .

1.1. Last minaret of Sofia (2010). Photo by author.

Wrists bloody, teeth clenched, feet bare,
Soil like a silk carpet,
  This hell is our heaven . . .
. . .
To live like a tree! Standing alone and free,
Brotherly, as in a forest,
  This is our longing . . . [11]

The destruction of Bulgaria's mosques and other Muslim architectural heritage is analogous to the devastation of Bulgaria's Muslim people. The war that brought an end to Ottoman rule triggered the massacre, mass flight, and emigration of the majority of the Muslim population. Not only was Ottoman Muslim rule terminated and the Muslim population forcibly removed, but the monuments of their civilization were also liquidated. While old maps may show Ottoman borders extending deep into the Balkans, it is often difficult to understand how those borders translated into human terms. Nowadays someone could easily spend a day, a week, a year, or even a lifetime in Sofia and never fully grasp that this city had a previous life as a Muslim town, with all that would entail. In order to treat the ensuing events and their impacts properly, it is imperative to establish certain facts.

First of all, there was a real Muslim presence in Bulgaria, and this presence was large for most of the duration of Ottoman rule: over a third of the population was Muslim. At its peak Muslims accounted for nearly half of the region's entire population. This was not simply a coterie of Muslim Ottoman officials subjugating the somnolent Bulgarian nation.

Second, this population was deeply rooted in the Balkan soil and not, as some would posit, a skittish bunch whose flight can be explained away by nomads' flimsy attachment to territory.

Third, this Muslim presence was diverse. Ethnic, linguistic, economic, and religious differences meant that Muslims in preindependence Bulgaria (known then by the Ottomans as the Rumelian and Danubian Provinces) had a wide range of experiences and lifestyles. The collective retribution meted out to them ignored this very important fact, causing suffering among Muslims with no connection whatsoever to the real or imagined feckless and cruel Ottoman administration.

The Ottoman imperial *millet* system encouraged identification and association along religious lines. This did not erase the diversity within these religious groupings, however, but allowed for substantial autonomy of the subordinate non-Muslim groups, with no attempt to eradicate identities and homogenize or "Turkify" the various Muslim ethnicities within the empire. The diverse attributes of the Balkan Muslims required various negotiations of identity and disparate paths to a subsequent assimilation.

Finally, Muslim interactions with Bulgarians were complicated. They were not defined by the slavery and tyranny of Bulgarian nationalist depictions but also did not resemble the enlightened tolerance fluff of Turkish nationalist nostalgic reverie. Alongside the many complicating tensions and fault lines running both ways caused by a number of factors, both internal and external, were positive points in the interactions of these populations, which often lived together by living apart. Thus it is interesting to note that the first moves toward the birth of a Bulgarian nation were not taken against the Ottomans but rather against their Greek coreligionists. These intraconfessional tremors preceded the interconfessional cataclysm of 1877, which shattered the mold and the everyday life of the preceding centuries.

THE BALKANS BEFORE THE TURKS

The area in southeast Europe between the Adriatic Sea and the Black Sea is commonly known as the Balkans. This name itself, through its etymology, hints at a past for the region that is generally not remembered with fondness in the collective memory of those who live there today. For, despite the pejorative noun more recently derived from it that denotes the mostly violent breakup of political territories (balkanization), the word "Balkan" is of Turkish origin and means, rather benignly, mountain or wooded mountains, to be more precise. For example, another Balkan region lies just east of the Caspian Sea in Turkmenistan. While the first Turks who used the word "Balkan" in southeast Europe probably had a specific mountain range in mind, the appellation has since expanded to include the entire region. But the Balkan region that concerns us here, like so many other regions of the world, is less a rigid geographic designation than a historic and cultural scheme. Ultimately, to know where the Balkans begin and where they end is to know something of the past. As Balkan scholar Maria Todorova succinctly put it, "It is . . . preposterous to look for an Ottoman legacy in the Balkans. The Balkans are the Ottoman legacy."[12]

The Ottomans, however, did not refer to their European dominions as the Balkans. They called their European territory collectively Rumeli or Urumeli, from the Turkish Rum İli, meaning the province of the Romans.[13] At the time when Turks and Greeks first encountered one another, the Greeks were at the head of the Eastern Roman Empire or Byzantine Empire as we prefer to call it today. For this reason the Greeks considered themselves Romans, an appellation that the Turks obligingly utilized for the Greeks and other Orthodox Christian subjects of the defunct Byzantine Empire.[14] The Turks took over large areas of the Eastern Roman Empire, a reminder of which was still visible in the name that the Turks gave to those lands just as the modern term, the Balkans, is a reminder of the Ottoman past in those same terrains.

These lands, situated on the edge of Europe and at the approach to Asia, have been crisscrossed throughout history by large movements of people from sundry directions. Migration and change have been perhaps the only constant in Balkan history. Just a snapshot of some of these early migrations should shatter any preconceived notions of the timelessness of any group's claim to territory in the Balkans. Greeks and Galatans (Celts) moved in and through the Balkans in the pre-Christian era. Goths coming from the Baltic Sea area settled in the Balkans in the third century before moving on to Spain at the advance of the (possibly Turkic) Huns in the fifth century. In the sixth century Slavs migrated to the Balkans from the Russian forests, followed by (definitely Turkic) Bolgars coming from the Volga region in the seventh century.

The vast Central Asian steppes offered no clear physical barrier to migration, and various nomadic peoples moved in many directions across them. Turks moved into China, serving as soldiers for the Mongol Yuan dynasty, and participated in battles in locales as far-flung as Vietnam and Burma. They also entered India, creating the ruling dynasty known to the world as the Mughals. It might be helpful to picture westward Central Asian migrations following two general routes. The first passed north of the Caspian Sea and Black Sea across the great Eurasian steppe. The second passed south of the Caspian Sea and Black Sea to enter the Middle East and Asia Minor (Anatolia). The first route was followed by migrations such as that of the Oğuz, who moved into the Balkans by crossing north of the Black Sea as early as the tenth century, followed by the Pechenegs in the eleventh century, and the Kipchaks and Torks in the eleventh and twelfth centuries. Finally, Genghis Khan and his descendants used both routes in the thirteenth century during the meteoric Mongol expansion. The Turkish entry into Anatolia in the eleventh century and subsequently into the Balkans in the fourteenth century was not a historic anomaly—it was only one of many similar migrations that took place over the centuries. The Turks' invasion of Europe has been treated as something of an exception because the migrants did not melt into preexisting populations as previous incursions from the steppe had done. Rather, they constructed a strong political dynasty that overturned the given political order with a different faith at its core—Islam.

We tend to assume that Islam is part and parcel of being Turkish, a subject discussed later. It should be pointed out, however, that the first Turkic people to enter the Balkans were not Muslims; nor were the first Muslims to arrive in the Balkans Turks.[15] Islam's existence in the Balkan Peninsula actually predated the arrival of the Turks and the Ottoman Empire: Arab Muslim traders, soldiers, and missionaries had already created a Muslim presence in the Balkans centuries before the Ottoman conquest. It was not altogether uncommon to see Muslim Arab traders on the Adriatic coast as early as the eighth century. And before the Turks besieged Constantinople, Muslim Arabs had attempted to conquer the Byzantine capital on several occasions, failing each time.

The original Bolgars were a Turkic-descended people who originated in Central Asia near the Volga.[16] One part of the Bolgars stayed in the Volga Basin, adopted Islam, and founded the Volga Bulgar Khanate, which was quite powerful until it gave way to the Mongols under the Golden Horde. The other part moved into the Balkans in the seventh century as pagans and eventually adopted Christianity. As noted, such large migrations were part of larger trends of massive movements of people through the region. The westward migrations from Central Asia and Siberia involved various tribes and peoples, many of whom were ethnically Turkic. Often compelling reasons spurred them to migrate westward, such as retreat from advancing conquerors like Attila the Hun and later Genghis Khan. While first practicing Central Asian style paganism, usually defined by a belief in a sky god, they later adopted religions from the pantheon already existing in the region. Some of these Turkic tribes, such as the Bolgars and the Gagauz Turks, adopted Christianity. The Orthodox Christian Gagauz Turks (most likely from the Turkish "Gök Oğuz") are still found in the northern basin of the Black Sea in Romania. Other Turkic groups adopted other religions. The Uyghurs of Central Asia, prior to adopting Islam, were followers of Manichaeism, whereas the Khazars of the western steppe lands and Crimea converted to Judaism in the seventh century and created a powerful state north of the Black Sea. The Tuvan Turks north of today's Mongolia practice the yellow hat form of Tibetan Buddhism. The existence of such pagan, Buddhist, Christian, and Jewish Turks refutes the notion that being Muslim is inherent in being Turkish. This is an important point, because the demonization of the Turks in the Balkans has had so much to do with religion.

The Bolgars, or proto-Bulgars as they are also known, first crossed the Danube in AD 681, led by Asperuch, son of Kubrat. Asperuch's intentions of settling his people in the lands south of the Danube required him to subdue the Slavic tribes that had migrated to the Balkans a century before. He did so by cooperating with the Slavs against the Byzantines. This Turco-Slav alliance had enough success against the Byzantines to force them into signing a peace treaty that ensured the consolidation of the first Bulgarian state. The Turkic Bulgars, probably because of their military prowess vis-à-vis the sedentary and agricultural Slavs, provided the muscle of the alliance and ruled over the Slavic masses in present-day Bulgaria. Because of the numerical superiority of the Slavs, by the ninth century the Bulgars had been assimilated into the people they ruled by adopting the language of their subjects, the Slavs. An analogous situation occurred with the various Germanic elites across Europe, such as the Vandals, Ostrogoths, Visigoths, Franks, Burgundians, and Lombards, who assimilated to the people they ruled in Spain, Germany, France, and Italy.[17] Khan Boris I shopped around for a faith between the Catholic Germans and the Orthodox Greeks, trying to secure as much independence as possible for his state's new religion, and was able to secure a patriarchate for Bulgaria. The Bulgars, now to be understood as the Slavicized Turkic elites and their Slavic subjects, adopted Christianity from the Orthodox Greek rite in 865.[18] The Bulgarian people had become linguistically and religiously one. However, the Turkic origins of the celebrated heroes of the first Bulgarian Empire still pose uncomfortable questions for Bulgarian nationalists who look upon their Turkish neighbors with blind hostility or have naïve notions of Bulgarian purity.

Over the centuries the Bulgarians and the Byzantines clashed in numerous battles, sometimes victorious and sometimes defeated. The Bulgarian Khan Krum famously had the skull of the Byzantine emperor Nicephorus I, who was killed in battle, lined with silver and made into his drinking cup, a common ritual to celebrate important victories in Central Asia. The First Bulgarian Empire was a serious threat to the Byzantines on their western front at the same time as the Turks were encroaching upon the eastern front. On more than one occasion the Bulgarians advanced to the Theodosian walls of Constantinople but, like many before them, were discouraged by the city's daunting bulwarks. In the closing years of the first millennium and the opening years of the second millennium, the Bulgarian Empire suffered a series of defeats at the hands of the Byzantines. By 1018 the First Bulgarian Empire was no more. The Byzantine emperor, Basil the Bulgar Slayer, had effectively annexed Bulgaria to the Byzantine Empire. Bulgaria became a Byzantine province, and the Bulgarian Patriarchate was abolished.

In 1186 the beginnings of the second Bulgarian Empire were marked by a revolt and the coming to power of the Shishman family. The crusaders in the third crusade (1189–1192) helped to consolidate Bulgarian gains against the Byzantines, whereas the fourth crusade (1202–1204) and the sacking of Constantinople severely weakened the Byzantine Empire, subsequently reducing it to a second-rate power.

ENTER THE OTTOMANS

The major turning point in the history of the Balkans was the arrival of the Ottomans, which triggered a large demographic change through the settlement of Anatolian Turks in strategic areas, and Islam became the religion of state power.[19] The Turks coming from the route south of the Black Sea, though, were to have a lasting impact on the Balkans. Initial waves of Turkish westward migration from Central Asia into Anatolia in the eighth century were assimilated into Byzantine civilization. Later, as the number of Turkish tribes entering Anatolia increased, they pushed further westward, bringing them into the Balkans. Turkish tribesmen were used as mercenaries in the Byzantine army, which embarked on countless campaigns in the Bulgarian lands.[20] Ironically, it was the Byzantine emperor John Cantecuzenus who solicited the aid of Ottoman Turkish tribes on his European front in 1345 and dispatched the Byzantine navy to transport them.[21]

Many may think of the Ottoman Empire as being strictly Middle Eastern. But in fact the Ottoman Empire, while having its initial start in northwestern Anatolia as one of dozens of Turkic principalities trying to advance in the chaos left by the receding Byzantine Empire and Selçuk Empire, quickly moved into the Balkans. Its rapid advance made it a largely Balkan, or European, empire whose rule only later extended into Asia Minor, the Arab Levant, and North Africa. Serbia came under Ottoman rule in 1389 and Bulgaria in 1396 under Sultan Beyazıt I, also known as the Thunderbolt (Yıldırım), whereas the Levant, Baghdad, Egypt, and the Hejaz only fell under Ottoman domination between 1512 and 1530. It was the Balkan provinces that provided the majority of Ottoman wealth, labor, military might, and agricultural output. The Balkans were, in effect, the empire's true core—its beating heart. Furthermore, because the Ottoman Empire became a Balkan empire early in its existence, it essentially began as an empire in which a minority of Muslim

Turks governed a majority Christian population. Only later, through expansion to the Arab south and retreat in the north, did the Ottoman Empire take on its definitive Muslim character, featuring an overwhelmingly Muslim population.

Like all empires, the Ottoman Empire had to develop a system by which it could govern diverse peoples and create manageable and peaceable relations among its subjects. Earlier Islamic precedents had established a theological foundation based on a modus vivendi with People of the Book. Christians and Jews were offered security and considerable autonomy in exchange for the recognition of a Muslim right to govern and the payment of a special tax. The Ottomans adapted this Islam-mandated relationship with non-Muslim subjects to their specific needs. The resulting system divided the Ottoman subject peoples by religion as Greek Orthodox Christians, Armenian Christians, and Jews. The Muslims held the predominant position over these divisions, which were eventually called millets, although the Muslims frequently referred to the non-Muslim people of their empire as *rayah*, which literally means flock. Although Christians carried out the bulk of Ottoman bureaucracy at an early stage, only Muslim subjects could scale the imperial ladder to the pinnacle of administrative positions regardless of which part of the empire they came from. In effect, considerable social mobility was attainable within the empire for anyone willing to convert to Islam.

Peaceful coexistence was secured by granting non-Muslims considerable autonomy and respecting their customs under the oversight of the millet leader, who was a patriarch of the Christian faiths or the Jewish grand rabbi in the capital of Constantinople. The heads of the millets became powerful individuals who were authorized to collect taxes (by force if necessary) for the administration of their respective religious communities. This was especially true with regard to the Greek patriarch. Before the Turkish conquest, the Byzantines had divided power between emperor and patriarch. The emperor was the secular leader of the empire, while the patriarch was its spiritual head. However, defeat at Ottoman hands meant the end of the royal line. The sultan was the new head of state, but the patriarch's responsibilities were actually increased. In effect, the patriarch took on new secular duties and became not only the head of the Orthodox Christian spiritual community but, to a certain degree, its lay leader as well. As Byzantine scholar Steven Runciman put it, this new, nonspiritual aspect of the patriarch's job description naturally entailed "the weakening of the spiritual enterprise of the institution."[22] Tax collection, the doling out of important positions, and responsibility for administering not only the churches but also any efforts toward promoting the community's secular education were all part of the patriarch's duties.

Given its many expenses, including regular extortion of more payments by the Ottoman rulers, the constantly impecunious patriarchy became increasingly corrupted. While the patriarch was an important person within the community, in the end the relative weakness of the institution meant that the Ottomans tended not to view it as posing a serious threat. Except for some petty persecutions, they left the patriarchy largely to its own devices.

Because the Ottoman worldview was dominated by a religious paradigm, the Ottomans were for the most part indifferent to ethnic differences. They thus had little knowledge of the ethnic composition of the territories they ruled and even less inclination to seek such information. Their subjects were lumped into fairly broad religious categories, often ignoring important distinctions within these communities. But the millets were far from homogeneous.

Within the Orthodox Christian millet significant cleavages prevented unity and later became exacerbated, such as divisions among Greeks, Bulgarians, and Serbians. The Orthodox Christian millet included many linguistically and ethnically distinct groups. For example, the Bulgars and Serbs had both possessed their own patriarchs and church administrations prior to 1776–1777 when the Greek patriarch secured the sultan's approval to eliminate the Serbian patriarchy and the Bulgarian archbishopric in Ohrid, thereby bringing all Balkan Christians under his control and purview.[23] This meant that the patriarch would have power to appoint the local religious leaders throughout the Balkans. The appointments suffered from corruption, as positions were bought and sold. From then on, Greek bishops were increasingly imposed on the resentful Bulgarians and Serbs until it became impossible to find the liturgy performed in Church Slavonic anywhere in Bulgaria. Instead religious services were performed in Greek, despite the congregation's long association with a national church and its maternal tongue. This attitude toward non-Greeks among the Orthodox hierarchy was proof, as Richard Crampton stated, that "non-Greeks were in effect second-class citizens in a second-class millet."[24]

The Ottoman rulers were not the only ones to view people in terms of religious identity. Until the second half of the nineteenth century, the people of the other millets were also often not overtly aware of ethnic distinctions and tended to view their fellow Ottoman subjects according to creed. Ethnic and linguistic differences were not yet the primary means of self-identification, and the Ottoman millet system affirmed religion-based worldviews throughout the empire. It was not at all uncommon for people to view themselves according to their religion prior to the ethnolinguistic awakenings that became part and parcel of the age of nationalism. Similar patterns of identification have been witnessed elsewhere throughout Europe and beyond.

As members of the predominant millet, the Muslims held certain advantages and privileges over the other millets. In theory, non-Muslims were not allowed to construct their houses near mosques and their religious buildings were subject to height restrictions. They were required to dismount from horses in the presence of Muslims and were not allowed to carry arms. Church bells were forbidden, and wooden clappers were employed in their place. Furthermore, certain sartorial restrictions were stipulated, such as the prohibition against wearing green for non-Muslims. The intent of such restrictions in urban planning and dress, combined with significant legal autonomy, was to separate Muslims and non-Muslims in their social lives. Their interactions, at least in cities, were essentially limited to the economic sphere. Yet economic interaction was often enough to develop social relations and even friendships. Preserving distinctions between groups was in the interests of not only the empire, which extracted higher taxes from non-Muslims, but also the subordinate non-Muslim groups. They naturally feared losing members of their flocks to Islam, which, as the religion of the state and the gateway to increased social mobility (including a lower tax burden), had a special allure. Later during Ottoman rule these arrangements had the effect of entrenching positions that depended on the continuation of the system. They hindered the integration of the Ottoman people and the creation of an Ottoman national, which was an important yet unattainable goal toward the last century of the empire, due to the rise of ethnic nationalism.[25]

The Ottoman system certainly gave preference to Muslims. Some scholars including Cathie Carmichael have insisted that the millet system was akin to apartheid. While the comparison may be intriguing in that non-Muslims were marginalized as far as sharing state power is concerned, some important distinctions should be made.[26] First, the system was not racially or ethnically based and therefore did not imply that individuals were inferior by birth. In fact, many of the Ottoman ruling elite were members of the former ruling Balkan elites who had converted to Islam. Second, it was possible to enter the privileged Muslim group via conversion. While that is not ideal by the standards of the twenty-first century, it is better than no opportunity for advancement whatsoever such as was found in apartheid South Africa. Third, unlike the apartheid system, the suppressed groups in the Ottoman Empire were often wealthier and better-educated than the ruling Muslim community. This was especially the case in the waning century of the empire, when Christians had more opportunities to engage in international trade, could avoid military service at a prime age for the accumulation of education and wealth, benefited more than Muslims from the opening of schools by foreign powers, and often enjoyed the protection of these same foreign powers in legal situations. Carmichael's comparison illustrates the overreach into hyperbole when assessing the Ottoman arrangements. The system was far from the best of possible worlds, no doubt, but an assessment with some perspective is needed.

While the restrictions that non-Muslims faced in the Ottoman Empire have received much attention and perhaps been overly dramatized in certain nationalist renderings, it should be understood that these restrictions were only intermittently enforced and often allowed to lapse entirely.[27] By the time of the Tanzimat reforms (the modernizing reforms enacted in the early nineteenth century) most of the legal restrictions had been waived. For example, in 1829 the restrictions on clothing were abolished; except for religious clerics, all state servants dressed similarly.[28] It would therefore be misleading to see the millet system as fixed or to attempt to define the Ottoman Empire primarily by a snapshot of the millet system during episodes of its most stringent application. In sum, the system was often flexible, ever-changing, and not legally extant as such at the birth of the empire or during its final exhalation. Five centuries of Ottoman rule cannot be reduced to the millet system alone. This being said, the millet system had a strong impact in reinforcing confessional self-identification, thereby organizing the way the state viewed its subjects and the way they saw each other.

The Ottoman Empire existed for over five hundred years, during which periods and episodes of intolerance and intercommunal violence occurred. Under certain circumstances the Ottoman rulers might hold their non-Muslim subjects in contempt,[29] while at the same time availing themselves of their services. Yet the Ottomans do not fare poorly when compared to their European contemporaries as far as the treatment of minorities is concerned, especially before Napoleonic reforms swept through Europe.[30] Ottoman tolerance was an economical exigency in ruling over diverse subjects and guaranteeing their peaceful cohabitation and subservience. Tolerance was desired because it was the least costly means to arrive at a peaceful outcome. The millet system can best be summarized by three words: separate, unequal, and protected.[31]

To avoid essentializing is a knife that cuts both ways, and it would also be incorrect to characterize the millet system and the Ottoman Empire (as is often the case in nostalgic Turkish narratives) as being founded on and imbued with tolerance, especially a tolerance rooted in Islam or Islamic principles. Tolerance still implies something of the vertical relationship between Muslims and non-Muslims. It was not acceptance and was not equality. In reality, the Ottoman rule was more defined by autonomy, not by some enlightened tolerance favoring diversity, which is nowadays celebrated in liberal humanist circles.

Yet Turkish renderings of the past that exaggerate the degree and nature of Ottoman tolerance nurture anti-Turkish sentiments of betrayal and injustice on the part of those rebellious subjects. Similarly, histrionic stories of Ottoman cruelty and barbarity serve to justify violence and absolve the rebels of any moral responsibility for the extremely bloody nature of the independence movements. Here, then, is a clear example of history with a purpose.

ETHNICITY IN OTTOMAN BULGARIA

Because the Ottomans were not concerned with national identities, ethnic definitions were not used frequently in their documents. For this reason, in the absence of detailed documentation about ethnic makeup, scholars have only been able to make reasoned guesses. The difficulty has special application for the Muslim and Orthodox millets, which were the largest and the most ethnically diverse in the empire. Among other ethnicities, the Orthodox millet was composed of Greeks, Bulgarians, Serbs, Romanians (Wallachians and Moldovans), Turks, Albanians, and Arabs. In the Muslim millet we find Turks, Arabs, Kurds, Albanians, Bosnaks, Greeks, Pomaks, Gypsies, Circassians, Tatars, Turcomans, Torbeš, Donmehs (converted Jews), and others.

The millet system had reinforced a religious base for notions of identity, especially among the ruling elite, so existing demographic record keeping is largely framed in religious categories. From time to time documents surface that reference differences within the Muslim millet, such as mentions of Kurds, nomadic tribes, Circassians, and Gypsies.[32] These are relatively rare, however, and most Ottoman documents obscure to a great extent the ethnic makeup of the Balkans throughout the Ottoman period.

Adherents of Islam identified themselves as Muslims, whereas the Balkan Christians and many in the West often called the Muslims Turks. For a long period the concepts of Muslim and Turk were synonymous in the West, although these Muslims may have belonged to a wide range of ethnic categories. Even after Christians had adopted the language of ethnicity and nationalism, they continued to see Muslims "in the undifferentiated religious community discourse."[33] Throughout this work I refer to the refugees who are the main subject of this research as Muslims unless a specific ethnicity is ascertainable. It should also be understood that quotations from Western observers referring to "Turks" are not making an ethnic distinction.

While ethnic identity was not particularly salient within the Ottoman Empire, it would be false to think that the only source of self-identification was religious (although it certainly was the most prominent). In addition to religion, people might have felt identity based upon loyalty to the sultan or loyalty to the institutions of self-governance, the values of an ethnic culture, and regional identities such as their locality or community of origin.[34] Ethnicity did not feature largely in the records that elevated religious-based identity, but this does not imply that ethnic markers did not exist. Ethnicity, and for that matter regional identities, might be visible in dress—the color of a sash or the pattern of an embroidery, food, language, music, architecture, furnishings, accents, and more. The multiple layers of identity available would give the refugees in question some flexibility in their assimilation as well as suggest some lingering differences that could have impeded their later assimilation if the refugees or the state had sought to highlight differences rather than similarities.

Because of coexistence engendered by imperial structures, the populations of empires have dynamic opportunities for mobility across the imperial terrains, so that substantial levels of migration and mixing take place. This was especially true in the Ottoman Empire, where no feudal boundaries or landed aristocracy existed. Ottoman subjects were even freer to move about their empire than their counterparts in other European empires.[35] Migration was always an important feature within the Ottoman Empire, where large numbers of people still lived a nomadic lifestyle, some with migration patterns that extended across Anatolia and into the Balkans.[36] Even though ethnic Turks had started to enter the Balkans as early as the thirteenth century, the period of greatest Muslim immigration into the Balkans was during the great expansion of the Ottoman Empire in the fifteenth and sixteenth centuries.[37] In addition to voluntary migration, forced exile or migration was a policy that contributed to the large numbers of Muslims found in the Balkans. It was deemed necessary to integrate the far-flung provinces more closely with the empire, increase government representation in strategic areas, and promote demographic ratios beneficial to the center. For this reason Muslims from Anatolia were settled in the Balkans, while some of the non-Muslims in the new territories were transferred to Anatolia, although the larger trend was toward Rumelia.[38]

One of the reasons why the state wanted to move more people to Rumelia was simple economics: the Rumelian lands were more fertile and more profitable. During the period of Suleiman the Magnificent, the provinces within Rumelia brought in considerably more revenue to the state coffers than all the provinces of Anatolia combined.[39] Despite the theoretical separation of Ottoman subjects brought about by the millet system, a significant amount of demographic intermixing took place due to the high mobility of Muslim subjects and the manipulation of settlement patterns via Ottoman *sürgün* (exile by the state), whereby the various Muslim ethnicities would live alongside various Christian ethnic groups and Jews.

Under sürgün local judges were empowered to force whole villages to resettle in areas designated by the central authorities. They were supposed to be fit enough to endure the move and were required to take their chattel with them. Moreover, entire nomadic tribes were forced to move. The exiles would be granted a reprieve from tax-paying for a few years, but resistance, which was not uncommon, was punished.[40] As the demographics of the region were altered in favor of more diversity, the seeds were sown for future conflict, in an era where homogeneity would be coveted as the ideal.[41]

The extent to which the Muslim presence in the Balkans was a result of immigration or conversion has been the subject of heated and often very unscholarly debate between nationalist historians in the Balkans and Turkey. Muslims speaking Serbo-Croatian (Bosnaks), Greek, Bulgarian (Pomaks), and Albanian, among other European languages living in the Ottoman Balkans, clearly were not the descendants of Turkish migrants. Clearly, then, conversion was one way in which a Muslim presence developed in the Balkans. However, the extent to which conversion took place has become extremely important in Bulgarian nationalist discourses. Such discourses have insisted that Turkish-speaking Bulgarian Muslims were ethnically Bulgarian, yet converts to Islam (and most likely forced converts at that) who had forgotten their real language were nevertheless at their core Bulgarian. Therefore, toward the end of the Communist regime in Bulgaria efforts to force name changes upon Bulgarian Turks, among other Bulgarization programs, were considered justifiable. (Such nationalization programs ultimately provoked a massive Turkish emigration from Bulgaria in 1989.) Turkish explanations during the same period, in contrast, tend to insist on large migrations of Anatolian Muslims to the Balkans, especially Bulgaria, to account for the large Muslim presence,[42] which was at its core ethnically Turkish and not subject to re-Bulgarization.[43]

Ultimately the question of conversion is highly complicated. Often conversions were voluntary, but sometimes they were forced. It is interesting to note that the two areas in the Balkans with the highest number of conversions to Islam, Bosnia and Albania, were the European regions farthest from the influence of Istanbul. In any event, by the nineteenth century conversions were rare occurrences. In fact, rather than forcing conversion upon Christians, the Ottomans erected various hurdles that made conversion to Islam more difficult, as seen by the Salonika Incident discussed at the end of the chapter.

Discussion of conversion to Islam in the Balkans is often emotionally charged due to one very specific early Ottoman policy known as *devşirme*. This was a military recruit system, whereby Balkan villages were forced to give up young boys to the state to serve in the Ottoman army, who would then be reeducated as Muslims. On its face the idea of forcing parents to give up their children to the state to be converted to a different religion sounds rather horrible. But the devşirme is more complicated than it seems at first glance, and its scale is undoubtedly exaggerated in Balkan nationalist narratives. The last levy, for example, took place in 1685.[44] In any event, the devşirme could hardly be said to account for the large Muslim population in the Balkans. Ultimately, ancestry is difficult to determine, because migration and religious and linguistic conversion both occurred. All this renders it difficult to make reality conform to the neat and simplistic nationalistic renderings so often defining history in the Balkans.

POPULATION FIGURES IN THE DANUBE PROVINCE

The country we know today as Bulgaria became part of the Ottoman Empire in 1396. The names used by the Ottomans for this territory varied, as well as the way in which it was divided and subdivided over time. For the purposes of this study, it is best called Rumelia, which included the Province of Edirne found today in modern Turkey and the Danube Province, which included Dobruca in present-day Romania and Niş in present-day Serbia (Edirne Vilayeti and Tuna Vilayeti in Turkish). Modern-day Bulgaria was formed from these two provinces of the Danube and Rumelia (created later under the Treaty of Berlin). The Ottoman provinces of Edirne and the Danube were created in 1864 as part of a modernization program spearheaded by the governor, Mithat Paşa, to increase the control of the central government by reducing the power of local chiefs, who were not only governing the territories poorly but also disobeying the wishes of Istanbul.[45]

Several factors contribute to the difficulty of discussing demographics in the Ottoman Balkans. First and foremost, accurate, objective, and comprehensive data are hard to come by. While some counts were undertaken at various intervals, the Ottomans did not conduct a true official census until after the end of the nineteenth century. Various counts were taken primarily to assess tax and conscription liabilities, meaning that they only counted males. In tandem with the state's desire for modernization and centralization in the nineteenth century came an increased need for reliable data. Yet for the most part these counts remained deficient. Moreover, the Ottomans mostly identified people solely by millet and not by ethnicity, leaving a murky picture of Ottoman demographics. Ottoman subjects who resisted paying more taxes or hoped to avoid recruitment into the army were often reluctant to cooperate with population counters. With that in mind, the government conducted its census-taking efforts with secrecy, producing far from comprehensive results.[46]

The census of 1831 suffered from a large undercount, whereas the 1844 census is missing or destroyed. The count of 1866 is also clearly short on numbers and has not been fully studied. European ethnological studies also cannot be considered a reliable source because they were often based on erroneous data, bias, or plain imagination.[47] Non-Ottoman surveys are often plainly tendentious—various European, Russian, and Balkan demographic studies sought to produce numbers to benefit their respective political agendas.[48] The Russians, for example, presented demographic numbers for Bulgaria at the Istanbul conference that were wildly inaccurate.[49]

In addition to the lack and questionability of data, the changing borders (both external and internal) of the Ottoman Empire must be taken into account when examining overall population figures. Because the borders and the populations within them were constantly changing, any set of data is only a snapshot in a long process of demographic change and cannot be considered representative for the empire's duration or even for the century in which it was taken, especially given the frequent wars that accompanied the drawn out years of the Ottoman demise.

Shrinking Ottoman territory in the Balkans resulted in an increasing ratio of Muslims to Christians as Ottoman Muslims essentially chased the moving borders to stay under the sultan's suzerainty. "Ottoman Europe" was a highly fluid concept, expanding until 1699 and shrinking thereafter. Moreover, the areas from which the Ottoman Empire first retreated generally had relatively lower densities of Muslims. In short, claims about population figures must be approached with great care. A respected author on the Balkans, Mark Mazower, makes the absolute but erroneous claim that Muslims never exceeded 20 percent of the population of

Ottoman Europe,[50] yet such a percentage would only be true for the Ottoman Europe at its most expansive point geographically. We must always qualify claims of quantitative dimensions when speaking of Ottoman populations. Around 20 percent of Ottoman Europe was Muslim in 1500, and about 25 percent was Muslim in 1600.[51] Because of shrinking borders, conversions, and migrations, Ottoman Europe was over one-third Muslim by 1800.[52] Muslims were the clear majority in the small vestige of Ottoman Europe by the turn of the century. Ottoman Muslims had been spread throughout the shrinking Ottoman Balkans. Only a few areas such as the interior of Montenegro had virtually no Muslims. Albania, Bosnia, and northeastern Bulgaria boasted large Muslim majorities, whereas in other parts they lived as minorities in majority-Christian districts.[53]

From 1866 to 1873, the period preceding the Russo-Ottoman War, the most detailed population count up to that time was conducted in the Danube Province under the governorship of Mithat Paşa, although it failed to count women. According to this census, the Muslim population of the province was around 40 percent, representing the majority group in most cities.[54] Yet the census appears to have excluded the nomads and newly settled immigrants such as Circassians and Tatars, who were exempted from taxes and military service and not deemed important enough to count.[55]

These Circassian and Tatar immigrants numbered well over 1 million, which would translate into a virtual parity between Muslims and non-Muslims in the Danube Province on the eve of the 1877–1878 war. In the entire Ottoman Balkans of 1876 (Eastern Thrace, Bulgaria, Albania, Northern Greece, Macedonia, Serbia, and Bosnia), according to E. G. Ravenstein, Muslims constituted 43 percent of the population.[56] In the provinces that constituted Ottoman Bulgaria this ratio was closer to 50 percent of the over 3 million inhabitants of the region. This large Muslim presence was to be subjected to a war and subsequently to a major reduction.

MUSLIM DIVERSITY IN THE RUMELIA AND DANUBE PROVINCES

Muslims in the Balkans were quite diverse in terms of ethnicity, language, class, and sect, which may have made their presence more fragile.[57] Even in the Danube Province Muslims were far from being a uniform group;

tangible differences existed. As has already been mentioned, the most obvious distinctions were based on language and ethnicity. Moreover, each Muslim group had a distinct past.

Yet the question of Muslim identities and pasts in the Balkans has been obscured by a "constant, obligatory falsification" since the creation of the Balkan nation-states, which attained a level of disconcerting senselessness during the Communist regimes. As Alexandre Popovic states, "Supply and demand of an image of the past of each of these groups of Muslims has varied enormously over time according to the periods and the regimes in place."[58] So, before speaking of Muslims in Bulgaria as a whole, it is useful to reexamine the diversity of the Muslim groups in Ottoman Bulgaria.

The largest Muslim ethnic group in Bulgaria was clearly the Turks. The Turks in the Balkans, much like those in Anatolia, did not yet self-identify as Turks. Although they would have most likely referred to their language as Turkish, they spoke a dialect known as Rumeli Turkish rather than Ottoman Turkish, which was the court language used only by educated Ottoman Muslims, who were relatively scarce in the Balkans and virtually nonexistent following the wars responsible for the creation of the Balkan nation-states.

Europeans at that time preferred to subsume all the ethnic Turks as well as other Muslims under an indistinct category as Turks, confounding a religious and ethnic designation. But they did not refer to Gagauz Turks (a group of ethnic Turks who had migrated from Anatolia in the thirteenth century and adopted Orthodox Christianity) as Turks.[59]

In addition to ethnic Turks were perhaps 400,000 Pomaks (Bulgarian-speaking Muslims) residing primarily around the Rhodope Mountains in the south of the Danube Province in areas that were difficult to access.[60] Some Pomaks were also centered around the region of Pleven in the north.[61] Interestingly, the Pomaks were known to have called themselves "Turci," whereas they called the Turks "Üruci." This is probably more an indication of their desire to be accepted as Muslims than an ethnic affirmation.[62] In fact, autochthonous Muslim groups such as Pomaks, Bosnaks, and Albanians who had some concept of their identity before conversion to Islam maintained this ethnic consciousness to some degree afterward.[63] The Pomaks, for example, maintained ethnic Slavic customs, but as Muslims in a fairly closed-off community.

Gypsies, today more properly known as Roma, originated in northern India. They are another example of migration crossing to the west and into the Balkans. They began arriving in the Balkans as early as the ninth century, during the Byzantine Empire, although the largest migrations into Bulgaria date between the thirteenth and fourteenth centuries. They had attained such large numbers in the Byzantine Empire that a part of Greece was even dubbed "Little Egypt" by Byzantine rulers.[64] In the fifteenth century the Gypsies in Bulgaria were primarily Christian, which indicates that they had most likely settled there during the time of the Byzantine Empire. However, many Gypsies entered the Balkans as auxiliaries to the Ottoman army, where they were engaged in such occupations as building roads, transporting cannons, and producing gunpowder. Other Gypsies joined the army as fighters themselves.[65] By the nineteenth century the majority of Gypsies in Bulgaria (which had the greatest number of Gypsies in the Ottoman Balkans) and in the Ottoman Empire in general were Muslims.[66]

Muslim Gypsies, who were more numerous than Christian Gypsies, were most often found in cities in their own separate quarters. Contrary to popular notions, they were generally sedentary. In addition to working at the jobs traditionally associated with them, as musicians, horse breeders, and metalworkers, they also worked as artisans, seasonal farmhands and military auxiliaries. However, they were not integrated with the rest of the Muslim Ottomans.

The Ottoman Gypsies most likely saw conversion as a way to escape the prejudices engendered under the Byzantines and take advantage of the socioeconomic opportunities available to Muslims in the Ottoman Empire. They were not entirely successful in this regard, however, as the Ottomans did not accept them as full members of the Muslim community. In fact, the Roma were the one group that the Ottomans did see in ethnic terms rather than religious terms.[67] Often their religious observance was considered insufficient. In fact, they regularly had to prove their religion by performing the necessary obligations in front of tax collectors in order to avoid paying the special tax incumbent upon non-Muslims. Their early service in the Ottoman army having been forgotten, only after 1874 were Gypsies drafted into the army again.[68]

Except for considering them to be the best musicians, in general both Muslims and Christians held negative attitudes toward the Gypsies; typically, Muslim Gypsies would be buried in separate corners of Muslim cemeteries, for example. Yet the large-scale persecution that they faced in western Europe did not take place under the Ottomans. In addition to these sundry groups of Muslims, we can also find limited references to Iranians, Kurds, and Albanians in the provinces of the Danube and Rumelia.[69]

At the beginning of the 1877–1878 Russo-Turkish War Muslims had a large presence throughout the Danube region. They were a clear majority in the northeast, thanks in part to Circassian and Tatar migrations. On the Black Sea coast from the Danube Basin southward to Varna, Muslims composed nearly 60 percent of the population.[70] They were also dominant in urban centers, even in western Bulgaria, where the Muslim presence was at its weakest. In the Rhodope Mountains in the south, where the Pomaks were primarily located, they tended to live in smaller villages, whereas the Turks dominated the towns. The Turks and Pomaks were understood to be older inhabitants in the province, whereas the Circassians and Tatars were the newcomers. The Gypsies, of whom the majority were Muslim, were seen as distinct both by the state and by the other Balkan Muslims and Christians.

Most of the Muslims in preindependence Bulgaria would probably fall under the rubric "Sunni" by today's classification and thus be under the authority of the Sheikh ul-Islam in Istanbul. However, these religious categorizations were blurry, somewhat permeable, and often overlapping throughout much of the Ottoman period, resulting in a surprising diversity in Islamic thought and practice in the Ottoman Empire. The Sunnis themselves would have had diverse localized regional practices that resembled more folk-Islam versions rather than a strict and structured Islamic practice.

Other Muslim groups included the Shia-oriented Alevi sect as well as the various mystical Sufi orders, such as the Baktaşi (the primary Sufi order of the Janissaries) Nakşibendi, Kadiri, and Kızılbaşı, who were originally nomadic Turcomans forced to settle in the Balkan frontier zone.[71] The Kızılbaşı presence, for example, stretched from the Danube to the Rhodope Mountains, with higher concentrations in Deliorman and Dobruca. The Sufis were known to be less strict about the duties and prohibitions of official Islam. For example, Friday prayers, the veiling of women, and the proscription against alcohol were not as rigorously observed.[72] The strong Sufi presence meant that folk Islam was commonplace in Rumelia and pluralism reigned. No major Islamic learning centers were ever developed in the Balkans, which remained free of doctrinal strife.[73]

Like their Bulgarian Christian counterparts, members of the Balkan Muslim population were both rich and poor. Both Christian and Muslim groups had developed elites with contacts in Istanbul, as well as in Russia for the Bulgarian Christians. It is possible to divide the Muslims into five large socioeconomic categories: (1) large property owners: beys and ağas; (2) civil servants, such as soldiers, police, and general administrative officials; (3) clergy; (4) merchants and artisans; and (5) small tenant farmers.[74] These various classes of people would have had different relations with the state and different attitudes to proposed reforms. They would also have had somewhat differing fates during the coming war.

In Bulgaria the Muslims tended to dominate the large property-owning class as well as the bureaucracy. Naturally, this situation contributed to animosity toward the Muslims, as the disparities in land holdings aroused jealousies. Gypsies were often the artisans, especially in metallurgy, whereas the Turks were dominant in the leather trade.[75] The economic disparity among Muslims was vast: the poorest of the Muslims might have been poorer than the poorest of the Christians. While Bulgarian Christians may have been envious of Muslim wealth, the reality is that the economic situation of Ottoman Muslims in Bulgaria was highly variable.

The Turkish language appealed to Muslims throughout the Balkans, as seen in the large lexicon borrowed from Turkish in other Balkan languages. Turkish, along with Greek, became the major lingua franca for trade and administrative purposes among the various groups in the Balkan Peninsula.[76] However, locals did not abandon their mother tongues. Except for community leaders, inhabitants of isolated villages of Christians or Muslims would have little use for either Turkish or Greek.[77] In mixed villages and towns, however, it was not at all uncommon for Turks to be familiar with Bulgarian and vice versa.

TATARS AND CIRCASSIANS: BITTER TRANSPLANTS

The Black Sea was once essentially an Ottoman lake: Muslim populations lived on all its shores. Crimean Tatars were a branch of the Golden Horde and were the dominant population in the Crimean Peninsula. Only much later in the history of the Golden Horde did the Crimean Tatars fall into the Ottoman orbit. Similarly, the people inhabiting the eastern shore of the Black Sea were primarily Muslim, a multiplicity of tribes and ethnicities who were dubbed Circassians. Russia's southward expansion totally changed life for both of these populations, resulting in large-scale emigration under distressing conditions and leaving a legacy of trauma and bitterness. Many Tatars and Circassians, forced to emigrate at the point of a Russian bayonet, found themselves in Ottoman Bulgaria. This both increased the Muslim-Christian ratio and created new ethnic tensions.

The Crimean Tatars, as a political force, were already spent by the fourteenth century, as dissension and divisiveness weakened them in the face of the meteoric Russians. They were absorbed into the Ottoman Empire as a vassal state in the fifteenth century but stayed more or less autonomous. The Ottomans were forced to recognize Crimean independence in the Treaty of Küçük Kaynarca in 1774. Catherine the Great finally annexed Crimea to Russia in 1783. The Tatars remained its majority population, despite Russian colonization, until the aftermath of the Crimean War of 1853–1856, during which Great Britain, France, and the Ottoman Empire allied to fight the Russians. Russian defeat led to recrimination against a Tatar population seen as a fifth column for the Ottomans. The result was a massive emigration of Tatars from Crimea and the Russian confiscation of Tatar lands.[78] While some of these Tatars migrated to Anatolia, around 150,000 of the approximately 595,000 Tatar refugees from Crimea and Kazan moved to areas in the Danube Province.[79] The vast majority of these settled in villages in central Dobruca in the Danubian basin (the Turks dominated the coastline of this region), which was essentially the land closest to Crimea.[80] The Ottomans hoped that by settling Tatars in Dobruca they would be able to fortify their position against Russia's approach to the Danube. As the departure of Tatars created an economic and agricultural vacuum, Russia solicited Bulgarians to immigrate and take their place. Many Bulgarians took up the Russian offer, causing a decrease in the Bulgarian population and a further diminution of the proportion of Christians to Muslims in the province.

The large Tatar migration was followed by an even larger flight of Circassian refugees due to Russian expansion and conquest in the Caucasus.

The term "Circassian" (Turkish "Çerkes") from the Mongolian word "Jerkes," meaning "one who blocks the path," was applied to a diverse group of people living on the coast and in the highlands of the eastern Black Sea region.[81] It is something of a blanket term, referring to an ethnically diverse group of peoples speaking a number of languages, primarily the Adyge and Karbadian peoples from the Northern Caucasus, possibly including the Abkhaz, Ingusheti, Ossetians, and Georgians among others.[82] They have lost their differentiation in the diaspora, coming to accept the more general designation "Circassian."

The Russians wanted a clear supply line to the south in hopes of conquering Persia and wresting India from the English. They distrusted the Caucasian highlanders and were not content to have them as vassals. Moreover, they wanted the lands for settling the Don Cossacks. In the end, around 1.2 million Circassians were forced to flee their homelands. Approximately three-fourths of these settled in the Ottoman Empire, which was grossly unprepared for such a large number of immigrants.[83] Resistance had been fierce during the long decades of Russian expansion into the Caucasus, and Russian brutality became intolerable, as entire villages were razed.

The string of defeats at the hands of the Russians culminated in a last major defeat in 1864. Life for many Circassians was made unbearable, and they were sometimes sent off elsewhere within the Russian Empire. At other times, they might be offered the choice of moving to the Ottoman Empire. If they accepted, they were then piled onto overloaded boats to test their fate in new lands.[84] Although the Ottomans were keen on having new residents for a chronically underpopulated Anatolia, the majority of Circassian refugees preferred to settle in the Empire's Balkan regions, where they would be in a more familiar climate. About 700,000 Circassian immigrants to the Balkans between 1864 and 1877 further increased the Muslim-Christian ratio. Unlike the Tatars, however, they did not speak a Turkic language, so the path to their assimilation would be more challenging. Because of their previous experiences with the Russians, the Circassians were filled with animosity toward them, which may have led to tense relations with the Slavic-Christian Bulgarians. They were often more loyal to their tribe than to the sultan, which caused concern for the Ottoman administrators, who often considered them a menace to stability.

BULGARIAN JEWRY

The Jews are the final group in Ottoman Bulgaria that merits discussion. While they never lived in large numbers in the Rumelia, their place within the Ottoman quilt is of interest, lest we think of the events in strictly Christian-Muslim terms. Jews most likely first arrived in these lands after the Roman conquest, as evidence dates to the second century AD. New arrivals continued throughout the Bulgarian and Byzantine Empires. At this point, the Jews of Bulgaria were Romaniote, meaning Greek speakers. In the fourteenth and fifteenth centuries Yiddish-speaking Ashkenazi Jews immigrated from north of the Danube due to conditions in Europe at that time. Finally, at the invitation of Sultan Beyazit II, Spanish-speaking Sephardic Jews immigrated to the Ottoman Empire after being banished from Spain.

The Jews of Bulgaria lived in the larger towns, and new immigrants tended to settle where they found Jewish communities already in existence. The Sephardic Jews became the largest Jewish community in Bulgaria as elsewhere in the Ottoman Empire. Despite earlier tensions, the Romaniotes and Ashkenazim, for the most part, chose to accept the Sephardic norms if not to assimilate entirely.[85] Given the Ottoman system of autonomy and their relatively small numbers, Jews were not pressured to convert to Islam. Quite to the contrary: many Jews who had been forced to convert to Christianity were allowed to reconvert to the religion of their forebears. Jews in the Ottoman Empire became invested in the empire's well-being. Many of them engaged in trade, lending for profit, and tax-farming, ultimately contributing to the integration of the Ottoman Empire into Europe, at least in the realms of commerce and finance.

Jews in Ottoman Bulgaria fared much better than Jews in Russia or Europe. The Ottomans' presence prevented any widespread persecution of Jews by the Christians. Yet this close working relationship between the Ottomans and Jews fed into increasingly hostile attitudes toward Jews on the part of the Bulgarians. Incitements against Jews, including the blood libel, were printed in the Bulgarian-language émigré press originating in Russia and Romania.[86] The advent of Balkan nationalism, imbued at times with anti-Semitism, only served to intensify Jewish identification with the Ottoman state.[87]

Outside of the Ottoman Empire, Europe's Ashkenazi Jews had taken an increasingly condescending attitude toward the Ottoman Jews, whom they considered greatly fallen from their Andalusian glory days and in dire need of revitalization. Although the European Jews outside of the Ottoman Empire viewed Balkan independence movements with some apprehension, only after witnessing Russian and Bulgarian behavior in the war did they reevaluate their position and belatedly come to recognize the benefits of Ottoman governance.[88]

CHRISTIAN-MUSLIM RELATIONS

An overreliance on Bulgarian nationalist interpretations of the conditions in Bulgaria before national independence would lead us to believe that the situation for Bulgarian Christians was intolerable. No rayah people were "so completely under the wheels of the Turkish chariot as were the Bulgars."[89] In these renderings, Ottoman rule was marked by poverty, cruelty, and cultural annihilation. It is true that before the arrival of the Ottomans Bulgarian was an important literary language, which by the nineteenth century had become little known even by Slavic-language experts.[90] Enhanced scrutiny often uncovers shades of gray. For example, Bulgarians were giving up their language not because they were abandoning Bulgarian for Turkish but rather because they were becoming Hellenized. Yet, according to many Bulgarian historians, Ottoman rule was supposed to have been responsible for the corruption and disappearance of the Bulgarian language. Thus Bulgarian national histories refer to Ottoman rule as the Turkish yoke and state that the Turkish overlords were the objects of a widespread hatred among Bulgarians. Turkish historians, in contrast, continue to promote the idea that ungrateful minorities took advantage of benevolent Ottoman tolerance.

We might wonder about the inevitability of massive violence. Once again, the situation is more complex than nationalistic narratives imply. Turkish-Bulgarian interactions varied according to multiple factors, which is not to say that hostility was nonexistent but rather to suggest that a more complex analysis is required. Tension ran across many fault lines and for many reasons. Many Muslims felt increasingly bitter about their situation and directed their resentment toward the Bulgarian Christians as well as the local rulers. Nor were the Bulgarians unified in their opposition to Ottoman rule, as many Bulgarian Christians benefited from their position in Ottoman society. These Bulgarians were more likely to seek gradual changes through the system, rather than blowing it up altogether.

Several issues were causing these matters to come to the surface, including disparity in land ownership, suspicions based on demographic change caused by immigration of Muslim refugees from places such as the Crimea and the Caucasus, corruption and abuses in local governance, envy caused by the protected status of Christians under the capitulations regime, the deteriorating status of Muslims under the Tanzimat reforms, and the unfulfilled promise of reforms for equality and fairer governance. These were all exacerbated by European meddling in Ottoman affairs, especially through the creation of a cadre of nationalist-minded Bulgarians sponsored by the Russian Empire.

Muslims and Christians often inhabited different geographic areas. For example, the Bulgarians tended to live in the hills and mountains in smaller villages, while the Turks lived in the coastal areas and cities. In cities, where economic disparity was more visible and class distinctions could be confounded with religion,[91] Muslim-Christian relations were apparently worse off than in the rural areas.[92] Interactions in the cities between Muslims and Christians were most common in, although not limited to, the market, because they tended to live in separate quarters.[93] Some tombs of saints were visited by both Muslim and Christian pilgrims.[94] Despite the propinquity of the two groups, however, the lack of interaction resulted in mutual ignorance. Educated Bulgarians knew next to nothing about Islam and equated any manifestation of it with "religious fanaticism,"[95] while Muslims were uneducated about Christian beliefs and practices. The groups theoretically were supposed to be separate according to the millet system, but was the separation only due to the millet system? Were Christians and Jews always eager to mix with Muslims and with each other? It seems more likely that the Christians, the Jews, and the Muslims for the most were content to be separate, except in cases where an opportunity for political economic advancement was impeded.

Yet Bernard Lewis's assertion that the difference between Muslims and Christians was uncrossable—"all Muslims are brothers, all non-Muslims are strangers"—oversimplifies relations greatly.[96] Such essentializing based on an overreliance on religious texts and legal statutes should be resisted, because it fails to take into account a reality based on day-to-day living. The truth is that our understanding of the situation is murky, because the reality was complex, and variegated. In a discussion on this subject Rossitsa Gradeva, the esteemed Bulgarian scholar of Ottoman history, expressed her own perplexity about the exact situation: "You know, I've given this question a lot of thought, and sometimes I think that they [Christians and Muslims in Bulgaria] interacted a lot, but then at other times I come to the conclusion that they hardly interacted at all."[97] Perhaps, then, it is safest to accept that Muslim-Christian relations in the Balkans varied greatly depending on the time and the place and that blanket statements will always be riddled with holes.

As Ottoman rule progressed over the centuries, Bulgarians often migrated from the cities to the countryside to escape dealings with the Ottoman administrators—especially the tax collectors. Muslims took over these abandoned towns or created their own new cities, which were then populated by coreligionist migrants from other areas. The majority of cities in Bulgaria had a Muslim majority,[98] even in the northwestern part of the province, where virtually no Turks lived in villages.[99] This dynamic underwent a major change in independent—royal and Communist—Bulgaria: by the twentieth century the vast majority of Muslims living in Bulgaria were rural.[100]

Land distribution was an important point of friction between Muslims and Bulgarian Christians. While they only reached demographic parity in the decade preceding the war in 1877, the Muslims had long held ownership of the majority of land (around 60 percent), especially the majority of good farming land and large estates (*çiftliks*). Many of the large estate holders were Turks who lived in the cities while managing their estates from afar. These estates had been formed over time through a system wherein smaller holdings of public land were incorporated into larger estates, often falling into the hands of corrupt local authorities. Yet unfair land distribution was exacerbated by the overall shortage of land under cultivation due to insecurity and lack of resources. The Ottoman state was blamed for this situation. Due to the absenteeism of the large estate holders and increasing competition from European agricultural producers, these large estates had become less profitable and were gradually being sold off, often to small Bulgarian farmers.[101]

The expansion of the Russian Empire, not to mention the Austro-Hungarian Empire, came at the expense of Muslims in the Ottoman Empire and on its periphery. A great movement of peoples accompanied Russian expansion. In the nineteenth century alone the Russians and Ottomans engaged in four major wars, which all had demographic impacts.[102] Incoming refugees undoubtedly exacerbated tensions in Muslim-Christian relations. The Nobel Prize–winning Serb novelist Ivo Andrić describes the dynamic landscape of Muslim emigration and its effects on Muslim-Christian relations in the Balkans:

> In the last few years especially—at the end of the eighteenth and the beginning of the nineteenth century—events and changes had come rather fast and thick. Indeed, there was a regular assault of events from every quarter, a clashing and a tumble that ranged all over Europe and the great Turkish Empire and reached even into this little valley, settling here like flood water or a sand drift. Ever since the Turks had withdrawn from Hungary, the relations between the Ottoman Empire and the Christian world had grown steadily worse and more complex, as had conditions in general. The warriors of the great Empire, the agas and spahis, who had been forced to relinquish their rich estates on the fertile Hungarian plain and to return to their cramped and poor country, were bitter and resentful of everything Christian; and while they multiplied the number of mouths that had to be fed, the number of hands available for work remained as before.
>
> On the other hand, these same wars of the eighteenth century that were easing the Turks out of the neighboring Christian lands and bringing them back to Bosnia, filled the local rayah—or subject Christians—with bold new hopes and opened up daring new horizons; and this too was bound to influence the attitude of the rayah to their imperial overlord, the Turk. Both sides—if one may speak of two sides at this stage of the struggle—fought each in its own way, and with the means that were suited to the times and circumstances. The Turks elected repression and force, the Christians fought back with passive resistance, cunning, and conspiracy, or readiness to conspire.

> The Turks defended their right to live and their way of life, the Christians fought to gain those rights. The rayah was getting "uppish" and was no longer what it used to be. This conflict of interests, beliefs, yearning, and hopes produced a convulsive atmosphere which the long Turkish wars with Venice, Austria and Russia made only tenser and more constricting. In Bosnia the mood grew somber and brooding, clashes became more frequent, life more difficult; order and sense of security waned by the day.[103]

Immigrants to the Ottoman Empire were offered exemption from military service and taxes for twelve years if they settled in Anatolia and six years if they settled in the Balkans. Yet about a third of the Circassians and Tatars chose the Balkans, mostly Bulgaria.[104] The influx of Tatars and Circassians, numbering over 700,000, created a definitive shift in the ratio of Muslims and Christians in Bulgaria in favor of the Muslims, who were approaching parity. In addition, Muslim fertility rates began to rise significantly after the 1850s.[105] The increasing numbers of Muslims in Bulgaria no doubt caught the attention of Bulgarian Christians, especially as the Circassians had become notorious for their raiding, even though they robbed both Christians and Muslims. Brigandage, whether practiced by Muslims or Christians, had become increasingly commonplace throughout the Balkans, which was an indication of the state's inability to control the security situation. The Christian brigands have often been granted the mantle of incipient nationalists in nationalist hagiographies, although such attribution is baseless.[106]

Many Christians in the Balkans abhorred the Ottoman governance due to feckless administration and seemingly arbitrary and onerous taxation. Ottoman rule was largely decentralized, so the responsibility for such bad governance primarily lay with provincial rulers, known as *ayan*, who were only loosely under the direction of Istanbul and were often impervious to the wishes and dictates of the central government. Indeed, they tried to turn the areas under their charge into their own fiefdoms. Muslims and Christians both suffered from corrupt and inefficient local governors, but the Christians naturally suffered more, given their inferior millet status. Naturally, the poor of either millet would have suffered the most. Several revolts against Ottoman authority in the Bulgarian lands took place in the nineteenth century. The most famous of these were in Tirnova in 1835, Niş in 1841, and Vidin in 1851. At the heart of these revolts, which were directed less against Istanbul than against the local administration, were grievances about taxation and raids. Tax rates were very high for Bulgarian peasants, and taxes were collected in an inconsistent and confusing way. The Bulgarians were liable for a plethora of taxes and also subject to official seizures, additional customs, and corvée.[107]

Consequently, some Bulgars began to emigrate from the Ottoman Empire to the Russian Empire. Some left to avoid retaliation for the revolts, while others sought to avoid the burdens of Ottoman administration. The Russians often invited these Bulgarians to take the place of the fleeing Tatars. The Ottomans, fearful of losing the revenue from the Bulgarians, initiated a reform in the tax code in 1852 and granted increased autonomy to village administration.[108] It is instructive to note that the Bulgarians had made appeals to the sultan for protection from the local rulers, who tried to hinder the communication of these grievances to the central government. This clearly was less a question of widespread hatred of the Ottoman Empire than of protest against the fecklessness, violence, and corruption of local government. The eighteenth century was a nadir in the central government's control over the peripheral governors, which hindered the sultan from carrying out desired policies throughout the Balkans.

Concomitant with the central government's weakness in terms of its provincial governors was its weakness vis-à-vis the European powers. Losses on the battlefield and a sense that the Ottoman state was trailing behind the Europeans spurred a modernization effort, which began in 1839 with the Gülhane Decree and continued intermittently until the demise of the Ottoman state. This modernization involved the creation of a new military using European methods and the reorganization of the administration of the empire, largely in the direction of increasing centralization. Centralization also meant that the state was increasing its interference in the lives of religious and ethnic communities.[109] This led to drastic changes in the way the empire viewed its non-Muslim subjects.

The consequences of these reforms, known as Tanzimat or reorderings, proved to be momentous throughout the Ottoman lands, certainly not excluding the part of the empire with the highest Christian density—the Balkans. The Tanzimat reforms greatly benefited the Bulgarian

Christians, who were henceforth equal under the law. The centralization of the empire, especially under the governorship of Mithat Paşa, ushered in a new era of economic prosperity.[110] Bulgarian farmers and shepherds, for example, were the main suppliers of wool and food, especially wheat, for the sultan's new army.[111] Bulgarian leatherwork was being sold throughout the Middle East,[112] and Bulgarian merchant colonies had spread to Istanbul, Odessa, Bucharest, and other cities.[113] In essence an incipient Bulgarian commercial elite was responsible for financing a cultural renaissance with political implications. This was furthered by newfound educational opportunities for Bulgarians both in the Ottoman system, even though they still faced discrimination in acquiring Ottoman posts,[114] and in Russia, where a new class of nationally minded Bulgarians was being formed. These new centers of wealth, power, and ideas were challenges to the old Ottoman models.

As members of a new Bulgarian elite were educated and came to develop their own religious worldview, which had only been deepened through the millet system, they often saw themselves as connected to Europe and its civilization. They viewed Europe as superior to the Ottoman Empire, so they began to develop a sense of an unrealized superiority to the Muslims. The Ottoman state, in their view, had prevented them from acquiring the development and refinement of Europe.[115]

At the same time, under the general trajectory of the Tanzimat reforms, the Ottomans sought to increase the capital's authority in the provinces. In Bulgaria this meant the appointment of Mithat Paşa as governor of the Danube Province. Initially, his appointment to Rumelia was seen as a punishment, because of the difficult task of restoring order. He suppressed rebellion harshly but built infrastructure and strengthened institutions. He also increased the participation of local notables, including ethnic Bulgarians, in hopes that more participation by local leaders regardless of ethnicity or religion would help put an end to demands for autonomy.[116] His efforts included a bilingual Turkish-Bulgarian newspaper, *Tuna-Dunav* (The Danube), which he hoped would combat Russian printed propaganda and help inspire unity between Muslims and Christians in the Bulgarian provinces. It was published from 1865 until the war began in 1877. Over time Mithat Paşa proved himself to be extremely competent and was eventually promoted to grand vizier, to implement the policies that he had pursued in the Balkans across the whole empire.

The modern Russian writer Boris Akunin, in his historical-detective novel about the Russo-Turkish War of 1877, describes Mithat Paşa, "the great Turkish reformer":

> "Just lend a brief ear to this Midhat's service record." Mizinov took out a separate sheet of paper and coughed to clear his throat. "At that time he was the governor general of the Danubian Vilajet. Under his patronage [they] established a stagecoach service in those parts, built railways, and even set up a network of islahans—charitable educational establishments for orphan children from both the Muslim and Christian confessions."
>
> "Did he indeed?" Fandorin remarked.
>
> "Yes. A most praiseworthy initiative, is it not? Overall, the scale of Midhat Pasha's. . . . activities was so great that a genuine danger arose of Bulgaria escaping from the sphere of Russian influence. Our ambassador in Constantinople, Nikolai Pavlovich Gnatiev, used all his influence with Sultan Abdul-Aziz and eventually managed to have the excessively zealous governor recalled. After that, Midhat became chairman of the council of state and steered through a law introducing universal public education—a remarkable law, and also, by the way, one that we still do not have here in Russia. . . ."
>
> "I see you are p-perfectly enamored of this man," Erast Petrovich said, interrupting the general.
>
> "You mean Midhat? Absolutely," said Mizinov with a shrug. "And I would be more than glad to see him at the head of a Russian government. But he's not a Russian, he's a Turk."[117]

Despite promises of equality and progress, the Tanzimat and other reforms met resistance and resentment from Muslim quarters. Provincial governors and local rulers protested the encroachment of the state's will in their prerogatives. Land reforms upset the wealthy ağas.[118] Moreover, the Muslims had developed a sense of entitlement as a result of their long-held superior position within the empire.[119] They could not easily accept an equal, and thus diminished, status.[120]

The insult of diminished status within the empire was compounded by special treatment and protection that the Christians often received through the capitulations regime. The capitulations were a series of agreements that gave European powers certain protective rights over non-Muslim Ottoman subjects. It began with France's right to protect European travelers and was later expanded to other Christians. The Russians gained the right to protect Orthodox subjects, including the Bulgarians. This was followed by a scramble between European powers for minorities whom they could sponsor within the empire. Hence these minorities could often bypass normal Ottoman administration and enjoy lower customs fees and beneficial commercial positions vis-à-vis the Muslims. Western powers became increasingly meddlesome in the affairs of the Ottoman Empire. The emergence of a booming Christian merchant class entailed a widening economic gulf between Muslims and Christians after 1856. The Muslims became increasingly resentful of what they saw as a privileged position enjoyed by Christians due to the protections that they enjoyed from the capitulations and exemption from military service.[121] While the European powers continuously pressured the Ottomans for internal reform, they were cynical in their encouragement and did not hope to see the reforms succeed.[122]

One incident in particular shines a light on the tensions that existed between the Muslim and non-Muslim communities on the eve of Bulgarian independence. In 1875 Stephana, a Christian Bulgarian girl in a Macedonian village, sought to convert to Islam. After her father passed away, she claimed a spiritual conversion to Islam. In the Ottoman Empire of 1875, however, conversion to Islam was a bureaucratic matter that required appearances before a council to determine whether the applicants were sane and acting of their own free will. If approved, the applicants would then have to appear before a judge and their own kin. The closest place where Stephana could undertake the process was in Salonika. Stephana's mother was opposed to her conversion, so she also headed to Salonika to prevent it from taking place. In front of a crowd of Muslim onlookers at the Salonika train station, the mother persuaded a group of Christians to pry her daughter from her Muslim escorts. They whisked her off to the American consulate, from whence she relocated to a nearby house. As news and rumors spread quickly among the city's Muslims, a crowd gathered outside of the consulate to rescue the Bulgarian girl. The Muslim paşa and local police chief tried to disperse the crowd with reassurances that the girl would be retrieved, but the crowd was not mollified. French consul Jules Moulin and German consul Henry Abbott approached the area but were directed to a mosque courtyard, where they barricaded themselves against the mob. Attempts by local Muslim officials to find the missing Bulgarian girl and stave off the crowd were unsuccessful. The crowd finally succeeded in penetrating the barricade and shooting the two foreign consuls.

The Ottoman authorities moved quickly to try to punish the guilty parties to avoid any more foreign excitement and meddling. The Ottoman Christians, though, were panicked. Rumors were running rampant, and tensions were increasing. Muslim religious students (*softas*) in Istanbul began to sell religious books in order to buy arms, which was in turn followed by nervous Christians in Istanbul arming themselves. Foreigners feared a bloodletting in the city. The softas' real target, it turned out, was the sultan. On May 10 and 11, 1876, the softas filled the streets demanding the heads of the sultan, the grand vizier, the Russian ambassador Nikolai Ignatiev, and, surprisingly, the murderers of the consuls in Salonika. As the softas advanced toward the Sublime Porte on May 12, the sultan finally relented by changing his grand vizier.[123]

The Salonika Incident is emblematic of the tensions that were bubbling in the Balkans prior to the Bulgarian Horrors of 1876: communal anxieties and suspicions, foreign interference, weak governance, sensational press, and the beginnings of civilian pressure on the Sublime Porte. Unfortunately, worse was to come.

TOWARD BULGARIAN INDEPENDENCE

When the scholar of medieval Byzantium and Bulgaria Steven Runciman noted that "Bulgarian history must always be read with Constantinople in sight,"[124] he clearly had in mind more than simply the first and second Bulgarian empires. A reading of the history of modern Bulgaria, too, must not stray too far from considering Constantinople.

In 1762 the Bulgarian monk known as Father Paisi completed his Slavonic-Bulgarian history, creating the first outline of a Bulgarian national history and identity. The manuscript was copied by hand and spread among interested Bulgarian speakers. Paisi glorified the history of the Bulgarian tsars and their victories in battle. The work was important not as a factual history but because it called upon Bulgarians to be proud of their Bulgarian past and its traditions and awakened a Bulgarian consciousness. Father Paisi reproached those Bulgars who had abandoned the Bulgarian language in favor of Greek: "And some there be that do not want to know about their own Bulgarian people, but have turned to a foreign culture and a foreign language and do not care for their own Bulgarian language but learned to read and speak in Greek and are ashamed to call themselves Bulgars—O you senseless and foolish people! Why are you ashamed to call yourselves Bulgars and why do you not read and speak your own language?"[125]

This was not, as we might expect, a vitriolic protest against Turkish rule. The book became influential in large part due to the rise of an affluent economic class of Bulgarians who competed with Greek traders and were eager to find an argument to combat the hint of inferiority that they felt vis-à-vis the Greeks.[126] Eventually it was used as a textbook in Bulgarian schools in the 1840s, where its sway was broadened.[127] In 1876 the Czech Slavicist Konstantin Jireček published a more comprehensive and factual history of the Bulgarians, but by then Paisi's place in Bulgarian history was settled.[128]

Before gaining or even seeking national independence from Ottoman rule, the Bulgars had first to rid themselves of Greek domination within the Orthodox millet. As mentioned earlier, all Orthodox Christians in the empire had been deprived of independent leadership and placed under the authority of the ecumenical patriarchate in Constantinople which was dominated by Greeks. The Bulgarian national liturgical language had fallen into disuse and was replaced by Greek, although this was not the demotic Greek spoken by contemporary Greeks, who probably found their own liturgy somewhat incomprehensible. Positions within the church were bought and sold. Greek priests received preferential treatment in the appointments, even though they were unable to converse with their congregations. In fact, one of the major grievances cited in the Niş revolts was that the people could not communicate with their priest. Furthermore, Orthodox Bulgarians were liable for taxes to the ecumenical patriarch, which in the early part of the nineteenth century were double the Ottoman state taxes.[129] The agitation against the ecumenical patriarch had no doctrinal dispute at its foundation—it was a purely political movement.

The Bulgarians' lack of a patriarch whom they viewed as their own added to the sense of their national suffering. Their political dependence was combined with a lack of spiritual independence. When the Islahat Firman was proclaimed in 1856, declaring all Ottoman subjects equal under the law, many Bulgarians saw these reforms in terms of equality between Bulgarians and Greeks rather than between Muslims and Christians. In this context, it is understandable why not only some Muslims but also some Christians who had advantageous positions opposed the reforms, such as Greeks and especially the Greek clergy who had a dominant position in the church led from Constantinople. They feared the undermining of their authority and resources.[130]

At the same time as these changes were taking place, increasing contact between Bulgarians and Russians (originally via the training of Bulgarian priests in Russia) aroused the first sense of Slavic awareness. Demands for more autonomy from the ecumenical patriarchate followed. Few if any of their demands were met, so they sent petitions to the sultan, asking for his intervention. The Bulgarians were finally allowed to construct a Bulgarian church in Istanbul in 1849 and started agitating for their own millet in 1856.[131] The Russians declined to sponsor this petition for fear of splitting the Orthodox world. Eventually discussions were held between the patriarch and Bulgarian representatives with the sultan's encouragement. In 1860, as an act of defiance, the patriarch's name was replaced with the sultan's name in a prayer read in the Bulgarian church in Constantinople, where, in the middle of the nineteenth century, more Bulgarians lived than in any other city in Bulgaria proper.[132] Bulgarian disobedience against the patriarch became a common occurrence, culminating with the Bulgarians expelling Greek bishops and priests in 1866.

After the Serbs and Greeks achieved national independence, they severed ties with the ecumenical patriarch of Constantinople and no longer paid tribute to the patriarchate. Hence the Bulgarians became his last and largest source of revenue. Because many Greeks still lived in the Danube region, especially in the cities of Plovdiv and Varna, the patriarch was not inclined to allow the Bulgarians to split. After the insurrection in Crete, the Greeks had lost favor with the Ottomans. The sultan sided with the Bulgarians.

In 1870 the sultan issued a firman recognizing the Bulgarian Church under a Bulgarian Exarchate. It allowed any congregation to join the

Bulgarian Exarchate with a two-thirds vote. This had the effect of sketching rough borders for the future Bulgarian state. Although the Bulgarian Exarchate was still nominally under the ecumenical patriarchate, the patriarch refused to accept the sultan's decision and declared a schism. However, the facts were already established on the ground. A Bulgarian Church had already come into being, and Bulgarians had acquired their own representative with the Ottomans in Istanbul. Before the Bulgarian nationalist movement took aim at the sultan, it had the ethnically Greek patriarch in its sights. Some Bulgarians had bigger aspirations, but national independence for most was not even on the horizon, although it was to be achieved within ten years.[133]

Russian interest in Bulgaria was rather late in coming. The Bulgarians were viewed as non-Slavic Huns or Avars who had adopted some aspects of the Slavic language until as late as the 1820s, when Ukrainian Iurii Ivanovich Gutsa-Venelin took a particular interest in Bulgarians and published a book making the bold assertion that Bulgarians were in fact Slavs. This claim provoked criticism from leaders in both the Russian and Habsburg Empires but was celebrated in Bulgaria, adding to the awakening of a Bulgarian ethnic consciousness as Slavs. Gutsa-Venelin's writing, however fantastical, offered the Bulgarians an escape from the notion that they were somehow related to their Turkish oppressors. By claiming that the Bulgarians enjoyed a purely Slavic and even heroic past, Gutsa-Venelin removed the stigma and shame of being related to the Turks and instantly provided the small Bulgarian elite with a more acceptable version of their past.[134]

Gutsa-Venelin's writings coincided with the Russo-Turkish War of 1829, when Russia advanced deep within Ottoman Balkan territory in Bulgaria and increased contacts between Russians and Bulgarians. As feelings of solidarity with first their Orthodox and later their Slavic kin gained ground among Russian intellectuals and nationalists, they tried to increase their engagement and support. However, the burgeoning Russian pan-Slav concern about the Bulgarians was not matched by Bulgarian interest in or knowledge of Russia.[135]

As Russia asserted its claim of protection over Orthodox Christians in the Ottoman Empire, many of the Russian tsars believed in their divine mission to defend fellow Orthodox believers. For his part, the ecumenical patriarch resisted Russian encroachment on his turf.[136] Russia, in turn, tried to maintain the patriarch's role and avoid fissures within Ottoman Orthodox Christianity, even though they often had conflicting goals. The patriarch, who enjoyed a powerful role within the empire, preferred the status quo, whereas the Russians promoted a change in power relations. They sought to assert a position of domination over the Ottomans without giving rise to any national or liberal movements modeled on French principles espoused by many Balkan national elites.[137] The Balkan nationalists, who were often resentful of Russian paternalism, had little desire to model their independent states on a Russian autocratic model. This was an additional reason for Russia's hesitancy in pursuing the formation of independent states in the Balkans.[138]

During the Crimean War, Russian policy makers discussed fomenting uprisings in the Balkans and assumed that these would naturally occur the moment Russian troops crossed the borders. Small numbers of Bulgarians volunteered to serve on the Russian side in that war. In truth, though, the Russians had little knowledge of the disposition of the Bulgarian people. They did not want to get dragged into a war that might bring about the disintegration of the Ottoman Empire, an event for which they were still unprepared.[139]

The Crimean War was a monumental defeat for the Russians. Their claim to the protection of Orthodox Ottomans was curtailed to such a degree that Great Britain became a mediator between the ecumenical patriarch and the Romanian Orthodox Christians. From that point onward, Russia's focus shifted toward Slavdom and away from Orthodoxy. The Russians were also forced to concede the right to have military ships enter the Black Sea. Furthermore, the Crimean War had far-reaching domestic consequences, including fiscal calamity and the end of serfdom. The Russians had originally concentrated most of their energy in the Balkans on Serbia, but Serbian nationalists had shown too much interest in revolutionary movements and ideologies, of which the Russians disapproved. In short, the Russians had realized that they could not control Serbia.[140]

The debacle of the Crimean War increased the Russian Empire's inclination to maintain the status quo in the Balkans, whereas Russian pan-Slavists became more active in supporting the education and creation of Balkan Slavic groups with an affinity for Russia and its political system. In 1858 the Moscow Benevolent Society was formed and helped finance

Bulgarian students in Russia. This gave Russia better contacts within Bulgaria and helped Russia to understand Bulgarian conditions better.

Both moderate and radical Bulgarian nationalists existed. Because the moderates had benefited from the economic prosperity in Bulgaria over the preceding decades, they espoused slow progress but not independence. Russia opposed radically minded Bulgarian nationalists because they were more difficult to control. In the end, nationalist attempts to attain change in Bulgaria ended in failure more often than in other parts of the Ottoman Balkans.

Bulgaria was closer to the center of the Ottoman Empire and could be monitored much more closely, so Bulgarians seeking radical change often operated outside of Ottoman control in Romania, Odessa, and Serbia. These more radical nationalists envisioned the uprising of the Christian peasantry and formed secret societies with that aim in mind. These clandestine revolutionaries were usually members of the booming merchant class, who were the least likely to feel oppression by the Muslims. They nonetheless equated the Muslims with the power of the state and directed all of their dissatisfaction in that direction.[141] Their aims gradually became more uncompromising. In 1867, for example, the clandestine central Bulgarian committee published a memoir proposing a dual Turco-Bulgarian Empire modeled on the Austro-Hungarian model.[142] Under such a scheme the Bulgarians would have had a national assembly and other autonomous institutions, while the sultan would be crowned tsar in the Bulgarians' historic capital of Tarnovo.[143] Such propositions were short lived. As the situation progressed, the nationalists' aspirations became uncompromising. Yet, understanding their weakness relative to the empire, they realized that they needed a foreign patron and were increasingly successful in being noticed by the European powers. Russian aid, though, made the most sense.[144]

It was only after the 1870 Franco-Prussian War that Russia was able to rid itself of its obligations under the Treaty of Paris. France, Britain's partner against Russian expansion, had been crucially weakened and could no longer aid Britain in enforcing the treaty. Britain alone could do little and felt great anxiety over Russia's increased activity in the Black Sea and Central Asia, whereas the Russian Empire considered the Black Sea its vulnerable underbelly and was determined to improve its position there. As the Black Sea gained in importance for both Russia and

Britain, especially after the opening of the Suez Canal in 1869, so did the geostrategic importance of the Balkan territories bordering it.

In 1875 a revolt of Christian peasants in Bosnia turned into an all-out war in Serbia in 1876. Pan-Slav enthusiasts from Russia joined in the fight against the Ottomans, who were able to send troops and put down the rebellion despite the empire's declaration of bankruptcy in 1875. At this time the more radical Bulgarian nationalists saw an opening for their planned uprising, which was ultimately to be a catalyst for a cataclysmic change in the demographics of the province and the empire.

Two

BAG AND BAGGAGE

The ancestor of every action is a thought.

Ralph Waldo Emerson "Spiritual Laws" (*Essays: The First Series*)

Where are you going, infidel? How dare you tread this sacred soil? This land is Bulgarian; yours is in the deserts of Asia. Go and rot there!

Ivan Vazov, *Under the Yoke*

I wish I had at least been able to help you kill a few Turks.... It does not suffice to humiliate them; they should be destroyed.

Voltaire writing to Catherine the Great (quoted in John Trumpbour "The Clash of Civilizations")

At the beginning of Leo (Lev) Nikolaevich Tolstoi's posthumously published work *Hadji Murad*, the narrator is returning home one fine midsummer day following the hay harvest. His eyes and nostrils are filled with enchantment by the resplendent variety of blossoms, which he describes in great detail, along his path. He gathers enough for a bouquet and then on a ditch bank he spots,

> [i]n full bloom, a beautiful thistle plant of the crimson kind, which in our neighborhood they call "Tartar," and carefully avoid when mowing—or, if they do happen to cut it down, throw out from among the grass for fear of pricking their hands. Thinking to pick

> this thistle and put it in the centre of my nosegay, I climbed down into the ditch, and.... set to work to pluck the flower. But this proved a very difficult task. Not only did the stalk prick on every side.... but it was so tough that I had to struggle with it for nearly five minutes, breaking the fibres one by one; and when I had at last plucked it, the stalk was all frayed, and the flower itself no longer seemed so fresh and beautiful. Moreover, owing to its coarseness and stiffness, it did not seem in place among the delicate blossoms of my nosegay. I felt sorry to have vainly destroyed a flower that looked beautiful in its proper place, and I threw it away....
>
> "But what energy and tenacity! With what determination it defended itself, and how dearly it sold its life!" thought I to myself, recollecting the effort it had cost me to pluck the flower.[1]

The narrator then continues his walk home through plowed fields, cleaned completely of weeds and even blades of grass. Nothing but black soil is to be seen. The scene causes him to reflect upon human nature: "Ah, what a destructive creature is man.... How many different plant-lives he destroys to support his own existence!" He begins to look for some sign of life as consolation in the desolation of the tilled field:

> In front of me, to the right of the road, I saw some kind of little clump, and drawing nearer I found it was the same kind of thistle as that which I had vainly plucked and thrown away. This "Tartar" plant had three branches. One was broken, and stuck out like the stump of a mutilated arm. Each of the other two bore a flower, once red but now blackened. One stalk was broken and a half of it hung down with a soiled flower at its tip. The other, though also soiled with black mud, still stood erect. Evidently a cartwheel had passed over the plant, but it had risen again and that was why, though erect, it stood twisted to one side, as if a piece of its body had been torn from it, its bowels had been drawn out, an arm torn off, and one of its eyes plucked out; and yet it stood firm and did not surrender to man, who had destroyed all its brothers around it.

Behind Tolstoi's thinly veiled metaphor about Russian conquest of Muslim lands is a rebuke to the violence of war as well as to its seemingly frivolous purposes. The thistle was destroyed in the vain creation of a bouquet, just as European imperialism glibly sought to put jewel after jewel in its crown. The Ottoman Empire had three limbs—in Asia, Africa, and Europe—much like the second thistle, and after the numerous wars of contraction in the Balkans, its European branch was also broken, "like the stump of a mutilated arm."

For Europe, the nineteenth century was one of its most peaceful times, but this is primarily because it was busy exporting war to the rest of the world pursuing conquest and scrambling for territory. Undergirding the strategic and economic motives was a powerful discursive incitement to conquest informed by the principles of religion and enlightenment. At the core of these ideas was the debasement of those to be subjugated, but these same ideas also implied the bumptious elevation of the would-be conqueror and his rule. With the dismantling of the Ottoman Empire as the goal, the Turk came under special opprobrium. The notion that civilization was a European invention as well as a European gift spurred nations on to all sorts of quixotic *missions civilisatrices*. Knights errant ranging from the English poet Lord Byron to T. E. Lawrence felt ennobled in the wars of their countries to oust the Turk, shielded by a self-righteous call to civilization yet blinded from viewing the conflicts with any sense of objectivity and fairness.

In this chapter I explore the ways in which the Turkish exit from Europe was conceived in the minds of Europeans before it was carried out. The atrocities committed by the Ottomans in their suppression of a violent Bulgarian uprising created a firestorm of enthusiasm for an end to the Turkish presence in Europe. Objecting voices were lost in the din, and the ranks of the Turkophobes momentarily swelled enough to push their governments to action in the case of Russia or inaction in the case of Britain. Ultimately, though, this goal—only abstract for most of Europe—was to have a concrete and bloody result in the Balkans, where European intellectual currents of nationalism and Orientalism were tributaries flowing into a Balkan torrent of vengeance.

THE APRIL RISING AND THE BULGARIAN HORRORS

In July 1875 Serbians in Bosnia-Herzegovina staged a revolt against Ottoman rule, encouraged and supported by the Russian state and individual pan-Slav enthusiasts. Up to this point, Serbia had been the linchpin of Russian policy in the Balkans. Only later were Russian attention and might directed to Bulgaria's cause.

When the Ottomans sent troops to quell the rebellion in Serbia, Bulgarian revolutionaries saw a fortuitous occasion for their own national ambitions. Many Bulgarian individuals had been receiving training and education under Russian tutelage in Moscow, Bucharest, Odessa, Constantinople, and elsewhere. They had developed networks of secret societies and revolutionary fraternities. Earlier uprisings, including one that had called for the burning of Constantinople,[2] had ended in abject failure. But in April 1876 agitation for new action culminated in a plan for a general uprising on May 12. Events preempted these plans, however, as several conspirators were arrested and some Ottoman police were murdered.

Expecting their plot to be uncovered, the Bulgarian revolutionaries expedited their call for uprising to May 2 (April 20 in the Julian Orthodox calendar). The uprising essentially entailed attacks on prominent Muslims in many villages in the center of the province. As news of the uprising spread, Bulgarian attacks on Muslim lives and property expanded, and many houses were burned.[3] In Koprovishtitsa, for example, the entire Gypsy population, including women and children, was murdered.[4] One estimate puts the number of Muslim deaths at one thousand and the number of houses destroyed at three thousand.[5] News of the uprising reached Ottoman authorities in Plovdiv, and the few troops at their disposal were dispatched to the areas of uprising. On their way, these troops encountered many Muslims who were fleeing the violence and who related what they had witnessed and heard.

Although the Ottomans diverted some regular troops from Niş and Vidin, they were unable to muster enough regular troops to cope with the uprising because most of the empire's Balkan forces were deployed in the war with Serbia. But the Bulgarian revolutionaries had overlooked the possibility that the Ottomans might send in irregular forces, which is exactly what they did. The governor of Edirne granted permission to local officials to recruit irregular forces, known as *başıbozuks*, from the local population. A number of these were Turks. Considering that the southern rim of the uprising was in the Rhodope Mountains, however, it can be safely assumed that many if not the majority of these başıbozuks were in fact Pomaks. It is also widely acknowledged that a considerable number of those employed to suppress the uprisings were Circassians. These men had become especially inured to violence by their experience fighting the Russian expansion in the Caucasus. Furthermore, having only recently migrated to the Balkans, they were known to have developed little loyalty to the Ottoman state, especially relative to their fierce tribal loyalties.

This mix of irregular forces, with some support from the available regular troops, attacked Bulgarian towns and villages, committing acts of violence, pillage, and destruction against the Christian inhabitants. The village of Batak is still the most infamous of the Bulgarian villages from this brutal suppression. It was an entirely Christian village whose inhabitants had entered into a dispute with Muslims of neighboring villages about property rights over timber located between the villages that they had been felling. Feelings between the Christians and Muslims had hardened to such an extent that Batak became one of the centers for the April Uprising. Leading up to it, the villagers of Batak, both men and women, had been arming themselves and engaging in military training.[6] During the uprising the villagers of Batak used these weapons against Muslims of the surrounding villages. When the başıbozuks arrived to put down the uprising, they were met with fire from the Christians. The Muslims eventually put down the uprising—with stunning brutality. The uprising and its brutal suppression are a formative moment in Bulgarian national history, but Bulgarian historiography has yet to come to terms with the fact that the Slavic Pomaks figured prominently in the Bulgarian Horrors.[7]

By June a trickle of accounts about the excessive harshness of the suppression began to pour into the capital of the Ottoman Empire and from there spread even farther afield. The British, like the Ottomans, had initially been skeptical about the carnage. Ottoman officials, after their experiences over the course of the century, had developed a tendency to view any agitation in the Balkans as yet another Russian intrigue. Being latecomers themselves to notions of nationalism, they could not fully grasp nationalist motivations.[8] As reports from foreign correspondents reached European readers, concern about the situation turned into public outrage. At that time the franchise had just been extended in Britain, and with few other issues around which British consensus could be built the Bulgarian atrocities were low-hanging fruit for British politicians to harvest.[9]

2.1. *The Bulgarian Martyresses* by Konstantin Egorovich Makovskii (1877). Public domain: Wikimedia Commons.

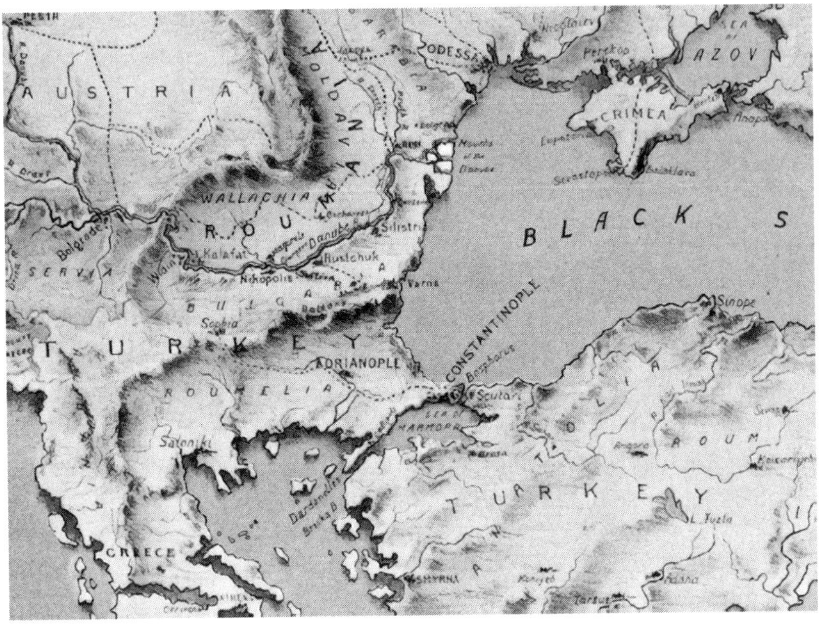

2.2. *Seat of War: Turkey and Rumelia* from *Historical Narrative of the Turko-Russian War* (1886), 109.

Originally Britain's envoy in Constantinople had encouraged the Porte to act swiftly and without mercy. In a letter dated May 7, he wrote, "About 5,000 troops have been dispatched from here and I believe no exertion should be spared for assuring the immediate suppression of a movement which, if allowed to spread, will become extremely serious."[10]

Benjamin Disraeli, who was British prime minister at the time, was inclined to support Ottoman territorial integrity as part of a long-standing British policy. He was suspected of holding his position of sympathy for the Muslim empire because he was of Jewish origin (his family became Anglican when he was a boy). At that time Jews and Muslims were thought to have natural affinities—a fact that highlights a much-changed Western view regarding Jewish-Muslim relations. Disraeli offered tepid and equivocal support to the Ottomans despite a barrage of histrionic questioning in Parliament. William Gladstone became his archnemesis in Parliament. His scathing and crusading rhetoric encapsulated feelings of British outrage engendered by the "nauseating profusion of detail" found in the writings of American correspondent Januarius MacGahan,[11] who broke the story in the West while writing for the *London Daily News*. The reporter's offer to cover the story for other newspapers was originally declined because of his "reputation for sensational proclivities."[12] Gladstone, determined to make the Bulgarian issue central in the electoral campaign for the seat recently vacated by Disraeli, published a pamphlet entitled *The Bulgarian Horrors and the Question of the East* in which he condemned the Turks with much vitriol and urged a change in British policy.

In the year and a half that followed the April Uprising, approximately two hundred different European newspapers published more than three thousand articles denouncing the Bulgarian atrocities.[13] European public opinion came out vociferously against the Ottomans, and respected European intellectuals and writers such as Victor Hugo, Oscar Wilde, Giuseppe Garibaldi, Charles Darwin, and Fyodor Mikhailovich Dostoevskii publicly denounced the Turks. Outcry, however was reserved for Ottoman crimes. The atrocities that Christian empires committed, such as those resulting from the Opium Wars in China, the Indian Mutiny, Russian expansion in the Caucasus and Central Asia, and frontier expansion in North America and Australia, failed to engender similar just sentiments. Atatürk later noted this hypocrisy: "When a Turk was killed, nobody raised an eyebrow, but when a Turk killed someone, they raised a ruckus."[14]

Russian public opinion was also outraged, as the Ottoman massacres were heavily publicized.[15] The Russian state had only eased censorship in 1860. Before that date public opinion had little influence on state policy. Now the interplay between state policies and public sentiment entered new territory. Russian and in particular pan-Slav and nationalist public opinion exerted immense pressure on the tsar. The first news in the Russian Empire on the "Bulgarian Massacres" was published in Odessa on May 10, 1876. Shortly afterward reports were echoed in the major Russian newspapers and periodicals. Pan-Slav and pan-Orthodox support for the Bulgarians was bubbling. Dostoevskii included reference to the Bulgarian Horrors in his novel *The Brothers Karamazov*:

> "By the way, a Bulgarian I met lately in Moscow," Ivan went on, seeming not to hear his brother's words, "told me about the crimes committed by Turks and Circassians in all parts of Bulgaria through fear of a general rising of the Slavs. They burn

villages, murder, outrage women and children, they nail their prisoners by the ears to the fences, leave them so till morning, and in the morning they hang them—all sorts of things you can't imagine. People talk sometimes of bestial cruelty, but that's a great injustice and insult to the beasts; a beast can never be so cruel as a man, so artistically cruel. The tiger only tears and gnaws, that's all he can do. He would never think of nailing people by the ears, even if he were able to do it. These Turks took a pleasure in torturing children,—too; cutting the unborn child from the mother's womb, and tossing babies up in the air and catching them on the points of their bayonets before their mothers' eyes. Doing it before the mothers' eyes was what gave zest to the amusement. Here is another scene that I thought very interesting. Imagine a trembling mother with her baby in her arms, a circle of invading Turks around her. They've planned a diversion: they pet the baby, laugh to make it laugh. They succeed, the baby laughs. At that moment a Turk points a pistol four inches from the baby's face. The baby laughs with glee, holds out its little hands to the pistol, and he pulls the trigger in the baby's face and blows out its brains. Artistic, wasn't it? By the way, Turks are particularly fond of sweet things, they say."[16]

Among Russian intellectuals the situation was referred to as a "war of races" and a "war of extermination." One Russian paper stated that "Turkey and the Turkish Başıbozuks have opened a war of extermination against our poor Bulgarian brothers. If so then the Turks are guilty. In order to punish the guilty and save the Bulgarians from the hands of the savage Asian herds, the Turks must be driven from the European soil."[17]

The hysteria generated by the press was contagious. The acclaimed Russian writer Ivan Sergeevich Turgenev, far from being a pan-Slavist, was still incensed enough to compose a poem directed at the queen of England, in which the queen is at leisure watching a game of croquet on the grounds of her castle at Windsor when the croquet balls suddenly morph into the heads of Bulgarian peasants. She summons a doctor, who blames her fit of madness on the London press. Turgenev then alludes to English complicity in the massacres. After being read aloud at

Peterhof, Turgenev's poem, in part inspired by the Queen of Hearts in Lewis Carroll's in *Alice's Adventures in Wonderland* (1865), "[flew] around all Russia" in handwritten copies, although it was not published in Russia. Nor was its translation (done via a French version by author Henry James, Turgenev's friend) published in Britain. In both countries there was serious apprehension about fanning the flames and irritating the other power. It was finally first published in America in October 1876.[18]

She sees, as in vision, the balls disappear,
And corpse-heads, all ghastly and bleeding,
Roll toward her, where speechless and pallid with fear,
She shudders, and watches their speeding.

Heads frosted, and heads of the young and the fair;
Heads of children, whose innocent prattle
Was drowned in the hell-storm that swept through the air
When their village was sacked in the battle.

And lo! the Queen's daughter—youngest fairest of all,
Instead of the red ball, is throwing
A babe's gory head, which comes rolling, to fall
At her feet, with its lifeblood still flowing!

She calls her physician to come to her aid,
"Quick, quick!" she cries, "quick to my cure!"
He quietly answers: "You may well be afraid,
You've been reading the papers, I'm sure.

"THE TIMES with Bulgarian horrors is filled—
Tells of Servian martyrs and Christian despair;
No wonder your majesty dreams of the killed;
Take these drops, and come in from the chill of the air."

She's housed: but as plunged in a revery still,
She sits with her eyes cast reflectively down,
O horror! her heart with new terror grows chill,
For she sees to her knees the blood spread on her gown!

"Quick! Wash it away, for I fain would forget,
Wash! Wash, British rivers and waters, this gore!"
No, no, haughty Queen, though that stain is still wet,
'Tis of innocent blood, and will fade never more![19]

Not all Russians were so easily drawn into a pan-Slavist furor. For example, at the end of his novel *Anna Karenina* Leo Tolstoi, by then a pacifist, treated the various Slavonic committees and Russian volunteers going to fight on behalf of the Serbs in 1876 with an unveiled disdain. He clearly resented the effort by the press to make public opinion demand war:

> "That's where you're mistaken, *batiushka*," said the latter [Katavasof]. "There may be cases when government doesn't carry out the will of its citizens, and then society declares its own will."
>
> But Sergei Ivanovitch did not approve of this reply. He frowned as Katavasof spoke, and said sternly,
>
> "You put the question all wrong. Here there is no declaration of war, but simply an expression of human, of Christian sympathy. Our brethren, men of the same blood, the same faith are butchered. Well! We do not look upon them only as men and as co-religionists, but purely as women, children, old men. The feelings are stirred, and the whole Russian people fly to help check these horrors. Suppose you were walking in the street and saw a drunken man beating a woman or a child. I think you would not stop to ask whether war has been declared before you attacked the man, and protected the object of his fury."
>
> "No; but I would not kill him."
>
> "Yes, you might even kill him."
>
> "I don't know. If I saw such a sight, I might yield to the immediate feeling. I cannot tell how it would be. But in the oppression of the Slavs, there is not, and cannot be, such a powerful motive."
>
> "Perhaps not for you, but other people think differently," said Sergei Ivanovitch angrily. "The people still keep the tradition of sympathy with brethren of the orthodox faith, who are groaning under the yoke of the infidel. They have heard of their terrible sufferings, and are aroused."

> "That may be," answered Levin in a conciliatory tone, "only I don't see it. I myself am one of the people, and I don't feel it."[20]

The debate in Tolstoi's literary endeavor spilled over into his real life. By the time that the passages of the novel were ready for publishing in 1877, the press uproar concerning the Bulgarian Horrors was at its height. His publisher Mikhail Nikiforovich Katkov, a well-know pan-Slavist, refused to publish Tolstoi's passages concerning the war and pan-Slavism. Tolstoi, for his part, refused to alter them. In the end, Katkov published a mere statement to conclude the novel, while Tolstoi published his conclusion separately as a pamphlet.

In Britain ultimately the reporting of MacGahan, corroborated with detailed descriptions by another journalist, Eugene Schuyler, who had set out on the journey to Batak with an expressed desire to vilify the Turks.[21] A third, more dispassionate report by Walter Baring aroused public passions.[22] These reporters generally estimated the damage at partial or total destruction of sixty villages and the deaths of 12,000–15,000 Bulgarians while bandying about rumored numbers of thirty thousand and even one hundred thousand dead.[23]

These figures have come under suspicion when they have come under scrutiny. None of the aforementioned reporters spoke proficient Bulgarian, although they were accompanied by some interpreters as well as Russian prince Aleksei Nikolaevich Tsertelev.[24] None of them personally visited more than ten villages. They also failed to take into consideration that many Bulgarians from this region were itinerant agricultural workers who spent the springs and summers in Romania and Hungary and that many had merely fled to the mountains in fear and would return later. The reporters also used the unreasonably high number of ten people to a household to make their estimates of village population and deaths, instead of a more reasonable five.[25] In any event, the true number killed in the massacres in Bulgaria is most likely less than the number who died in massacres in Mount Lebanon or Damascus during roughly the same period. What made the reports so consequential in the case of Bulgaria is that they were sensationalized by the press and utilized by the Russians to advance their geostrategic interests.[26]

The main thrust of Ottoman diplomacy at this time was to ensure the support of the British against Russian aggression (as had been the case in the Crimean War of 1854), but that policy was now under attack inside Britain. The British government was charged with being in some way responsible for the atrocities because it had given protection to such a malevolent empire.[27]

Given the importance of British military backing, it was imperative for the Ottomans to stay on good terms with the English. As the British complained about the Bulgarian Horrors, their Ottoman counterparts lamented that every minute detail of Christian suffering was published in Europe while the suffering of Muslims in the initial uprising garnered no European attention or sympathy. The war with Serbia was over by September, and the Ottomans, who accepted an unfavorable armistice despite their advantageous military position, diverted regular troops to Bulgaria to impose order, albeit too late to affect European public opinion.[28] The Ottomans also tried and punished certain individuals implicated in the Bulgarian Horrors.

The European powers, mostly at the behest of Russia, tried to impose a reform program on the Ottomans that would have divided the Balkans into various autonomous Christian principalities and states. The British, who claimed that the proposals were an infringement on the Ottoman Empire's sovereignty, were reluctant to excite their own Muslim subjects in India and therefore tended to side with the Ottomans at the conference. The Ottomans assumed that the minorities were already benefiting from autonomy. Furthermore, they had become chary of demands for territorial autonomy based on their experience with Greek independence, which was the lens that colored all Ottoman views on this subject.[29]

Assuming that the British would not allow the Russians to attack unhindered, the Ottomans refused to sign off on the Russian plan. They also promulgated the empire's first constitution on December 19, 1876, and thereby declared that the reform proposals of the European powers had immediately become superfluous and unnecessary.

The Europeans, though, were reluctant to accept any reform proposals originating from the Ottomans themselves.[30] Moreover, Russian politics and interests at that time did not favor compromise.[31] As negotiations over reform continued, the Russians arranged a deal with the Austrian Empire, whereby Austria would remain neutral in the event of war in exchange for the cession of Bosnia-Herzegovina. The Russians were reluctant to enter a war that might invoke foreign intervention, as had happened in the Crimean War, and thus sought to buy protection on their western flank. They were also nervous that Russian action in the Balkans in favor of their Orthodox and Slav kin might be countered by appeals from the sultan for the loyalties of Muslims within the Russian Empire.[32]

As negotiations proved fruitless and the Russian Empire felt increasingly sure that the British would not come to the rescue of the Ottomans, the mobilization of troops that had begun in the fall of 1876 hastened. Russia severed diplomatic ties with the Ottomans on April 23, 1877, and declared war on the following day, finally crossing the Danube on June 15. The Russian plan of war was occupation of Bulgaria with the "unconditional liquidation of Ottoman rule in the Balkan peninsula" and a military advance to "Constantinople itself."[33]

IMAGINING A EUROPE WITHOUT TURKS

The presence of Muslims in Europe was objectionable to many in Christian Europe. In its heyday, the Ottoman Empire expanded northward as far as the gates of Vienna, eliciting great fear throughout Europe. Unlike marauding Christian troops and expanding European empires, which had also trampled across Europe leaving destruction in their wake, the Ottoman expansion in Europe proved particularly menacing because they were different—they were Muslims.

Although Europe was already cleft by numerous fissures, such as the sectarian Protestant-Catholic-Orthodox divides, European identity was nevertheless largely shaped in opposition to non-Christian others. The Jews and Gypsies were the others within, the scapegoats of Europe: "The Jews poisoned the wells, the gypsies brought the plague."[34] The Moors and Turks were the others without. The Moors had been mostly expelled by the end of the fifteenth century and had already been on the retreat for centuries before that. So the Turks, who remained the representatives of Islam for Europe, became the necessary "other" for the creation of a European "us." In many ways, this other became the focus of a European anxiety that morphed into fear, dislike, and at times hatred. The idea of expelling the Turks from Europe was a direct consequence of their otherness: those who are considered others cannot fully belong, and their presence creates a dissonance that must be resolved.

The impulse to expel the Turks from Europe had a long history. It was greatly influenced and colored by the crusades and the crusading ethic, which continued to have a strong appeal in Europe as both historic precedent and unfinished business. Originally the crusader discourse encouraged taking back the Holy Land from the Turks, whom Pope Urban II called an "accursed race" and "slave of the demons,"[35] and such tropes were repeatedly voiced long after. One leading proponent of war against the Ottomans and liberation of the Bulgarians, William Thomas Stead, wrote, "I felt that I was called to preach a new crusade. Not against Islam, which I reverenced, but against the Turks who disgraced humanity. I realized the feelings of Peter the Hermit. God was with me."[36] Crusading language was actually becoming an increasing part of Western discourse, inevitably employed in grand conflicts between Christians and Muslims. As late as the First World War, when Britain and the Ottomans engaged each other militarily for the first time in almost a century, British soldiers were canonized both in the press and in official propaganda as modern crusaders and the operation in Palestine was seen as "the Last Crusade."[37] The crusades thus were an ominous historical motif for the fate of Muslims living in the Balkans.

Yet here an important point needs to be emphasized: the expulsion of the Muslims from the Balkans was imagined before it was realized. After five hundred years of Ottoman presence in the Balkans, Muslims had become a demographic fact of life. Their expulsion was bound to take a human toll. Indeed, the desire to rid Europe of a Muslim presence was at first only imaginary but was ultimately "an imaginaire of death."[38] This imagined elimination of the other was a foundational prerequisite for mass violence leading to ethnic cleansing.

The idea of a Muslim-free Balkan Peninsula was buttressed by the process of otherizing the Turks—who remained, despite centuries of life in the Balkans, "Asiatic." At its most extreme, this otherization devolved into dehumanization and from there to bestialization. The bestialization of the enemy demonstrates the potential for violence. As French sociologist Jacques Semelin has indicated, "A massacre ensues when the victims have been dehumanized. . . . The killing starts with the use of words disqualifying his humanity." The very word "massacre" betrays an inhumane meaning, given that it originated with the slaughter of animals.[39]

Some scholars have suggested that pre-1878 thinkers did not fully understand the consequences of establishing a nation-state on top of a population that was ethnically and confessionally heterogeneous.[40] Yet the suggestion that those who made such exhortations to liberate the Christians or rid Europe of the Turkish yoke were ignorant of the human suffering that would inevitably ensue is untrue. In 1865 the Austrian geographer Johann Vincenz Goehlert clearly pronounced the corollary: "The more the individual nations gain their independence, the more the Mohammedans, and especially the Ottomans, are displaced from their homes."[41]

While a desire for Christian emancipation from Turkish rule was a familiar motif among Europeans of the epoch, it was accompanied by a sordid desire to expel the Turk and do violence against him. According to the chorus of a popular song in Greece in 1821, "The Turk shall live no longer, neither in the Morea, nor in the whole earth."[42]

Gladstone, who roused much excitement in Britain after the Bulgarian Horrors, was especially prominent in his condemnation of the Turk: "What spectacle did these Sultans offer to the world—a dynasty of worn-out and impotent debauchees, who let loose on mankind a horde of uncontrollable wild beasts."[43] It was, for Gladstone, "not a question of Mahometanism simply," for the Turkish "race" was especially vile. The Turks were not, he wrote, "the mild Mahometans of India, nor the chivalrous Saladins of Syria, nor the cultured Moors of Spain. They were, upon the whole, from the black day when they first entered Europe, the one great anti-human species of humanity."[44]

Gladstone made it crystal clear in his pamphlet what he thought the solution should be: the Turks should "carry away their abuses in the only possible manner, namely by carrying off themselves . . . one and all, bag and baggage."[45]

The phrase "bag and baggage" subsequently became synonymous with the expulsion of the Turks from Europe. It falls into a category of English vocabulary known as legal doublets. These standardized phrases are formed by putting two synonyms side by side in order to eradicate any ambiguity that might leave wiggle room for lawyers to make a case based on nuanced language.[46] Gladstone's choice of the phrase, which entered

English usage in the fifteenth century, was a clear demand for the Turks to clear out of Bulgaria leaving nothing behind.

Gladstone came under criticism for this reckless rhetoric. His critics better understood the demographic reality in Bulgaria and realized that people could not simply be uprooted from their land without grave consequences. One Englishman wrote quite presciently about the removal of Turks from Europe:

> They have more people to "remove"—that is to starve or kill, for in this case they prefer removal to another world to subjection and degradation in this—than from the whole population of the kingdoms of Holland, Denmark and Greece; . . . so that if every man, woman, and child were swept out of that "cock-pit of Europe," it would not equal the "removal" of the Turks, "one and all, bag and baggage," from their homes and heritage in Europe.
>
> The human mind fails to realise such an Aceldama. "The field of blood" is too vast for any range but that of a demon's vision. As the Slavs, Cossacks, and Calmucks advance they will pass over ravaged fields, burnt villages and ruined towns. . . . It will be a conflict for dear life, and whatever else the Turk may do he will "die hard."[47]

This reprimand and similar objections caused Gladstone to climb down from his bluster, albeit only a trifle. Trying to backtrack on his "bag and baggage" statement, he explained that he had meant only the Turkish administrators. He conceded that relations between a Christian majority and Muslim minority in an independent Bulgaria might be difficult but referred to Greece as a case in point: such a problem had already been solved there and could be solved in Bulgaria as well.[48] Gladstone must have been unaware of the irony of the statement: Greek independence in 1832 resulted in the death and expulsion of the native Muslim population rather than its peaceable coexistence with the Greeks.[49]

Scottish philosopher Thomas Carlyle also called for "the immediate and summary expulsion of the Turk from Europe," with the naïve view that the Muslims who were not part of the administration could stay unmolested. He predicted that "the peaceful Mongol inhabitants would . . . be left in peace and treated with perfect equity. . . . but the governing Turk with all his Pashas and Bashi Bazouks, should be ordered to disappear from Europe and never to return."[50]

But the simple fact that Gladstone, Carlyle, and others were remiss in overlooking was that—as demographics played an important role in the ability of the Ottomans to maintain their rule—the overturning of their rule was to have an inevitable demographic facet. Simply put, the suggestion of a change in administration only rang a bit disingenuous.[51]

Disraeli responded by pointing out how foolish the idea of expelling the Turks from Europe was: "Let others follow Mr. Gladstone's example and recall any preposterous notion they may have had that you can suddenly turn all the Turks out of Europe." Later he made it clear that indiscriminate violence would be necessary for such a crude proposition: "If we are told that our political duty is by force to expel the Turks to the other side of the Bosphorous, then politics ceases to be an art, statesmanship becomes a mere mockery . . . we had better at once resolve ourselves into one of those revolutionary clubs which settle all political and social questions with the same ease as the Hun."[52]

Other contemporaries were also acutely aware of the heterogeneous nature of Bulgaria and what the consequences of an end to the Ottoman administration would entail. Lord Edward Derby, the foreign minister, explained in July 1877 to deputations seeking to end Britain's siding with the Ottomans that Christian emancipation was absurd. He pointed out that Balkan villages were mixed, with oppressors and oppressed on both sides, and that "when the exaggerations and inventions had been gone through, both Christians and Muslims would appear in the same bad light."[53]

In 1862 Ottoman grand vizier Ali Paşa predicted chaos and endless civil war to the French foreign minister, quite accurately it turned out. "If all the national demands in Turkey are freely recognized, think for a moment what will be. . . . One portion will require a whole century and rivers of blood in order to create a stable situation."[54]

The Ottoman Muslims in the Balkans whose fate hung in the balance were aware of the discussions and attitudes in Europe and Russia and were rightly concerned. The English consul, R. Reade, reported to his superior: "I also hear that they [the Muslims] are very well aware of the 'speeches and writings' in England, advancing their expulsion from Europe" and "are convinced that the Russians will only come here to drive them out of Europe, and they say, 'in that case what have we to live for'?"[55]

The concerns of commoners in a distant territory were not the concerns of the policy makers in European capitals—who, rather, were increasingly building empires overseas in the lands of people who were culturally different. The intellectuals of Europe devised ways of viewing these people, whether indigenous Americans or Australians, Africans, Asians, Indians, or Middle Eastern Muslims, that justified and even encouraged European states to interfere in local politics or to seek conquest in the lofty name of "civilization." These people were somehow inferior and in desperate need of proper administration, which the Europeans were willing to generously provide. But the history of European colonialism demonstrated that, once in control of new territories, the Europeans instituted economic and social policies, usually backed by racist theories, that left them in a position to exploit local resources and workers. European conquest was buttressed by European discourses of superiority, which not only justified ruling over other nationalities but demanded it as the duty of the civilized. This phenomenon was documented by Edward Said and given the name "Orientalism."[56]

Whether with an eye to economic benefits, strategic positions, or national glory, many European states hoped to be able to wrest territories from the Ottomans and append them to their own empires. However, for the most part tension between the Europeans prevented outright annexation of Ottoman territories eyed greedily by various European powers. Ottoman diplomacy skillfully focused on balancing these rivals to maintain territorial integrity. When Ottoman diplomacy failed on this count, the result was usually a concession of territory or sovereignty.

Greece was the first Ottoman territory to become independent as a result of interference by European powers, and the revolution that led to Greek independence was a harbinger for the Balkans, where other ethnonationalist calls for independence would follow. Secret revolutionary societies and European intervention led to Ottoman defeat and the creation of a new nation-state. At the same time, local Muslim communities were destroyed in bloody massacres. Muslim men, women, and children were slaughtered in cold blood, whether they were Ottoman officials or simple commoners. Estimates put the number of Muslim deaths around 25,000 during the Greek revolution.[57]

> Neither sex nor age was spared. Women and children were tortured before being put to death. So great was the slaughter that Kolokotrones himself says that when he entered the town [of Tripoliza], from the gate of the citadel his horse's hoofs never touched the ground. His path of triumph was carpeted with corpses. At the end of two days, the wretched remnant of the Mussulmans were deliberately collected, to the number of some two thousand souls, of every age and sex, but principally women and children, were led out to a ravine in the neighboring mountains, and there butchered like cattle.[58]

Athens was conquered by the Ottoman Empire in 1468. In the three and a half centuries of Turkish rule, a Muslim community of over 50,000 had developed.[59] The Napoleonic wars gave impetus to an emerging Greek nationalism with Napoleon's eventual arrival in Dalmatia. When the uprisings in the Greek Morea and some of the Aegean islands began, Muslims started to emigrate toward Anatolia.

The European Enlightenment was an age of archaeological discovery that brought antiquity into vogue—especially an interest in ancient Greek civilization, known as philhellenism. For many Europeans the rediscovery of ancient civilizations in the eastern Mediterranean world was yet another example of the offensiveness of Turkish existence: "The barbarian power, which has been for centuries seated in the very heart of the Old World, which has in its brute clutch the most famous countries of classical and religious antiquity and many of the most fruitful and beautiful regions of the earth . . . ignorantly holding in its possession one half of the history of the whole world."[60]

Voltaire expressed his fervent wish that "the Turkish barbarians be chased away immediately out of the country of Xenophon, Socrates, Plato, Sophocles and Euripides. If we wanted, it could be done soon but seven crusades of superstition have been undertaken and a crusade of honor will never take place. We know almost no city built by them; they let decay the most beautiful establishments of Antiquity, they reign over ruins."[61]

Europeans developed the idea, which ultimately proved naïve, that if the Turkish patina could be removed new Aristotles and Aeschyluses would bob to the surface. When the Greek revolution was finally won thanks to the intervention of the English, Russians, and French, the European powers decided, over the objections of the Porte, that the Muslim communities of the Morea would have to go.[62] The Ottomans were to learn with every subsequent independence movement that the local Muslim inhabitants would be faced with existential peril.

RUSSIAN ORIENTALISM AND THE DREAM OF CONSTANTINOPLE

An important backdrop to Russia's war with the Ottomans in 1877 is the development of Russian Orientalism, the ways in which Russia came to view the Muslim peoples to its east and south and justify their conquest. Yet Russia's notions about the Asiatic "other" were closely tied to its relationship with western Europe as well as to pan-Slavism, Russian imperial expansion, and the Russian retaking of lands for Christianity, of which the city of Constantinople would be the jewel in the tsar's crown. These strands of thought became thickly entangled with geopolitical objectives and had a persistent weight in public debates and on state policy.

Unfortunately, many Turkish scholars avail themselves of simplistic references to pan-Slavism to explain the violence against Muslims in the Russo-Turkish War of 1877–1878. What is of interest here is a brief examination of the evolution of these ideas and how changed strategic circumstances often converged with the alteration of political ideology and the reinterpretation of history. Many Russians observing events transpire in 1877 believed that with the Russian army approaching Constantinople they were witnessing the advent of a new age and the fulfillment of Russian destiny, but this just goes to show to what extent history is interpreted for the present.

Of all the myriad sieges that have ever been attempted to take the gilded city of Constantinople, only the Ottomans under Mehmet II, dubbed the Conqueror, were successful. (In the case of the crusading Latins, the doors were opened for them.) The fall of Constantinople was a watershed in European history writing, even though the writing had been on the wall for some time anyway. Between the meteoric expansion of the Arabs starting in the late sixth century and the lapping waves of incursion from the steppe starting in the tenth century, the eastern fringe of European civilization had already undergone momentous transformation. The eastern Mediterranean world was now part of a new Islamic civilization. To the north of the Black Sea, steppe nomads patrolled the vast plains where Europe shades into Asia. The year 1453 could not escape the attention of Europe, as it underscored to what extent the barbarians were at the gates.

Russia had become an important member of a Byzanto-Orthodox civilization radiating from Constantinople. Its conversion to the Orthodox cross was secured, at least in lore, by the otherworldly atmosphere of the great Cathedral Church of Hagia Sophia, which had been erected in 537. According to legend, Vladimir, the grand prince of Kiev, in search of a monotheistic state religion, sent emissaries to study the religions of neighboring peoples. Ambassadors from Islam, Judaism, Catholicism, and Orthodoxy all made their cases. While the grand prince was attracted to Islam because of its authoritarian nature, he felt that prohibitions against drink and pork went against the grain of the Russian people. In Constantinople the emissaries fell under the spell of Hagia Sophia and reported: "We knew not whether we were in heaven or on earth. For on earth there is no such splendour or beauty, and we are at a loss how to describe it. We only know that God dwells there among men."[63] Vladimir, as a consequence, was baptized in 980 in the Crimean city of Kherson on the Black Sea, and his people (forcibly) followed suit back in Kiev. Russia was thenceforth connected to the Eastern Orthodox ecumene and to the Byzantine Empire that watched over it.

Russia, despite the belief of many of its elites that their country was a vital part of Christendom, missed out on some of the momentous events that shaped European civilization. It was often on hostile terms with its Catholic neighbors and took no part in the crusades to the Holy Land. Squeezed as it was between pagan Lithuania and the encroaching steppe tribes, it often felt isolated and abandoned by its coreligionists. While relations with the various steppe peoples ranged from hostilities to trade and alliances, the expansion of the Mongols fundamentally altered the trajectory of Russian history. The Mongol incursions that began in 1223 culminated in the sacking of Kiev in 1240. For the next 240 years the Russians were under the suzerainty of the Golden Horde.

The Golden Horde did not try to incorporate the Russian lands into their empire as the Mongols did in China or Persia. Rather, the ruling families retained their positions and the famous Mongol tolerance of religion was shown to the Orthodox Church, which was exempted from taxation. But the princes had to pay tribute to the great khans, whose capital was at Sarai on the Volga, and Tatar tax collectors earned the invective of people. The Tatars pitted the princes one against another through diplomatic and military alliances, a fact that played a large role in the development of the great Russian cities. This period became known as the Mongol yoke (or sometimes Tatar yoke). The Russians tended to call their rulers Tatars (although they had both Mongol and Turkic elements). This appellation eventually was stretched to cover all Muslims, much in the way western Europeans referred to Muslims generally as Turks.

The Russian princes now bowed before a Mongol khan, and the natural development of Russia was arrested. Russia's intimate encounter with the so-called Orient was another experience that set it apart from western Europe. The Tatars were primarily pagan at the time of conquest, as their conversion to Islam is usually dated around 1280. Nevertheless, Russian exposure to Tatar rule shaped Russian attitudes about their Muslim neighbors to the east and south.

At the time of Russia's subjugation, Russian writers were largely silent on the question of Mongol rule;[64] however, once Russia had freed itself from the Golden Horde, or rather once the Golden Horde had disintegrated because of intra-Mongol feuds, the Russian line against the Mongols actually became harsher.[65]

The disparaging language that Russians learned to employ against the Tatars was religious in tone and was borrowed from the Byzantines, who had developed it through their encounters with Islam. After Moscow had turned the tables on the Golden Horde, Russian rule quickly expanded as far as the Volga River. Although Russian expansion at this point was strategic in nature and offered the promise of war booty, it was buttressed by a notion of holy war. Some scholars believe that for Greeks and Russians in particular a concept of holy war failed to develop because neither had participated in the crusades. For many Russians the behavior of the crusaders in Constantinople in the fourth crusade blackened the entire effort. Their anger was coupled with the fact that the West had made no similar effort to help liberate Russia from the Mongol occupation, as had supposedly been done for the Holy Land.[66]

Yet, as shown by Adam Knobler, a rationale for "holy war" did in fact exist in Russia and the Byzantine world and was not very different from its Catholic counterpart. One of the primary objectives of Russian holy war was the reconquest of Christian land lost to infidels. Orthodoxy's hostility to Islam, though, tended to be milder than that of Rome.[67] Moscow considered the conversion of the "godless Saracens" to be an important state goal in which initial expulsions were followed by efforts to convert the Tatars in order to assimilate them and thereby root out opposition to Russian rule.[68] But the coeval horrors of the Spanish Inquisition on the opposite end of Europe were not repeated in Russia's new territories.

Russia missed out on the transformational European developments of the Renaissance and the Reformation. Whether this was due to Russia's Byzantine heritage, the Mongol yoke, or other circumstances is debatable. But Russia's failure to be involved in these major trends, along with the cultural implications bequeathed to it by the Byzantines and the Golden Horde, left it culturally, not just geographically, on the fringe of Europe. This was a situation that Peter the Great (1672–1725) endeavored to change. He tried to steer the great Russian ship onto an unambiguously Western course, by zealously adopting Western models that made Russia for the first time a major player on the European stage. Westernizing reforms always met with resistance in Russia. Peter subjugated the clergy and made enemies of those conservatives who thought he was leading an uncontaminated Russia into "Babylonian Captivity."[69] Ultimately, the question of Russia's position vis-à-vis Europe, while continually raised, has never received a definitive answer.

The shadow of Byzantium always loomed in Russia, offering a model of greatness on its own terms. Thus the more Russian power developed, the greater was the pull of Constantine the Great's crown. And as Peter the Great's reign opened new strategic horizons, it also served to connect Russia to the Byzantine past in novel ways. So, while much attention has been paid to Peter's western front, his efforts to the south are often neglected.

In 1696 the tsar led his troops into battle in a failed attempt against the Ottomans to take the Turkish fortress at Taganrog on the Sea of Azov. Peter barely escaped from the battle, but in a second effort one year later the Russian troops prevailed over the Turks and set the bells ringing throughout European Christendom.[70] Peter's victory boosted his prestige throughout Europe as well as at home. The Russians quickly set out to build a port at Taganrog. From there, with imaginations unbounded, they could make out Constantinople through the fog of the Black Sea, which had been for centuries a Turkish lake. What's more, the warm waters of the Mediterranean beckoned, promising trading wealth and prestige. The Russian victory at the Sea of Azov endured more in Russian aspirations to glory than in the ephemeral base on the Sea of Azov, which was returned to the Ottomans in 1711.

Nevertheless, a dream of retaking Constantinople for Russia was born. It was a dream others had dreamed before: "For more than 2000 years the leading minds of the world have dreamt of Constantinople. Dreamt of it in visions of splendor as did the Russians of Kief and Smolensk in mid-medieval days when they thought of Tsargrad—the city of Emperors. Dreamt of it in golden dreams as did the bankers of Venice and Genoa in the twelfth century. . . . Dreamed of it as did the minstrels of western Europe when they sang of the beauty of Byzantine palaces and the pleasures of life in Byzantium."[71] But it became, briefly, a Russian obsession.

While this objective was probably spurred by strategic interests, as far as the statesmen were concerned, we cannot discount the strong cultural, historical, and religious seduction underlying it. "Is not Constantine's town your inheritance?" Peter was asked.[72] Perhaps Peter would realize his birthright as the "new Constantine," a designation that was employed to confer legitimacy on Muscovite princes.[73] Russia's destiny was being reinterpreted.

Not as widely known is that pagan Rus marched on Constantinople two times in its pre-Christian era with hopes of loot from what was at that time a city at the zenith of its glory. In 860 Viking Rus, a fleet led by the first Kievan rulers, Askold and Dir, attacked Constantinople. In 907 Oleg, who had brought together Kiev and Novgorod, headed a force of 80,000 men and 2,000 ships in an assault on the city.[74] This was followed by more attempts under both Igor, in 941 and again in 944, and his son, Prince Sviatoslav, in 970. His army of Russians, Pechenegs, and Magyars passed through Bulgaria, shattering the Bulgarian defenses, and moved on to Thrace, where they camped for the winter. Although urged on to Constantinople, the Russians got no farther than Lule-Burgas, where the Byzantines halted their defense with a crushing defeat.[75] Again in 1043 the newly Christianized Russians sailed a fleet down the Dnieper to attack Constantinople over a commercial dispute. The Russians were beaten yet mollified by the marriage of a Byzantine princess to the son of the Russian prince, and it would require almost another eight hundred years before they approached Constantinople again.[76]

After Russia's conversion to Christianity, contacts with Constantinople accelerated as Russian monks, pilgrims, diplomats, artisans, and traders visited the city. The power structure in Orthodoxy was more diffuse than that of Rome, yet Constantinople remained the center of the Orthodox universe until its conquest in 1453. The end of the Byzantine Empire was seen as catastrophic throughout the Christian world, especially in Russia. But, as a silver lining, the Turks' arrival in Constantinople freed Moscow from the city's orbit, allowing it to chart its own path. While for the Balkan Slavs the authority of the ecumenical patriarch increased after 1453, as the Ottomans looked to him as the head of Orthodox Christians in the empire, the Russian Orthodox Church declared complete independence from the ecumenical patriarch of Constantinople in 1470.[77]

Russia, with its Slavonic liturgy, became increasingly cut off from its Byzantine godfather. The Russian church became the preserve of a national cultural life in Russia, and the capital, Moscow, was now the guardian of an undefiled faith. The fall of Byzantium was seen by some as God's punishment for a willingness to subordinate Orthodoxy to the Latins in Rome. Moscow, then, was the natural heir. The monk Philoetheus of Pskov proclaimed its divine pedigree sometime between 1510 and 1521: "A new and third Rome has sprung up in the North, illuminating the whole universe like a sun. The Third Rome will stand to the end of history, for it is the last Rome. Moscow has no successor; a fourth Rome shall not be."[78] The ecumenical patriarch of Constantinople echoed this claim in 1588: "Since the first Rome fell through the Apollinarian heresy and the second Rome which is Constantinople, is held by the infidel Turks, so then the great Russian Tsardom . . . which is more pious than previous kingdoms, is the third Rome."[79]

Over time the original intention behind the Third Rome idea was muddied, and it undoubtedly received more than its due share of credit in explaining Russian foreign policy. The letter of Philoetheus was only put in print form in 1861, but it quickly garnered mythological force within Russia's reinterpretations of its own history.[80]

Russia, now freed from the Golden Horde, was bolstering its claims to legitimacy by connecting itself in a very transparent manner to the imperial crown of Byzantium. The niece of the last Byzantine emperor, Zoe Palaeologina, was married to the Russian grand prince Ivan III in 1472, and Russia adopted the twin eagle emblem from the Byzantines. Such a gambit of bestowing the regal authority of a long defunct dynasty on an incumbent ruler finds great precedent in history. The desire to be connected somehow to the great events of Troy was common throughout the classical world. The Roman poet Virgil, for example, recounted the founding of Rome by Aeneas, who had survived the fall of Troy and thus conferred upon Rome the authority and prestige of Priam and Achilles. The Third Rome doctrine, then, was not originally a call to retake a fallen Constantinople but rather an attempt to accrue legitimacy for an ascendant Moscow. As such, this proclamation did not exert any influence on Russian foreign policy in the sixteenth and seventeenth centuries.

Only in the eighteenth century, under Peter the Great, did Russia begin to assert itself as a European power, and it was precisely in this period that the legacy of the Byzantine Empire was increasingly given voice in the country's external policies. As Lindsey Hughes states, "The 'Third Rome' doctrine had its strongest practical appeal not in the sixteenth century, when it was formulated as a more or less abstract idea, but in the eighteenth, when it became plausible to act upon it. Peter was the first Russian ruler to 'don the mantle of liberator of the Balkan Christians.'"[81]

Peter was implored to come as savior by Dionysius, the deposed patriarch of Constantinople: "Serbs and Bulgarians, Wallachs and Moldavians—all of us are expecting help from your Holy Tsardom. Do not drowse, arise and come to save us!"[82] Peter, however, while generous with words for his Orthodox kin, was more interested in what they could do for him rather than vice versa. He wrote to the Balkan Christians: "I am taking upon myself a heavy burden for the sake of the love of God, for which reason I have entered into war with the Turkish realm. . . . because the Turks have trampled on our faith, taken our churches and lands by cunning, pillaged and destroyed many of our churches and monasteries."[83] While he raised the issue of freedom of religion for Orthodox Christians in negotiations with the Ottomans, nothing about it was included in the treaty with the Turks. In 1711 Peter encouraged Orthodox Christians to rise up against the Muslim oppressors to aid him in his war against the Ottomans, yet he found no such aid forthcoming.[84]

The truth is that Russia feared Austrian intervention in the Balkans; not even being in possession of the Black Sea littoral, Russia could do little to effect big changes in Ottoman Europe. With Peter the Great's push for Westernization, which coincided with wars with the Ottomans on its southern front, Russia came around to viewing crusading in more Western terms, and engagements with the Ottomans were seen increasingly in this context. In Peter's campaign of 1711 he invoked Constantine the Great as the Russians hoisted standards bearing the cross and the declaration "Under This Sign We Conquer."[85]

Under Catherine the Great (1729–1796), Russia continued to expand into formerly Ottoman territories. This expansion coincided with the tsaritsa's fantasy of a restored Byzantium under Russian guidance. In 1769, as part of a larger assault against the Ottomans, Catherine sent a Russian squadron from the Baltic Sea around the coast of Europe through the Strait of Gibraltar (a first in Russian history). Her intention was to incite the Greeks to rebellion, force the Dardanelles, and attack Constantinople. While those efforts came to naught, the ground war with the Russians ended in severe defeat for the Ottomans. Russia was now firmly ensconced on the Black Sea, with Crimea as a protectorate. In addition, Russia was granted certain privileges regarding the Ottoman Orthodox Christians in the Treaty of Küçük Kaynarca.

An expanding Russia included an increasing number of Muslims within its borders. Hostility toward Islam was commonplace in the Russian Empire and was often a matter of state policy. It was during Catherine's reign that the term "Mongol yoke" entered the Russian vocabulary, and with it came tales of oppression by the barbarians.[86] Muslims were under pressure to convert to Christianity and did not have the same property rights as Christians. There were restrictions against building mosques, and Muslims were not allowed to go on pilgrimage to Mecca. Finally, in 1773, Catherine the Great proclaimed the edict of "The Toleration of All Faiths," which ended many of the discriminatory practices. With the intention of exercising more effective control over her Muslim subjects, she created institutions such as the Orenberg Assembly, in order to regulate Islam and bring it under the purview of the Russian state. This even involved the subsidization of mosque building and efforts to convert pagan nomads to Islam with the intention of forcing them to relinquish their nomadic lifestyle.

Catherine won the Crimea outright in a second war with the Ottomans. For Catherine's closest advisor the Crimea was a first step to something much bigger. Prince Grigorii Aleksandrovich Potyomkin, who had been schooled in Greek and was a devotee of the Orthodox Church, was quite taken with the fact that Constantinople had been the center of Orthodox Christianity. He won Catherine over to his idea of restoring the Byzantine Empire. This "Greek Project," as it came to be known, was never clearly articulated but became something of an obsession for both Catherine and Potyomkin. The tsaritsa even had her second grandson, born in 1779, named Constantine. Her imperial expectation for her grandson was evident: she had medals struck to commemorate his birth, depicting the Hagia Sophia in Constantinople, and had him raised by Greek nurses with Greek playmates so that he would speak Greek fluently.[87]

The idea of restoring antiquity, especially Hellenic Greece, had a great deal of traction in the Romanticism of western Europe. It was influential in garnering public support for European actions in support of Greek independence from Turkish rule. For Russia, the Greek capital most worthy of restoration was not the Athens of Socrates and Sophocles, with its mathematicians, astronomers, and doctors, its democracy and rationalism—rather, it was the Greece of Constantine and Justinian, of monks and theologians, of Cyril and Methodius.

Nikolai Iakovlevich Danilevskii (1822–1885) believed that Greek civilization had culminated in the Byzantine period and that the Slavs were its heirs. He for one viewed the Turkish occupation of the Balkans as God's mercy on the Slavs, because Ottoman rule insulated them from the corrosive influence of the West.[88] Russia lacked the ties to antiquity that had developed in the West. The Western church's insistence on Latin built intellectual bridges to the study of ancient civilization that had no equivalents in the Orthodox churches in Russia and the Balkans, which learned their religion through translation, not in Greek itself. These connections were bolstered by unique historical connections to Bulgaria.

Bulgaria became the cradle of written Slavic culture when the Slavonic clergy were given shelter by King Boris I (the title for Bulgaria's rulers changed from khan to king with the adoption of Christianity) after Moravia's return to the Latin rite. The spread of Christianity among the

Slavs owes much to the efforts of saints Cyril and Methodius, who, coming from Thessaloniki, were both Byzantine and Slavonic. Toward the end of the ninth century they developed the Glagolitic script for the Slavonic liturgy. The Cyrillic alphabet was later developed in Bulgaria, using Greek majuscule letters with Glagolitic borrowings. Because Bulgaria was the center of Slavic Christendom, it was there that Kievan Rus acquired its books on religion and its alphabet following its own conversion to Christianity at the end of the tenth century. In fact, Slavonic, whose origins can be traced to Bulgaria, still held sway among the literati of Russia until the eighteenth century.[89]

Russia's special historical relationship with Constantinople as well as Bulgaria was important to the pan-Slavists such as Iurii Gutsa-Venelin, who viewed these areas as the classical lands of Slavonic culture. This was a connection that neither Britain nor France could claim. The essence of a reestablishment of the past was also inherent in Russian efforts to liberate Bulgaria and Constantinople, returning both of them to the Orthodox fold.

Adding to Russian ambitions for the grandeur of empire by expansion, the nineteenth century brought a new element of Slavic solidarity to Russian politics. This followed on the heels of Romantic nationalism, which was already beginning to impact the way that Europe viewed nations and what markers should inspire solidarity. The Byzantine-era connections between Russia and the southern Slavs had been largely neglected following the Ottoman conquests. But new theories in historical linguistics and ethnography were uncovering links among the Slavs. Originally pan-Slavism got its start among Czech intellectuals in the Austrian Empire, where the question of a Slavic role in the state had become increasingly important. Pan-Slavs attempted to increase ties among the various Slavic groups at the beginning of the nineteenth century. In political terms, the ideas ranged from cultural contacts among Slavs in general, to an improved standing for Slavs in the Austrian Empire, to some form of Slavic confederation. When pan-Slavism was taken up in Russia, it was often subordinated to Russian nationalism and an injured national pride, becoming a vehicle for Russian Messianism. Closer political ties among Slavs were imagined with Russia, the largest and only independent Slav state, as the natural leader of whatever polity might emerge. As Hans Kohn wrote, "Pan-Slavism in the first half of the nineteenth century was a movement of the Western Slavs born out of their cultural awakening and their political weakness. In the second half of the century it became a predominantly Russian movement, rooted in a feeling of spiritual and material grandeur and in a consciousness of historical destiny."[90]

While pan-Slavism was not popular in the Russian court or government, a small educated group of Russians, facing condescending European attitudes, sought to justify Russia, which was powerful and large, albeit backward. As a result, Russian thinkers tried to craft an identity for Russia by highlighting its uniqueness without agreeing to any suggestion of inferiority. They formulated a destiny for Russia through its greatness. Pan-Slavism had a variety of adherents in Russia. Some were of a more religious bent, while others considered themselves rational and scientific—but, regardless, Constantinople exuded an irresistible allure.

A pan-Slavist Russian poet who saw the liberation of the southern Slavs and the retaking of Constantinople as one and the same was Fyodor Ivanovich Tiutchev (1803–1873), who is often mentioned together with Aleksandr Sergeevich Pushkin and Mikhail Iurevich Lermontov as one of Russia's greatest nineteenth-century poets. For Tiutchev, Russia was under constant threat from Western conspiracy but would ultimately triumph in creating a pan-Slav empire with its capital at Constantinople. During the Russo-Turkish War of 1829, he wrote a poem that ended with an image of the Russian conquest of Constantinople:

> Voiceless midnight! All is silent.
> Just then the moon broke through the clouds,
> and over the gates of Istamboul
> The shield of Oleg flashed.[91]

In 1848 Tiutchev published another poem claiming Constantinople for Russia, which begins:

> Moscow, Peter's city, and Constantine's city
> Are the holy capitals of the Russian realm.
> But where its outer limit, where its border,
> To north, to east, to south and where the sun sets?
> Destiny will unmask them in future times.[92]

When the Crimean War broke out, Tiutchev was elated. He believed that Russia would not only win the war but celebrate victory in Constantinople. He published a poem calling for a Russian advance on Constantinople:

Arise, O Rus! The hour is near!
Arise to do Christ's service!
Is it not time, while crossing yourself,
To ring Byzantium's bells?

Now let the church bell sound ring out
And all the east resound!
It summons and awakens you—
Arise, take heart, to arms![93]

In another poem Tiutchev prophesied Constantinople's incorporation into a Russian Empire:

When Byzantium is restored to us
The ancient vaults of Saint Sophia
Will shelter the altar of Christ anew.
Kneel then before it, O Tsar of Russia—
You will arise all Slavdom's Tsar!

What once was promised by the fates
Belonged to her in the cradle,
What was bequeathed by centuries
And faith of all her Tsars,

What once the followers of Oleg
Went forth with swords to conquer,
What Catherine's double-headed eagle
Once sheltered with its wing—

No, you (the coward) will not rob us of scepter
And crown of Byzantium
The universal fate of Russia,
No, you will not usurp![94]

Of course, at the end of the Crimean War, Russians were not ringing bells triumphantly in Hagia Sophia. Rather, Russia suffered a humiliating defeat against the combined forces of Britain, France, and the Ottoman Empire. Many in Russia viewed the fact that both England and France came to the Ottomans' rescue as treachery of the highest order. Fyodor Dostoevskii (1821–1881) penned the following lines:

> The Christian uniting with the Turk against Christ.
> The Christian—a defender of Mohammed.
> Shame on you—apostates of the cross.[95]

The humiliation of defeat had the effect of alienating many Russians from Europe, who subsequently found refuge in Russian pan-Slavism and its implied expansionist aims. Because of Russian bitterness over the defeat, pan-Slavism acquired strains of xenophobia and chauvinism. Many Russians felt that the Crimean War demonstrated the hostility of Europe toward Russia, because Europeans would never consider Russia part of the European family. But alienation from Europe also transformed attitudes toward the Orient negatively.

Russia had borrowed Orientalist discourse from the French, British, and Germans, but what set Russian Orientalism apart from others was that it was heavily impacted by Russia's experiences with the West even more than by its own contacts with the Orient. Russia's precarious position on the margins of Europe was troubling to its own self-image. When Russians spoke about the barbarous Muslim Turks, they were attempting to reaffirm Russia's place within the civilized West by creating a foil to emphasize their own level of civilization.[96] The Crimean War left Russia feeling ever more the outsider. As a result, its attitudes to both the West and the Orient became more hostile.

Reports of the Bulgarian Horrors reached the Russian public and caused a loud outcry. The Russian government, which was not controlled by pan-Slavists, came under intense pressure for war as pan-Slavism reached its peak in Russia. "Never have there been as many Slavophiles in Russia as now," one pan-Slavist declared. Even Turgenev, who rejected pan-Slavism, wrote the poem "Croquet at Windsor" (quoted earlier). The tsar, who had loosened the Russian state's control over the press and journalists, was now subject to its effects. "Every gory detail gave them for months an effective instrument to the emotional mobilization of the public against the government."[97] In the end the tsar capitulated to the deafening pan-Slav roar and declared war.

In the Russian press, the use of "holy war" language regarding the Ottoman Empire increased significantly throughout 1876–1877 as a response to reports of Turkish cruelty in the Balkans.[98] The conflict was often depicted as a war between Orthodoxy and Islam waged in order to bring "the arrogant moon" of the Ottoman Empire to its knees.[99] The notion of a Russian holy war was underscored by the importance of retaking lands lost to the Christian patrimony. The Russians, as heirs to Byzantium, adopted this premise for their expansions against Muslim neighbors. Beginning with Kazan on through to Bulgaria, the Russians considered their actions in terms of the "liberation" of their Orthodox kin and the "recovery" of lands for Christianity.[100] Russia viewed its role in the Balkans as the legacy of those earlier expansions against Muslims. Just as the war against the Ottomans was about to begin, the pro-war *Moskovskie Vedomosti* (*Moscow News*) connected the historical dots: "For over 650 years the Russian people have fought against the Mongolian Tatars, Turks and other Mohammedan peoples—for Christianity and our freedom, for the Greeks, Serbs, Bulgarians, Georgians and Armenians."[101]

Unfortunately, in the Balkans the emancipation of Christians and expulsion of Turks became interchangeable notions, for, while only implicit and not openly declared, the doctrines of national liberation of the incipient Balkan states entailed the elimination of Muslims from these territories.[102] The Russians viewed this war with the Turks as the "final solution" to the Eastern Question.

Dostoevskii, "the greatest prophet of Slavophilism" and also its "last outstanding spokesman," was enthusiastic about the war and the prospect of Russia taking Constantinople.[103] He had followed press reports about the Bulgarian Horrors and believed that as many as 60,000 Bulgarians had died.[104] Based on what he read, he created the Bulgarian survivor of the massacre in his novel *The Brothers Karamazov*. Dostoevskii, who was capable of great refinement when considering the human soul, was, in the words of Hans Kohn, "a bigoted fanatic without any originality when he approached the problems. . . . of Russia's relationship to Europe."[105] His prejudices with regard to Europe affected his view of the Turks, whom he called "profane Hagarite Mohammedans." According to Dostoevskii, the

Turks were "this savage, vile Muslim horde, a sworn enemy of civilization." He further expressed his hope that "these bloodsucker Turks break their necks."[106]

One pan-Slav supporter, General Rostislav Andreevich Fadeev (1824–1883), promoted the idea of a Constantinople, purged of Turks, as the capital of a Slavic confederation.[107] It is unlikely that Dostoevskii would have let Turks remain in his Russian-controlled Constantinople, as he had supported the deportation of Crimean Tatars and their replacement by Russians.[108] He rejected the idea of even sharing Constantinople with other Slavs: "Constantinople must be ours, conquered by us, Russians, from the Turks and remain ours forever. She must belong to us alone."[109]

Dostoevskii spelled out the basis for such a claim:

> Thus in the name of what, by virtue of what moral right could Russia claim Constantinople from Europe?—Precisely as a leader of Orthodoxy, as its protectress and guardian—a role designated to her ever since Ivan III, who placed her symbol and the Byzantine double-headed eagle above the ancient coat of arms of Russia, a role which unquestionably revealed itself only after Peter the Great when Russia became the real and sole protectress of Orthodoxy and of the people adhering to it. Such is the ground, such is the right to ancient Constantinople.[110]

After the war and the disappointment of the Berlin Treaty, pan-Slav fever subsided. The government repressed outspoken pan-Slavs. Russia turned increasingly away from Europe and to the East. Even Dostoevskii seems to have accepted that Constantinople would not become Russian any time soon. The next tsar, Nikolai II, said, "I do not concern myself with Constantinople. My eyes are directed towards China."[111]

Only after Russia's loss to Japan in 1905 did pan-Slavism have a brief rebirth. The Russians set their sights once again on Tsargrad, even signing the secret "Constantinople agreement" with Britain and France as part of a pact to vivisect the Ottoman Empire in the First World War. Russia had finally secured the acquiescence of Great Britain for a Russian Constantinople as well as Russian control of the straits and the Sea of Marmara.[112] But Russia never got as close to Constantinople in the First World War as it did in 1878.

CONQUEST TO MURDER: VICTIMHOOD IN THE BALKANS

The European powers came to rule over Muslim populations in colonies in North Africa, sub-Saharan Africa, Southeast Asia, the Indian subcontinent, and Central Asia. After conquering these lands, they often co-opted local notables and collected tribute. They exploited resources and the workforce for the benefit of the metropole. In most cases the Europeans gave preference to the monotheistic Muslims over pagans. From Peru to India, having people to rule over was the point of empire. Europe was not in the practice of eliminating Muslims from the lands that they conquered as long as they would submit to European rule. Orientalism, the West's essentialized and patronizing view of the East, was a justification for conquest and rule, not for elimination. The presence of a Turkish Empire that aspired to sit at the same table as other European powers was disconcerting. They lambasted the Turkish administration for being degenerate and despotic. All the while, Europe assumed that it might one day carve up the Ottoman territories and bring its civilizing administration to them. It is not just that Europe was justified in conquering these territories—it was obligated to do so! This justification for conquest, however, does not fully explain the situation in the Ottoman Balkans. There it was more than just an issue of the Turks' suitability to govern: their very suitability to live in those lands was called into question. Europe developed a justification to conquer Muslims, while the Balkan Christians developed a justification to kill them. Europe imagined a Europe free of the Ottomans, while the Balkan Christians realized their liquidation.

The Orientalist ways in which Europe viewed the Turkish Muslims were not likely to have a direct penetration among the Balkan masses. Average Balkan Christians not only were unlikely to be literate, with access to European thought, but were much more likely to be concerned with the day-to-day worries of peasants. Instead, it was the burgeoning class of Balkan intellectuals, a great many of whom were émigré students or merchants, who led the awakening of Balkan nationalism. These intellectuals certainly were in contact with European and Russian ideas about the Turks, and they played a large role in reinterpreting European Orientalism from a context where Europeans Christians ruled over Muslims to a context where European Christians were under the rule of Muslims.

Balkan nationalisms were based on ethnicity and religion but were also defined by a crude anti-Turkism, which had been developed and encouraged in the West, as it fit in with Russian imperialist and pan-Slavist thinking.[113]

Nationalist Balkan intellectuals eagerly consumed the anti-Turk concepts—naturally they readily agreed with the concept of the cruel, barbarous Turk and the inferiority of his Islamic civilization. Especially grating was the notion that these inferior Turks should rule over European peoples with gilded pasts. These newly emerging Balkan elites, many of whom had traveled in Europe and witnessed its economic and military might, stood in awe of these states. In the West, though, because the Balkans were an integral part of the Ottoman Empire, the Balkan people, even the Christians, were viewed as barbaric.[114] The Balkan elites felt great anxiety because of this and were driven to distance themselves from any association with the barbaric Orient. Identities of Christians throughout the Balkans became aligned with western Europe in stark opposition to Islam, which was exemplified by the backward and corrupt Ottoman Empire.

The birth of Balkan nationalism was accompanied by a sense of victimhood vis-à-vis Turkish rule. This alone was enough to explain any economic or cultural backwardness, and this concretization of national suffering could show the way to rebirth. Dependence on the notion of Ottoman rule as a black period, "slavery," or the "yoke" has been a stubborn fact in Bulgarian national historiography. "Yoke," "long nightmare," "slavery," and "cultural annihilation" are common tropes, although they are for the most part exaggerations.[115] The "Catastrophe Theory," as Machiel Kiel has dubbed it, is especially resilient in Bulgaria.[116] Anton Donchev's novel *Time of Parting*, for example, describes seventeenth-century Bulgaria: "Then there was a drumming in my ears, and I understood my first truth. And it was that all over the Bulgarian lands, whosoever spoke Bulgarian suffered and groaned under the heel of the Turk."[117]

This view of the Ottoman period as entirely destructive to Balkan culture is repeated as dogma even in academic works for which it is largely irrelevant, no matter how clichéd it has become and regardless of new scholarship. The collapse of communism has provided a more open arena for historical debates throughout the Balkans, and Bulgaria has witnessed short-lived moments of historical reevaluation, yet for the most part Bulgarian historiography remains mired in parochialism and nationalism.[118] Kiel gives a fine example of the Catastrophe Theory of the conquest of Bulgaria by the "Ottoman Hordes," which was

> accompanied with never seen cruelty, blood-thirstiness, lust for booty, inhuman and full of religious fanaticism.... The cities were plundered and burnt, villages wiped out and cultivated fields turned to wilderness.... [If the leaders and learned people did not accept Islam, they could choose to] sacrifice their inflexible head to the yatagan or in the best case to drag their chains to the far land of Asia Minor.... But the Bulgarians, whose creative genius had reached such a level of science and art, whose arms did make the great Byzantine empire and the whole Balkans tremble with fear, never bowed their heads and were never assimilated. One of the main reasons why they preserved their national feeling at this horrible time was the mass of people possessed already a civilization high above the level of the conquerors.[119]

Each of the Balkan nations has created its own version of the Catastrophe Theory, which has much to do with their respective histories and mythologies. Greek history speaks of the "Turkish Slavery," Serbian history of the bloody fields of Kosovo, and Bulgarian history of the "Turkish yoke." By the time the Ottomans began to conquer in the Balkans, the Greeks and Bulgarians were already only shadows of their former glories. The Greeks had long lost their Anatolian provinces, and the Latin crusaders had caused irreparable damage to the Byzantine Empire during the fourth crusade. In fact, the empire based at Constantinople was only spared from being swallowed up by the Ottomans a hundred years earlier by the sudden arrival of Tamerlane and his defeat of Sultan Beyazıt I. Only a few small provinces such as Trebizond and Crete and the city state of Constantinople remained. The year 1453 is a watershed in Greek history, marking the definitive end of the Eastern Roman Empire. By contrast, the Serbian state was the great power in the Balkans of that period, having achieved the zenith of its might just as it was about to square off with the Ottoman forces. The Battle of Kosovo (1389), while technically a draw, marked a sudden change in the trajectory of the Serbian nation.

Seen in the long run as a defeat, it was all the more painful because it interrupted the glory destined for the Serbian Empire.

For the Bulgarians, however, the golden age in their history was clearly the First Bulgarian Empire (681–1018). It achieved its apogee under Boris's son Simeon (864–927), stretching from across the peninsula from the Black Sea to the Adriatic, including most of Serbia, Albania, and Macedonia. Throughout its existence, it challenged the Byzantine Empire to its south, sometimes victorious and sometimes defeated, in a multitude of battles. It eyed with envy the capital of Constantinople and approached the city's walls on more than one occasion. But ultimately it succumbed to the Greek-ruled Byzantine Empire in 1018 and became subjugated to Constantinople. The independence of the Bulgarian church was abolished in favor of the ecumenical patriarch in Constantinople, and a policy of Hellenization was pursued. This situation endured until 1185 when a successful revolt against the Byzantines once again secured Bulgarian independence and a new royal family was enthroned. The Bulgarian Patriarchate was reestablished, this time in Veliko Tarnovo. This Second Bulgarian Empire, while a culturally rich period in Bulgarian history, was never able to achieve the glory of the first empire.

The Bulgarian state was rife with petty infighting and fissiparous tendencies and by 1371 had effectively split into three or possibly five separate statelets. Ivan Shishman ruled the larger part from Veliko Tarnovo, while his half-brother, Ivan Stratsimır, governed in the northwest, and a Bulgarian nobleman named Ivanko ruled over the area the Turks effectively named Dobruca after his father Dobrotitsa. The days of Bulgarian might were past, whereas the Serbian state was ascendant. By the time the Ottomans actually arrived to conquer Bulgaria, there was no longer a unified state to confront it. The Ottomans skillfully played against the divisions, and the weak Bulgarians went out with a whimper and ignominy. No one battle can be singled out as the end of a free Bulgaria, just spasmodic decay. Making matters worse for Bulgarian historiography, the Bulgarian rulers did not perish heroically in an unforgettable battle as did the last Greek emperor or suffer the bloody fate of treachery like the Serb leader. Both Stratisimir and Shishman had become vassals of the sultan before falling into disfavor. Shishman was ingloriously left to languish in prison after the Turkish capture of Veliko Tarnovo, while his son apparently converted to Islam and became a governor on the Anatolian

Black Sea coast. Stratisimir was taken captive after the fall of Vidin and imprisoned in Bursa, where he was murdered. As for Ivanko, after making treaties with the Ottomans, he eventually perished in an insignificant mopping-up operation. Perhaps that the Catastrophe Theory has held on the longest and strongest in Bulgaria of all Balkan states is cover for the fact that Bulgaria's resistance to incorporation into the Ottoman Empire was one of the Balkans' weakest.[120]

While I have already discussed the nature of Ottoman rule in chapter 1, it is interesting to note that the post-Ottoman world and its independence movements have not been the subject of scrutiny from a postcolonial perspective. One intriguing commonality can be seen in the violent lust for vengeance among some anticolonial revolutionaries in the second half of the twentieth century and the Balkan revolutionaries in the second half of the nineteenth century. Among twentieth-century anticolonial intellectuals, Martinique-born Franz Fanon, in particular, embodied a cult of vengeance to satisfy the victim's humiliation—a catharsis for the nation. In his advocacy of violent liberation he echoed the anti-Turkish radicalism of the previous century. "Violence," Fanon wrote, "is a cleansing force. It frees the native from his inferiority complex and from his despair and inaction; it makes him fearless and restores his self-respect."[121] Because Fanon considered violence to be the language of the oppressor, the only language he understands, he saw no distinction between French civilians in Algeria and French police and military. To him, the civilian was as complicit as the police officer or soldier. For Fanon, violence would be an expression of national solidarity, stimulating a national rebirth.

In the Balkans the revolutionaries viewed matters with a venom similar to that of Fanon. The Turk and his rule became the source of all present unhappiness; his going away would allow for the return to the glories of a supposed golden age. "The creation of nation-states in the Balkans, since the start of the 19th century, was realized directly against the Ottoman Empire and against the 'Turks.'"[122] European discourse had clearly affected the burgeoning Bulgarian intellectual class, for those Bulgarians who were educated by the pan-Slavists in Moscow became the most radical in their hatred of the Turk and the instigators of violent revolt against him. In the Balkans a sense of a common past suffering was amplified and then instrumentalized in order to awaken resentment and fear.

Balkan discourses concerning the Ottoman Empire partook of all the European stereotypes about the inferiority of Islamic civilization and the barbarous and cruel nature of the Turk. However, they added the critical element of victimhood, which would justify not only the overthrow of Turkish rule but the expulsion of the population from the territory, if needs be, by violent means. The Balkans, then, is where Edward Said meets Franz Fanon. The language of inferiority and dehumanization is coupled with claims of suffering and humiliation.

In Bulgaria, even among the leaders of the Bulgarian nationalists, known as the Apostles, opinions differed on what was to be done with the Turks.[123] Lyuben Karavelov, for example, considered the Turkish people and the Turkish government to be synonymous. "A Turk is a Turk, and neither God nor the devil can make a human being of him." He also stated that "Bulgaria will be delivered only when the Turk, the Chorbadzhii [wealthy landownders] and the bishop are hanged on a willow tree."[124] Georgi Rakovski, too, proposed the eviction of Muslims from Bulgaria. He urged his co-nationals to take vengeance and let Turkish heads roll.[125] In contrast, Vasil Levski, who was executed by the Ottomans in 1873, saw a distinction between the Turkish government and Turks themselves and envisioned a Bulgaria free of the sultan and the Chorbadzhii in which ordinary Turks could take part. Others like Hristo Botev vacillated between Karavelov's views and Levski's. Ultimately, the trend was toward radicalization, especially after the suppression of the April Uprising, so that even if the Bulgarian revolutionaries' stated objective was regime change, "for the great masses, it was a question of chasing the Turks out of the country."[126]

Perhaps the clearest example of the Catastrophe Theory and its consequences is to be found in the epic poem *The Mountain Wreath*, composed in 1847 by Montenegrin Petar II Petrović-Njegoš. It begins with a retelling of the Ottomans' devastating entry into Europe:

> The Dragon see, with seven mantles red,
> Wielding two swords and crownèd with two crowns;
> Great-grandchild of the faithless Turk, with Koran!
> Behind him hordes of that accursèd breed,
> That they may devastate the whole wide earth,

As locusts pestilent lay waste the fields! . . .
Osman—infernal dream—was monarch crown'd;
The pale moon wedded, she his apple fair;
From whom sprang Orkan, Europe's evil guest;
And now Byzantium's realm is nothing more
Than the youthful Theodora's dowry . . .
From out far Asia where they have their nest,
This Devil's brood doth gulp the nations up; . . .
I see my people sleep a deadly sleep,
No parent's hand to wipe away my tears;
God's Heaven is shut above my head,
Giving no answer to my cries and prayers.
This world is now become a hell.[127]

The plot details the struggle of the Montenegrins to be free, yet in their obsession with freedom they become obsessed with their supposed enemy:

Thou dost not eat nor canst thou fall asleep;
Thou turnest o'er great thoughts within thy mind;
Thy crowding dreams are ever of the Turk.

The solution, however, leaves no room for compromise:

And to this struggle no end shall ever be,
Until the Turk has disappeared—or we!

The Muslims appeal for coexistence:

Small enough is this our land,
Yet two faiths there still may be,
As in one sàhan soups agree.
Let us still as brothers live,
Of further love no need have we!

But they are rebuffed:

Fain would we, but it cannot be;
Such love as this were laughing-stock!
No mutual love doth light our eyes,
A brother's glance we ne'er exchange,
Our looks are those of vengeful hate;
What saith the heart, the eyes must state!

In the end the Muslims are slaughtered:

No single seeing eye, no tongue of Turk,
Escap'd to tell his tale another day!
We put them all unto the sword, . . .
We put to fire the Turkish houses,
That there might be nor stick nor trace
Of these true servants of the Devil!
From Cettigné to Tcheklitche we hied,
There in full flight the Turks espied;
A certain number were by us mow'd down,
And all their houses we did set ablaze;
Of all their mosques both great and small
We left but one accursèd heap,
For passing folk to cast their glance of scorn.

The Montenegrins rejoice in what they have accomplished:

And now for thee throughout our parts
Is not a trace of e'en one single Turk—
At least thou'lt find not any Turkish ear—
Bodies headless, ruins, ashes views man here!

The *Mountain Wreath* has held an important position in Serbian literature but has come under critical rereading in light of the horrible events that followed the breakup of Yugoslavia. As one analyst, for example, noted, "There was another side to *The Mountain Wreath* far more sinister than its praise of tyrannicide. . . . the poem was also a paean to ethnic cleansing . . . it helps explain how Serbian (might we not say

'Balkan'?) national consciousness has been moulded and how ideas of national liberation are inextricably linked with killing your neighbour and burning his village."[128] Nor is *The Mountain Wreath* unique in post-Ottoman literatures. Defeat of the cruel Turk justifies cruelty. The qualities that the Balkan nationalists purport to hate in their Turkish masters become their adopted traits. Here is Ivan Vazov giving voice to such a sentiment:

> Cruelty is an element inherent in our Bulgarian nature, it has become part and parcel of us and it is absorbed with the first breath of air, together with the poisoned milk of our mothers in slavery. Don't talk to me about exceptional times, don't explain this horrible expression of our national character by the political storms raging in our country. No history of any European revolution in the 19th century has recorded such ruthless beastliness and mean cruelty. None of these revolutions has its Knare, Staropatits with their beastly tortures! Rivers of blood have flowed, thousands of heads have fallen, thrones and kingdoms have been ruined and those events have been only terrible but not disgusting in their cruelty. To kill an armed and dangerous enemy is pardonable, it is the law of nature, the cruel natural law of self-defence, despite the fact that Count Tolstoy considers it a crime incompatible with the high ideal of Christianity. But to torture or make others torture a bound and defenceless victim without no need or point, often without knowing the victim, that is the barbarity of a cannibal which can be explained only by the lowest possible cultural level; and since we are Europeans, and a progressive people, how otherwise could we interpret this same ugly phenomenon if not by that is inherent in our souls, a feeling of cruelty and pitilessness towards our brother instilled in us since childhood?[129]

The discourses that were prominent in the orbit of the Bulgarian intellectuals were certainly adapted and reinterpreted in order to insinuate themselves at the local level where they were ultimately grafted.[130] National catastrophe, an unrealized superiority, and Orientalism were ideas that crystallized for the average population when faced with the prospect of plunder in war. As Mark Biondich says, "War is a transformative phenomenon and civil conflict often transforms local and personal grievances into lethal violence."[131]

Simple self-interest and greed were motivation enough to set in motion the aforementioned grievances. "Men profit from the fact that a country's social and political climate designates this or that category of individuals as 'enemies' in order to relieve them of their wealth, even if it means killing."[132] Because, in addition to their association with the regime, Muslims were seen as wealthy haves and haves-too-much, especially when it came to land, making them opportune targets for robbery. When order breaks down as war breaks out, individual motives for violence may tend toward the settling of personal scores.

But when violence takes on massive scales, it is important to understand the larger social dynamic at play. With Russia entering a war against the Ottomans, ostensibly to support the national aims of the Bulgarians, an occasion appeared wherein Russia and the Bulgarians could both meet objectives—ideological and cynical. The Bulgarians would achieve the creation of a nation-state and the expropriation of wealth and property. The Russians would provide assistance to their suffering Slavic kin and, given that outright annexation of Bulgarian territory (as in the Polish case) would have provoked war with the other European powers, would gain a second-best alternative—the creation of a pliable Slavic state in the heart of the Balkans. In this they were able to find sufficient motivation to change the demographics of the Danube Province in order to create the nation-state of Bulgaria.

Sociologist Michael Mann has pointed out the conflictive structure that stems from notions of territory and sovereignty. When rival ethnonational groups make claims for sovereignty and elicit outside backing (from Russia in this case), the conflict enters a "danger zone": "the weaker actor [may decide] to fight rather than submit because he benefits from some external support." When outside pressures such as war bolster the external support, a high risk for ethnic cleansing results.[133]

War has been the catalyst for many horrible events. It mobilizes groups, "pitting the cohesion of the self against the enemy 'them.' The figures of the enemy constructed in peacetime become realities in wartime. . . . This is unfortunate for all those who have already been depicted as enemies!"[134] The Russo-Turkish War of 1877–1878 would prove greatly unfortunate for Muslims living in the Danube region, who, having been maligned and dehumanized in centuries-old European discourse, were "far away from Christian sympathy, the objects of Christian hate."[135]

Three

MASSACRE AND EXPULSION

> The Danube is our water of life. If the Danube were to go away, our homeland could not survive.... Wherever you dig along the Danube's bank, you'll find the bones of your father or your brother. The rising silt that makes the Danube's waters murky is the very substance of her defenders' bodies.
>
> Namık Kemal, *Vatan Yahut Silestre*

> The obligation to emigrate from the lands of unbelief will continue right up to the Day of Judgment.
>
> Averroes (quoted in Richard Fletcher, *Moorish Spain*)

In Kazanlak, Bulgaria, "the world seem[ed] dotted with roses." For mile after endless mile, all the fields were thick in flower. It was the "garden of European Turkey."[1] Turk and Bulgar alike diligently worked the fields, plucking rose blossoms, which they distilled into the renowned attar of roses and sent to far-off destinations, including the sultan's harem. It is said that a wandering Turk brought a rose tree from Tunisia and planted it in the Tundja valley at the foot of the Balkan mountain range. The transplant thrived there, where the maroon soil was indifferent yet peculiar and somehow capable of yielding that most exquisite essence. Four thousand pounds of roses were required for the production of just one pound of attar. In June, when the rose blossoms blazed in riotous color, a gentle wind could carry the perfume as far as fifty miles.[2]

3.1. *Two Hawks (Başıbozuks)* by Vasilii Vasilevich Vereshchagin (1879). Public domain: Wikimedia Commons.

By the end of summer 1877, after Turkish rule had been forever pushed far from the banks of the Danube and the remnants of Muslim life there were made precarious, the prosperous valley had been reduced to a desert and the rose gardens were laid waste. Muslim men had been carried off to gravel pits, ditches, cherry orchards, and rose plantations, where they were tied up with unbound turbans, the red sashes that they had been wearing around their waists, or pilfered Ottoman telegraph cable, back-to-back in pairs or in groups of up to five. The men were then slaughtered, kneeling in prayerlike prostration.

At one such horrific scene, on Friday, August 10, 1877, set amid the rose bushes of the Tundja valley, a Bulgarian priest named Pop Stefan "was reading prayers during the whole of the massacre." Dormuş, a Muslim Gypsy, bound and awaiting certain death, recognized the priest, who was an acquaintance. He begged the priest to intercede like a good neighbor, which the priest refused to do, saying, "Neighborhood is at an end." Then, as the 35-year-old Muslim Gypsy testified: "When our turn came we were led off to the edge of a rose plantation. Some of us wanted to kneel with our bodies upright, but we were forced to bend them down with our faces to the ground, like the others." After shots were fired and Dormuş's companions were killed, the officer in charge commanded "Redjo" (Bulgarian for "Cut"). "The soldiers and Bulgarians together set upon us with swords and yataghans. I heard the noise of hacking in all directions, and the murderers giving a gasp as they delivered each blow." After receiving severe cuts to the neck, shoulder, and head, Dormuş pretended to be dead. "When the work was over, the Bulgarians called out 'Umrelli' ('They are dead'). They then went away, shouting something about 'Rossia,' which I took to be 'Long live the Emperor of Russia,' and adding 'Amen.' They fired shots as they went off."[3]

As similar massacres were repeated there and elsewhere, the Balkan soil took on a "dark red hue as if saturated with blood." During later investigations of similar massacres, the clothing, including "fezzes [which] lay scattered about" like rotting fallen fruit,[4] identified the corpses as Muslims. Plumes of smoke wafted from abandoned villages in the deserted countryside, and "everywhere a horribly mingled smell of attar roses and putrefied human flesh" sickened the senses and troubled the soul.[5]

A Russian officer passing through a nearby village to get his first sight of some Bulgarian troops that had joined up with the Russians was struck by an odd sight, which along with other scenes caused him some uneasiness: "As I passed the Sheinova redoubts, I was struck with the sight of slaughtered Turks. They lay here, in front of the trenches, in long, even lines, as though they had lain down in drill. . . . such even files of corpses, exactly as though they had been mowed down, I never beheld anywhere else."[6]

Given that its social fabric was already being strained by alterations to the demographic, legal, and diplomatic situation, the Danube Province was unable to withstand the outbreak of violence and was finally torn into irreparable tatters by the Russo-Turkish War of 1877–1878. This conflict created a chaotic atmosphere that allowed the Bulgarians to rob and then massacre the very same Muslims with whom they had lived for hundreds of years. The war nearly allowed the Russian Empire to bring to fruition a European dream that had been entertained for centuries—the expulsion of the Turks from Europe.

During the war noncombatant Ottoman Muslims suffered all manner of mass violence at the hands of Bulgarians, Cossacks, and even Russian regular forces. As news spread of the treatment that some Ottoman Muslims had endured, panic spread throughout the province, causing mass flight. Flight, however, was an option fraught with peril, for there was little time to gather possessions and little coordination. Furthermore, the largest movement of people took place in an especially cold winter. Many who were fleeing the Russians and Cossacks were attacked en route by Bulgarians, while greater numbers succumbed to hunger, cold, and disease in impromptu refugee camps, on snowy trails, and in open cattle wagons. Of those who made it to safety, few were ever able to return to their birthplaces; instead, they were to begin life anew as refugees in their sultan's diminished domains.

The 1877–1878 Russo-Turkish Ottoman War resulted not only in the redrawing of lines on the map but also in major demographic changes, due to the mass violence, intimidation, and flight experienced by the Muslims in the Danube and Rumelia Provinces. In Turkish the war is known as the War of '93 (Doksanüç Harbi), referring to the Hijra calendar year 1293.[7] In Bulgaria it is known as the War of Independence, in Russia as the War of Liberation, and by contemporaries in western Europe as the War of the Orient. Yet whatever the name, by the end of the war, 55 percent of the Muslim population had vanished like butterflies in a tempest, but this was the bloody requirement of nationalism–a homogenized population. Often the violence was ad hoc, sometimes encouraged and even organized, and nearly always it was ignored by the Russian troops, who had virtually taken possession of the territory. While the War of '93 was a fatal blow for an Ottoman presence in Europe and was the largest case of the destruction of a European Muslim community, surpassing even the death toll in 1990s Bosnia, the mass elimination and expulsion of these Muslims have received shockingly little attention. This is all the more striking in view of the vogue for studies of ethnic violence and genocide and the similar sociological patterns found in other cases of mass ethnic violence.

This chapter shows that the violence against Ottoman Muslims in Bulgaria during the Russo-Turkish War of 1877–1878 bears the sociological imprint of an ethnic cleansing. Moreover, the demographic consequences of this violence are investigated here in order to gain an idea of the scope of the resulting human suffering. Indeed, given the scale and intensity of the violence and expulsion, the main questions that this study poses concerning memory and forgetting become even more salient.

WAR AND THE EXPULSION OF THE TURK FROM EUROPE

Upon declaring war, the Russians made preparations to cross the Danube. This they accomplished on June 22, 1877, in Galați in Dobruca. The Ottomans had wrongly anticipated a crossing between Ruse and Nikopol. Due to the superior railroad system in Romania, the Russians were able to concentrate a large number of troops there more quickly. Despite initial heavy fighting, the Ottoman commanders pulled back, allowing the Russians to advance rapidly and occupy Dobruca. Many of the Muslim inhabitants fled or were evacuated, mostly to Mecidiye and Varna in the east. The tsar then called upon the Bulgarians to join the Russian army in the war of liberation.[8]

On June 26 Russia crossed the Danube again at Sistova, this time in force, with the intent to occupy the south and press onward to Istanbul. With only intermittent yet bloody fighting, the Ottomans for the most part ceded ground in retreat. By July the Russian forces controlled the Bulgarian countryside, and on July 20 they began the siege on Pleven. The fortress at Pleven became the major obstacle for Russian success in the war as it was, to the surprise of all, able to hold out until December 11. The delay caused by Ottoman doggedness in the face of the siege discouraged the other Balkan states, which had wanted to join the Russian attack in exchange for territory, from entering the war.[9] The only other lengthy siege was in Ruse.

An initial shock for the Russians, perhaps greater than the weakness of Turkish defenses, was discovering that average Bulgarian peasants possessed higher standards of living than their Russian counterparts. One Russian called it "a prosperity from which Russian peasants are as far away as from the star in heaven." Another Russian officer said, "God help our peasant in achieving this sort of well-being within fifty years. But I know for certain that in the next hundred years we shall not have it..... There was no reason to liberate the Bulgarians; they are better off here than the ruling Turks."[10] Misgivings developed as many Russian officers were quickly disenchanted with the ungrateful, uncouth Bulgarians that they thought they were there to save.

The Ottoman 3rd Army was stationed in the east, and the Turks continued to hold fortresses in Ruse, Silistra, Shumen, and Varna. This line of fortresses became a safe haven for refugees fleeing to the Black Sea coast and were not relinquished until after the armistice. However, city after city, including Sofia, Pazardzhik, and Plovdiv, fell throughout January.

The rapidity with which the Russians advanced through Bulgaria indicates that Ottoman military resistance was generally quickly overcome. Thus few Muslim civilians would have been killed as a direct result of warfare; moreover, no primary source indicates a large number of civilian casualties from battle.[11] On the contrary, the huge number of deaths was a result of violence against civilians and the cold, hunger, and disease that accompanied displacement. Virtually as soon as the Russians crossed the Danube, excesses were reported. Although Russia was the first European state formally to recognize the Red Crescent (which first became active in this war),[12] one of the first Russian salvos was the shelling of a civilian hospital draped with the Red Crescent flag. The Ottoman Empire, which was a signatory to the Geneva Conventions, had notified the International Committee of the Red Cross on November 16, 1876, of its intention to replace the Red Cross with a Red Crescent on the flags and armbands of neutral personnel. While Russia acquiesced, it expressed concern that the national emblem of the crescent might be confused with the crescent of neutrality. Interestingly, Austria proposed putting the cross and crescent together to demonstrate that, while these two religious symbols might be antagonistic on the field of battle, they were in accord in the humane treatment of the sick and the injured.[13]

The organized massacres committed at the very outset of the war should give second thoughts to those who suggest that the violence against Muslim civilians escalated as the war dragged on. By June 28 Bulgarians in Sistova had painted crosses on their doors, reminiscent of Passover, so that their homes would not be attacked. Nevertheless, the Turkish homes and quarters were sacked: "The Turkish homes were opened and half-way destroyed. Through their shattered windows, one could see heaps of rubble, debris of all nature, garbage. The furniture was hacked to pieces and the clothing was shredded, the walls gutted, the books torn up, the trees in the gardens were felled, the domestic animals had been slaughtered."[14]

The more immediate threats and attacks on Muslim persons and property were amplified by assaults on the community through the destruction of mosques and cemeteries. We have a description of the destruction of the mosque in Sistova at the very start of the war:

3.2. *Artillery Fire at Ruse.* From *Historical Narrative of the Turko-Russian War* (1886).

> The Bulgarians proved themselves even more ferocious. They had broken or tipped over the tombstones in the Muslim cemeteries. In order to avoid the repetition of similar actions, the Russians had to put guards at these places of rest. The cemeteries are at the same time more simplistic and more poetic in Turkey than in any other country of the world. There the trees and the flowers play their role of peace, planted and sown randomly amid the tombs, in charming disorder. The cypresses shade the graves of the Muslims, made of columns on which were inscribed some Quranic verses and topped by a type of marble head, decorated with a red fez with blue tassel. The simple tombs of women are hidden under heaps of flowers. The virgins get roses. The grass grows densely between the graves, all of which point toward Mecca.[15]

Alexandre Toumarkine has classified the persecution of Muslims into three degrees, as exemplified throughout this chapter: (1) intimidation, such as threats and the defilement of mosques and cemeteries, (2) pillage, such as theft of goods, animals, and clothing, burning of houses, and destruction of crops and orchards, and (3) physical aggression, including mutilation, rape, murder, summary execution, immolation of villagers inside their homes or mosques, and mutilation of corpses.[16]

Before giving a much more detailed picture of the process of destruction of the Muslims in Bulgaria, I wish to consider the question of responsibility. While some may point to civilian deaths as a natural state of war, such an approach seems to condone the destruction of civilians as a legitimate act of war—making massacre akin to self-defense.[17] Others impute the excessive violence to the savage character of the Balkan people.[18] This type of condescending equivocation is found in the Carnegie report on the Balkan Wars, which stated, "Burning of villages and exodus of vanquished populations are normal and habitual events of wars and insurrections in the Balkans."[19]

During war, when the state can no longer enforce peace between the various communities, local actors are naturally freed to become entrepreneurs of violence. They set about settling scores with neighbors or just getting while the getting is good, whether this means goods they envied or females they lusted for. As a consequence, violence multiplies.[20] Franz Kafka more succinctly describes the onset of violence when war breaks out, "It is an inundation. War has opened the floodgates of Evil. The props supporting human existence are caving in."[21]

However, as American political scientist Donald Horowitz has demonstrated, while events such as war may serve as a catalyst to violence, ethnic hatred is insufficient to create mass violence; rather, these actions only take on magnitude if they are mobilized and organized, possibly with the support of state institutions. Naturally, we can expect some improvisation, but "the climate of impunity created by those who gave the massacres their thrust would make such excesses not only possible, but still more probable by actors. . . . intoxicated by their power."[22]

The British ambassador Sir Henry Layard, who is an important figure in this story, the French ambassador Hughes Fournier, and many other observers felt that they were witnessing a deliberate policy of extermination. As Layard remarked at the time,

> No such war of massacre and destruction had been carried on for centuries. It is waged on the hateful principles of religious persecution in the name of Christianity. . . . Flourishing

provinces have been reduced to a desert, and populations of different races and creed . . . have been taught the lesson of mutual extermination . . . all the accumulated evils and vices of Turkish misrule had not produced such results as these . . . [and] no war of modern times has produced so much misery and desolation.[23]

Queen Victoria herself became convinced of the motives for the war:

> Under the cloak of RELIGION and under the pretence of obtaining just treatment for the so-called "Christians" of the principalities, but who are far worse than the Mussulmans, and who moreover had been excited to revolt by General Ignatieff, who prevented regular troops being sent out to quell the revolt, leading to the so-called "Bulgarian atrocities" as the irregular troops were sent out, this war of extermination (for that it is) has been iniquitously commenced![24]

Justin McCarthy points to a great deal of circumstantial evidence to suggest a deliberate policy to kill and expel the Muslims.[25] For example, the speed with which the war progressed meant that coordination was necessary for the mass expulsion to be effected. In fact, the Russians had a pattern for using Cossacks and Russian-educated Bulgarians to ensure the liquidation of the Muslims.

Vladimir Aleksandrovich Cherkasskii, who had been appointed by the tsar to head the civilian administration during the Russian occupation of Bulgaria, ordered the disarmament of Muslims prior to the Russian crossing of the Danube. He wrote a letter from Romania dated May 30, 1877:

> [Great importance] was seen in the necessary disarmament of the Muslims to prevent the bloody confrontations between the different nationalities of the Balkan peninsula . . . as soon as our troops cross the Danube, immediate disarmament should be undertaken. By fulfilling this important measure at the earliest time . . . [we] will show that, in the territory we occupy, our government does not tolerate the carrying of arms by one part of the population, which has on so many occasions splattered defenseless Christians with blood. . . .

> The Muslim population, which has so often abused its right, should undergo disarmament. As for the disarmament of the Bulgarian population, there is no need to resort to it, because having been disarmed for so long by the Turks they do not possess weapons in large quantities and they need [what little they have] to repel the potential attempts on the part of the Muslims at new attacks against the Christians.[26]

In his instructions about how the disarmament was to be carried out, Cherkasskii disallowed house searches and violating the sanctity of harems. However, he noted that Muslims inevitably would have weapons, so one could estimate a certain amount of arms according to the number of homes in a given village or quarter. He instructed that, in the case of noncompliance by the Turks, they could always make use of "the best local Christian inhabitants" to point out the number of weapons held by the Muslims.[27] According to Cherkasskii's instructions, the collected weapons were to be put in the military depots or placed under the guard of troops.

The disarmament of Muslims did not prevent intercommunal violence; rather, it was done in such a way as to encourage violence against Muslims. The Russians or Cossacks would routinely surround villages and disarm the Muslim population, demanding, with a promise of protection, that Muslims bring all their arms within a very short deadline to a designated spot, such as the local government building or a mosque in the village itself or in a nearby large town. Suspicion of noncompliance was a pretext for raids on Muslim dwellings, despite Cherkasskii's proscription. Raids were actually opportunities to search for and confiscate valuables and to make arrests leading to summary executions of Muslims pleading their innocence. Once the Muslim arms had been turned over to the Russian forces, the Muslims would be given safe-conduct passes to return to their villages. The confiscated weapons were then used to arm the Bulgarians of the same village or neighboring villages.

Aleksandr Vasilevich Vereshchagin, the son of the famous Russian artist Vasilii Vasilevich Vereshchagin, watched in one village as the local mullah instructed the village's Muslim inhabitants to gather all arms in the town center. Oxen pulled in five cartloads of weapons. "What manner of gun is there that is not here!" he exclaimed as he described all the different decorations on the guns and swords. "The Bulgarians crowd around the weapons and devour them with their eyes. Evidently, they would very much like to share all these spoils." He had the weapons stored in the town konak (government house), but during the night the town's Bulgarians rushed in and stole them all.[28] In some villages Bulgarians tried to help their Muslim neighbors by interceding with the Russians or by warning of imminent danger when it seemed no longer possible to help otherwise. In the village of Yakuboğlu, for example, the local Bulgarians refused to set fire to the Muslim houses as Cossacks had encouraged them to do.[29]

However, the enticement to plunder with impunity was too great for most Bulgarians to resist. Robbery became a means to compromise the sense of morality among the Bulgarians and thereby firmly position the Bulgarian peasantry on the Russian side. In a classic of Bulgarian literature, *Bai Ganyo*, the eponymous hero and his friend seem to hint at the dirty little secret of how fortunes were made during the war:

> "When I hear the word 'Cossack' I get the shivers."
>
> "You get the shivers, eh?" whispered Bai Ganyo softly with a wink. "But when the Russians came, who was it that cleaned out the cattle from the Turkish villages, eh? Since when do you have those riches, eh? Speak up!"
>
> "Well, but you, too, Bai Ganyo," whispered Bai Mihal. "Truth to tell, you've had the water mills since the Russian occupation, haven't you? Tell me; isn't that so?"
>
> "Come now, one can't even have a simple conversation with you. What's done is done."[30]

In a climate of incitement and impunity, the slippery slope from robbery to far worse deeds was precipitous indeed. When the killing started, a dynamic of its own was unleashed in support of personal agendas, interests, and vendettas. Actions against the Muslim population were encouraged by a group of Russian-educated Bulgarians whose aim was to take revenge on the Muslims for the violent suppression of the April Uprising. These Bulgarians, many of whom had been living for some time in Romania, called themselves the "Avengers" and were otherwise known as the Bulgarian Legion. They were recruited, paid, and officered by Russians in Bucharest and were filled with a passionate hatred of the Turks.[31] Approximately 4,000–7,500 of these young Bulgarians crossed the Romanian frontier to join the Russian army shortly after it entered into Bulgarian territory, while more Bulgarians were being organized into militias in Ploesti, Romania.[32] For the most part they were part of General Iosif Vladimirovich Gurko's advance force. Their presence in many instances could be gleaned from the fact that when dressed as Russian soldiers or Cossacks they could speak Bulgarian and Turkish. Bent on vengeance, they hunted down Ottoman officials with any role in the Bulgarian atrocities.

The fate of the *kaymakam* of Kazanlak, Akif Efendi, for example, illustrates what Ottoman officials might expect after the arrival of the Russians. While detained by the Russians, he was overheard conversing with a Bulgarian, who urged him to give up Islam. He responded, "Should I cover myself with filth to save a spoonful of blood? God forbid! Is there no executioner to finish me? If you have not a sword, a hatchet will do; so let my soul be free at once." The witness who overheard the conversation then heard the blows of swords falling from two attackers.

> Akif Effendi then got up into the cart and began to pray and to recite verses from the Koran with great fervency. The two men pulled him out again and continued striking him till he was silent. He then got into the cart a second time, and again was dragged out and beaten, He then called for water, saying, "I will not be killed till you have given me water; so will you kill me." Water was brought, and as he stretched out his neck to drink he said, "Kill me now, now is the time."[33]

The kaymakam was beaten throughout the night until it seemed that he might be dead, but the next morning he was seen bound and being led to a carriage. He was next seen entering the next village in a carriage, escorted by Bulgarians and Cossacks, but with no officers in sight. He came in and out of a consciousness. His teeth had been knocked out and he was bleeding from both his mouth and nose. A Cossack was occasionally whipping him with a cowhide. When the carriage arrived at Kazanlak, Bulgarians of all ranks surrounded the cart, where they mocked the kaymakam with a fake reverence and then spat on him and abused him with foul language. The cart went to the government konak, where the kaymakam was lifted out and laid on the floor. He was speechless and barely conscious. Nearly a week later the kaymakam was seen outside, escorted by Cossacks. An acquaintance approached and had the following brief conversation with him:

> EMIN EFFENDI.—Thank God we have met.
> AKIF EFFENDI.—Are you alive then?
> EMIN EFFENDI.—Praise be to God, I am. Were you kept at the khan?
> AKIF EFFENDI.—I have been brought from Shipka.
> EMIN EFFENDI.—What for?
> AKIF EFFENDI.—I do not know.
> EMIN EFFENDI.—What is the blood upon you?
> AKIF EFFENDI.—Do not ask me; every joint in my body feels dislocated.
> EMIN EFFENDI.—What was it done for?
> AKIF EFFENDI.—Because I let out the Bashi-Bazouks.[34]

Days later, some Cossacks ordered a Muslim named Mehmet Arnavutoğlu to hitch his oxen to the cart and come to the konak where the kaymakam was held. He and another local Muslim were told to go in and get Akif Efendi. They brought him out weakened and barefoot as instructed and headed in the direction of Tarnovo, as the Cossacks had demanded:

> The Kaïmakam sat silent in the cart. Crowds of Bulgarians, many women and children among them, and Cossacks, gathered on the way and followed us, but there were no cries or insults. When we came to a mulberry-tree which was on the left of the road in the public way, just outside the town, we were made to drive the cart under it. One of the Cossacks then produced a cord, a new one, and said to me, in Turkish, "Put it round his neck." The Cossack had a drawn sword, and his manner was threatening. I had no resource but to do as I was bid. I was then made to tie the other end of the cord to a branch of the tree overhead. The Kaïmakam, from first to last, said not a word. He now and then looked about from side to side. The order was

> then given to me to drive on. I did so, and the Kaïmakam was left hanging. His arms were not tied, and he put up his hands toward the rope, but they dropped immediately, and he died almost without a struggle.[35]

The Bulgarian Legion actively incited Bulgarian peasants to attack Muslims after creating a sense of impunity by spreading rumors of exaggerated Russian military successes. What started out principally as robbery and pillage along with occasional rapes and scattered murders, committed sometimes by Cossacks or more often by Bulgarians from the same or outside villages, degenerated into widespread violence when news of the Russian defeat at Stara Zagora was confirmed. In order to prevent reprisals for their abuse of the Muslims, given that the Russians were retreating and the Ottomans advancing, "a deliberate attempt was made to exterminate the adult male population." The massacres took place in the presence of the Russians. One such massacre in Shipka involved from five hundred to six hundred Muslim men.[36]

The Russian troops sometimes guaranteed the safety of Muslim civilians but generally turned a blind eye to the proceedings. One Russian soldier, responding to the pleas of Muslim villagers from Balvan for Russian intercession, said, "During the insurrection last year you killed the Bulgarians and plundered and burnt the monastery, for this reason they now retaliate." He then walked off, leaving the village to the Bulgarians.[37] In many cases the Cossacks allowed the Bulgarian peasants to keep the pillaged items without taking any for themselves, which raises suspicion: the Cossacks were notorious for their looting, so such behavior bespoke an unusual discipline. This was documented in the villages of Hidibey, Büкümlük, and Stara Zagora among a great many others.[38] In Stara Zagora, where the Russian troops brought in Bulgarians from other villages "of the baser sort, who were intent on revenge and plunder," a Russian officer surveyed the destruction through his field glasses, according to an American missionary's report:

> These outside Bulgarians, assisted by a few of a similar character in town, began to plunder Turkish shops in the market. They did not at first take any lives, but they entered the mosques, took valuable copies of the Koran, tore them in pieces

> and besmeared them with tar, and stuck them on the walls. Presently becoming insolent, they took Turkish citizens who were obnoxious to them, and some, with or without forms of the law, they hewed in pieces with their axes.[39]

According to a Russian in another village, "Throngs of Bulgarians, red, perspiring, breathless, hurry from house to house, plunder, quarrel among themselves, and heap up their asses and their little horses, from their tails to their very ears, with the stolen booty."[40]

In the words of one journalist, the Russians and Cossacks "were their [the Bulgarians'] accomplices throughout, and encouraged and protected the perpetration of these outrages even when they did not share in their commission."[41] Despite the behavior of the Bulgarians, the Russians continued to disarm the Turks and arm the Bulgarians, as noted by a correspondent for the *Times* of London, after citing Russian frustrations with Bulgarian behavior:

> It has sometimes been urged in excuse for these wretches that they had been debauched by centuries of Turkish misrule; but there had been nothing for centuries previous to the war, capable of developing such a hell of evil passions in the Bulgarian population, had there not been something essentially vicious in the very nature of that population. . . . Yet these were the men whom the Russians systematically armed as they advanced in the country, after first taking all the weapons from the unfortunate Mussulmans, who were thus left defenceless. It was hardly possible that the results should have been other than they were.[42]

Prince Cherkasskii, as head of the civil administration of occupied Bulgaria, was already concerned by midsummer with the way things were developing. He included the following in a report:

> Despite the graceful and statesmanlike words of his Majesty the Emperor, found in the proclamation [concerning] the full protection of the law to all inhabitants of the Balkan Peninsula, peacefully remaining in their dwellings in the parts of Bulgaria occupied by our troops, the crossing of Russian troops over the

Danube was a signal for the immediate, and almost to a man, flight of the entire Muslim population from the places that our troops have occupied. A prevalent and frightful rupture in the local population between Bulgarians and Turks, Christians and Mohammedans, took shape in plain view of all and at its fullest weight. The flight of yesterday's lords and oppressors induced the Bulgarian population into some kind of intoxication, which, unfortunately, pushed them toward reprisals against the entire Muslim population. Turkish homes, first in Sistova, and then in Tirnova and other places, were pillaged by Bulgarians; in the rear of our troops near Sistova, at Tirnova and Gabrovo armed gangs of Bulgarians were formed who robbed and murdered Turks wherever they might encounter them. That our forces freed and provided protection to the Turks who stayed peacefully in their villages and asked for nothing more than protection from the Bulgarians sparked the latter into a rage that I personally witnessed in Tirnova during the release of Turkish deputies to their homes who had come to request protection from Your Highness. In that very same Tirnova, near which the headquarters of the army was stationed, a sinister rumor about the impending burning of the Turkish quarters floated about for many days, and several deliberate fires set in individual homes showed that, without a watchful eye on the population, the implementation of some malefactors' intentions would easily take place, clearly endangering numerous military stores and supplies, which were already located in Tirnova. To our great misfortune, it is necessary here to mention that members of the priesthood participated in the armed gangs who robbed and murdered the Muslim population, which demonstrates that the reprisals of the Bulgarians against the Turks were not only made by the lower classes but were justified by the more developed classes of society.

I was forced by similar circumstances to point out, in a memorandum given to Your Highness on July 4 in Tirnova, the acrimony dividing the local population, one part of which strove to annihilate the other, and having explained that, judging by the way things were going, such a rupture was not going to settle down but rather was likely to evolve further and further.[43]

Benjamin Lieberman and Peter Holquist insist that the Russians had no deliberate policy of extermination and had instructed their soldiers in the laws of war. Lieberman further says that it should have mattered little to a multiethnic empire such as Russia whether Muslims remained in Bulgaria. He argues that Circassians were indeed targeted but not other Muslims and cites reports of some Russians caring for refugees in Edirne and encouraging them to return home.[44] (Other accounts, though, report instances of Russians withholding aid from starving masses, even when resources were at their disposal.) The contentions of Lieberman and Holquist seem no more than anecdotal in the face of the sheer scale of events and testimonies indicating broad patterns of behavior of Russians, Cossacks, and Bulgarians. The majority of those testifying to the Rhodope Commission pointed a finger at the Russians rather than the Bulgarians and told many stories of Russian misdeeds. Furthermore, in seeking a rational explanation for Russian behavior, we should consider that Russian annexation of the Bulgarian provinces was simply impossible: such a move would undoubtedly have spurred the kind of alliance that guaranteed Russia's defeat in the Crimean War. Rather than expanding its empire and collecting taxes or tribute from Muslims, such as it had been doing in the Caucasus and Central Asia, Russia's goal was to have a tractable Slavic state in the Balkans. It was therefore important to have an overwhelming Slavic majority. Holquist, who maintains Russia's innocence in terms of policy, does concede that "Russian units either helped foment atrocities by Bulgarians or stood by passively when they occurred."[45] British ambassador Layard expressed his concerns in August:

> It would scarcely be proper to accuse Russian Generals and the Russian Government of deliberately encouraging or sanctioning the extermination of the Mahommedans of Bulgaria; but I fear there are influential persons who believe that the only way to russianize Bulgaria, and to reduce the province to a complete state of dependency on Russia, is to destroy or remove the whole of the Mussulman population from it. There are even some in England who appear to think that this is the best mode of settling the Turkish question. . . . If Russia succeeds in reducing Bulgaria to the condition of a Russian province she will, no doubt, accomplish her object of putting an end to a mixed population.[46]

While no document containing an extermination order per se has been unearthed, and probably never will be, we can still conclude that the expulsion of the Muslims was in some way sanctioned. While it may not have been premeditated by the Russians, it was certainly not unwelcome.

Layard was very much alarmed that the Russians offered no guarantee of safety to the Muslim populations. In telegram after telegram he asked London to demand that the Russians issue such a decree in order to stop the overwhelming flow of refugees. The Ottoman grand vizier also implored the Russians to make such a proclamation.[47] But the Russians insisted that any decree on this matter other than the one that they had made at the beginning of the war would be superfluous. Prince Cherkasskii declared his opposition to a new proclamation in a letter to the Russian minister of war: "For the establishment of order, what is needed is not words but force." He wanted Russians to form his police force, not Bulgarians: "It is impossible to rely on a local police force made up of Bulgarians. They would be the ones raping the Muslims and there would not be any witnesses or informants on the police."[48] Cherkasskii never received the Russian forces that he requested.

Layard was convinced that "it was the settled policy of the dominant party to drive the Mohammedans out of Bulgaria and Rumelia." He felt that his conviction was supported by Prince Aleksei Tseretelev's response to that accusation: "The departure of the greater part of the Turkish population to Asia would greatly facilitate our work in Bulgaria and Thrace."[49]

It is difficult to discern whether the Russian government had a settled policy. On the one hand, we can observe a pattern of action on the part of Russians, Cossacks, and Bulgarians and a lack of response by the Russians that would have demonstrated their opposition to the unfolding situation regarding the refugee problem. The civil administration of the occupation, headed by Prince Cherkasskii, was underfunded and undermanned. He constantly expressed his frustration with the military leaders who left him without resources and clear instructions for dealing with the many problems he faced, including large numbers of refugees and continuing communal violence. Why the Russian leadership in the war wanted to keep subordinates in the dark about such an important question is open to speculation. Was it incompetence, lack of a plan, or something more sinister?

In the immediate time frame of that period, however, having fewer Turks around was beneficial to Russian war aims, because they would not have to worry about an insurgency in the rear. Moreover, the throngs of refugees made things more difficult for the Ottoman forces in the war zone. It is possible that the Russians were therefore eager to rid themselves of a potential nuisance by scaring the Turks into leaving. Prince Cherkasskii discussed the return of Turks to their homes in a letter in July:

> It is our good fortune that they are not returning, and we should encourage them not to do so. Given that we have not yet secured our communications, our only salvation is the absence of any Turks on our first primary artery between the Danube and Tirnova. Once they get started [returning] here, it will be far worse for us. Believe me and do not encourage them to return. Without encouragement they won't come back on their own. At least they don't bother us too much with this. Thank God![50]

In response to his letter, Adjutant General Dmitrii Alekseevich Miliutin made it clear that at his level he was unaware of any policy to respond to the emerging refugee crisis, as higher-ups refused to announce any decisions:

> Nobody here knows what to do with the prisoners [of war] and the Turkish families that have been brought here. . . .
>
> The surrounding inhabitants have yet to see any proclamation. . . . The question of what to do with the Turks who have been brought to the local military leaders has clearly not been thought through. . . .
>
> I have already written about the Turkish population, about entire families brought with children, cattle, and property. Now, as they count such families in the hundreds, we will be advancing to the west, we will have to maintain under arrest and feed thousands, [if not] hundreds of thousands, of families. Is it conceivable to send the entire Turkish population of Bulgaria to Russia? And how can you make that agree with the proclamation that the Muslim population should quietly stay in its place?

> In the end, I would not want to be the one who has to decide this question. I am not going to get involved in its resolution and I expect that similar general questions will already have been discussed and settled in the plan of the Commander-in-Chief.... But in the meantime, at this critical juncture, things are not being dealt with: hundreds of families can be found in the open air with their children, livestock, and property, threatened with a cold death.[51]

The Russian troops may have been under orders to eliminate the possibility of the return of Turkish refugees by burning down Turkish homes and villages. The Austrian delegate to the Rhodope Commission pointed out to his English colleague the deliberate nature of the destruction of Turkish villages:

> We visited about a dozen burnt villages outside and within the Russian lines; the sight of these once prosperous villages, now utterly destroyed, made a great impression on all the members of the Commission.
>
> It was pointed out by Colonel Raab that all this destruction must have been done purposely, as the houses are all separate, and must have been fired by design; he also said he could find no trace of cannon shot ... isolated farmhouses are all burnt, and even the stacks at a distance from the dwellings; in fact it is a scene of desolation impossible almost to describe, and which exceeds belief if one had not seen it.... I never witnessed such a systematic complete destruction.[52]

An Italian journalist who was accompanying the Russian army noted that needless destruction followed in the wake of the Russians, calling into question their blaming such activities on the Bulgarians:

> But there was something terrible that marked the march of the army—fire: everywhere were seen large columns of smoke, quite often one would think from a distance that it hailed from a serious battle. I found one, two, four, several houses burning or already burned in Akşehir, Iaidzi, Kosna, Radan, Kucina, and

> Borus. The Russians said that the fires were started by the Bulgarians. In Akşehir I saw Russian soldiers coming out of a house that was beginning to burn. Then a Bulgarian came along to contemplate the spectacle with fearful satisfaction: in any event it is sure that the Turkish houses burned.[53]

Cossacks receive a large portion of the blame for indiscriminate violence, including the rapes of Muslim women and attacks on women and children. Wounds from sabers and lances were an indication of Cossack attacks because these were the weapons they normally wielded, and it was not uncommon to find such wounds on children and women. Incidents of Cossacks disarming and murdering entire villages were reported.[54] Whether they played a role by participating actively themselves in massacres, rapes, and theft of property, inciting others to carry them out, or simply looking on, their presence seems to have been synonymous with atrocities against Ottoman Muslims.[55]

The sultan sent Izzet Bey to Grand Duke Nikolai, commander of the Russian forces, in order to ask for better treatment of civilians and an end to the "barbarous acts" of the Bulgarians and the Cossacks. In their meeting the grand duke first responded to Izzet Bey's accusations by accusing the Turks of atrocities then reflected awhile and said, "I know perfectly well that the Bulgarians are barbarians, and that before the arrival of our troops in the villages they commit atrocities, but never in the presence of our troops." At this, Izzet Bey replied that "the Bulgarians don't have lances or sabers and the hospitals in Sumla [Shumen] and Razgrad contain a large number of infants, women, and elderly wounded with these weapons."[56]

The Russian regular forces were also responsible for some attacks against civilians. Again we have a Russian officer eyewitness who relates the following senseless act of cruelty:

> A group of soldiers forms not far from me. I step up and look: in their midst, on the ground, lies an old, gray-haired Turk, as dried up as a mummy. Leaning on his elbow, he gazes confidingly at the good-natured soldiers, dips some honey out of a basket that lies beside him with his finger, licks it, and is, apparently, perfectly happy: at all events his face is expressive of a certain naive, childlike joy.

The soldiers look on and make their comments.

"The idea of his undertaking to fight!" remarks one, smiling, as he leans against his comrade's shoulder from behind.

"How in the world could he fight, as he is simply one of the inhabitants," returns the other.

After looking at the Turk, and inwardly commending the soldiers for having shown hospitality to their enemy, although not with their own honey, I go back. I have not yet reached my tent when I hear behind me a piercing cry, like the wail of a child. I glance back: those same soldiers are dragging the Turk by the feet, at a run, across the road to the fence.

The poor old man clutches at the earth, with all his feeble power, and digs his fingers into the dusty road. While I am trying to overtake them, they have made an end of the Turk: his shaved and aged skull, covered with sparse white hairs, presents a formless mass, and his eyes have leaped from their sockets.

"Why have you killed him?" I shout to the soldiers.

"He was a bashi-buzuk, your Honor!"[57]

While it is sometimes difficult to distinguish between Russian regulars and Cossacks in the documents, in some cases it is clear that Russian regular forces were involved in the destruction of villages. Bombardment by cannon and artillery indicated Russian regular troop action—many villages of no strategic importance were destroyed. In other reports Russian regulars are specifically pointed out as having provided cover for Bulgarians to enter and destroy villages.[58]

One scholar, James Reid, makes the absurd statement that a majority of the Muslim refugees were fleeing from Circassian depredations. While Circassian bandits were sometimes seen as the saviors by Muslims in peril, at other times they did indeed cause some Muslims (and non-Muslims) to flee before looting villages. However, Reid's statement ignores the overwhelming number of reports and accounts that point to Bulgarian, Cossack, and Russian violence.[59] Moreover, there were reports of Bulgarians dressing up as başıbozuks in order to pillage with impunity.[60]

After the onset of violence, many Bulgarians became committed to a Bulgaria without Muslims. The expulsion of the Muslims would not only free up lands and allow for the expropriation of Muslim property but would also give Bulgarians an ascendant position in the political order that was to be. They were often given weapons confiscated from the Muslims and then used these same weapons on the Muslims. Pillage was widespread; Bulgaria had "more Muslim land than the Christian peasants could covet." Indeed, national liberty was in a sense the legalization of the theft and expropriation of Muslim property made unalterable by the nonpresence of Muslims in the land.[61] Theft and murder were interlinked in massacres committed by Bulgarians, which happens to be a common feature of other cases of ethnic cleansing.[62]

Summary execution and rape were also prominent features of the violence when Bulgarians occupied Muslim quarters and villages. Sometimes the men were used as slave labor in projects such as tearing down fortifications before being murdered. In the case of a village called Uflahanli, they were marched into the woods in groups of ten or twenty and slaughtered.[63] When massacres did occur in secluded places, the men were usually told that they were being taken to work on such projects so that they would willingly walk to the sites of their imminent death. In towns trials of Muslims resulted in numerous death sentences, which were eagerly carried out. Muslim villagers were greatly panicked as they awaited unknowingly who would be charged, tried, and inevitably executed next. The following report describes the degeneration of such trials into legitimated murder:

> The Bulgarian Provisional Government at Eski Zagra [Stara Zagora], as soon as constituted, hanged six Turks and shot four others, after trial by court-martial. . . . Next day others were executed, and yet others the next day, the formalities of trial being less in each case, until, at last, Turks were taken out of the city and killed by any Bulgarian who chose to do so, without form of trial. Ten Turks in one batch were so disposed of, the executioners hacking them down with swords so dull that three or four blows were needed in each case.[64]

While Muslim men were targeted for massacre, rape was a weapon used against Muslim women (just as happened in Bosnia one hundred years later). Women who had come into contact with Bulgarians and later became refugees often accused the Bulgarians, Cossacks, and even Russians of such crimes. In the village of Muflis, 25-year-old Zeineb described how the women of the village were brought together:

> [A]s soon as we had been brought to this place, the Cossacks and Bulgarians began to take off the veils of us females, and to carry off those who were good-looking. They said openly that it was in order to violate them. The women and girls tore their hair and begged to be killed rather than dishonoured. The Bulgarians pointed out to the Cossacks the prettiest girls. Some of the women who were carried off related when they came back that the Cossacks and Tchorbadjis had taken them to houses and gardens where they had been pressed to drink wine and to submit to their fate.[65]

Not all the raped women were allowed to live. Near Nova Zagora, for instance, numerous bodies of women and children were discovered in the woods: "The position of the bodies of the women, as well as the fact that they lay singly on the ground at intervals through the wood, sufficiently showed what had been their fate before death. Some of the women had dead children lying near them. Their dress was Turkish beyond doubt."[66]

An English doctor describes an even more gruesome sight of the corpses of one hundred and twenty women and children in a beech forest, reflecting that "it was but too easy to observe what had taken place":

> We counted 122 skulls, of which from 20–25 were those of young children. All the clothing to be seen was such as is worn by Turkish women and children. . . . Many of the skulls had been extensively fractured by blows from blunt instruments. In three cases it was clear that the throat had been cut. . . . In one case the abdomen had been opened in such a manner as to bear out the assertion . . . [that it was] the body of a woman from which had been taken the child she was bearing. Close by were small remains, which may have been those of an unborn child. Some of the women had their arms outstretched clutching their clothes, which had been drawn over their heads. In several cases it was evident that mutilation had been practised, the private parts

> having been cut away before and behind. In two cases certainly, and seemingly in others, the breasts had been removed. At one spot was found the body of a woman encircling with her arms that of a young child, both skulls being fractured. At another was the body of a woman in the prone position, the hands stretched downwards in the evident attempt to protect herself from outrage, the thighs abducted, the legs flexed, the abdomen and other parts horribly mutilated.[67]

In many accounts the women were locked up in barns or other buildings, where they were raped repeatedly, often before being murdered. An Englishman in the service of the Turkish Compassionate Fund heard repeated and corroborating stories of rape, one of which he related:

> The Bulgarians, with a few Cossacks—some say two Cossack officers—came to the village.... They appear to have collected all the young women and children in one or two large houses, to have taken all the men outside the village and shot them, and to have continued pillaging and burning.... All accounts agree that the unhappy girls and young women, who were kept prisoners in these houses, were daily and hourly ravished, that fifteen of them were killed, and that a very large number were taken away to the mountains when the Bulgarians retreated.[68]

The body of one of these dead women was graphically depicted:

> The death of one young woman could only have occurred two or three days ago at the farthest. It is painful and revolting to give one's reasons for being thus able to fix the date, but I must briefly say that the flesh was still adhering to the almost skeleton remains, and what had not been devoured by the dogs was quite fresh-looking.... I can never forget that woman's face. I was accompanied by the correspondent of the "Daily Telegraph," and by our servants, as well as by a Turkish Major and an escort of two or three soldiers. We all stood round that awful sight without saying a word. Her face, which the dogs had respected and left intact, was most strikingly beautiful, with a delicacy of

> outline and a perfect contour of cheek and chin that was only heightened by the pallor of death. Her mouth, which was small and beautifully formed, was slightly open, and her teeth visible, her eyes closed and long fringed lashes lying on her cheek. There was just a faint expression of pain on the forehead, and her hair was lying all round her head like a rich brown wavy halo. She was entirely nude, and her throat had been cut with one clean, deep cut, which must have severed the jugular and windpipe immediately. We also found the remains of women and children in a well. How many there were it was difficult to say, as we did not get them up.[69]

Rape is more than the release of the male sex drive. It is a "sexual manifestation of aggression," and a means to encourage flight of refugees and destroy any desire to return. More than an attack on the individual female, rape in these circumstances is an act of terror against the community.[70] It was a clear means to intimidate the Muslim population in Bulgaria, because the raped women felt that they had lost their honor. Some of the women were raped in front of their children or their tied-up husbands. As two Muslim women who had suffered rape at the hands of Russian soldiers testified, "Rather than give us bread, give us poison!"[71] Another Muslim woman, Nazik from Kazanlak, was locked up in a barn with her children and other villagers. After the Bulgarians came in and tied up the men, they dragged all the women to the surrounding fields, where they "ravaged" them. After they were moved to another village, the rapes continued. According to Nazik, "Not a week has passed without some one of us women being forced to submit to the worst indignities. And if we resisted, which we knew to be useless, beating, beating, beating! We have become like animals, and have forgotten what it is to feel shame."[72]

Cruelty took on extreme manifestations. Breasts were cut off, people were beheaded. One newspaper correspondent in Bulgaria relates how a Bulgarian in Kazanlak had proudly nailed to the wall of his home seven fingers from four Muslim or Jewish infants as some type of trophy. His claim that they were taken from dead children was debunked by a doctor at the trial, who pointed out that the fingers were covered with blood, which indicated that they had in fact been cut off live children.[73]

While not Muslim and not part of the Ottoman military forces, the Ottoman Jewish population in Bulgaria came under attack as well, echoing centuries of Christian violence against Jews and foreshadowing the pogroms that were about to wreak havoc on Jewish life in the near future in the aftermath of the tsar's assassination in 1881. According to Mary Neuburger, the hostility that already was bubbling in Russia against Russian Jews was transferred to the Ottoman Jews, who were believed to be on a similar socioeconomic level as the Jews of Russia and Poland because of an anti-Semitic belief in an inherent Jewish tendency to exploitation. Moreover, Russians often harbored a suspicion of Jews as agents of the Ottoman Empire. Russia's treatment of its own Jews combined with the promise of reform in the Ottoman Empire meant that diaspora Jews outside of the Ottoman Empire were likely to side with the sultan over the tsar.[74] While many Jews who had the means were able to escape to Istanbul, many others remained. The numerous Jewish casualties complicate the view of a strictly Muslim-Christian conflict.[75]

By early July attacks on civilians and the destruction of mosques had already been reported. As news of Russian, Cossack, and Bulgarian cruelties spread, so did the instances of flight. Accounts of massacre, theft, and rape spread quickly and caused entire villages and quarters to empty. An English diplomat reported to his superior in mid-July from Pazardzhik:

> From beyond the Balkans, news arrives to us in an undeniable manner, that little by little as the Russian army is advancing the Bulgars, or the miserable people calling themselves Bulgars, massacre the unfortunate Muslims, an inoffensive people, men, women, and children, refugees whose sad fate renders them worthy of pity. But true or false, this news is propagated and believed everywhere in the southern Balkans.[76]

The ensuing refugee caravans were often attacked. This, in fact, was the general pattern. For if the expulsion of the Turk was the goal, then "columns of refugees [were] not a consequence of massacres, but their prime objective."[77] One Englishman who witnessed empty village after empty village lamented an early occasion of mass flight from the areas around Lovech, south of Pleven: "Here a spectacle presented itself, such

FLIGHT OF THE TURKS. FUGITIVES IN A TURKISH VILLAGE.

3.3. *Flight of the Turks.* From Edmund Ollier, *Cassel's Illustrated History of the Russo-Turkish War* (1877–79), 468.

as I have never before witnessed. Heaven grant that such another scene may never more present itself to me":

> As far as the eye could reach—a distance of several miles, for we were on the top of a hill—the road was covered with refugees toiling their weary way along the burning road, terror-stricken, footsore, starving, hopeless. There were thousands of bullock wagons, bearing pots, pans, babies, women, wooden bowls, fowls, benches, sacks and faggots, all huddled and heaped together in one apparently inextricable mass. Leading the oxen

3.4. *An Exodus* by Montagu Irving. From *Camp and Studio* (1892), 130.

which toiled along was usually the father of the family, but frequently the wife with her heavy woolen yashmak on, in that blazing sun. But even these poor people would not have troubled me so much had they been the only ones on the road, for they had their carts in which to sleep and their goods about them. Unhappily they were not alone in that helpless, hopeless crowd which for four long hours passed.... Thousands upon thousands were endeavouring to carry their all with them. There were poor old women of sixty years struggling along under the burden of pots and pans—the only property they had in the wide world—stopping now and then to rest, and then continuing their way, crying and sobbing with fatigue and grief; mothers, who ought to have had every care, such was their condition, toiling along with babies on their backs and with babies at their side, each infant carrying something belonging to what had been the household ware, or helping to drive, perhaps, a calf or a goat or a sheep. Then there would come by a young girl, holding her yashmak up, so that the strangers might not see her face, driving two or three bullocks; and then a widow with her young family about her, all

> helping to urge a troop of donkeys and goats to move over the road. There were old men hobbling along, helping on their way equally old women; and coming down the side of a hill I saw a fine old fellow of about sixty-five years, I should say, carrying on his back an ancient shriveled dame, who, I suppose was his wife.
>
> Misery reigned supreme: these thousands, flying from the relentless Cossacks, had left their homes, their little crops, to save their lives, and, as they toiled over the pitiless road, they presented the most awfully depressing spectacle it is possible to conceive. . . . These helpless women and children knew full well what the Russians had done on the other side of Loftcha [Lovech], and they preferred to perish on the road to running the risk of coming into contact with Cossack civilisation.[78]

Indeed, whether committed by Russians, Cossacks, or Bulgarians, attacks against Muslim civilians or their property and heritage served to empty vast stretches of Bulgaria of a Muslim presence. One British journalist passing through a Turkish village witnessed the effects of such a process:

> On my way here I passed Bolwan, a village named in the Turkish circular as one of the spots where outrage and murder were committed by the Bulgars. My route did not take me through it, but I saw enough to rouse curiosity, and stopped. The settlement had been large, containing perhaps two hundred and fifty cottages—the official enumeration made four hundred. Of these the greater part were inhabited by Turks. Fine harvests encircled the place, rolling in waves from the high ground about to a stretch of turf surrounded by orchards and houses. Several broad roads traversed the village. I wandered all about it. Where a Turkish house had stood amongst its fruit-trees, charred posts, black rafters, heaps of ashes, lay on the ground. Here and there, but seldom, the quaint framework of the dwelling partly remained, whilst the very beams had often vanished, leaving no more than a foot-deep layer of charcoal. Even the orchards had been burnt or hacked. A few sodden rags lay about the weed-grown path, and a score of dogs, abandoned and starving, skulked among the ruins.

> The Bulgarian huts were unharmed, of course. Behind one of them I saw two Cossack ponies tied; their masters left the winepot and came to stare at me with a kind of swaggering curiosity.[79]

British ambassador Layard reported as early as July to his government that the Muslims had come to believe that the Russians had the intention of exterminating them:

> The shocking outrages which, there can scarcely be any doubt, have been committed upon them, either by the Russians or the Bulgarians under their protection, have struck terror amongst the Mussulman populations. They are now flying, as the Russians advance to escape the fate of their brethren, and are seeking refuge in the Turkish fortresses and Constantinople.[80]

Muslim villages were singled out, and in mixed cities Muslim quarters were targeted. The Russians would only graze their animals on Turkish not Bulgarian crops.[81] In something like the reenactment of the Passover, Christian neighbors would mark their doors with crosses in chalk to protect themselves and their homes.[82] Neighborliness degenerated: many Turks said that that they knew their attackers.[83] The wealthier families usually were able to flee early with their goods. When they remained behind, however, they were pointed out by the local Bulgarians and tortured by the Cossacks to get them to reveal where they had hidden their valuables.[84]

In February refugees who had been hiding in the Rhodope Mountains were induced to come down and return to their homes by a promise of safety, but they were plundered and attacked. Bulgarians and Russian soldiers raped the women.[85] In March it was reported that villages were still being burned after two months of Russian occupation—even as late as May there were reports of Russian attacks on villages.

FLIGHT AND THE BEGINNINGS OF A REFUGEE CRISIS

The Muslims were greatly demoralized by the Ottoman Army's failures in the battlefield. Reports of attacks against innocent civilians generated fear, and fear resulted in flight. The first to flee were typically the large landholders, clergy, and administrators, whose assets were most mobile and who would also adjust most poorly to a new Bulgarian-dominated regime.[86] However, the decision to flee was much more difficult for the rest of the Muslim population. For those who depended on their plots of land to make ends meet and who had little more in life than an attachment to the lands they tilled, abandoning those fields, especially before the harvest, was an economic disaster. For most, leaving meant the rupture of social ties and personal contacts and, quite naturally, worries about what a kind of future they would have in an unknown land. Rumors about Russian and Bulgarian atrocities circulated, but in some cases the villagers simply could not believe what they were hearing.

In Stara Zagora the governing town council convened a meeting to discuss the option of flight. One of those present relates the difficulty of the decision in a couplet:

> Neither courage to stay, nor strength for the road
> Our feet bound with grief, with fear are we froze.[87]

In the end, the council told the villagers to go to their farms and get their oxen and carts. Whole villages were evacuated, attempting to hold out until after harvest time when possible.[88]

The fleeing masses proved to be militarily beneficial to the Russian advance. Refugees escaping from the Russians packed roads and trains, thereby hindering the movement of Ottoman troops and their supplies and diverting valuable resources to caring for the refugees.

> The retreat of the Turkish forces had brought fresh misery upon these poor people, and again they were following to the rear, but still clinging to the skirts of the army, in the hope that the retreat might be merely temporary. The train of arabas [wagons] which carried their families and the few household effects which remained to them formed a serious embarrassment to the movements of the troops. The roads in this part of the country were usually narrow and bad and when an advance or retreat became necessary they were found constantly blocked by the country carts of the peasants.[89]

3.5. *Fleeing. Illustrated London News* (1877).

3.6. *Turkish Refugees Fleeing toward Shumen. Illustrated London News* (1877).

In fact, the impeded movement of Ottoman supporting forces prevented an Ottoman sortie from Pleven.[90] The refugees' inundation of the railroads from Edirne prevented important supplies from reaching the army in Plovdiv just at the moment when the war and the empire hung in the balance.[91] These refugees had little time to prepare for their departure. Their main objective was simply to avoid crossing paths with the Bulgarians and Cossacks. They often seemed to lack direction and certainly lacked shelter and food. The conditions in which they found themselves were often very dire and became more so as winter arrived. Journalist Wentworth Huyshe, traveling in September, mentioned that in the vicinity where Bulgarians were living quite comfortably amid the misery: "No less than 60,000 semi-starved Turkish families, fugitives from the Danube bank, from Sistova, Tirnova, and the Jantra valley were camped in the fields about the town. How these poor creatures kept alive . . . was a mystery to us. Many hundreds, probably, died in their quiet resigned Turkish way, yielding to destiny and making no fuss about it."[92]

A warm autumn lingered and the portent of a harsh winter caused one American correspondent embedded with the Russians to shudder:

> The meadows are still green, although the leaves on the mountain trees are dead and brown and, as we rode along, the air was as soft as in springtime. Bulgarians were trooping down laden with the plunder of the Turkish houses, even to the iron window bars. . . . Suddenly, and without warning, while we were enjoying the warm weather, arose a cold north wind, blowing furiously. The clouds which had been drifting over the mountains whirled about, gathered and settled, and a cold rain fell, which turned soon to snow, and in a few moments the spring landscape was transformed to a winter one, and everything was white with snow. All that afternoon and during the night the storm continued at intervals, and as I write there are two or three inches of snow on the ground. Conditions are anything but pleasant.[93]

The winter of 1877 was entirely unforgiving: snow piled eighteen inches deep on the road to Sofia and three feet high farther north, and chilly temperatures dipped as low as negative nine degrees Celsius. After complaining about the cold, a Frenchman with the Russian army said,

"Yet we should not complain about this drop of the temperature, because without it the numerous Turkish corpses that still clutter Pleven would be capable of generating the plague and a number of epidemics."[94]

When news was announced that the Russians were on their way to Sofia and that the Ottoman state would not be putting up resistance, the population shook with fear. The people gathered whatever they could and got on the road; where they were going, they knew not. The caravan of refugees fleeing the Russian advance from Sofia accrued fresh additions from each village it passed until it stretched out twenty miles and contained over two hundred thousand people.[95] The road was so crowded that the arabas were often forced to a standstill in what surely must have been a traffic jam of incomparable stress and fear. If new convoys wanted to join the larger mass of refugees, they could wait up to twelve days to do so, and many froze to death underneath their own arabas while waiting.[96] The cold was fatal, and the road was strewn with bodies and belongings. A Frenchman traveling with the Russians, seemingly unaware of the massacres and rapes of Muslims after Russian occupation, puts the blame for the wintry deaths of Muslims in flight on the Ottoman government for having evacuated villages and towns as the Russians approached. However, his descriptions of the march leading toward Harmanlı offer a chilling account of the fate of Muslim refugees in the winter of 1877:

> We have had to endure along this whole stage of the journey a painful and terrible spectacle, well made to merit execration for the war and its authors.
>
> Over the entire long road of sixty kilometers and in the fields bordering the railway are spread out numerous Turkish corpses, women, children, and old men dead of hunger and cold. We counted nearly 600 of them during this lugubrious march.
>
> These unfortunate victims of Turkish fanaticism belong to the population of Philippopoli [Plovdiv] and the surrounding villages, who, at the approach of the Russians, received a formal order to evacuate their homes and flee as quickly as possible to Adrianople [Edirne] and Constantinople.
>
> One can see what a horrible situation these unfortunate residents find themselves in, obliged to traverse a country covered in snow and exposed to a glacial temperature! . . .

The cadavers abound on the road. Wherever the Turks camped—the spot is easy to recognize by the bits of straw and tatters littering the ground—one comes across the bodies of these unfortunate people, who couldn't stand the freezing cold and the overwhelming hunger.

Nothing is more horrible to contemplate than these bodies remaining without a burial, blackened, bloated, desiccated by the cold, stretched out among the corpses of cows and buffaloes, sheep and goats, because for some time a kind of bovine disease has inflicted the livestock in all regions of Bulgaria.

What a woeful image I have and will always have before my eyes of this sorrowful march through the horrible camps, which the Cossacks, in their picturesque and imaginative language have nicknamed "The Camp of Death!"

As I have already said, I only see the bodies of old men, women, and children in these fields of death, not a single lad or man in the prime of life; all without wounds, dead of cold and hunger. Some are piled up in heaps of five or six people, having tried to warm themselves and to provide each other with a bit of warm contact; mothers stretched out on tattered blankets, still holding their children pressed against their breasts; two young girls hugging closely with arms intertwined lay stretched out face down against the earth: on first glance one might think they were merely sleeping; old men with long white beards, bearers of a venerable physiognomy and marked with the kind of oriental cachet one finds in the paintings of Descamps; a young girl of the rarest beauty with long wavy black hair, dressed in a black jacket with golden embroidery and big blue pants had, just before dying, pulled down the thin veil over her face, which she still held in her clenched hands and which the wind had ripped to shreds.

Some of these victims . . . fell in the path covered in mud, and—horrible detail—the heavy carts had more or less crushed them.

I saw an unfortunate old man, dressed in the robe of a dervish, who had fallen in a rut and whose head had been smashed by the wheels of a cart; for, it is a sad thing to say, these fugitives

> were taken by such a delirium of flight that every morning upon leaving their camp of the previous night they fled as quick as possible, leaving the corpses behind unburied.
>
> At Kayadjik, a small village located on the Oskyizli river, just two hours from Haskoy [Haskova], the approach ramps of the bridge and the crevices of the rocks that border the right bank are full of corpses of these wretches who huddled there to spare themselves a little from the freezing gusts of night.
>
> The ground is littered with blankets, rags, and innumerable prayer books, and next to the body of a Gypsy woman with dazzling white enamel teeth I noticed a small square mirror framed in chiseled leather.[97]

This vulnerable mass of refugees moving at a snail's pace along iced-over roads fell victim to one of the largest and most tragic episodes of the Ottoman expulsion from Bulgaria. General Gurko advancing from Sofia, General Mikhail Dmitrievich Skobelev from Shipka, and retreating Ottoman troops all intersected with the enormous caravan of 60,000 refugees and up to 20,000 carts. The women walked in front, while the men plodded along in the rear to protect them. Refugees from the incident gave simple testimony of what happened. As consul-general Henry Fawcett summarized after listening to numerous firsthand accounts,

> Your Excellency has only to read the depositions taken by the Commission to understand the ruthless barbarities practised by a savage soldiery on helpless women and children; anything more horrible than the butchery at Harmanli I cannot imagine ever happened in the history of the world. Consider a line of from 15,000 to 20,000 arabas laden with household goods, with men and children struggling through the deep snow being suddenly attacked by wild horsemen. The [Muslim] men with their knives and a few guns did their best and kept the cavalry off till night fall, next morning infantry and artillery appeared upon the scene, and if testimony given in the most simple manner is to be believed, commenced firing grape and musketry on this helpless mass of human beings.[98]

Hope was lost, and panic spread among the refugees. While some refugees tried to fight off the Russians to give time for their families to flee, in the end the able-bodied abandoned the elderly, the ill, and the infants to be massacred by Cossacks and Russians and plundered by Bulgarians, who "mercilessly put to death all those who had not yet perished of cold."[99] Survivors testified to direct attacks on civilians by the Russian troops; indeed, one Mustafa from Haskovo told of being at Harmanlı with his wife and his son's family when three Russians on horseback attacked his daughter-in-law. His son fled; his wife tried to intervene, but the Russians killed her with a saber. The Russians then took away the daughter-in-law, leaving Mustafa to carry away the corpse of his wife on his back to a place where he could bury her.[100]

A Polish Hussar trying to catch up with his Russian brigade came upon the scene:

> Long lines of carriages parked on the big road attracted my attention again. As I approached I was frozen with dread. The darkness of the eve was no longer there, alas! to hide the horrors of these somber convoys. In each carriage was a human corpse! Here it was an old man with a long beard, his head leaning on his chest, farther on a young woman who was pressing convulsively her nursling against her frozen breast. . . .
>
> A few versts farther, on the edge of the road, the remains of a vast camp: carriages, buffaloes, tents, broken dishes, tattered fabrics were strewn on the ground; and everywhere dead bodies, of men, of children, of old men, of women, one of whom with long red hair stretched on her back offered the hideous image of murder and rape, such as I had never seen until then except in sinister paintings.
>
> A quantity of corpses was completely buried under the snow; a dead hand or foot emerging from underneath the ground was the only indication of their burial place.
>
> I was the lone living being in this immense cemetery and a poignant anguish squeezed my throat. . . .
>
> At the gates of Haskieu [Haskova], I saw a group of old women kneeling in poses of prayer, and I approached them with respect to not trouble their contemplation. Useless precaution!

> They were inanimate corpses that nothing could trouble . . . the unfortunate women were kneeling to implore the pity of God or that of men, but it was death that had surprised them and left them there in the middle of the rode like real statues of desolation and despair.[101]

Refugee corpses littered the road from Plovdiv to Edirne, dubbed "The Road of Desolation" by one reporter: "Never did I feel so utterly helpless," he wrote as he described "baby faces half covered with snow [that] look out innocently and peacefully, frozen at their mother's breasts."[102] The Polish hussar met Januarius MacGahan at Harmanlı and asked him if he was joining them in the campaign. "Oh, yes, I've never seen a war like this. I've done wars of succession, famous for their massacres and cruelties, but the spectacle of the road between Philippopoli [Plovidv] and Adrianople [Edirne] surpasses in horror everything I've ever seen." The Pole then asked, "Do you hold us accountable for these atrocities?" MacGahan replied, "Oh no, it's destiny; but it's horrible, horrible!"[103]

It is curious that MacGahan was thunderous in his attribution of blame in the Bulgarian Horrors but said that a massacre that surpassed anything he had ever seen was just part of war. Later in his writing he stated that it "should for all future time be known as 'the Road of Death.'"[104]

Wondering about the fate of the Turks, journalist Archibald Forbes traveled through this grim trail of death and desolation in January and related the horrific scene that he witnessed: "Scarcely had we left the outskirts of Phillopolis [Plovdiv] when the dreaded solution to our oft-discussed problem presented itself in all the horror of death, blood and misery unspeakable. Our first day's ride was full thirty miles long, and not a kilometer of it was there that did not lie among corpses, dead animals, broken arabas, piles of rags and stray tatters of cast-off clothing." He tells of seeing corpses of Bulgarian peasants and

> dignified old Turks, their white beards clotted with blood, their hands closed on their bare breasts. . . . The men had died violent deaths, but it had been cold and privation which accounted for the dead women and children who had been frozen to death, and now lay in the snow as if still alive. From the muddy water of the

ditches tiny hands and feet were visible, and baby-faces looked out from the snow that had covered them.[105]

An American officer with the Russian army also recounts the horrific scene:

> For three successive days we marched through the remnants of this caravan, scattered over a length of seventy miles,—broken wagons, scattered contents, dead animals; here a man and his wife, who had stretched a blanket in the snow and lain down to die side by side; there a stately old Turk, with flowing white beard, green turban, and brightly figured robe, lying by the ditch with his throat cut from ear to ear; and again a naked little infant frozen stiff in the snow with its eyes upturned to heaven. Our blood curdled as we saw a Bulgarian clot, grinning and staring at us from the road-side, who answered as we asked him who murdered those two Turks lying a few feet from us:
>
> "Nashe bratte!" (Our brothers, we did it.)[106]

The desperation of the situation inspired even mothers to give up their children in terrifying ways. According to one witness,

> In a cemetery on the outskirts of Sofia, I saw a refugee woman. At her side were two girls and a son around seven or eight years old. The woman cried out, "I can look after myself with these two girls, but is there one merciful enough to take this boy?" At that time someone answered, "I will do it." The poor woman, as she was sending the boy away, brought down a violent slap on the back of his neck. Those present asked, "Woman, why are you hitting the child?" To which she responded, "Let the pain remain in his heart, so that he will not forget his mother. That's why I slapped him." When she said this, the hearts of those listening were stung.[107]

As Forbes continued his journey, he caught up with a caravan of refugees. Miles of straggling, emaciated, and dread-filled refugees continued southward through the snow. One mother in particular caught his attention:

> I watched a mother slowly leading a miserable sick child which lagged continually. Both were half naked, and both were emaciated to the last degree. The last vehicle of the araba train was nearly out of sight. The mother tried to urge on the child, fast losing patience as the dusk began to fall. With a sob and a gasp she caught the child to her breast, then threw it from her into the snow on the roadside, and hurried on without daring to glance over her shoulders.[108]

Many more children were thrown to the wayside. Russian General Skobelev told one English observer that when he arrived at the head of the regiment he

> soon saw a baby by the roadside. He ordered a soldier to pick it up, and before he reached the next town nearly every soldier in the regiment had a child in his arms, which had been thrown away by its parents in their mad flight. At this town he seized a sufficient number of carts to carry these children to a Turkish village in the mountains where there was hope that the people might feed them. What their fate was he could not tell.[109]

The next day Forbes caught up with the main part of the caravan and estimated that it contained over fifteen thousand carts with oxen still attached. There were no Turks, however, just swarms of Bulgarian peasants happily plundering the remains. Another journalist documented the act of despoilment by Bulgarians:

> I know that they have murdered great numbers of Turks, and do not doubt that they have done worse. A peasantry who in broad daylight, before a crowd of lookers-on, could deliberately strip the dead, and then leisurely fold and take away the hideous rags, stiff with blood, are not to be restrained by any impulses of humanity. They are now armed with the plunder of Turkish

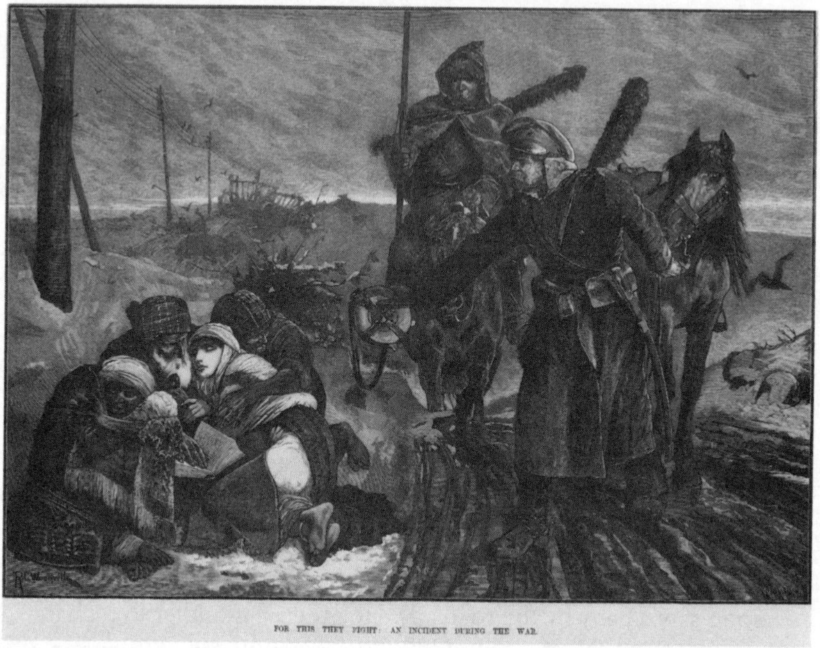

3.7. *An Incident during the War* by Richard Caton Woodville Jr. *Illustrated London News* (1878).

camps and the weapons taken from the Mussulman population. The Russian officers do not interfere with them, although they view their proceedings with disgust.[110]

The area all around this road was covered with debris:

The ground itself, covered with thousands upon thousands of objects, . . . indicated that there had been an immense and vertiginous panic and not a simple encampment.

Everywhere and on every side, torn paper, thousands of Qurans written on yellow paper with golden illumination, silken blankets with golden embroidery, clusters of wool cloth, heavy pottery, iron plates bent from long years of use, gourds, kegs, screens for oats, stools, slippers, wooden shoes, in a word, everything that these poor fugitives owned, all of these objects covered in mud, dirtied, withered by rain and snow, and, in the middle

> of this solitude, bands of Bulgars gleaning these sinister spoils like birds of prey.[111]

The British consul general Fawcett, after having traveled through Bulgaria, exclaimed: "What horde of savages has passed over this smiling land? Have Attila and his Huns come to life again? The answer is, that all that has happened has been the presence for three short weeks of a detachment of the great army of . . . the Tzar of holy Russia."[112] An Ottoman journalist in Shumen ended his article bitterly: "Oh Lord have mercy! What kind of civilization is this? Can this truly be the nineteenth century? What has become of humanity? Where are the rules of war? And what use are they to civilization? . . . Alas, mankind has seriously lost its way."[113]

Refugees often hoped to escape danger by riding a train to safety. However, the railway system of the Ottoman Empire was not well developed. The railways were often built by European companies, whose governments had objectives other than reinforcing the Balkan connection to Istanbul, so Balkan railways were often more oriented toward Vienna than toward the Ottoman capital. Moreover, much construction was done on the cheap. Outside of the larger cities all train stations were made of wood; only the train station in Istanbul had platforms. The train stations for Edirne, Plovdiv, and Pazardzhik, for example, were miles out of town in order to avoid the costs of bridges over the Maritsa River and of land purchases in nearby towns. The bridges that did exist were made of wood and were often overtaken by water during the thaws. The contract for the rails was on a per-mile basis, so the rail paths were unnecessarily winding.[114] Worse yet, because of the way the rails were put together, under the very best of conditions only six trains a day could make the round trip between Edirne and the capital.[115] That said, the following rail lines existed in Bulgaria: Edirne–Istanbul, Sofia–Plovdiv–Pazardzhik–Edirne, Edirne–Sliven–Burgas, Edirne–Aleksandropolis, Edirne–Thessaloniki–Skopje–Mitroviçe, and Ruse–Varna.[116]

The rail journey between Edirne and Istanbul alone could take six to eight days, although many of the refugees would hope to board a train farther out than Edirne. Pazardzhik, which was located halfway between Edirne and Plovdiv, became the most important stop for refugees arriving on foot or by cart and was inundated with refugees following the fall of

3.8. *The Road to Constantinople* by Sydney P. Hall. *Graphic* (March 9, 1878).

Pleven. The Ottoman official in Plovdiv begged for more trains because "[t]he necessary number of wagons have still not arrived, and the local refugees, up to 15,000 men, women and children have been sobbing and wailing for two to three days as they wait for the arrival of the next train while sleeping on blankets of snow in the station. All the while, destitute women and children continue to pile into the station."[117]

Ten miles per hour was a common speed for trains, and for the most part the tracks were single lines, which meant more frequent stops. The average train pulled twenty to thirty wagons,[118] many of which were open cattle cars, in the bitter cold, and at train stops "corpse after corpse came out of the trucks."[119] Derailments were not unknown, and railway stations were packed, fights breaking out as people tried to get on the trains.

Mithat Paşa wrote of one family at Pazardzhik that was unable to get a place on a departing train: "Stricken with despair, the old men, the women, and the children sat down on the rails, preferring to be crushed by the wheels of the machine rather than continue suffering. Force had to be employed to snatch them away from a certain death."[120]

A Scottish newspaper described another incident on the road between Plovdiv and Edirne: "A vast crowd of panic-stricken people placed themselves across the lines and the train was forced to stop, then they clambered on to the roofs of the waggons and clung to the wheels imploring to be taken away. Many were hurt, and the shrieks and lamentations of the women when they were left behind was heartrending."[121]

Layard gives us an idea of the horror of the voyage by train:

> Trains, with from 8,000 to 10,000 of these wretched fugitives, have been arriving daily at Constantinople. Only open trucks can, in most cases, be provided for them. The weather has been intensely cold, the snow falling heavily. The poor creatures are packed together standing, and are thus kept sometimes for more than twenty-four hours without food or shelter. As the trains arrive at the stations the bodies of men, women, and children, frozen to death, or who have succumbed to illness, are dragged out of the wagons. Even the tops of the closed carriages are occupied by the women and children, who in some instances, numbed by the cold, roll off and are killed.[122]

A British aide-de-camp reported on the train voyages of refugees, where single train lines meant additional delays as the trains had to wait at designated areas to pass one another, and where people were so tightly packed in the open cattle cars that they could not move or even remove the dead:

> The difficulty of transporting this moving population, for such it is, is enormous, and consequently, trains of these wretched people were kept waiting days and nights, utterly exposed to the incessant snow and driving blasts, scantily clad, and half starving. One train I saw where the people had remained packed for four days in the wagons without moving. Such was their terror that nothing would persuade them to leave the carriages for fear of losing their places. As dysentery, and diarrhea was extremely prevalent among them, the filth and stench, as may be imagined, was appalling.[123]

An English officer described a train ride that he witnessed from Edirne to Istanbul:

> It would be impossible even to attempt to describe the misery these wretched refugees underwent during their transit from Adrianople [Edirne], which lasted seldom less than four days, and frequently, on account of the accidents, extending over seven and eight. They experienced every kind of weather, snow, frost, wind and rain. I need hardly add that many succumbed to these hardships. Every morning the dead were collected and buried by scratching the earth over the remains of a wife, daughter, or child, lost on the road. Many of the children who died were simply thrown out, either by the side of the line or into one of the numerous train crosses. Mothers too have even killed their offspring. One day, not 100 yards from a train, and in view of all, a woman took her two children about five and three years old, and plunged a dagger into each of their hearts. In interrogation, she stated "She had done so to prevent the possibility of their experiencing the misery she had already gone through, the wretchedness she was now enduring, and that still loomed in the distance."[124]

The Russo-Turkish war of 1877–1878 unleashed a cataclysmic loss for the Muslims living in the Ottoman territories that were to become Bulgaria. In a climate of fear and panic, huge numbers of Muslims fled toward safety by foot and by train, but the pathway there was perilous; a cold winter, lack of food, and the onslaught of disease probably killed more Muslims than the massacres that caused their flight.

FOR THOSE WHO STAYED AND THE RHODOPE UPRISING

The shrinking Ottoman Empire was giving way to Balkan nation-states. While other European empires looked on with pleasure, each would find, in time, that it too was not eternal. Shrinking empires in the era of nation-states resulted in situations of human leftovers. Dawn Chatty noted this new development: "Displacement no longer merely refers to people moving across borders, but of borders moving across people . . . who are found not to 'belong' within the newly determined territorial boundaries."[125]

For those Muslims who stayed put or did not move far enough to be outside of the new Bulgarian state, a new set of circumstances had come into being after the war. Violence continued as late as 1879, as state power was slow to be consolidated. However, even when security of life was guaranteed, the Muslims of Bulgaria clearly felt unwelcome and unwanted. Muslims were now a clear minority in an incipient Bulgarian nation-state. Land tenure and assurances of property rights were tenuous. Moreover, Muslims were gravely concerned about their linguistic and religious rights. Conscription into the Bulgarian army, where they would be fed pork products and be required to wear crosses and train for war against the only ostensible enemy, the Ottoman Empire, was greatly resented. Rice farming on the Danube, an occupation primarily engaged in by Muslims, was banned. Mosques and other markers of their heritage were demolished for the modernizing purposes of city planning. The Bulgarians were on the fast track to European-style modernity. While not every policy was undertaken to spite the Muslim population, after the horrors of war trust between the communities had broken down. The young Bulgarian state worried about losing a desperately needed tax base and offered concessions to the Muslim community on questions of military service and education. However, now secure in their person yet feeling insecure in their cultural and religious rights, Muslims continued to emigrate toward the Ottoman Empire over the ensuing decades.

Some refugees who were not able to make it out of the country decided to make a stand and put up a fight along with other Muslim inhabitants of the Rhodope Mountains. In the mountainous Rhodope region the locals had followed news of the war by gathering information from refugees and others who were passing through. This was an area where many Pomak Muslims lived, especially in the west, whereas Turkish Muslims tended to be found in the east. The war itself did not intrude into the difficult terrain, which was home to the highest point in Bulgaria. If anything, the Rhodopes were seen as more of an obstacle on the way to the Aegean Sea than a path eagerly trodden. The news of the war brought by the refugees was not encouraging: violence, rape, and pillage.[126] By January 1878 the Ottomans were defeated north of the Rhodopes, and Edirne was taken by the Russians. The remnants of Suleiman Paşa's army were cut off from Ottoman territory. They decided to try to pass through the mountains in difficult winter conditions in order to return to Ottoman-controlled territory; tens of thousands of refugees went with them. While the Russians had no particular interest in occupying the Rhodopes in the winter, the appearance of the defeated Ottomans and the masses of refugees, some of whom had fled from the massacres at Harmanlı, caused the local inhabitants to panic. Many of them too decided to tag along with the army and flee to the Aegean coast.

In the meantime Bulgarian groups raided and burned villages, which Russians occasionally bombarded.[127] Most of the Rhodopes fell within the Russian side in agreement with the Edirne ceasefire, even though Russian troops had not been able to physically occupy them. Rather than surrender their weapons to the Russians, the local Muslims and refugees decided to resist, in what would be known as the Rhodope Insurgency.

While not a very important part of the war, the Rhodope Insurgency lasted seven years and demonstrated that the refugees were not just passive subjects of events. The insurgency started in February with skirmishes against Bulgarians. Over 500 inhabitants of the Turkish villages around Haskovo were joined by refugees who took up arms and went into the mountains to fight against the Bulgarians. Their stated aim at first was to protect their villages from the kinds of massacres and pillage that had occurred elsewhere. In April the Russians demanded that the Rhodope Muslims lay down their arms, to which the Muslims answered that they would only do so under a guarantee from the international powers or a firman from the Porte. In response, the Russians bombarded the villages continuously for seven days and seven nights.[128]

In April the Muslims engaged a Russian-Cossack force, which they repelled.[129] The fighting increased as reinforcements joined both sides but the fighting did not result in any definitive conclusion. The participants of the uprising appealed for support to both the Ottoman government, which was already overwhelmed with the situation in the capital, and to Great Britain, which was not about to meddle in the affair. The insurgency spread from the Rhodopes westward and inspired smaller uprisings; however, it never was sustained at a high level. For their part, the Russians were not eager to fight in the Rhodopes, although they sent Bulgarian battalions of up to 20,000 soldiers into fight.

The leadership of the insurgency was unclear. At times letters were signed by village leaders, while at other times an English adventurer named Stanislaw Bower Graham St. Clair, going under the name Hidayet Paşa, seemed to have taken a leadership role. He was most likely anti-Russian given his Polish ancestry, but interestingly he professed discipleship to Ali Suavi (see chapter 4).[130] St. Clair eventually left the Rhodopes under inauspicious circumstances. Later Ahmet Ağa Tamrashliya, a figure who played a role in the Bulgarian Horrors, became something of a leader. The insurrection eventually declared its own Rhodope state, the Tamrash Republic, but after the Bulgarian annexation of Eastern Rumelia in 1885 the new lines incorporated most of the territory in the Ottoman Empire and the insurrection subsided.

An international commission was sent in July 1878 to investigate the situation of the Muslim refugees in the Rhodopes and surrounding areas, who numbered between 100,000 and 120,000. It was hoped that the refugees in these areas would be able to return to their homes, although the Russians had already stated that they opposed their return. In the summer the Russians had been involved in the destruction of Turkish villages in the area. In other parts of the region the commission came across thousands of refugees "reduced to the last state of distress."[131] They also heard testimonies representing the tens of thousands of refugees who fled the Russian advance. They wished to go home but feared the Russians too greatly to do so.

Some Muslims who remained in Bulgaria after the war made their feelings clear about their situation: "Our goal is not only to make known that we do not want to be separated from our country and our property, nor to be subjected to the sort of vicissitudes of the Muslims of Walachia and Moldovia, Serbia, the Morea, and the Caucasus, but to ask for sufficient guarantees of our life, our property and our honour."[132]

THE MEANING OF INDEPENDENCE: NO MORE TURKS

Nikos Kazantzakis wrote a novel called *Freedom and Death* depicting the struggle for Greek independence from Turkish rule in nineteenth-century Crete and the violent breakdown of intercommunal life. An old Cretan grandfather who has seen much over the years greets a young Greek, Mitros, from Rumelia, with a summary of anti-Turkish sentiments described above: "You've no more Turks in your land. You're lucky!"[133]

In his short story "Old Yotso Is Watching" the towering Bulgarian national writer Ivan Vazov portrays a Bulgarian who goes blind just prior to the Russo-Turkish War. His memory was haunted by images of red fezzes, turbans, whips, and cruel Turks. The only flicker of light left in his heart was to behold a free Bulgaria, which he referred to as "the Bulgarian thing." Living in a remote part of Bulgaria, he missed out on the drama and violence of the war. But when the conflict was over, people came and told Old Yotso that he was now liberated. "[B]ut he was blind, he could not see Liberation nor feel it. For him Liberation was expressed in the words: 'there are no more Turks.'"[134]

Yotso could hear nothing out of the ordinary in the conversations among the peasants. Life, with all its struggles, continued: "They were the same people with the same passions, misfortunes, and poverty as before." He yearned to see liberation with his own eyes to be convinced it was real. Not being able to see a liberated Bulgaria, he sank into apathy. Finally, four years after the war a county officer was visiting the village. Old Yotso became excited again. He insisted on going to the house where this Bulgarian official was staying. This Bulgarian "Pasha" had a sword, and epaulets. When Yotso finally got his meeting with the county officer, he fingered the silver epaulets on the officer's shoulder and made the sign of the cross with tears in his eyes. "To the old man it seemed that for the first time in five years he had been able to see for a minute and had seen 'the Bulgarian thing,' a ray of 'Bulgaria,' and he was fully convinced there were no more Turks and there was freedom in the world. . . . Apart from this event, everything was as before."[135]

Mitros's reply to the old Cretan grandfather mentioned above belied a certain letdown: "We have no Turks, certainly, . . . but we have big landowners, police and politicians. Don't ask me about them, old man."[136]

In the aftermath of so much destruction and the scarring of society by participating in or witnessing such events, the naïve expectations of independence inevitably encountered disappointment. Ultimately, the new state when exercising its power will evince authoritarian streaks that can alienate its own citizenry. Such a reality inspired Vazov to have his character in the short story "Father Nestor" compare the new independent Bulgarian government with the departed Ottomans: "Maybe the Turks weren't so bad after all."[137]

For his part, Leo Tolstoi believed that the Bulgarians were even worse off than before. In a conversation with an Armenian nationalist he advised against an insurgency based on the Bulgarian experience. It was clear that, after the war was over, Tolstoi had not had a change of heart or mind:

> Even granting that it is all true [Ottoman oppression of Armenians], still no doubt some Armenians share in the oppression. What I mean is that of the more influential and wealthy of them squeeze their own people not less than the Turks or the Kurds do . . . the question is not one of nationality! . . . You say that Raffi and other writers see no escape for the Turkish Armenians but by an insurrection? But what will come of it? Will the condition of the people be improved? Take a striking example—Bulgaria. A friend of mine, who knows, tells me that under Turkey, Bulgaria was better off than now after its emancipation. At any rate the common people lived better. That is a fact well worth considering . . . and do not forget that the Bulgarian insurrection only succeeded by a pure accident. The result might easily have been quite different, as has often happened elsewhere.[138]

The meaning of "national independence" might not be more than the simple knowledge that while the new head of state, to use Franklin Roosevelt's famous words, "may be a son of a bitch, at least he's our son of a bitch."[139] The aims of nationalism had been met for Bulgaria. Their own people wore epaulets and carried swords, but otherwise for most Bulgarians things changed little: life continued as before. For the Turks, however, things changed a great deal, as they had deserted their lands, the lands of their forebears, under considerable duress.

The carnage of war fell heavily upon the Muslims. Of course, Bulgarian civilians also suffered massacres and depredations in the war. However, I have focused on Muslim suffering here because ultimately this work is about conceiving an idea of a Europe without Muslims, putting into practice this idea during the Russo-Turkish War of 1877–1878, and remembering (or rather forgetting) these events in the Turkish Republic. It does not minimize the suffering of other groups to say that in the end the greater brunt was borne by the Muslims because in the end it was they who were cleansed from Bulgaria. Perhaps if the Ottomans had been the superior force and the Muslims had been seized with the idea of expelling the other, it might have turned out differently and the Bulgarians would have been removed; for indeed both sides were consumed by fear. As British consul Blunt stated, "The Bulgarians are afraid that the Turks, if successful, will massacre them, while the Turks attribute the same intention to the Bulgarians should the Russians be victorious."[140]

The Ottoman Empire, though, was a multiethnic empire organized around religious communities and had opted for co-cultivation during the preceding five hundred years instead of monoculture. It was not worse than the empires that preceded it and in many respects better than the ones that followed it, because it lacked the racist tenets of European colonialism, offered more autonomy to its communities, and did not prevent those from the nonruling classes from acquiring wealth. But the heterogeneity fostered by empire was bloodily giving way to a new era of the modern state, bolstered by national liberty and its implicit, if not vaunted, ideal of modernity via homogeneity. The Ottomans simply could not balance national claims with the need to centralize administration.

The overall trend of what took place for Ottoman Muslims during the War of '93 is clear, yet reckoning with the quantitative dimensions poses significant challenges. Estimates of the number of Muslim victims vary. As noted in chapter 1, no accurate census figures exist. However, we can be sure that the scale of suffering was massive. According to Justin McCarthy, during and immediately after the war, 262,000 Bulgarian Muslims—17 percent of the total Muslim population of Bulgaria—were either murdered or died from dangers associated with their eviction. Another 515,000 Muslims—34 percent of the Muslim population—left their homes never to return and thus became refugees in the Ottoman Empire.[141] Kemal Karpat, another expert in Ottoman demographics, estimates between 250,000 and 300,000 dead during the war, whereas Richard Frucht says that 216,000 were killed and that about 50 percent of the Muslim population migrated or were killed. At the high end, Nedim İpek, a Turkish specialist in Ottoman migrations, estimates that 500,000 were killed or died from hunger or disease and 1 million emigrated.[142] Bulgarian estimates tend to be lower, such as Todor Valchev's estimate that only 350,000 Muslim refugees left Bulgaria between 1877 and 1912.[143]

For the most part, Bulgarian historiography tends to deny the scale of the tragedy, if not the atrocities themselves. Prominent historian of Bulgarıa Richard Crampton, for example, says that only 150,000 refugees were created as a result of the war, a big part of which returned to Bulgaria after the fighting came to a halt.[144] Such a low number is pure fantasy given the documents, including the Refugee Commission report, which puts the number well over 300,000, and the International Council of Health Report, which estimates at least 150,000 deaths and 350,000 refugees. As the following chapter shows, more than Crampton's estimated number of refugees were huddled in Istanbul alone at one time.

The Muslim population had been least affected in the east. In 1881 five-sevenths of the eastern districts still had Muslim majorities,[145] although after 1885 even these began to emigrate in large numbers. Immediately before the war, approximately 50 percent of the population was Muslim. In 1878 Muslims were only 26 percent. This number continued to decline: Muslims constituted 19 percent of the population in 1880; 17 percent in 1892; 14 percent in 1900; and only 11.5 percent in 1910.[146] At the same time, Muslim heritage was being lost through the orderly destruction of mosques and cemeteries.

The fate of Muslims in Bulgaria was not a unique phenomenon but rather a large, if not the largest, example of a trend that had already affected Muslims of the Ottoman Empire in previously lost territories and would still await many future Muslims in the remaining mixed territories. The virus of nationalism had infected the body politic, and much death and destruction would be the consequence.

While some question the notion that the dispossession of Muslims and their emigration from Bulgaria were part of a homogenization program, the final result was nothing other than a complete overhaul of the demographics of the region. Muslims bore the brunt of the Ottoman debacle, and their absence was necessary for the creation of a Bulgarian nation-state, which was not interested in assuming responsibility for a large Turkish population within its borders. Therefore, "it was best to eject unwanted or menacing groups when they threatened to weaken the beleaguered nation."[147]

While these Muslims differed among each other in class, ethnicity, language, sect, and so on, they were targeted and therefore frightened because of an identity they shared—being Muslims. This identity became politicized, securitized, and ultimately attacked, leading to death and exile. Many died, and others found themselves refugees in the same state yet a different land. Journalist Archibald Forbes traveled through Bulgaria after the war. Documenting the void, he remarked, "Now the whole region was Bulgarian pure and simple, since the Turkish inhabitants with rare exceptions had gone away bag and baggage."[148]

While nationalism is often seen as a companion of democracy and modernization, it also has a senseless tribal element that seems to be the exact opposite of human progress. Nationalism eschews nuance and empathy, exalts homogenization, and is fed by sweeping generalities and hubristic exclusivism. It is unsurprising that most nationalist characters in literature are flat and insipid. This can be seen in the Bulgarian patriot Insarov in Ivan Turgenev's *On the Eve* (1860), in Boycho Ognyanov in Ivan Vazov's *Under the Yoke* (1888), and in Captain Mikhaelos in Nikos Kazantzakis's *Freedom and Death* (1953), whose blind obsession with Cretan independence from the Turks leads him to ignore the consequences of his actions not only for the Muslim population of the island but also for his fellow Christians, who must pay for his reckless fixation. Kazantzakis unwittingly makes the Turkish governor the more sympathetic character in the novel.[149]

However, in his masterpiece *Zorba the Greek* (1946) Kazantzakis gives voice to incredibly poignant words through his bon-vivant protagonist, Alexis Zorba, a Macedonian Greek who participated in the Cretan War of Independence. Zorba engages the nameless narrator in a discussion on the origin and consequences of nationalism, posing powerful questions that resonate not only with the theme of this book but far beyond. It is worth quoting the passage at some length:

> Zorba turned round and gave me a mocking look.
>
> "And now I suppose, boss, you think I'm going to start and tell you how many Turks' heads I've lopped off, and how many of their ears I've pickled in spirits—that's the custom in Crete. Well, I shan't! I don't like to, I'm ashamed. What sort of madness comes over us? . . . Today I'm a bit more level-headed, and I ask myself: What sort of madness comes over us to make us throw ourselves on another man, when he's done nothing to us, and bite him, cut his nose off, tear his ear out, run him through the guts—and all the time, calling on the Almighty to help us! Does it mean we want the Almighty to go and cut off noses and ears and rip people up?
>
> "But at the time, you see, my blood was hot in my veins! How could I stop to examine the whys and the wherefores? To think things out properly and fairly, a fellow's got to be calm and old and toothless: When you're an old gaffer with no teeth, it's easy to say: 'Damn it, boys, you mustn't bite!' But, when you've got all thirty two teeth. . . . A man's a savage beast when he's young; yes, boss, a savage, man-eating beast!"
>
> He shook his head.
>
> "Oh, he eats sheep, too, and hens and pigs, but if he doesn't eat men his belly's not satisfied."
>
> He added as he crushed out his cigarette in the coffee saucer:
>
> "No, his belly's not satisfied. Now, what does the old owl have to say to that, eh?"
>
> He did not wait for an answer.
>
> "What can you say, I wonder?" he continued, weighing me up. "As far as I can see, your lordship's never been hungry, never killed, never stolen, never committed adultery. What can you know of the world? You've got an innocent's brain and your skin never even felt the sun," he muttered with obvious scorn.
>
> I felt ashamed of my delicate hands, my pale face and my life which had not been bespattered with mud and blood.

"All right!" said Zorba, sweeping his heavy hand across the table as if wiping a sponge across it. "All right! There's one thing, though I'd like to ask you. You must've gone through hundreds of books, perhaps you know the answer . . ."

"Go ahead, Zorba, what is it?"

"There's a sort of miracle happening here, boss. A funny sort of miracle which puzzles me. All that business—those lousy tricks, thefts and that slaughter of ours—I mean of us rebels—all that brought Prince George to Crete. Liberty!"

He looked at me with his eyes wide open in amazement.

"It's a mystery," he murmured, "a great mystery! So, if we want liberty in this bad world, we've got to have all those murders, all those lousy tricks, have we? I tell you, if I began to go over all the bloody villainy and all the murders we did, you'd have your hair stand on end. And yet, the result of all that, what's it been? Liberty! Instead of wiping us out with a thunderbolt, God gives us liberty! I just don't understand!"

He looked at me, as if calling for help. I could see that this problem had tormented him a lot and that he could not get to the bottom of it.

"Do you understand?" he asked me with anguish.

Understand what? Tell him what? Either that what we call God does not exist, or else that what we call murders and villainy is necessary for the struggle and for the liberation of the world . . .

I tried hard to find for Zorba another, simpler way of explaining it. "How does a plant sprout and grow into a flower on manure and muck? Say to yourself, Zorba, that the manure and muck is man and the flower liberty."

"But the seed?" cried Zorba, striking his fist on the table. "For a plant to sprout there must be a seed. Who's put such a seed in our entrails? And why doesn't this seed produce flowers from kindness and honesty? Why must it have blood and filth?"

I shook my head.

"I don't know," I said.

"Who does?"

"No one."[150]

Four

REFUGE AND RESETTLEMENT

Every one who has tried to describe the stream of homeless, frost-bitten, and starving refugees which has been flowing towards the capital in terror of the advancing Russian, has confessed that it is indescribable. . . . The unspeakable Turk is unspeakable just now in his misery, if nothing else.

World Daily Press, February 5, 1878

It was estimated that some three hundred thousand reached Constantinople in such a piteous state that instead of plundering the unprotected city, they lay down and died in the streets and mosques.

George Washburn, *Fifty Years in Constantinople and Recollections of Robert College*

At five o'clock on March 3, 1878, Russian grand duke Nikolai rode his horse past Orthodox priests draped in green and gold and an altar bedecked with religious artifacts and icons that had been specially sent in from Saint Petersburg for the occasion. A large icon of the Virgin, which had hung in the tent of Russia's most celebrated general, Aleksandr Vasilevich Suvorov—the general who never lost a battle—stood out conspicuously. In the grand duke's wake rode Ottoman minister of war Rauf Paşa and grand vizier Savfet Paşa, both wearing grim expressions—they had just signed the humiliating Treaty of San Stefano. Savfet Paşa, it was said by one reporter, "would talk of nothing but the refugees," deflecting any

4.1. *Announcing the Treaty of Peace to the Russian Troops at San Stefano.* From Edmund Ollier, *Cassel's Illustrated History of the Russo-Turkish War* (1877–79).

other conversation by asking, "Have you seen any of the poor refugees from the interior?"[1]

The grand duke rode out to his beaming soldiers, taking off his hat. He stood high in the saddle, made the sign of the cross, and then shouted in a thundering voice "Mir!" (peace). The Russian troops erupted in enthusiastic rejoicing, darkening the sky with the frenzied launch of their caps into the air. And as "hurrahs" continued to thunder for a long time, running up and down the flanks, the dusk's last embers lit the evening and the call to prayer was sounded. The grand duke lifted his finger, directing the attention of all to the minarets of Istanbul, which pierced the horizon, and said, "Here is Constantinople!"[2]

Only nine days earlier the Russians had first glimpsed Istanbul's multitudinous minarets capped with crescent moons reflecting the golden rays of sunrise. A hastily agreed-upon armistice had been signed on January 31 at Edirne that required the Ottomans to evacuate their remaining fortresses in Bulgaria and stipulated that a final agreement would include autonomy for Bulgaria and Bosnia, total independence for Romania and

Serbia, and new Russian rights in the Bosphorus Straits. The Russians also reserved the right to renew aggressions if they thought the Ottomans were not implementing the agreement; in any case, their troops continued to advance.

The Ottomans were forced to concede the approach of a few thousand Russian troops to the Theodosian walls that had protected the city for more than a millennium. They set up camp there in San Stefano (Yeşilköy). Evoking a scene reminiscent of the crusaders upon reaching Jerusalem, some soldiers began to embrace one another, while others fell to their knees in religious awe and began to cross themselves fervently and feverishly. The fulfillment of the Russian prophecy that one day "Tsargrad" would belong to the Russians and that they would worship in Hagia Sophia was finally within reach.[3] The grand duke went to the heights of San Stefano, accompanied by Alexander of Battenberg, who recounted that upon seeing Constantinople with Saint Sophia and its minarets "tears filled the Grand Duke's eyes. What satisfaction it must give him to stand at the gates of Constantinople with his army!"[4] No Russian commander had every been closer to the "Queen of Cities." Nicholas wrote to his brother, the tsar, "We must go to the centre, to Tsargrad, and there finish the holy cause you have assumed."[5]

The public mood in Britain's capital, however, had swung decidedly against any further Russian advance. The English term "jingoism" was coined in an atmosphere of Russophobia in a ditty sung by crowds in London.[6] The chorus went:

> We don't want to fight,
> But by jingo if we do,
> We've got the ships,
> We've got the men,
> We've got the money too.
> We've fought the bear before,
> And if we're Britons true,
> The Russians shall not have Constantinople![7]

An English naval fleet stationed at Besika Bay, against the sultan's wish and in violation of the Straits Convention, moved into the Dardanelles. An angered tsar, despite the armistice, wanted his brother to seize the city. He telegraphed the grand duke: "I leave you the numbers and moment to occupy."[8]

But the Russian numbers were small compared to those masses guarding the city walls; moreover, they were exhausted and the supply lines were stretched thin. They could not be certain that the Austrians would stay on the sidelines; nor could they predict the reaction of the city's inhabitants to an occupation. Most worrisome of all was the sentiment that Britain and Russia were sliding toward war. On March 24 the grand duke arrived by train and began negotiations with the Ottomans, who were unsure of British support in the event that the Russians renewed aggressions and unsure of British intentions toward the sultan. Moreover, the sultan, who had already made preparations to flee the city, was fearful of provoking the Russians further and caved in to the Treaty of San Stefano. The Russian advance had finally come to an end. When General Skobelev learned that the Russians would not take Constantinople, he broke into tears.

Yet for the next several months Russian troops stood stationed outside the walls of Constantinople. It was not a pleasant experience for them, especially when the icy cold began to thaw and disease began to make itself known. But most of all, the Russians suffered, in the "gloomy, idiotic San Stefano life," from "hellish boredom."[9]

Lucky soldiers would occasionally be permitted a chance to escape the boredom and enter the old city. A Don Cossack recounts his trip to Hagia Sophia:

> We received permission to enter Constantinople. Of course, I didn't fail to take advantage of this and the next day I boarded a ferry with a comrade. Approaching Constantinople I was in awe of the grandiosity of the picture. Quaint homes, walls overgrown with moss, gardens, mosques, towers, minarets—everything taken together presented a particularly marvelous view. The sea and the multitude of ships with multicolored flags accentuated the beauty of the fairytale decoration, then the setting sun blanketed both the city and the sea with a blood-red reflux. We were given a boat, and along with a translator headed toward the shore. . . . Upon the following day we set out for the cathedral of Saint Sophia.

> From the grimy outside it smacked of a dirty horse stable, but the inside resembled a hospital without precedence. Up to three thousand Turkish families infected with typhus took shelter in its walls. The view of everything from the choir was fantastical. Mosaics, delicate marble work, gigantic columns, the Sultan's golden lodge, enormous circles around prayers written in gold, the floor, strewn with thousands of ill people wearing colorful costumes—all of it had the look as if it were concocted, as if it were out of some fairytale.... The atmosphere was stifling, and I ran outside to avoid suffocating.[10]

Many visitors passed through Istanbul that difficult spring. They were all highly troubled by what they witnessed. One of them was none other than former president of the United States and Civil War hero Ulysses S. Grant, who was taking a cruise around the Mediterranean. He was affected by what he witnessed: "But the sight is wretched enough. In a small portion of the city is stored away in the Mosques and public buildings probably more than a hundred thousand refugees, men women and children, who have fled to the Capital before a conquering Army. They are fed entirely by charity and mostly by foreigners. What is to become of them is sad to think of."[11]

Whereas the Russians had approached Constantinople in triumph, delivering the Bulgarians from the Turks, the erstwhile Muslim residents of Bulgaria were now in dire straits. Neither flight from the advancing Russian Army and Bulgarian depredations nor the end of war brought an end to Muslim misery. Even as these Ottoman Muslims, now displaced from their homelands, arrived at the remnant of Ottoman Europe, they still had many difficulties to endure. Istanbul and Edirne were the primary destinations for the refugees in flight; however, even those who arrived at what was left of the "well-protected domains" had to suffer a difficult winter in Istanbul, outbreaks of disease, evacuations, dashed hopes of a return home, and an eventual resettlement in Anatolia. The refugees created considerable challenges to a government whose capacity to cope was already under considerable duress due to the debacle in the Balkans. The government's resources and organizational capacity to deal with hundreds of thousands of refugees, the outbreak of disease, an attempted coup d'état, and the resettlement of these refugees were being greatly tried. However, through much improvisation, some planning, and the contributions of civil society, these masses of people whose homelands were lost to them began life anew in a new Ottoman society in the plateaux and coasts of Anatolia—a society that was much more Muslim than it had theretofore been. However, partly because of the government's efforts to resettle the refugees in a timely manner, they were able to more quickly and fully assimilate into their new environs—a major factor in their weak group memory and identity.

IN SEARCH OF REFUGE

Fearing danger from the advancing Russian armies with their Cossack irregulars and a newly armed Bulgarian population, hundreds of thousands of Ottoman Muslims were forced out of their homes or abandoned them in search of safety. These refugees, depending on the origin of their flight, traversed a series of points on their way to the safety of the sultan's protection. The movements of displaced Muslims typically unfolded according to the following patterns. For Muslims in Dobruca and the northern towns and villages, the nearest points of safety were Shumen and Varna, cities where Ottoman forts held out throughout the war and were only evacuated after the armistice had been signed. From Varna refugees took ferryboats to Istanbul and Turkish cities on the Black Sea and Marmara coasts. Varna, along with Pomorie (close to Burgas), and Constanta were the major Black Sea port cities for the evacuation of Muslim refugees.

Some Muslims in the west fled to Macedonia and even Albania or to the Aegean ports of Thessaloniki and Kavala, where they could board boats sailing to the capital, or cities on Anatolia's Mediterranean shore. Muslims in Sofia and central and southern Bulgaria sought to reach Plovdiv and wait for trains going to Edirne. From Edirne train lines extended to Burgas, Istanbul, Alexandroupoli, and Thessaloniki.

Refugees who journeyed through cities such as Shumen, Varna, and Edirne, which became more or less temporary transit points on the way to Istanbul and Anatolia, often occupied the abandoned homes of Muslims who had fled ahead of them. As they subsequently moved on to another destination, a new wave of refugees would often take over these homes being left behind. Moreover, in addition to reoccupying abandoned homes, in city after city the refugees were welcomed into the homes of local Muslim populations.[12]

As a general rule, those in the best economic situation were able to leave first. They often worked as religious officials, administrators, or wealthy landlords, meaning that they possessed more mobile assets and were therefore more able to purchase train tickets away from danger and onward to Istanbul. These wealthier and earlier Muslim refugees were often accompanied by Jews and Greeks,[13] whose dealings in commerce meant that they had much to fear from envious pillaging Bulgarians. The Jews and Muslims were usually viewed by the Bulgarians as synonymous.[14] As noted, many of these Jewish refugees were descendants of the Spanish Jews who had fled from Andalusia alongside the Moors. They were thus to relive their ancestors' Andalusian exodus in the Balkans, but this time with Turks.

Given the means of these earliest arrivals to Istanbul, and their desire not to impose a burden on the state, they rented apartments and began to adjust to their new lives in the empire's capital.[15] They were well received by the state and the populace, although some property owners tried to swindle them by raising rents steeply. The first report of refugees arriving in Istanbul dates to July 1877 and concerns a group of about five hundred people.[16]

Officials from the Ottoman military administration and the municipality met these earliest incoming groups of refugees at the train station. Men, women, children, and their belongings were loaded on oxcarts and transported to their destinations. When one of these early groups arrived at the Sirkeci station, it was transported by sailboat to Kabataş. During this boat ride, an emissary from Abdülhamid II boarded the boat and passed along the sultan's regards.[17]

The refugee presence in Istanbul began to grow heavy by autumn after the massacres in Stara Zagora, Nova Zagora, and Kazanlak, and large concentrations of refugees had developed in Tarnovo, Hadımköy, Çorlu, Plovdiv, and Pazardzhik. That October the Şeker Bayram (Eid al-Fitr celebration at the end of Ramadan) had lost its gaiety:

> There was the usual display of fine dress among the people, only that its chief extravagance was seen among the children, who at

4.2. *Arrival of Turkish Refugees at Constantinople. Illustrated London News* (1878).

> five years old and upward blazed in the uniform of major-generals or in blue satin ball-dresses. But this has been a rainy Bairam, and furthermore, among the gaily-dressed people on the streets one continually meets gaunt men, all in rags . . . 25 thousand refugees in the city, whose fate when winter comes, already causes anxiety. Altogether, it has not been a happy Bairam for the Turks.[18]

The rapidly waning fortunes and crumbling battlefield positions of the Ottomans translated into Russian breakthroughs and Bulgarian brutality. The Russian advance only came to an end with the Treaty of San Stefano, signed on March 3, 1878. As the Russian army pressed on, terror and panic seized the Muslim population and precipitated their vast displacement. The decision to abandon homes and villages was difficult and oftentimes made collectively as communities. Many hoped to reap the autumn harvest before leaving, but this was not always possible or wise. Unlike the earlier incoming refugees, the subsequent waves were less well-off and less prepared, often leaving suddenly and taking very

4.3. *Arrival of Train of Fugitives at Constantinople* by M. Kauffman. *Le Monde Illustré* (1877).

little with them. They did not have adequate means to buy train or ferry tickets or to procure housing and food once they arrived at their destinations. Some of these refugees arrived already scarred by violence. Many women and children had suffered brutality and bore wounds from Cossack lances and Bulgarian knives. Disturbingly, many of the women and girls had been "outraged."[19]

News of the refugees' grim state in Edirne had reached the capital. The constant inflow of refugees to Edirne was clogging the roads needed by the military, and the authorities thought it best to evacuate Edirne of its refugees, who were to move on to the empire's capital. Preparations were made to receive them upon arrival at Sirkeci train station in Istanbul, but the city could not be prepared for what it was about to witness. "Who does not remember the arrival of the first refugee train at the station in Stamboul?"[20]

Under an alternating rain and snow, a devoted crowd dressed in fine clothing had assembled to provide soup and succor for the incoming refugees:

> Constantinople never saw a more remarkable assemblage of people, ladies and gentlemen, than that which waited at the railway station for the train which was announced to bring the first detachment of fugitives from Adrianople [Edirne]. On a day of December, when heavy rain contended with heavy snow, and a boisterous wind with both, the looked for train slowly drew up at the platform, the actual state of its freight, for the moment, hidden beneath a covering of snow. For a moment—for a moment only—the deceitful pall screening the inexpressible horrors beneath—there was a hope that rumour had magnified the sufferings of the fugitives. The eye quickly belied the hope, and it was seen that the roofs of the carriages, the tender, the buffers, every point to which a human being could cling, was occupied by people stupefied by cold and want of food, many frost-bitten, many more ill, not a few dying, others already dead. How many had dropped from these exposed positions on the way will never be known. Then each carriage from within disgorged, with difficulty, its freight, disclosing in the process every form of suffering from exposure, from cold, and from hunger, as well as the corpses of those who had died on the journey—some from exhaustion, some, apparently, from suffocation in the densely packed vehicles.[21]

Another witness confirms the "heartbreaking spectacle":

> On the roofs of the wagons, from the locomotive until the very last car, stretched out a large shroud of snow that covered up the human masses; the happiest among them were those parked in the cattle wagons. The disembarkation was undertaken with great difficulty. From the depths of the wagons we pulled out here and there a cadaver buried among the living. Women, children, with frozen feet, were carried off on stretchers: they had not eaten for thirty-six hours.[22]

In early January Ali Efendi, a correspondent for the Ottoman-language *Basiret* daily newspaper, was one of those who had come to witness the arrival of refugees. He wrote about these "guests of God":

4.4. *Arrival of Train of Refugees. Graphic* (February 16, 1878).

> The hearts of those who go to Sirkeci station and see the condition of these poor people melt even if they are of stone. Especially the violent trembling and moaning of the bare headed and barefoot little children and the women weeping, without thought for themselves, asking help in the name of God from their fellow citizens for the protection of their beloved children, and the soul-rending condition of the sick and the powerlessness of the old makes us feel that this places a great duty both legal and humane on the men of the state.[23]

At first the refugees were placed pell-mell wherever there was shelter; the primary goal was to get them out of the cold. They were packed into some of the cities more spacious buildings—mosques, khans, schools, imperial residences, and private homes. Three mosques in particular were used as provisional shelters for the incoming refugees: Hekimoğlu Ali Paşa Camii, Fatih Mehmet Camii, and Laleli Camii. They were later moved to other shelters where there was space. Those who were to be sent out of Istanbul were sent to Yeni Camii to wait.

The visible presence of refugees in Istanbul finally brought home to the population in Istanbul the desperate military situation of the empire. The Russian occupation of Edirne on October 22 sped up the rate of refugee immigration to Istanbul; however, the fall of Pleven on December 11 was the catalyst for the complete inundation of the city by refugees.[24]

In the words of the French consul based in Edirne, the situation began to take on "frightening proportions."[25] Indeed, from January 15 to January 24 up to eighty thousand refugees arrived in Istanbul on ferries, by foot, and in more than thirty overflowing trains, pulling over a thousand wagons.[26] A foreign resident at the time described the shocking nature of the refugee tsunami:

> The completeness of the collapse of the Turkish defence is daily brought home to us by the sight of the refugees. . . . The refugees, with their wagons and household effects, fill the road for fifty miles from the city. They crowd into the city by special trains sent down the railroad. . . . Every train which arrives has a certain number of aged men, or of feeble women, or of tiny babies, who have froze to death during the terrible journey from Adrianople [Edirne]. Arrived in the city, these poor villagers know not where to go, and wander about the streets ankle deep in snow, or curl up in miserable, shivering heaps under friendly porches. The suddenness of their appearance and the number in which they come defy all effort to provide for them, and many of them die in the streets.[27]

The precarious condition of the arriving refugees was a great concern. One man working for one of the foreign charity organizations provided this desperate description:

> Yesterday there were known to be 15,000 women and children out in the snow at Chorlu, and three more trains full are hourly expected to arrive at Constantinople. It is not known where they are to be placed for shelter. The snow lies several inches deep on the ground and is still falling. The cold is intense. All that can possibly be done is being effected . . . , but many lives are being sacrificed which it will be impossible to save. The spectacle here

> is simply horrible—indescribable. More money is needed. The refugees require clothing, food, lodging, everything.[28]

By the middle of January the number of refugees in Istanbul, a city with a population of 600,000–700,000 before the war, had risen by 150,000, with 25,000 to 30,000 refugees still strewn along the Edirne–Istanbul train line; 200,000 refugees in Ruse; 40,000 at Kavala; over 25,000 in Varna, "packed like herrings in a barrel" in the konaks, mosques, and schools;[29] and hundreds of thousands more on the move elsewhere.

In order to alleviate some of the acute problems caused by the lack of shelter, the government began to move some refugees to the countryside at the end of January. However, their number in Istanbul actually increased to 200,000 by early March. Essentially, as refugees were evacuated from Istanbul, their places were immediately filled or exceeded by newly arriving refugees. Despite minor efforts to move refugees out of the capital, and after temporary decreases, the number was still close to 200,000 even as late as June. Following the Berlin Conference, which ended on July 13, the number continued to hover at around 120,000 until October 1878, before finally falling to around 60,000 by the end of the year. The number stayed in the tens of thousands for years afterward.[30]

In February an aid worker gave the following account of the general situation of refugees in Istanbul:

> Their numbers have been daily added to. Long trains of arabas, packed with women and children, and of foot passengers, half clothed and starving, have been moving unceasingly by various routes upon this central point, until the already crowded capital has been inundated with a new and strange population, without support. The Mosques and other public buildings, as well as private houses, are overflowing with fugitives. The streets of Stamboul are strewn with whole families, who, struggling into the city, the hoped for haven of refuge, have fallen helpless and exhausted in the mud, and lie there without the simplest necessaries of life; in every open place swarm groups of hungry-eye, hollow-cheeked people, tall men, and women with babies in their arms and little children clinging to their skirts. To-day the fine weather hitherto prevailing has changed to snow

and rain and sleet, the effect of which on the refugees need hardly be described.[31]

The state's ability to cope with the large number of incoming refugees was strained to breaking point. The succeeding waves of refugees were not given the welcome received by the initial groups in July. Not only did they arrive with fewer resources for their survival, but the weather conditions were also more severe. As the pace of incoming refugee arrivals quickened throughout the fall and into the winter, the city's capacity was in no way able to keep up. While the first refugees had been transported to housing in carriages, the city eventually was forced to employ horse-drawn garbage collection carts to transport refugees from the train station to temporary destinations.[32] The financial burden imposed by the need to feed and house the refugees, as well as the lost revenues from the Balkan provinces, meant that the government was compelled to suspend its debt payments.[33]

The flood of refugees overwhelmed Sirkeci train station, the eastern terminus of the oft-romanticized Orient Express. For this reason, trains began unloading their passengers around Yedikule, about four miles from the city center, where the massive walls of Istanbul begin.[34] Later Çorlu, about sixty miles from Istanbul, became a collecting point for refugees before trains took them to the city.

In addition to the refugees arriving by train and ferry, some Balkan Muslims made the arduous journey to Istanbul on foot or with carts pulled by horses or oxen. These carts and draft animals became economic resources, as refugees were able to make a living by transporting goods, people, and even new waves of refugees across the city.

Although the government authorities were pessimistic about their ability to house the incoming masses, the state did make an effort to acquire housing for the refugees. The state's refugee commission identified empty houses and buildings, where refugees were transported. Some property owners, however, not wanting refugees housed in their empty properties, attempted to deceive authorities by hiring caretakers to occupy their vacant properties. Other Istanbulites made great efforts to accommodate refugees or find shelter for them. Some refugees even wrote to the newspaper to offer public thanks to their hosts for the hospitality provided.[35]

Some destitute refugees who had rags for clothing and had no food were taken in by a number of well-to-do Istanbul families.[36] Conditions in private residences were cramped, as they were often crammed full of people who had just suffered major trauma and were at the mercy of the kindness of strangers or totally dependent on a state without means:

> Some of the refugees were in good houses—the summer houses of Beys and Pashas at Hissar—and in some rooms there were as many as thirty, many without clothes or charcoal; one old woman, about a hundred years of age, had walked from Kesanlik [Kazanlak], and her feet were so swollen that they were feet no longer, and she would never walk again. In one room was an old father and an old mother, and four daughters, whose husbands had all been killed within a week. Each woman had one or two small children, and their babies were often wrapped in a bit of carpet and nothing else. At Candilli [Kandili], the Imaum Mehemet looked after the refugees very well; he was thoroughly honest and kind hearted.[37]

Ambassador Layard also praised the generosity of the people of Istanbul:

> To the credit of the Turkish families and in justice to them it must be added that according to their means they did their best to relieve their suffering coreligionists. There was scarcely a Turkish house, which in the course of the winter months was not plied with refugees. Handsome mansions, with costly decorations and furniture belonging to wealthy men of high descent and employed in high offices were in many instances given over to them. . . . It was with difficulty but not always that they were prevented from burning the doors and shutters to warm themselves during the rigour of a Constantinople winter.[38]

Other refugees, however, were not fortunate enough to find shelter and care in the winter. One pregnant woman arrived at night: "She sat herself down on a door-step to rest, and then in the darkness a new little life wailed itself into being, and then wailed itself out into the unknown. In the morning both the mother and her new-born babe were found dead, with snow for their couch and snow for their covering."[39]

In an attempt to remedy the severe shortage of shelter caused by the incoming refugees, on January 18 Sultan Abdülhamid II issued an edict stating that the homes, seaside mansions, and villas of all present, former, and deceased deputies, ministers, and civil servants as well as all madrasas, covered neighborhood mosques, dervish lodges (large and small), and the homes of all individuals, according to their ability to do so, must be made available for the sheltering of refugees.[40] In order to set an example, the sultan had already taken a large number of female and child refugees into his Beylerbey waterside palace.

Eventually refugees were also sheltered in other royal palaces, including the courtyard of Topkapı Palace. Public schools were so full of refugees at the beginning of 1878 that public education came to a complete standstill. Despite the evacuation of refugees from the schools in order to allow class work to resume, some refugees were still reported residing in schools as late as the end of 1878.

The beautiful mansions along the Bosphorus, according to the sultan's edict, were required to take in refugees as well, who were shipped free of charge to those waterfront homes. The bottom floors of state buildings were also put to use as shelter for refugees. The ground floors of police stations and post offices were teeming with refugees—a situation that caused a great interruption in the delivery of mail and thus became the subject of complaint by businesses and newspaper bosses.[41] When all of these places proved inadequate, farms belonging to the treasury and various foundations were opened for the purpose of accommodating the crowds of refugees. All the while, a deep nostalgia troubled those refugees ripped from their homes. As *Basiret* put it, the refugees "even if housed in the best mansion cannot forget the deep suffering and sadness, caused by the loss of their vatan [homeland]. In their hearts, there is always the longing for the vatan, on their tongue always the word vatan."[42]

BETWEEN A DOME AND A HARD PLACE: SHELTER AND SICKNESS IN THE MOSQUES

For the majority of refugees, mosques and other religious buildings were their primary haven. Before being moved to other locations, refugees were often taken, or went of their own accord, to mosques, Sufi lodges, madrasas, caravansaries, and other public and religious buildings. Both the interiors and courtyards of mosques were overflowing. The grand imperial mosques closest to Sirkeci train station and quay were inundated with newcomers to the city. As a visitor described it: "All the great mosques are filled with refugees. Under the gilded dome of St. Sophia they are packed in a great mass, and on the stone pavements of Sultan Ahmed, Suleimaniye, and Bayazid, they huddle together, and groan and weep in the helplessness of despair."[43] The large mosques in old Istanbul with expansive domes held the greatest numbers and because of the crowded conditions, filth, and suffering became ideal points for the transmission of disease. Yeni Camii was assigned on January 14 as a shelter for the refugees by the Ottoman Parliament and held up to 5,000 refugees. Initially refugees placed in Yeni Camii were designated to be sent on to the provinces.

Mahmud Paşa Camii had 1,000 refugees, while Laleli, Cezhade, Nur-i Osmaniye, and Süleymaniye had 2,000 to 3,000 refugees each. The Blue Mosque sheltered 4,000 individuals, and at its peak Hagia Sophia housed an astounding 12,000 refugees in February, which fell to 8,000 through March and April.[44]

The descriptions of the conditions inside the mosques at this time, especially Hagia Sophia, add detail to this otherwise little known episode in the history of such an important world monument. In one of the earliest descriptions of the refugees in Hagia Sophia, an English reporter visiting in January wrote:

> Those . . . who have visited Saint Sophia, and are acquainted with the difficulties which were formerly thrown in the way of visitors, would be somewhat surprised if they could visit it to-day. You need no firman now to obtain admission to the stately temple. To-day no haughty doorkeeper bids you thrust your unhallowed feet into the prescribed slippers before you set your foot upon the sacred floor. The pressure of relentless misery has broken down the barriers of conventionality, and if you are compassionate there is no Holy of Holies which you may not enter. The voice which was wont to say, "Take off thy shoes from thy feet, for the place whereon thou treadest is holy ground," says this no more, but invites you rather, in the name of humanity, to forget all differences of race or creed, and to mix freely with the

sufferers who rest under the shade of a temple which, though it has served both Christians and Mahometans, has always been devoted to the worship of one and the same God. The vast area of Saint Sophia . . . is almost entirely free from furniture of any kind. At one end of the church there are two large stone mihrabs or pulpits, and in each of these mihrabs two or three families were encamped. I could not learn why they had obtained this distinction over the vast crowd of refugees which comprised more than three thousand persons, and was encamped all over the matted floor of the mosque. I use the word "encamped," because each family had been careful to preserve its individuality. When a family possessed any baggage it had built a little semicircular wall of that baggage, within the protection of which it sat and crouched and lay. Who will doubt that even this wretched simulacrum of a home comforted the poor exiles who had made it. Even those who had no baggage wherewith to protect themselves occupied a little exclusive ring on the matted floor, and tried to look as if they were in their own house or tent. In the whole crowd there were not more than two hundred men, and most of them were lying down on rugs and mattresses, and were quite stricken down with fever. I do not think that any person who was suffering from small-pox had been allowed to enter the mosque, but there must have been three or four hundred, great and small, who were suffering from fever. The air was quite sweet, and the mosque was clean, the children, who were at least fifteen hundred in number, were also clean and some of their mothers who had been able to procure washing utensils and water were engaged in washing the children's clothes. In every corridor, and against every wall to which nails and string could be attached, long rows of children's clothes were hanging up to dry.

We spoke with many of the groups, and found no anger, no petulance, no impatience amongst them. I never knew what patience and resignation were until yesterday. Here were three thousand people who had lost almost everything they possessed, and who had been driven from homes to which they never can return, yet we heard from them no word of anger or even vexation. In one corner was a family, every male member of which had

> been killed. In another was a group of children whose father and mother had been carried dead out of the mosque on the previous day. In another a woman, herself fast yielding to the coming fever, watched by the fever stricken forms of her husband and children. Never have I seen such misery. Never have I seen such patience. We stayed a long time with these poor creatures, and then ascended to the lofty galleries which overlook the floor of the mosque. These galleries are so high that adults seem small when you look down upon them, but yesterday the children who were scattered over the floor in vast numbers looked no bigger than cats and dogs. The scene was terribly impressive. When last, four hundred and twenty-five years ago, a vast crowd of refugees was for the first time gathered together in the temple of the Divine Wisdom the splendour of the church mocked the misery of the fugitives. Saint Sophia has no such splendours to-day. The bare, cold, and discouloured walls harmonise with the squalor of the crowd which they enclose. When the Christians took refuge in the church, the faces of four colossal angels looked down on the suppliants from the lofty dome. The Turks have long since hidden the faces of these angels under a veil of white wash, but the wings are still visible, and it is easy to see where the faces of the angels have been. Let us trust that if the face of the Creator, like the faces of the angels, is for a time veiled from this suffering crowd, his mercy still lives, and will ere long shine forth upon them.[45]

The smaller Istanbul mosques were also harboring refugees,[46] while the Greek churches and island monasteries were full of Christian refugees.[47] In all, upward of 100,000 refugees were housed in the city's religious buildings at one time,[48] and the sultan constantly enquired about their status.[49] In addition to Istanbul's mosques, mosques in the Balkans, in Damascus and other Syrian cities, and even in Beirut provided shelter for refugees.[50]

The mosques, though, were not ideal refugee centers. The caretakers of the Blue Mosque literally took the mosque rugs out from underneath the refugees' feet—they did not want the carpets muddied, leaving the refugees nothing but the cold stone floors. A deputy of parliament representing Istanbul defended this action to the elected body, arguing that

4.5. *Refugees in a Gallery of the Mosque of Hagia Sophia* by Gyula Tornai (1861–1928). Courtesy Damien Peronnet / Art Digital Studio © Sotheby's.

the issue of the carpets was being overblown since there was not much room left to sit down anyway.[51]

In order to cook food and keep warm, refugees either lit fires inside the mosques (smoke inhalation resulted in some deaths) or more likely huddled together and tried to seal out outside air. Moreover, the number of toilets available was inadequate, so refugees ended up relieving themselves in the streets surrounding the mosques, in the courtyards, or in the mosques themselves. The stench in some of the mosques was so bad that visitors had a difficult time entering them.[52] However, an order to break the windows to facilitate ventilation was ignored.[53]

The physical toll of the perilous winter journey, combined with the lack of food and shelter, meant that sickness was taking hold among the weakened refugee population. The crowded, cold, unsanitary conditions of the mosques became incubators for disease that had sneaked into the city with the fugitives. However, as the temperatures warmed toward the end of winter and the beginning of spring, epidemic conditions began to threaten. One refugee who documented his experience in poetic stanzas lamented, "Ah, and from the cold and from the humidity/So many fell ill and died. Lord, what a pity!"[54] First smallpox attacked. It was found most commonly in the refugee children, but not unknown in adults and the elderly and was especially prevalent among Circassians and Gypsies.[55]

Typhus made an appearance in Hagia Sophia in mid-February and had grown to an epidemic scale by the end of the month, ravaging the refugee population. The mortality from the typhus attained 50 percent in some mosques and khans, and the hospitals could not cope with all the patients being brought in. Hagia Sophia was especially hard hit. In the months of March and April when it contained between 7,000 and 8,000 refugees, doctors could only find 3,000 who were not afflicted by the scourge. In those months alone they were pulling 30 to 60 dead bodies a day out of the mosque![56] Typhus continued to be a major concern until it began to recede toward the end of April and finally disappeared in July.

Other diseases such as respiratory infections and dysentery were common from the time the refugees appeared in the city, and many cases of frostbitten limbs were treated. But starvation was the most important cause of death and suffering after typhus, typhoid, and smallpox. The children and elderly who had lost their support networks had no one who could go look for food for them.[57] An Englishman residing in Istanbul at the time described the dreadful conditions: "Typhus fever and smallpox raged among them and infected the city. There was a scarcity of food and places to shelter them. It was altogether the most terrible experience that Constantinople had witnessed since the Turkish conquest."[58]

The mosques that had been converted from Byzantine churches tended to have less salubrious conditions than more modern Ottoman mosques, which usually but not always had larger openings and greater penetration of sunlight.[59] In March an English doctor was sent to inspect the situation in Hagia Sophia and the Blue Mosque. He reported that, while Hagia Sophia housed more refugees, it was better off than the Blue Mosque because it had more space and a greater number of entrances. However, Hagia Sophia's inhabitants were likely to be more destitute than those of the Blue Mosque. The doctor gave a detailed picture of life in the mosque built by Emperor Justinian:

> In St. Sofia the refugees are all placed on the ground floor, the large gallery being quite free. In the body of the mosque they

> are placed in transverse rows, squatting in family circles, having under them matting which is spread over the whole floor, and any articles of bedding which they may have been able to preserve in their flight. These are usually piled in a heap in the daytime, and serve as boundary lines between the various families. In addition to these, a few pots and pans, a handmill and a mangal, and in some instances a cartwheel, which seems to be kept as a souvenir of the old country, as a rule, comprises the inventory of their worldly goods.
>
> The refugees, who are all Turks [Muslims] are to be found in every conceivable nook with which the mosque abounds, and being huddled together, form hotbeds of those diseases which are so painfully making their presence felt.[60]

On a visit in February Ambassador Layard's wife noted the striking juxtaposition of sorrow and the spectacular setting: "Each family had installed itself in a group barricaded by their rugs &c &c—some were lying ill—some were huddled over their mangals—It was a curious contrast looking down on the misery & then looking up at the glorious building—the finest temple in the world—with its gold mosaics—& fine marbles."[61]

Disease was becoming fatal in the mosques and throughout the city, especially for infants: the refugees "seemed literally to melt away under [its] influence."[62] In March twenty-five people were dying each day in Hagia Sophia as well as in other mosques. In Nur-i Osmaniye and Mehmet Paşa, respectively, eight and nine deaths took place on one day alone. Typhoid, typhus, dysentery, pneumonia, and smallpox were the most prevalent and dangerous diseases. A Russian observer of the San Stefano Treaty negotiations visited Hagia Sophia and after commenting on the facade of the building reported that even entering the mosque was seen as dangerous because of disease:

> Inside we found a horrid scene. Both on the bottom floor and in the choir thousands of people of both sexes and of every age were bivouacked side-by-side in tattered rags; it was all Muslim families who had run away from our troops to Stambul. A good half

of these wretches were seriously ill, lying motionless, or thrown into a feverish delirium. It is very possible that among the dense heaps fallen on the floor were dead people. As we made our way through this horrid bivouac, we soon drew the attention of all to ourselves, and when we got to the center of the temple to look around, we were nearly surrounded by a tightly packed crowd who stared at us with murky concentration. It was amazing that not even one hand was extended to us for alms, as had been the case in the streets. Seeing these dark stares directed toward us, we decided that it might be better for us to leave. In that very minute, before we could budge, the crowd suddenly began to move to the sides: a slow-moving Turkish policeman appeared and with a great wave of his stick scattered the crowd before him. When he got to us, he indicated with his hand to follow him, which we obeyed with pleasure. The crowd silently gave way and we carefully maneuvered between the sick people lying on the floor (primarily women and children) and managed to get to fresh air.

The coachman explained to us that as soon as we entered the temple, the policeman approached him and, having learned that of three Russians one was in military uniform, he immediately went after us to help out. According to his words, among the crowds camping in the temple all possible contagious diseases were raging and every day they carry out several dead people: it is not recommended to enter the temple without an urgent need.

Our policeman-guide did not limit himself to leading us out of Hagia Sophia but went after us, evidently to protect us from some other thoughtless action. Going around under his supervision, we paid special attention to the square on the other side and the surrounding buildings of unquestionable antiquity.... From there we walked by foot (with the policeman and the coach driver following) to the big, magnificent mosque of Ahmed [the Blue Mosque] surrounded by six minarets (they usually have two or four). Inside we found the same congested, miserable fugitives as in Hagia Sophia and we went through it preceded by our volunteer body guards.[63]

A relief worker reported the situation in regard to smallpox:

> In St. Sophia, many children are lying, closely surrounded by the rest of the family, as well as by great numbers of other children, in various stages of this pestilent and dangerous disease. The mothers are most reluctant to let them go to the hospital, and many a time I have had to carry with my own hands out of the Mosque children robed in dirty rags and covered with the terrible evidences of confluent small-pox. . . . Typhoid and typhus are also sufficiently frequent to show that, as in the case of small-pox, we are on the verge of an epidemic which, if it once really breaks out, will rage amongst this crowded and ill-fed population with unprecedented violence.[64]

As disease spread in the city, it arrived at the opposite bank of the Bosphorus and Üsküdar by mid-March.[65] In mid-March 400 to 600 of Istanbul's refugees were dying daily, and 22,000 people were lining up at the hospital doors, where they might wait days to get inside.[66] Moreover, twenty-three doctors and thirteen nurses appointed to work with sick refugees had contracted diseases and died by April.[67]

Januarius MacGahan, the journalist whose sensational reporting on the Bulgarian Horrors created such an uproar in England, contracted typhoid fever in Istanbul from which he died later in June. The disease had even spread among the Russian troops stationed at San Stefano. On April 4 Ambassador Layard visited Hagia Sophia:

> Which like all the other large mosques in Stamboul, had been used by the Government for the reception of the Musulman refugees. The scene was one never to be forgotten. The pavement and galleries of that vast and magnificent building were covered by a mass of human beings, crouching together in the utmost squalor and misery. Confounded with them were the sick and the dying. The small-pox and other diseases had already began to wreck ravage amongst them. Every now and then a dead body was carried out of the building. The wretched creatures were grouped together in families around the little property they might have succeeded in saving. . . . Their sufferings were terrible

> but they were borne with a patience and resignation which were wonderful.[68]

A French traveler lent his impression of the horrid situation:

> In fact, the misery is terrible. The city is burdened with unfortunate refugees from the Balkans and Rhodopes. Distress is everywhere. In this first promenade through Istanbul, I encountered the specter of hunger in every corner of the street. I have never seen more frighteningly skinny people than I have today. Poor dark-skinned girls, veiled in black yatmaks, drag themselves along the walls like phantoms. Lying at the corners of streets, the Bulgarian Muslims, rich yesterday, are dying of hunger. . . . In the cemeteries and the courtyards of the mosques, the refugees, who camp with their wives and their children, are piled one on top of the other, half naked, gnawed at by fever, abandoned by the criminal carelessness of the government and the insufficiency of Christian charity. They are hardly fed; the sick go untreated, and the dead are only buried out of fear of the plague. Around the clear fountain of the mosque of Ahmed [Blue Mosque], and under the covered gallery that encircles the courtyard with a delicious fringe of Moorish arcades, the spectacle is heartbreaking. Last week, during a visit lasting a half-hour that a friend of mine from Pera was making here, six people died without any doctor having seen them, without anyone budging around them. One cannot beg with more dignity. The Turk who asks for alms does not abase himself; he stands straight, head held high, his large pale eyes open; with one simple gesture, he points at his family shivering from inanition and fever against a marble column, and he waits.[69]

Death and its trappings became a part of everyday life in the capital. By the end of April over 18,000 had died within the city from hunger, cold, and disease.[70] The cemeteries, much like the mosques, filled up, and burials for the refugee dead were forbidden in a great number of the city's cemeteries. Graveyards were supposed to be outside city walls, yet, because new cemeteries were not created, refugees buried their loved ones in places that had not been included in the ban, such as the cemeteries at Eyüp and Edirnekapı, or paid bribes in order to conduct clandestine burials.

> The health administration asked that burials no longer be conducted either in the city or on the edges of the suburbs. It was not listened to. Between the Greek quarter of Tatavia and the Turkish quarter of Cassim-Pacha exists a small Muslim cemetery. The overseer of the church of Tatavia has taken numerous steps in vain in order to prohibit [use of] this cemetery. Having failed, he placed a man to make note of the daily interments. This man stated that from Saturday to Monday evening, in forty-eight hours, 376 Muslim cadavers had been buried. The pits are barely dug: the bodies wrapped in a shroud, not shut in a casket, hardly covered by dirt.
>
> This little cemetery is now completely full. They continue to bury the dead, but in the gardens of the Christians located nearby, at the foot of the hill of Tatavia. Tuesday evening, as the sun was going down at half past six, they brought at one time twenty-eight Muslim corpses and interred them in the garden of Manoaki, despite the vehement vociferations of the Greek women of Tatavia.[71]

Corpses were often not disposed of quickly, lying out in the open for days at a time. This, in addition to the poorly executed burials, which left body parts exposed, only contributed to the spread of disease.[72] It was only later that new cemeteries were created to meet the demand, sometimes at a pace of two to three a day.

As spring arrived, the health situation only got worse. In a cable to the foreign secretary a few weeks after his visit to Hagia Sophia, Layard urged immediate efforts to forestall a major epidemic in the city:

> The atmosphere in the mosque of St. Sophia . . . is absolutely poisonous, and the condition of the place is beyond description. The Turkish government is only able to distribute food sufficient for the bare support of life to this vast crowd of starving human beings. . . . There is serious danger of a fatal epidemic breaking out in Constantinople unless the present state of things be speedily remedied.[73]

The Ottoman press speculated that such an epidemic could wipe out half of Constantinople's population.[74] It was this existential fear of plague that resulted for the first time in serious efforts to move the refugees out of the city.

Foremost among those encouraging evacuation of refugees from Istanbul were the foreign consuls. While they were genuinely concerned about the city's welfare, they were also worried about the damage that an epidemic would inflict on the commercial interests of their governments' subjects and the economy of the Ottoman Empire in general, as the imposition of a quarantine would be required.

Ambassador Layard, after concurring with other foreign consuls, proposed the creation of a commission of foreign and Ottoman functionaries to deal with moving refugees out of the city and to increase customs duties by 25 percent to help pay for the relocation of refugees.[75] Even though Layard's plan was not put into action, conditions had sufficiently frightened the Ottoman government that by late April it issued an evacuation order for refugees in Hagia Sophia, sending them on one rainy day to hastily constructed tent cities in Fenerbahçe and Alemdağ on the outskirts of the city, which could only shelter a fraction of them.[76]

Thirty thousand refugees were moved to these tent cities as well as to farms away from the crowded city centers. By late April sixty thousand refugees had been sent willy-nilly to other provinces within the empire. However, the anticipated alleviation did not take place; neither did the total number of refugees in the city diminish, as a continuous flow of new arrivals simply replaced those who had been evacuated. Hence the idea of settling the remaining refugees in other provinces was broached.[77]

The evacuations were carried out without much planning or forethought; the main concern was simply to move refugees away from populated areas such as old Istanbul. An observer provided an idea of how these evacuations were implemented:

> The filthy habits and the crowded condition of the refugees have been turning this city into a vast pest-house. In view of this fact the government has undertaken to send away the refugees. The minister of police doubtless received orders in council to execute this measure, and he has begun the work in a thoroughly characteristic manner. Without making arrangements with other

> departments of administration, consulting as to the means of providing for the people on arrival at their destination, or even fixing the troublesome details of their embarkation, he transmitted to his subordinates the order to send away the refugees ... every circumstance of the condition of the people on arrival at their destination [was left] to luck.
>
> Hence the refugees have been bundled into steamers, without food or traveling equipment, and the steamers have discharged the miserable crowd upon some convenient seacoast town, where, because no provision has been made to receive them, they are tenfold more miserable than before. Furthermore, in loading up the steamers, the police have been known to seize any chance passers in the street, and to drive them without mercy into the ships. No man or woman dressed in the costume of the villages is safe for a moment in the vicinity of a refugee steamer. The people have, therefore, signed a monster petition to the Sultan, setting forth these facts, and pointing out that many die of starvation after being landed from the steamers; and that husbands are torn from their wives and wives from husbands, children from parents, and parents from children, through the summary method of selection adopted by the police. The petitioners then beg to be allowed to remain in Constantinople under the shadow of the Sultan, until they can be restored in peace to their homes in Bulgaria.[78]

After Hagia Sophia and the other mosques were evacuated, a Mr. Bonkowski, who taught chemistry at the medical school, was hired to disinfect the mosques "as they are free of their refugee inmates."[79] First, straw mats, which covered the mosque floors and the dirt underneath them, were lightly sprinkled with water to reduce dust and were burned in the Turkish baths, rugs were disinfected, and latrines were covered up. Then the interior walls of the mosques were washed down with fire department hoses, starting with the domes, which caused black streaks to trail down the mosque walls. Next the mosques were fumigated, followed by a treatment of carbolic acid, and finally left to ventilate with all doors open for ten to fifteen days before being reopened for worship.[80]

However, the cleaning of the mosques proved to be a monumental and risky task:

> The refugees have been cleared out from St. Sophia, where they were so crowded that an epidemic of malignant typhus was raging among them. Men were hired to sweep out this magnificent mosque after the departure of the refugees, and they nearly all took the fever, in several cases with fatal result. The proof of the deadly character of the infection quite paralyzed the Government. Now, however, on the advice of physicians, the Turks are applying carbolic acid to the whole interior surface of the building. Fire engines are brought up to the windows and the disinfectant is thrown into the mosque by this means. All the other great mosques are to be cleared and cleansed in the same manner, after which the doors will be closed for two or three weeks. It is supposed that by that time the deadly atmosphere will be dispelled so the workmen can enter and complete the cleansing. But what a story this tells of the condition of the people who have for three months lived in these mosques![81]

Even after these initial evacuations, mosques continued to play a role as refugee shelters. As late as 1879 a visitor to a mosque in Plovdiv left the following poignant description:

> The first place that I saw was a mosque, in which 28 women and children had been placed for shelter. The windows were imperfectly filled up with straw. The women in all cases but one were widows. The children in many instances had lost both parents. The poor creatures were emaciated, uncared for, and hardly clothed. On the ground each little party of relatives had gathered a few sticks, and kindled miserable fires over the floor, which burnt up and burnt out in a few minutes. Round these the shivering women and children cowered, for the temperature was but a degree or two above freezing. The little children smiled in spite of their cold and misery, when spoken to. The women shewed their rags and told their stories, but there was neither loud clamour nor complaint.
>
> A sad token of the future, but too probably near at hand for many of them, was an empty coffin placed against the side of the wall of the mosque.[82]

The fascinating yet heartbreaking role that mosques played in the story of the refugees in 1877–1878 was to be revived again during the Balkan Wars of 1912–1913. Once again, the mosques of Istanbul became shelters for those displaced by war, weary from flight, and traumatized by personal experience. The history of the mosques of Istanbul, especially the story of Hagia Sophia, becoming refugee shelters has rarely garnered the attention that it merits. Even today a series of panels in the portico of this church-turned-mosque-turned-museum telling the biography of this important building neglects any mention of this most noble function.

By the end of May, although still persisting, disease had receded. Improved sanitary conditions and the increasing capacity of hospitals meant that deaths, while still occurring, had fallen from the highest points in April and early May. Death from disease, though, continued to rage elsewhere among refugees such as in Edirne and Ruse. With disease abating in the capital, the public becoming inured to seeing poor refugees in the streets, and foreign charitable donations drying up as attention to the issue decreased, soup kitchens were shutting their doors. Some predicted that the next winter could be worse for the refugees than the last one.

REVENGE AND REVOLT: ALI SUAVI AND THE FAILED COUP

The circumstances of their flight from Bulgaria and their deplorable stay in Istanbul generated feelings of hatred and revenge against the Bulgarians and Russians as well as a sense that the state had failed them and was continuing to fail them. Incompetence on the battlefield was compounded by a perceived diplomatic weakness and a lack of effort to restore the refugees to their homes. In short, despite the quiet and uncomplaining dignity praised by some foreign observers, an amorphous anger among the refugees was clearly seething.

After the ceasefire and the Treaty of San Stefano, the appearance of Russian soldiers strolling around Istanbul on days off caused heads to lower and fists to clench among the city's Muslims. For this reason the Russian soldiers primarily ventured to the Christian parts of town. For many Istanbulites, life continued as normal. Their fancy dress presented a striking contrast with the ragged and mendicant clothing of the refugee population.

Tales of Russian and Bulgarian cruelty passed directly from refugee mouths to the general population, awakening a sense of indignation. One traveler crossing the Bosphorus by boat encountered the fury caused by the refugees' condition:

> Their tales and proof of outrages committed by the Bulgarians and Cossacks upon Moslems have deeply moved the popular heart. The other day I was crossing the Bosphorous in a caique, and passed some lighters full of refugees, who looked so wretched that I said, "poor creatures." The Turkish boatman burst out with a vehemence which astonished me. "Yes, they are poor creatures, and the Great God will never bless the Russians who have made them poor creatures. May his curse follow them, and may they get from Him their deserts!"[83]

Many refugees were obsessed with avenging their suffering and humiliations:

> They are half naked and half starved, and tell the most extraordinary stories of the brutality of the Cossacks. They fill our streets, thirsting to take vengeance upon some one, and not very particular as to the race of the victims. These fellows are not at all anxious to conceal their regrets that they had to flee before they could kill the Bulgarians. Two of these men, who had been Bashi Bozouks under Reouf Pasha, sat near me on the steamer the other day, and talked in perfect unconcern of the plan which they had made to return to their village, after placing their women in safety. The object of their return was solely to massacre their Bulgarian neighbors, in order to deprive them of the benefits of the Russian victories; but when they carried out their purpose to return, they found the Cossacks already there, and were obliged to beat a hasty retreat. "Yes," said one of them, "the Russians were too soon for us; and now, every dog of those Bulgarians has put on a stovepipe hat, and struts about like a gentleman."[84]

The huge numbers of refugees in a precarious situation caused concern on the part of the authorities. The potential for a large disturbance to public order was duly noted:

> Constantinople is more and more assuming the character of a powder magazine. . . . They [the refugees, some of whom were armed] are all more or less cowed and harmless for the moment. But if some small disturbance should occur at any point the whole mass of these ruffians would be moved to action, and the limits which could be placed to their madness cannot be forecast.[85]

Theft of bread by starving refugees was reported, and highway robbery was on the rise to the point that it was dangerous to be on the outskirts of the city unescorted due to roving bands of refugees looking for anything to improve their lot. The Circassian refugees were especially noted for their banditry and violence, and the government took special pains to move them out of the city the quickest. However, the most serious event concerning refugees and public order occurred on May 20, 1878. Ali Suavi was a Young Ottoman intellectual who promoted positive associations with the word "Turk" and is considered, along with Namık Kemal, a forerunner of Turkish nationalists. Suavi thought it best for the empire to let its Arab and African provinces go and to retrench in what he considered the Turkish motherland (*vatan*): Anatolia and Rumelia.[86] Suavi organized a group of refugees who attempted an assault on Çırağan Palace to dethrone Sultan Abdülhamid II. This would be the first time in the history of the Ottoman Empire that civilians sought to remove the sultan.

Many Ottomans held the sultan accountable for the war debacle. In the second session of the Ottoman Parliament, which opened in November 1877, detailed criticisms were launched at the mismanagement of the war.[87] (After the January armistice Abdülhamid dissolved Parliament, which did not reconvene for thirty years.) Many refugees also laid blame on the sultan for their difficulties. Not only did he fail them in the war, but he failed them in a peace that ceded their lands to the Bulgarians. Even though Abdülhamid II was interested in encouraging an uprising in the Balkan states, he refused to support the insurgency in the Rhodopes. The sultan even pondered menacing Bulgaria with further emigration

Ali Suawi Effendi
Le grand Patriote Turc
مرحوم علی سعاوی

4.6. *Ali Suavi*. By Abdullah Frères. Public domain: Wikimedia Commons.

4.7. *Ali Suavi and the Failed Uprising. Journal Universel* (1841, no. 71, June 8, 1878).

in order to destroy the fledgling state's tax base, but he faced a lack of resources and European support to be capable of harboring any recidivist dreams. As far as the refugees were concerned, he was clearly unwilling to continue the fight to restore them to their lands and property.

Ali Suavi, a forty-year-old former Plovdiv high school teacher and part-time mosque preacher originally from Central Anatolia, tapped into these feelings of injustice and resentment against the sultan. He had for some time spoken out against Sultan Abdülhamid II's personal rule and absolutism and also condemned the sultan publicly for his conduct of the war and his failure to support the insurgency against the Russians in the Rhodope Mountains. Suavi was a prolific writer, expressing the fairly liberal notions of the compatibility of Islam and Westernism, and was at times associated with the Young Turks in exile. He was also known to be something of a populist, who supported representative government, as well as an intriguer and troublemaker.[88]

After having conspired in private with refugees, Ali Suavi published an article in the *Basiret* newspaper on the day before the coup attempt, signaling for them to gather the following day. On May 20 he armed a

4.8. Abdülhamid II. By W & D Downey Photographers.

group of between 200 and 500 people, primarily consisting of refugees from Plovdiv, and led them from the Mecidiyeköy Mosque to the palace, where the sultan was residing, with the aim of overthrowing Abdülhamid II and replacing him with his brother Murat V, who had been a supporter of constitutionalism. After the group forced entry into the palace, a battle ensued. Palace guards, soldiers, and the police defeated the insurgents. Ali Suavi was killed in the palace stairwell during the mêlée, and many of the refugees went down with him.[89] Some escaped and others were hanged, with the sultan's encouragement, and after his personal interrogation.

The coup attempt only heightened the sultan's paranoia about his personal safety: in order to prevent another coup attempt by disaffected refugees, he accelerated the efforts to move refugees out. The city was on edge, as more gunfire was heard that night and fires were started throughout, even at the Sublime Porte. The government increased security measures, making arrests throughout the city.

At first the sultan tried to keep a lid on news about the attempted coup, including shutting down *Basiret*, which had connections to Suavi and had given coverage to the refugee situation. In fact, the sultan was well known for his fondness for the censor and his desire to clamp down on dissident voices, which had become more assertive in the face of his military defeat. Despite efforts to prevent news of the coup attempt from spreading, word got out anyway. For many in the city, the only fault they could find with the conspirators was their inadequate organization; for many refugees, this failed coup disgraced their reputation. Some despondent refugees even sent the sultan formal written apologies, begging his forgiveness for the behavior of other refugees.[90]

Few things could spur the slow-to-act sultan to action as quickly as concerns about his own person. The Ali Suavi coup attempt was an important impetus for the state to settle refugees outside of Istanbul as it was realized that they posed a potential threat to public order and that their presence called into question the legitimacy of a government unable to protect them in their previous homes or provide for them in their new shelter. Another 180,000 refugees were quickly shuttled out of Istanbul.[91]

Hüseyin Raci Efendi, a refugee in Istanbul at the time, described the effect of these events on the refugees in verse:

[The coup attempt] threw the city into quite a bustle
All carried a burden, yet 'twas just a dry rustle

Helpless Turk, Pomak, and Gypsy
Are piled onto ferries without mercy

Wives torn from their husbands' side
And exiled to Asia, far and wide

> And then they to Anatolia jettison
> Both the Tatar and the Circassian
>
> Shipped off to a land of death without a care
> Their souls commended to certain destruction there.[92]

One contemporary observer summed up the state's attitude toward the refugees at this point:

> This affair affords food for reflection on the dangerous character of waiting between war and peace. The band . . . was composed of refugees, of whom there are many thousands in the city ready, because of their misery, to undertake any desperate enterprise. They are hungry and must have bread. The foreign soup kitchens and relief societies are closing up their work, and the only remedy which the Government can devise for the miseries of the refugees is to ship them to some other part of the empire where they will be out of sight but not out of suffering.[93]

THE RIGHT OF NO-RETURN

The Treaty of San Stefano that brought an end to the Russian advance toward Istanbul also begat a greater Bulgaria at the expense of the Ottoman presence in Europe. These newly drawn borders created a new potential Balkan power that would in theory be pliable to Russian leadership. This situation was unacceptable to the other European powers.

Even though Russia had plotted to create the largest Bulgaria possible, before and during the war it made promises that no such greater Bulgaria would be created. Given the ire of the other European states and Russia's overstretched position, it gave in to a new round of talks that would be presided over by the "honest broker" Otto von Bismarck in Berlin. The outcome of these talks was the Berlin Treaty, which redrew the Bulgarian borders, returning some land to the Ottoman Empire and dividing the remaining Bulgaria into the autonomous Bulgarian principality in the north, Eastern Rumelia, which was to remain under Ottoman sovereignty, and Macedonia, which was to remain under Ottoman rule. It codified the loss of Cyprus to Great Britain, Bosnia-Hercegovina to Austria-Hungary, the eastern province of Batumi, and Bessarabia (Moldova) to Russia, and Dobruca to Romania. To a great extent the treaty marked movement away from the idea of multiethnic and multireligious empires promoted in the Congress of Vienna and toward the notion of the ethno-nation-state.[94] The treaty linked the ethnic makeup of a population and sovereignty, fanning the flames of desire for national determination across the Balkan region as well as within the Ottoman Empire and setting Europe on the path to the First World War.

The circumstances of the refugees were not unknown to the European powers. Indeed, the English and French had sent many diplomatic cables on the issue. Furthermore, Muslims sent many petitions and requests to the Congress of Berlin, detailing their woes and asking for reparations. Some refugees directly petitioned Bismarck himself, prefacing their pleas with a description of their lot:

> Faced with mass massacres, isolated murders, pillage, rape, and fire, we had to flee, tracked on all sides like wild beasts, leaving the fields strewn with the bodies of our wives, our children, and our unlucky compatriots. The misery, the deprivations, and epidemics continued the work of extermination begun by hordes of savages unworthy of the human name.[95]

Some refugees begged for an end to depredations, for the return of livestock, and for the return of homes. Some wanted a clear indication of what to do: "Should we emigrate or should we resign ourselves to our sad fate?" Others, such as the inhabitants of Sultanyeri, rather than remain under the Russians, stated that they were prepared to emigrate en masse and pleaded for imperial bounty in "designat[ing] a land where we can live far from fear and terror."[96] They further expressed their disapproval of being made part of the new Bulgarian state and asked for redress from the powers.

Yet the Berlin Treaty failed to make explicit mention of the refugees. Rather, it dealt with the minority rights in the newly created Principality of Bulgaria, despite Russia's objection to the idea that the Balkan state constitutions must contain guarantees for minority rights. In the end, it stipulated equal protection and political rights for the minority groups of Bulgaria. The Ottomans hoped that Muslims in the new Bulgaria would possess sufficient security in person and property that they would not feel the need to immigrate to the Ottoman Empire. According to the treaty, Muslims could enter any profession, including the civil service. The Ottomans signed the treaty believing that the codification of certain guarantees for the remaining Muslim population would be fulfilled. However, given that no European power would be willing to intervene on behalf of the Muslim minority in Bulgaria as they had repeatedly done for the Christian minorities in the Ottoman territories, there was no enforcement of these stipulations. Thus the Bulgarian state was left more or less to do as it pleased.[97] Minority rights in Bulgaria were strengthened following defeat in the First World War and the imposition of the Treaty of Neuilly.[98] Yet the true implementation of rights for Bulgaria's Muslims has been inconsistent.

The Ottomans were eager for the refugees to return to their homes in the Balkans in order to alleviate the crowded and pestilent conditions in the capital and to prevent the Russians from reinforcing the Bulgarian population of Eastern Rumelia. The Ottomans assumed all along that most of the refugees would return to the Balkans at some point. This is why they were often referred to as "guests." With the signing of the peace treaty, many refugees began returning home. According to lists prepared in Istanbul in order of province, the refugees were to be sent back to their cities and villages. The refugees were gradually to return to their places of origin—first the refugees in Istanbul and Thrace, then the refugees in Anatolia.[99]

The state paid the railroad companies for transporting the refugees to Edirne, from whence they would go on to their homes. Local commissions were to resolve the issue of property and animals that had fallen into the hands of the Bulgarians. Because Russians still occupied these areas of return, the refugees needed to get permission from Russian authorities for passage into these occupied territories.

The Russians, though, had an insurgency on their hands in the Rhodope Mountains. This uprising, which included many refugees, sought independence from the incipient Bulgarian state and even threatened the Berlin Treaty. In order to encourage the insurgents to give up their resistance, the Europeans created a commission for the Muslim refugees of the Rhodopes. Under the guidance of the commission, the refugees could return to their homes and retake possession of their lands and goods.[100] By October 1878, however, the joint commission's work had already come to a standstill because of disagreements between the Russians and Ottomans.[101]

Beginning in June 1878, one hundred and fifty refugees a day took a train to return to their homes, but the Ottoman government wanted to speed things up and gave authority to issue four hundred official certificates per day. The treasury would pay for a one-way rail ticket for poorer refugees and assigned an increasing number of wagons to them. By August six thousand refugees had attempted to return.

The Russians made it extremely difficult for Muslims to return with onerous paperwork requirements and other stalling techniques. Bulgarians also did not want to give back the property and goods that they had acquired in the tumult of war.

While the Berlin Treaty made no mention of the refugees, it did state that property owners who had left the Bulgarian Principality could continue to administer their properties. In theory, refugees should have been able to return; in practice, they were not allowed to do so. The Russians not only refused to guarantee the safety of the returning refugees but made great efforts to prevent refugees from returning through insurmountable red tape and impossible deadlines. The Berlin Treaty provided no means to assure the repatriation of refugees or erstwhile property owners and left it entirely to the goodwill of the Russians and Bulgarians. Prince Dondukov-Korsakov could see no legal foundation to prevent refugees from returning to their lands, but "the return of these Turkish 'muadzhirs' threatened to give birth to serious complications, to create endless bureaucratic procedures and inevitable bloody confrontations with the local Christian population."[102]

However, it was not only a simple matter of not wanting Muslims to return to mixed villages and towns, because the Russians were opposed to Muslims returning even to places where Muslims had a numerical superiority over the Christians such as Ruse and Varna. Prince Dondukov-Korsakov appointed a commission to review the questions of return, but its members were motivated by a desire to make the return of Muslims to their abandoned homes even more difficult.[103]

The Russians announced that even Muslim refugees returning to all-Muslim villages would need to be vouched for by a Bulgarian who would guarantee that this Muslim would not commit any crime. Sometimes proof of income was required from Muslims whose farms had been seized by a Bulgarian. Muslims who had been large landholders in particular were prevented from returning to claim their lands, as Ottoman titles were not considered sufficient proof of ownership. Prince Dondukov-Korsakov announced that refugees would not be allowed to return to certain towns, such as Stara Zagora, Karlova, and Kalofer, and if they did somehow return they could be sent to military tribunals.

For their part, the Bulgarian population also sought to prevent refugees from ever returning to their homes, quarters, and farms. Refugees were often attacked on the road back to their homes. For instance, ten thousand refugees who tried to return to their homes hurried back to Plovdiv after some of them had been robbed and others treated cruelly by the Bulgarians.[104]

If refugees were able to get back to their villages, they often found that their homes had been burned or destroyed or were inhabited by Bulgarians. Such destruction of Muslim property continued as late as the end of 1878 with Russian help and into 1879 under Russian surveillance.[105]

The refugees' farms were now being tilled by Bulgarian farmers, and their herds were now being pastured by Bulgarian shepherds. Obviously, the Bulgarians were not simply going to give back the properties to the Muslims. The Bulgarian farmers even refused to share the harvests with the starving Muslims. With no food, land, or shelter, the refugees came to understand that they were no longer welcome in the land of their forebears.

After much effort to retake possession of their properties through the legal channels proposed by the Russians and much Russian temporizing and violence and intimidation on the part of the Bulgarians, who were now being armed and organized into an army, it became clear that a return to Bulgaria was improbable. Stories of thwarted attempts at return circulated in the capital, and the Ottoman state recognized that it was powerless to help Muslims go back. The historical record has proven something that was obvious to the Ottoman leaders: only force could bring about the repatriation of the refugees.[106]

"BY SEA"—BRITISH MEN-OF-WAR'S BOATS RESCUING WOMEN AND CHILDREN AT BOURGOS

THE RUSSIAN ADVANCE—FLYING BEFORE THE ENEMY

4.9. *Flying before the Enemy. Graphic* (February 16, 1878).

Rather than maintain the refugees in a state of limbo in refugee camps, the sultan and the state chose to settle the refugees permanently in Anatolia. A continuing migration of Muslims from Bulgaria to the Ottoman Empire took place, as life as a Muslim minority in the Bulgarian state was deemed intolerable by many. They would seek a new life in Anatolia under the protection of their sultan and caliph. A French observer described the scene of one such emigration at the port in Varna in September 1878:

> I attended new spectacles of exodus. As Varna is in daily communication with the Bosphorus, it is to its port that flows the crowd of Muslim refugees, Turkish families that the Liberator of the Christians has chased from Bulgaria. The dilapidated docks resemble an encampment of nomads . . . this long parade of unfortunate people, carrying off pell-mell the debris of their fortunes, "having abandoned many a thing of value in order to load up on things without worth." I have just seen these scenes

4.10. *Turkish Refugees from Eastern Rumelia* by Richard Caton Woodville Jr. *Illustrated London News* (1885).

with my own eyes, but sadder still contrasted with the surrounding gentle landscape, and by this dignity in misfortune that distinguishes the Ottoman among people. Not one tear, not one word of anger. The pale faces stay calm, almost serene. These strong men believe that complaining would be unbecoming. For is this not all written?

> The Nile has just unloaded two hundred refugees. When the heavy caique on which they are piled up comes to attach itself to the sides of the large vessel, the men, throwing themselves nimbly, climb aboard with a gleam in the eyes. Are they not escaping from the civilizing Christians? The women are afraid; they are the last left in the barges, weeping, letting out cries of distress, getting up with difficulty, staggering, falling back on the benches, readjusting their yamaks, clinging to the boatmen, climbing up the ladder while trembling, collapsing on the deck, bursting with laughter akin to a sob; then languidly lying down in piles in a corner, vanquished in advance, gracious, charming, indifferent to everything.[107]

RESETTLEMENT: ANATOLIA, THE NEW HOMELAND

The very real possibility of an epidemic wiping out Istanbul's population and placing the city in an international quarantine, the threat of another uprising of refugees against the government, and a realization that the refugees would not be able to return to their Balkan villages forced the Ottoman government to become serious about resettlement.

At first resettlement efforts were completely disorganized, and a great many suffered and even died on account of this. The main goal was just to get them out of the capital, where they posed a danger for the state. A traveler to Istanbul at this time related her brother's eyewitness account of one of these ferries taking refugees from Istanbul to Asia:

> Tom . . . had been to see what he described to me as "one of the most terrible scenes of human misery that can be imagined." The "Asia," a ship of 900 tons burden, was laden with two thousand refugees—men, women, and children—all bound for Chanak, Smyrna, Beyrout, and Larnaka. It was impossible to move on either of the decks without treading on some one. The poor creatures had no covering, no food, no room to move, and the ship itself was without ballast. The captain seemed half an idiot; the

> crew could understand no language but their own, which was unintelligible to everybody else.... Several died last night, and Tom said he felt sure many more deaths must shortly follow.[108]

The state transported refugees to Asian shores with few preparations for their upkeep after disembarkation. The first refugees to be shipped off to Anatolia suffered immensely:

> The effects of the war are being felt disastrously in Asia.... In the mosques of Istanbul and in the large fields where they camped, the refugees from the Balkans and Rhodopes were dying from hunger. In Asia, they were continuing to die; it's a pity to see. The Ottoman Government contents itself to transport them on its ships from the European side to the Asian side; and when it drops them off on the bank, it worries itself no more about them as if they never existed. At Brousse [Bursa] from time to time some handouts are made in the mosques, that's it. Across the countryside the fever and deprivations of all sorts continue to decimate these miserable people, whom the Christian and civilizing policy of Russia systematically expelled from Bulgaria and Roumelia.[109]

Over time organization improved and deliberate policies, with intended and unintended consequences, took shape. These settlement policies became increasingly well thought out and even ideologically based. Their clear purpose was to increase the security of the state by settling refugees in strategically important areas, such as at the opening of the Dardanelles or on the border with Bulgaria, as well as to move unwanted elements, such as the Circassians, far away from the capital.

Anatolia, which is now considered to be the heartland of the Turkish Republic, constituted a neglected, backward, and depopulated part of the empire. In fact, Sultan Abdülhamid II was influenced by reports emanating from Kastamonu and Ankara about the weakening of the empire there due to its decreasing Muslim population.[110]

The empire's economic and population strengths had been in the Balkans. Yet in view of the loss of a large chunk of the Balkan territories and the influx of Muslim refugees, a potential change in the fate of Anatolia was visible. The refugees began to be viewed as a means to repopulate and ultimately rejuvenate the economically backward Anatolian provinces of the empire, which would subsequently be seen as the Turkish homeland. In fact, the very notion of the vatan was produced in part by the existence of so many displaced people whose lands were forever lost to them. The inalienability of such lands was taken for granted, so the notion of a homeland acquired a new appreciation. As a *Basiret* journalist put it, "The Muhacirs' longing for their homeland [*vatan*] cannot be compensated by any gift that we here possess."[111] Moreover, Muslims now had a clear understanding that the continuation of their culture and faith was tied to territory, which was henceforth seen as being under threat.[112]

In the years surrounding the Russo-Turkish War of 1877–1878 movements of people caused by war originated not only in Bulgaria but in Bosnia and the Caucasus as well. This fact complicates efforts to identify with precision the quantitative dimensions of the multiethnic immigration and settlement of Anatolia. Rather than being the first refugees settled in Anatolia, these immigrants from Bulgaria were part of a longer-term trend. Their impact, however, would probably be the most significant in terms of affecting the state. What was clear to a European traveler in 1878 was also becoming clear to the Ottoman government:

> Yet, to what great work does this tremendous exodus seem to invite the Turkish government! If ever the project of Lamartine about the regeneration of Asia, a project much less chimerical than one normally thinks, should be fulfilled, is it not today? All that Anatolia is missing are the hands to work its wastelands, which are without number, these lands of a prodigious wealth, fallow for centuries.
>
> For now, here are those hands; the hardest-working farmers, the most sober laborers of Eastern Rumelia and Bulgaria, the Russians chase them, expel them as Muslims, as infidels, as barbarians. Let the Porte give these expatriates all the uncultivated fields of Anatolia; may it consecrate all its remaining resources for their proper settlement and may the palace continue to take them in, and from the very defeat of Turkey may come forth her regeneration. The banishment of Muslims from Europe by

> Russia would be for the Ottoman Empire what the revocation of the Edict of Nantes once was for England and Prussia.[113]

Utilizing ferries and a poor train network, refugees sent to Anatolia were primarily settled in the coastal towns along the Black, Marmara, Aegean, and Mediterranean seas, in western Anatolia, and on the central plateau. Bursa's population, for example, doubled between 1876 and 1906, while İzmir received some fifty thousand refugees.[114]

The government was concerned with finding land that could be used for farming and herding by the refugee immigrants. Refugee families played the role of pioneers in erecting villages and cities in Anatolia that, once created, were populated by larger numbers of incoming immigrants. Immigrants were given on average about twenty-six acres of land per household (often in malarial marshes or rocky wastelands, as the best lands, as a rule, were already occupied), seed, animals, and money for farm equipment. The refugee immigrants often had to wait long periods in difficult conditions while houses were constructed by themselves or through the contributions of local governments. Only after the war in Crete did the government actually prepare housing in advance of the refugees' arrival.[115] After 1878, due to an increasing scarcity of good land, they were also directed to migrant districts in towns and cities.[116]

The acclimatization of refugees to their new homeland was a long process full of great disappointment and hard labor. The government was late in realizing the arduous path to tapping the fecundity of the Anatolian soil:

> They [the government] thought they were in possession of a new country, where the human plant would, as soon as transplanted, send out deep-feeding roots, where the slightest work would be immediately rewarded a hundredfold; they didn't want to see the long years of patience and effort that would be required of the immigrants, before the first harvest would furnish them with their daily bread alone.[117]

The Balkan immigrants were concerned with equality and justice among themselves and thus often took responsibility for the division of farmlands. This resulted in common farm plots shaped in rectangles, as they were easier to measure and compare. In dividing the land, "with a string, a few older men measured equal widths along an old path, for which lots were then cast."[118] After time, as some immigrants were more successful than others, land was redistributed in favor of the rich.

While the Bulgarian state was busy changing place-names from Turkish names to more Bulgarian-sounding ones, Anatolian toponyms were being coined. The refugees founded new villages and gave them place-names based on the names of their abandoned villages in Bulgaria, the names of sultans (such as Mecidiye, Hamidiye, Selimiye, and Osmaniye), or aspects that clearly identified the village, such as Muhacirköy (Immigrantville).

The refugees were settled in urban sites only after 1878, often in isolated quarters or city outskirts. The three major cities that absorbed refugee immigrants were Istanbul, İzmir, and Ankara. By one estimate, 40 percent of refugees settled in these three cities alone.[119]

In the formulation of its settlement policies, the government was clearly concerned with the assimilation of the refugees and carried out policies to that end. For example, steps were taken to weaken the organizational capacity of incoming refugee groups, such as separating leaders, whether tribal chiefs, Sufi heads, or village ağas from their flocks. Generally speaking, because the Turks and Pomaks of Bulgaria were not tribal and therefore had no chief figure, the government preferred to treat them as households. When visible leaders existed, the government induced them to settle in Istanbul with pensions, stipends, awards, and other gifts and honors. Sufi leaders were also targeted for separation from their orders, because the government worried that Sufi orders had the potential not only to divide the loyalty of incoming refugees but also to hinder their assimilation and even create conflicts among the various Sufi orders as well.[120]

Perhaps the most important factor in weakening older forms of patronage was that the very basis of such relations—land—no longer existed in Anatolia. That is to say, with households being given plots of land, their dependency on and subordination to powerful landholding interests disintegrated.[121] The state's gift of land to the refugees was a clear factor in binding them to the state. Freed from subservience to a large landowner, the refugee immigrants created village assemblies that were a novelty in Anatolia.[122]

The efforts of the government to assimilate the refugees and co-opt their leaders into the system were not altogether novel: they were founded on similar unity policies that the government had used with communal leaders in Anatolia, Syria, and the Arabian Peninsula.[123]

In order not to overburden local villages, but with an effect that would obviously speed up assimilation, the state attempted to send no more than four immigrant households to one village. However, some immigrants insisted on staying together as their original communities. In these cases the state cut their food rations.[124] Such negotiations between the state and immigrants appear not to have been altogether uncommon. One group of Turkish immigrants from Bulgaria was sent to Syria by the state, but they decided to leave the lands given to them there and traveled to Antalya and petitioned the state to allow them to settle there. The state consented on the conditions that the locals agreed to this and that the immigrants paid their own resettlement expenses.[125]

Refugees were generally forbidden to move from the areas they were assigned to settle, although that appears to have happened quite often when they were sent to areas where conditions were miserable. Hunger, poor land, and strife with the locals and nomads caused some refugees to attempt to return to their homelands, but the Ottoman government discouraged such efforts with offers of provisions and housing.[126]

The government was also somewhat conscious of the diversity of the refugees, and the sultan encouraged reforms that would dilute ethnic divisions and strengthen solidarity among Muslims.[127] The government's refugee settlement policy stipulated the dispersion of non-Turkish Muslims so that they would not exceed 5 to 10 percent of the population in a given area.[128] No such effort was made to minimize interreligious tensions. In fact, the state made deliberate attempts to settle refugees in ways that would dilute the percentage of non-Muslims in areas where they were high.

Despite the intention to increase Muslim solidarity, the arrival of refugees in established villages created resentment among the natives. These resentments had an economic foundation, as the already poor inhabitants saw scarce government resources being diverted to the newly arriving refugees.[129] Local governments were often required to raise money that would be spent on aiding the implantation of the arriving refugees, leading to disputes about land. In addition, contentions between settling refugees and nomadic tribes arose, especially in western and southern

Anatolia, where the land was more fertile. Competing claims to property and usage rights between these groups caused the state to develop a clearer policy on immigration and citizenship.[130]

The government saw the refugee immigration as an opportunity to increase its efforts to sedentarize the empire's nomads. One means of doing so was by placing villages along the migratory routes of nomadic tribes with the hope of forcing them to give up their lifestyles. The disputes between tribes and settled refugees at times even escalated to the point of requiring the deployment of government forces to protect the settlers.[131] Refugee immigrant villages, autochthonous villages, and nomadic winter grounds for a while existed separately and apart but gradually opened up to each other. The groups learned from one another and adopted certain practices and technologies in agriculture and construction.

Abdülhamid II was deeply involved with issues relating to the refugees and their settlement. The refugee commission was almost directly under his authority. Its functions were interministerial, and the sultan appointed its members. One of the sultan's close advisors, Izzet Paşa, was a member of the commission, which indicates the sultan's close attention to its functions.[132] The sultan was quite concerned about security issues, especially his own, which might explain some of his interest in decapitating the refugees of their leadership as well as settling them out of Istanbul with an eye to minimizing ethnic tensions. While there is no pattern that accounts for every settlement, we can say that in general the refugees were permanently settled, thereby taking them out of a liminal state. This had a large impact on the weak formation of a social memory and group identity.

The refugees themselves were not mere bystanders in these processes. It is clear that they were not keen on moving to Asia, in view of the fact that many of them attempted returns to the Balkans. Moreover, they did not always accept the designated settlement areas. However, through negotiation with the state and because they had been deprived of their erstwhile leaders, ultimately they were settled and assimilated.

While state policies affected refugees, the state in turn was deeply affected by the refugees. The very complexion of the empire changed. For the first time in its history Istanbul became a majority Muslim city, and the empire itself became far more Muslim than it had ever been. For example, before the war Muslims constituted 60 percent of the empire's 35 million people. Following the Treaty of Berlin, Muslims were nearly

75 percent of the much-reduced population of 17 million.[133] By 1880 the population of the Ottoman Empire had reached 80 percent Muslim, and over the next twenty years hundreds of thousands more Muslims would immigrate to Ottoman lands.[134]

This demographic change had a large impact on the development and promotion of a pan-Islamic policy, which had been advocated by such figures as Jamal ad-Din Afghan. It became a staple of Sultan Abdülhamid II's domestic and international political platforms, because it became the easiest ideology around which the population could be mobilized. The sultan was apparently touched by the desperate stories of the refugees and felt solidarity with them and increasingly with Muslims in general. He viewed his role as caliph with renewed importance and promoted this title internationally.[135] This reflected a shift in the legitimacy of the empire; the legitimacy for governing that had theretofore been based on the notion of dynasty was now predicated on religious terms.

The state's refugee commission was given the responsibility of coordinating and overseeing the settlement of the refugees. In so doing, the commission divided Anatolia into seven regions. It designated where refugee immigrants would be settled and in theory provided rations for their survival and sent delegations to make sure that the plans were being implemented successfully. The commission expanded its mandate, so that by the First World War it was in charge of determining questions related to citizenship.[136] This role meant that the refugee commission eventually became an official participant in the question of identity within the Ottoman Empire.[137]

After the Crimean War the Ottoman state encouraged immigration to its territories regardless of religion. Immigrant families were given plots of land with exemptions from taxes and conscription. The exemption was for six years for those choosing to settle in Rumelia, whereas it was twelve years for those moving to Anatolia. As early as 1880 the Ottoman government began to change its immigration policy in favor of Muslim immigration.[138] By 1893 the sultan had embraced an exclusive immigration policy: henceforth only Muslim immigrants would be accepted. He outlined his reasoning thus:

> The time when we embraced intimately those of different religions is long past. We shall accept only immigrants who are

> our conationals and those who share the same religious beliefs. We must pay attention to strengthening the Turks. We should see to it that the surplus Muslim population of Bulgaria, Bosnia and Herzegovina is systematically brought and settled here. . . . We must strengthen the Turkish elements in Rumilia and especially in Anatolia and mold the Kurds and make them part of us. My predecessors who occupied the Turkish throne committed a grave error in not Ottomanizing [converting] the Slavs.[139]

The very name of the government commission dealing with the refugees was changed to Muhacirin-i Islamiye Komisyonu (Muslim Immigrant Commission), thus reflecting its newly minted Muslim nature.[140]

Balkan immigrants to Anatolia imported their way of doing things, leaving an impact on the lifestyle and economic sphere of Anatolia. They introduced new farming techniques and technologies such as growing potatoes, horse carts, better ploughs, dual-slanted tile roofs (rather than the customary local flat roof), and an acquaintance with railway transportation.[141]

Their experience with modernity was not only tied to railroads and ploughs but also to the fact that the Bulgarian Muslims had experienced the modernizing reforms of Mithat Paşa. Moreover, Kemal Karpat argues that the incoming refugees spurred the development of a middle class in Anatolia, given that they arrived in Anatolia without assets yet were very interested in regaining their previous status. Thus, through industry and ambition, they sought economic gain.[142]

CONCLUSION

The epic movement of people from Bulgaria to Istanbul and other parts of the remaining Ottoman lands had an impact on the larger population, who now realized the dire straits that the empire was in. The feeling that the empire was in precipitous decline was unavoidable and heartbreaking. The refugees brought with them appalling tales fraught with death and outrage. A new understanding of what the nationalist idea implied was developing in the makeshift refugee centers throughout the empire's capital and major port cities. Had the British fleet not loomed ominously in the waters just outside of Istanbul, Russia most likely would have attacked the city. We can only imagine with dread how the already bad situation could have deteriorated further.

Migration is the untold story of Turkey. Few might now think of the minarets of Istanbul in the same way as the Statue of Liberty, but countless people fleeing hearth and home, starting with Spain's Jews, have been greeted by the welcome sight of the Hagia Sophia and its minaret(s) overlooking the Sea of Marmara. Certainly, this aspect of the city deserves more attention. The situation inside of Hagia Sophia was especially heart-rending. It is hard to think of a single edifice of such magnitude and importance that has been the site of a similar drama on such a scale. Yet today, even within Hagia Sophia itself, no reminder of this episode is given.

The refugees were permanently settled in a relatively short time frame because their presence in the capital posed challenges to the health of the city and the security of the government. The final blow was struck by the unwillingness of the Berlin Conference to consider their plight and their return home. The need to resettle the refugees necessitated the development of state capacity to do so. Although uncoordinated at first, resettlement took on certain characteristics over time that sped up the assimilation of the refugees to their new homes. As chapter 5 shows, this assimilation became an important factor in the nonemergence of a trenchant memory or a separate identity.

Five

APHASIA AND AMNESIA

The Mohammedans have made the flight of the Prophet their chronological starting point. The past few weeks have witnessed a flight of another kind which must impress itself as deeply in the Moslem mind as ever the Hegira has done.

Western Daily Press, February 5, 1878

The refugees are a national reminder of our lost country.

Atatürk (quoted in Akçam, *From Empire to Republic*)

He had a past and was going to die and his memory was going to die. And another voice, the collective voice said, "We will outlive this individual and we will project a world of words with language and memory which will go on."

Carlos Fuentes (*Paris Review* 82 [Winter 1981])

Thirty-four years after the epic clash between the Russians and the Ottomans, the Balkans again erupted in war. This time the Balkan nation-states of Greece, Serbia, and Bulgaria colluded to declare war against the Ottoman Empire with the aim of expanding their territories. Things went badly for the Turks, who were already fighting off the Italian invasion of Libya, and it seemed, if but for a moment, that Bulgaria might capture Istanbul—a prospect that seriously worried the Russians, who still wanted the city for themselves. The Balkan Wars lasted from the autumn of 1912 to the summer of 1913 and re-created many of the humanitarian disasters seen in 1877–1878.

The Balkan Wars caught the world's attention, especially among Muslims, who, faced with the onslaught of imperialism and a gradual loss of sovereignty, were filled with a sense of gloom and doom. Most of the Muslim world had been gobbled up by European colonialism, but the Ottoman Empire was one of the few remaining sovereign Muslim states, which served to enhance the importance of the caliph residing in Istanbul. One person who was following events closely was Ahmed Shawqī, a 44-year-old Egyptian poet who was a formative figure in the development of Egyptian nationalism. He came to be known as the Prince of Poets in Egypt, but Shawqī was a literal embodiment of the Ottoman Empire, descended from Turks, Greeks, Kurds, and Circassians. His lineage made him fond of the Ottoman Empire, and he wrote many poems relating to Turkey. When the Ottomans lost Macedonia in the first Balkan War, Shawqī composed an elegy for the Ottomans in the Balkans, which he named, symbolically, the *New Andalusia*. The expulsion of Muslims from both sides of Europe was a theme ripe for comparison, and Shawqī gave voice to it in his first poetic mention of Spain, a country to which he would be exiled only two years later:

> Farewell, sister of Andalusia,[1]
> Islam and the caliphate have fallen from thee
> The Crescent moon has gone down from thy sky.
> Would that the heavens had folded up,
> And darkness enveloped all the globe.[2]
> Two nations have been afflicted by two wounds.
> One now flows, the other is ancient but still unhealed.
> Through you both the Muslims were fulfilled,
> In you both calamity was buried and the saber concealed.
> The grief of Andalusia remains unconsoled,
> yet again the Muslims prepare to don black for you, sister of
>   Andalusia.
> Between her fall and yours, many days have passed,
> some to our liking, others to our displeasure.
> The centuries have slipped by like a night,

and the conquering empires have been interrupted
like dreams.
Time does not spare the overseers of kingdoms,
if they are distracted, the blame must fall on them.
Oh Macedonia, the Muslims form a great tribe.
What is the situation on your territory of our aunts
and uncles?
It was our last home in the West; it has now disappeared.
Greetings to the Ottomans who are still found there.
Time imposes upon us the same attitude as Ṭāriq:[3]
Despair was behind you, and hope ahead.[4]

While Islam was brought into Europe in three main thrusts—by the Arabs through Sicily and the Iberian Peninsula, the Tatars in Russia along the Volga and in the Crimea, and the Turks in the Balkans—in the nineteenth century only the Muslims in the Ottoman Balkans retained their independence and remained in their lands. The Russian expansion to the east swallowed up the Tatars, requiring conversions to Christianity at first and leaving Muslim life precarious until Catherine the Great's edict on the tolerance of religion. The Reconquista of the Iberian peninsula took centuries to complete but nevertheless resulted in the banishment of Muslims from the lands of the Catholic kings.

The idea of the Spanish Reconquista as historic precedent for the demise of the Ottoman Balkans occurred to more than just Ahmed Shawqī. Yet for a long period the glories and demise of Islamic Spain had receded from memory, except among a few of the exiles. Libraries of Arab writings in Spain were burned, and many of the beauties of Islamic architecture were leveled. The learning of Arabic was denounced, and Spanish historians, availing themselves blindly of only the most bigoted sources, came to look upon the Muslim period as a dark hour ruled by "a ruthless warlike nation, hostile to science and polite literature."[5] Their national myths implied a built-in hostility toward Islam. Spain, they believed, had saved Europe from the barbarians. Only in the nineteenth century was interest in this chapter in the life of Islam renewed, at first by the publication of some Romantic and unscholarly works and then by the rediscovery, translation, and reprinting of a vast survey of Andalusia written by the Ottoman-born Arab scholar Aḥmad ibn Muḥammad al-Maqqarī (ca. 1578–1632). Al-Maqqarī was born in Tlemcen, which was then part of the Ottoman Empire, but spent his youth in Morocco, where he came to know the history and literature of Andalusia. His book, more than any other, restored awareness of the Muslim history of Andalusia.[6] Typical of traditional rhyming Arabic couplet-titles is the title of his work *Nafḥu al-Ṭīb min Ghosni al-Andalusī ar-Rattīb/wa Tarīkh Lisānu ad-Dīn Ibni al-Khaṭṭib* (Fragrant Smells from the Tender Shoots of Andalusia/ and the Biography of the Tongue of Religion, [Vizier] Ibn al-Khaṭṭib). It spans the entirety of the Islamic presence in, as al-Maqqarī puts it, "Andalus (may God restore it entire to the Muslims!)."[7] After a pilgrimage to Mecca, al-Maqqarī went to Damascus, a city that he quickly fell in love with. He decided to stay there longer to contemplate the beauty of the city: "While we passed the evenings in eloquent and learned conversations ... such among the company as were eager for science, and covetous of information, began to inquire about Andalus, and to entreat us to speak of its fertility and productions, to praise its excellences and advantages, to record passages of its history."[8]

Reluctant to leave his new friendships in Damascus, al-Maqqarī set off in 1628 for Cairo, where he could have access to the documents that he needed to compose his history of Andalusia. The work that he produced, however, was not widely circulated and gathered dust in Middle Eastern archives until being translated and published in London in 1840 and subsequently republished in Arabic in Holland in 1855.[9] Soon other books were written about Moorish Spain and then published in Arabic and Turkish. Throughout the Muslim world interest in the bygone glories of Islamic Iberia blossomed, and Abdülhamid II sent emissaries to Spain to track down more documents in 1886.

The demise of Muslim life in Andalusia, as in the Ottoman Balkans, was spasmodic and took place over centuries. The Muslims of Spain were gradually forced out of Europe into Africa. As Andalusia shrank, southern Spain and North Africa welcomed refugees. When Seville fell in 1248 after an 18-month siege, the emaciated Muslims were allowed to leave with what they could carry. Many of them took boats to North Africa or made the 100-mile trek to Granada. The fact that many Spanish Muslims converted to Christianity while continuing to profess Islam in secret and became known as Moriscos is widely known. Less well known are the many other Muslims who were allowed to remain openly

Muslim in reconquered parts of Spain under certain arrangements, called *fueros*, which held some resemblance to (and were possibly inspired by) the millet system. These Muslims were known as *mudéjares* (Turkish "Müdeccenler").[10]

The seizure of Constantinople in 1453 put Europe on edge, and Spain was eager to deal a blow against Islam, which it did in 1492 with its defeat of Granada. But the promises made to the defeated Muslims were quickly broken. By 1525 Muslims faced a choice of conversion or emigration, which required the payment of a tax, meaning that baptism was the only option for many.[11] By the late sixteenth century a major rivalry between Spain and the Ottoman Empire for control of the Mediterranean Sea was developing. The Moriscos were suspected of sympathy for the Turks, who had now moved as far as the Algerian coast. Finally Phillip II made the definitive decision to banish the Moriscos themselves, which was carried out from 1609 to 1614. According to estimates, nearly 300,000 people were expelled.[12] Any Moriscos that remained after that time faced the horrors of the Spanish Inquisition.

At the end of his work al-Maqqarī describes the siege and capitulation of Granada (which was attended by Christopher Columbus), the forceful conversions to Christianity of the remaining Muslims despite promises to protect their religion, the fateful decision by many Andalusian Muslims to quit Spain for Africa, and the difficulties that they faced in their migration:

> They were ultimately expelled from the territory of Andalus,—an event which took place in our times, in the year 1017 of the Hijra (A.D. 1610). Many thousands of the unfortunate emigrants went to Fez, thousands to Telemsán from Wahrán (Oran); the greater part took the road to Túnis. Few, however, reached the place of their destination; for they were assailed on the road by the Arabs and such as fear not God, and they were plundered and ill-treated, especially on the road to Fez and Telemsán. . . . A few went to Constantinople, to Egypt, Syria, and to other countries where Islam is predominant, and settled there, inhabiting now, as we have been told, the same places at which they first fixed their residence. God, indeed[,] is the master of all lands and dominions, and gives them to whomsoever he pleases.[13]

Austreibung der Mauren. Zeichnung von Conrad Ermisch.

5.1. *Expulsion of the Moors* by Conrad Ermisch (1855–1888).

The interest being generated about Islamic Spain coincided with the decline of the Ottoman Balkans; indeed, the line from Andalusia to Rumelia was visible. Contemporaries noted the similarities. In 1854 Ami Boué, an Austrian geologist who had done much work in the Balkans, alluded to the ethnic cleansing in fifteenth-century Spain, sounding an alarm about the fate of the Muslims in the Balkans:

> People often talk in the West about transporting all the Turks, in other words Muslims, to Asia in order to turn Turkey

> in Europe into a uniquely Christian empire. This would be a decree as inhumane as the expulsion of the Jews from Spain or of the Protestants from France, and indeed scarcely feasible since the Europeans always forget that in Turkey in Europe the Muslims are mostly Slavs or Albanians, whose right to the land is as ancient as that of their Christian compatriots.[14]

A Serbian scholar looking back saw the expulsion of Muslims from the Balkans very much in light of what happened to the Iberian Moors during the demise of Andalusia: "The liberation of Bulgarian lands in 1878 has in many cases very certainly taken on the trappings of a Spanish Reconquista. It provoked, as elsewhere, during each loss of Ottoman territory in Europe, mass migrations and emigrations of the Muslim populations of Bulgaria towards Turkey."[15]

More often than not, however, the Turks have failed to receive a sympathetic comparison with their coreligionists at the other end of Europe. In the preface to his eulogistic 1886 book on the Moors of Spain, Stanley Lane-Poole warned against comparisons of the Turkish Balkans and Muslim Andalusia:

> Those who are inclined to infer, from the picture here given of Moorish civilization that Mohammedanism is always on the side of culture and humanity, must turn to another volume in this series . . . to see what Mohammedan barbarism means. The fall of Granada happened within forty years of the conquest of Constantinople; but the gain to Islam in the east made no amends for the loss to Europe in the west: The Turks were incapable of founding a second Cordova.[16]

The romanticization of Moorish Spain sharply contrasts with the vilification of the Turkish Balkans. Neither view is soundly based, for the tolerance witnessed in both was based on pragmatism: a top-down arrangement that took into account the reality of three religions—Islam, Christianity, and Judaism—and diverse ethnicities populating the same territory. Discrimination existed in both cases, but so did autonomy for the communities. Naturally, intercommunal relations experienced ups and downs, as the stability of the system was tested by feuds for power among the Muslim leaders and challenges posed from abroad. Yet both Andalusia and the Ottoman Balkans were centers of coexistence in a comparatively intolerant Europe. From Córdoba to Constantinople, beautiful works of architecture and poetry were created, words were exchanged between lexicons, and thinkers pondered deep questions.[17] In both cases a more exclusive outlook overthrew the systems of coexistence, and in both cases waves of refugees were produced who with great nostalgia lamented their losses. The poet Abū al-Baqā' al-Rundī (1204–1285) composed the following after the fall of Seville:

> Ask Valencia what became of Murcia,
> And where is Jativa, or where is Jaen?
> Where is Cordoba, the seat of great learning,
> And how many scholars of high repute remain there?
> And where is Seville, the home of mirthful gatherings
> On its great river, cooling and brimful with water?
> These cities were the pillars of the country:
> Can a building remain when the pillars are missing?
> The white wells of ablution are weeping with sorrow,
> As a lover does when torn from his beloved:
> They weep over the remains of dwellings devoid of Muslims,
> Despoiled of Islam, now peopled by infidels!
> Those mosques have now been changed into churches,
> Where the bells are ringing and crosses are standing.
> Even the mihrabs weep, though made of cold stone,
> Oh heedless one, this is Fate's warning to you:
> If you slumber, Fate always stays awake.[18]

WHILE MEMORY SLEEPS, HISTORY REPEATS

In reference to his project to rid Europe of the Jews, Adolf Hitler reportedly quipped, "Who, after all, is today speaking of the destruction of the Armenians?" This quotation has served Armenian nationalist and diaspora claims that their removal from Anatolia was the fulcrum in the learning curve of numerous ethnic cleansings, culminating in the Holocaust. In other words, the Turks taught genocide to the Nazis. Andrew

Bell-Fialkoff goes a step further and cites the Turks in the nineteenth century as the first perpetrators of ethnic cleansing as a state goal, this time against Armenians and Greeks.[19]

Hitler's purported statement also reveals that the fate of Armenians in eastern Anatolia had been widely forgotten at that time. Since then, however, what once had been left at the wayside of memory has been pulled back into the larger public consciousness. Armenian identity, especially in the diaspora, is firmly tied to a sense of victimhood arising from those events. Without question, traumatic experiences can serve to cohere a community, yet those same experiences can be crippling as well. Victimhood may be leaned on like a crutch, even when the time for healing and moving on is long overdue.

Other groups too, such as Jews and Palestinians, are closely tied to their respective national traumas, while the tragedies of others pass into oblivion. When asked today "Who today remembers the Balkan Turks?" few will answer in the affirmative. The harrowing experiences of massacre, flight, refuge, and resettlement discussed in the preceding chapters are virtually unknown in the West as well as in Bulgaria and the rest of the Balkans. Most surprising of all, though, is that a general ignorance about these events prevails in Turkey today.

The Russo-Turkish War of 1877–1878 was one of two most important European wars of the second half of the nineteenth century, the other being the Franco-Prussian War of 1870. In the former the Russians reached the walls of Constantinople, in the latter the Prussians approached the walls of Paris. The major ramifications of Russo-Turkish War throughout Europe are reason enough for it to be better known. As a result of the war, the British negotiated the takeover of Cyprus from Ottoman rule; Serbia, Romania, and Bulgaria gained independence from the Ottomans; Romania acquired Dobruja in exchange for southern Bessarabia; and Bosnia was annexed by Austria as part of an agreement with Russia, which set the foundation for conflict leading directly to the First World War.

In western treatments of the Balkans, what happened to the Muslim inhabitants is usually not mentioned and the Turkish Empire remains, according to the general narration, a cruel and barbarous one. For example, while making no mention whatsoever of Turkish victims at the end of the Ottoman period, the traveling scholar Robert Kaplan's influential light-history book states that the Ottoman Empire died "amid a welter of cruelties directed against a host of small nations, struggling to break free."[20] If Muslim suffering and exodus are alluded to, this is only done fleetingly and with a transparent scorn for the scholars who dare mention them. Justin McCarthy's work on the Ottoman Muslims' fate in the nineteenth and twentieth centuries is considered unbalanced by Mark Mazower.[21] Stanford Shaw, according to Micha Glenny, "protests a little too much" in pointing out Bulgarian massacres of Muslims during the April Uprising, which likely caused more deaths than the subsequent Bulgarian Horrors, to which Glenny devotes significant detail.[22]

Sympathy toward Ottoman Muslim victims is often treated as a vice, challenging Jacques Semelin's assertion that in cases of massacre morality rests with those denouncing ethnic cleansings.[23] In the West generally, and in the Balkans definitively, the Turk is condemned to be the perpetual perpetrator and Turkish suffering is forever nullified or, at best, inserted as a footnote. In contrast, the Ottomans' mistreatment of and violence against their Christian populations attracts a great deal more attention, sympathy, and ink in the annals dealing with the wars accompanying the end of the Ottomans and the birth of the Balkan nation-states. Three nineteenth-century episodes in particular have gained a foothold in the Western image of the Turks: the Greek War of Independence, the Bulgarian Horrors, and the ethnic conflict with Armenians in the 1890s and 1915. Whereas Europeans have insisted that the violence associated with these events was deliberate state policy, they simply cannot contemplate or accept the internecine nature of these conflicts.[24] This is in stark contrast to the way the Russo-Turkish War of 1877–1878 has been portrayed: a fratricidal, bloody Balkan mess.

In the Balkan states the subject of the violent Ottoman Muslim expulsion from Bulgaria, as well as from Greece, Serbia, and elsewhere, has not yet been broached in any substantial way. The fact that the Ottoman architectural heritage in these nation-states was often destroyed following the disappearance of large Muslim populations had the intended consequence of wiping clean the historical slate, so to speak. In Bulgaria the state-led project of demolishing Muslim sites under the guise of "city-planning" means that outside of more densely Muslim areas the physical reminders of a different past, which elicit questions about that very past, are much reduced. Consequently, visitors and locals have little idea of a

Muslim existence before national independence. This is a clear example of what Mirko Grmek meant when he created the term "memoricide" to describe the effort not only to eliminate certain people from a given territory but "to annihilate any trace that might recall their erstwhile presence (schools, religious buildings and so on)."[25]

Innumerable specimens of Ottoman architecture have been destroyed from Hungary all the way to Edirne (the ruins of the sultan's summer palace are a prime example). This only adds to the myth that the Ottomans were inherently destructive as opposed to constructive.[26] Ironically, it is often the superb products of Ottoman creation that now draw tourists. Plovdiv, for instance, with its charming Muslim quarter, was named the 2019 European Capital of Culture. Yet Balkan nationalists are still consumed by a hatred for anything bespeaking a Muslim past. Today there is only one functioning mosque in each of the two major Balkan capitals, Belgrade and Sofia, while in Athens there is none at all, despite large Muslim populations augmented by immigrants. Proposals to build new mosques in these cities have been met with vehement protests and even attacks on Muslim residents (for example, in Belgrade in 2008, Sofia in 2011, Athens in 2013).

Balkan attitudes about the Muslim past are shaped by the historical narrative of a Turkish yoke, which perpetuates a victim mentality among Balkan Christians and thereby justifies any means (with an underlying implication of a justified violence) that might have (but will not be admitted to have) been employed to eliminate the Muslims from these territories. This is something of a rhetorical legerdemain, wherein the crime is denied and absolved at the same time. Here is how one Bulgarian historian treated the subject:

> The deep-reaching social upheaval blended in with stormy ethno-demographic changes. . . . The Turkish masses, aware of the coming end of their unreined supremacy, and unable to swallow the fact that they would have to live from then on as equals to yesterday's slaves of theirs, chose to leave altogether with the withdrawing Turkish forces. Quite a few of them had in the past killed Bulgarians, robbed their homes, raped their wives and daughters and burned their villages. The hour of atonement was nearing, and they preferred to flee rather than face retribution.[27]

This is very much along the lines of what George Orwell said concerning nationalists' penchant for looking the other way: "The nationalist not only does not disapprove of atrocities committed by his own side, he has a remarkable capacity for not even hearing about them."[28]

A typical attitude was on display when I participated in a conference on nationalities at Columbia University in 2011. After my presentation, a Greek woman asked without concealing her hostility, "Why should I feel sorry for these Turks? Were they not, after all, occupiers?" Indeed, rare is the nation that enters willingly into a serious conversation about the ethnic cleansing that took place at the founding of its state. Throughout the Americas little enthusiasm has been shown for delving into the destruction of the Native American populations. Nor have other nation-states eagerly embraced a reflection upon the violent homogenization projects that were part and parcel of their coming into being. The denials and silence within the Balkan region itself are not at all surprising.

Given the power of the narrative of victimhood which finds representatives in the Middle East (Jews, Armenians, and Palestinians, among others), we might expect that the massacre and exodus of Muslims during the Russo-Turkish War of 1877–1878 would form an integral part of a larger Turkish narrative. Furthermore, considering the enduring bitterness and endless claims and condemnation of Turkish crimes against the non-Muslim subject peoples as well as the incessant reproaches from the West about the fate of the Armenians, Turkish victimhood would seem to be a fitting response. In fact, in 1997 Turkey erected a monument to the Muslim victims of the "genocide" committed by Armenians in Iğdır, Turkey,[29] showing that Turkey is certainly not above the politicization of victimhood when it is useful. To this day awareness in Turkey of the human tragedy that was a crucial part of Bulgarian independence and Ottoman collapse is, apart from some specialized scholars, generally nonexistent. These events and sufferings have for the most part been collectively forgotten. In light of the scale of these events, which was by any standard massive, and their large role in shaping Ottoman/Turkish society and its political orientation, such forgetfulness is baffling. As mentioned in chapter 4, these refugees increased the Muslim proportion of the population in Istanbul and Anatolia, thus plowing the field for the dissemination of Abdülhamid's pan-Islamic policies. Moreover, the loss of Bulgaria meant that Anatolia was by default the new heart of the empire, and thus in this period can be seen the beginnings of its rebirth as the new "Turkish homeland," which was so essential to the Kemalist Turkification project. Interestingly, such a refocusing of imperial sentiment was not unprecedented. After having ceded Balkan territories to the Slavs after numerous wars, the later Byzantine Empire also recentered itself on the Eastern Provinces, especially Asia Minor, which resulted in the empire's gradual orientalization.[30]

All nations have traumas: some choose to deal with them by highlighting them, while others conceal them.[31] The major premise here is that in the case of Turkey these sufferings have been forgotten. Yet proving the absence of something, such as knowledge, is theoretically impossible and quite difficult in practice. My assertion that these events are generally forgotten—that is to say, not known and as a consequence not part of the framework that makes up the Turkish national narrative and identity—is based largely on anecdotal evidence, which has been reaffirmed through an investigation of the scant offering of Turkish-language sources on the subject. While many Turks living in the Turkish Republic today may be aware of distant ancestors from Bulgaria, few of them know the reasons, time frame, or conditions of their ancestors' emigrations. The situation is changing, as discussed later in this chapter.

"Muhacir," which originally referred to those of a lower class,[32] has come to designate Turkish citizens who have migrated from the Balkans.[33] Yet for most Turks today, Bulgarian Muhacirs are the Turks who emigrated from Bulgaria in 1989 during the last days of the Bulgarian Communist regime, which tried to stay afloat through a nationalist-inspired forced assimilation project of the Muslim minorities. Outside of specialized niches in Turkish academia or the more recent phenomenon of Rumelia associations, one generally does not encounter a Turk who knows or has even heard about these events. The Turkish-language sources that do exist tend to be obscure dissertations and graduate theses not easily accessed and certainly not targeted for mass readership. Generally, the few books discussing Turks in Bulgaria primarily focus on the late Communist period with only slight reference to the period that is the topic of this book (or no mention at all).

In one such work giving scant attention to events in 1877–1878, entitled *Urumeli'nin Gözyaşları* (*The Tears of Rumelia*), the author urges his readers in the introduction not to forget Turkish sufferings in the

Balkans: "I will not forget. Do you know why I won't forget? Because they make a great effort for us to forget. Whereas they never forget a single thing, and they don't let anyone else forget either."[34] For this writer, the constant accusations of Turkish crimes in the Balkans and Anatolia have inspired a search for victimhood.

The suffering and migrations of Muslims from the Balkans to Turkey have not been promoted in Turkish education. In an interview with Nedim İpek, one of the leading Turkish scholars on migrations in the late Ottoman and Turkish Republic periods, he told me that this subject was not taught in school when he was growing up.[35] I am not talking about a complete erasure. Turks are certainly aware of the Ottoman Balkans, even though this history was, in the words of Tanil Bora, "passed over and transcended, never mentioned," and ultimately forgotten by Turkey.[36] The vast majority of Turks view defeat in the Balkans in terms of territory—that is to say, the state's loss—rather than in terms of human suffering and the separation of Muslims from their hearths and homes. In one sense, then, the Turkish view coincides with the view of the Balkan nation-states: the end of the Ottoman Empire in Europe signified nothing more than a change in administration and a redrawing of lines on a map. A paucity of knowledge, however, is not evidence of a lack of curiosity. At the same conference mentioned earlier, a Turkish audience member of Tatar descent asked, "Why is it that we Turks don't have any idea about this [the violent forced exodus of Muslims from Bulgaria]?"

Why, then, have the Turks forgotten this tragic episode? Armenians, Jews, Palestinians, and other nations have turned their collective tragedies into ongoing suffering that never allows the trauma to subside, thereby forming the nucleus of a national identity. Their refrains of "never forget" and "never again" are cynically employed, more to justify a perpetual sense of victimization in order to maintain the cohesion of the community or promote the narrow goals of community leaders than to prevent the recurrence of similar actions against other groups in a broader context. Yet the Turks have not yet done so with the suffering of 1877–1878. Why is this so and why is Turkish memory about these traumatic experiences so weak?

The remainder of this chapter suggests some answers to these questions, although documenting the stillbirth of a memory is less straightforward than documenting the massacres and migrations in the preceding chapters. The multitude of factors that constitute memory and its formation, reception, and maintenance means that clear-cut answers are unlikely. That said, I have attempted to get at the heart of the matter. While the answers posited here might appear somewhat speculative, I believe that they lead us in the right direction and offer insights, which may be valuable for comparative studies in the future. Before tackling the questions directly, I would first like to suggest a framework for thinking about collective memory.

HISTORY AND MEMORY AND FORGETTING

Someone who can forget nothing has been the motif for no small amount of philosophical speculation and numerous works of fiction. In the great Argentine writer Jorge Luis Borges's story "Funes the Memorious,"[37] for example, the main character, after falling from a blue-gray horse, contracted the onerous condition of total recall wherein he could even remember the shapes of clouds at any and every moment. Only mentioned as an irrelevant side note, Funes was also paralyzed in the accident. Yet the paralysis is clearly a metaphor—such power of memory was a curse in disguise. German philosopher Friedrich Nietzsche also believed that an individual's ability to remember everything would be debilitating. Faced with the constant recollection of meaningful and meaningless minutiae such a person would be hopelessly burdened with a surfeit of the unimportant and loss of the essential capability of abstraction. For this reason he extolled human forgetfulness as vital to life itself: "It is possible to live almost without memory, indeed to live happily, as the animals show us; but without forgetting, it is utterly impossible to live at all."[38]

Human experiences are integral to humanness itself. Hence an exploration, beyond dictionary definitions, of the vocabulary of experience in search of the deeper meanings of the words we use to talk about our past is an endeavor of great human introspection. The writer Jamaica Kincaid pondered just such a question:

> What to call the thing that happened to me and all who look like me? Should I call it history? If so, what should history mean to someone like me? Should it be an idea, should it be an open

> wound and each breath I take in and expel healing and opening the wound again and again, over and over, or is it a moment that began . . . and has come to no end yet? Is it a collection of facts, all true and precise details, and, if so, when I come across these true and precise details, what should I do, how should I feel, where should I place myself?[39]

While memory and forgetting are seen as opposites, history and memory are seen in oppositional as well as complementary terms. Both history and memory refer to the past: while History (in capitalized form) is usually seen as the true, objective past, memory is a subjective recollection of the past. With such an approach, History can never be fully realized, only approximated, because all recollection is invariably subjective. A distinction therefore exists, although not always recognized, between History and history (lowercase "h"). The latter carries an aura of authority through the consensus of historians or through state endorsement but should not be mistaken for the unattainable true History. In a sense, then, history is inevitably fashioned from memory, and an important yet not the sole arbiter in what elevates memory to history is its connection to power.[40] When compared with history, memory becomes a type of subaltern, alternative, vernacular, or contested version of the past.[41] The official version can become institutionalized and dogmatic, yet this official, formal, consensus version of the past and the vernacular, subaltern, and contested version have a mutually influential relationship. The state can hammer into people's minds the selective recollection of certain events, yet the state is not impervious to the bubbling up of memories from the people that it purports to rule. In other words, "historians make use of memories, while narrators of memory are influenced by written history."[42]

Referring to memory as a collective act may sound strange because each person in reality only has individual memories; yet, since Maurice Halbwachs's pioneering essays on collective memory, it is now widely held that memory is an individual act undertaken in a social milieu.[43] To be sure, while no two individuals can share a cortex, memories nevertheless can be shared.[44] This act of sharing and then interpreting memories is what gives memory its inherent social aspect. Indeed, in telling one's story verbally through songs, pictures, or in written form some type of reception and interpretation of these memories is required. In addition, when the state or another entity with resources gets involved, the past can be converted into monuments or through some forms of physical ceremony and reenactment, which should serve to relate some historical event or phenomenon.

All these forms of recollection presuppose a semiotic environment wherein meaning is created and conveyed via society. The past is discussed, recalled, interpreted and reinterpreted, invented, contested, rejected, restored, forgotten, and recovered all through social means in groups. Through the various and manifold social mediums a residue of knowledge about the past is inculcated in society and its members. Society, through the development of a set of cultural cues, becomes the reservoir where individuals may go to "retrieve" recollections in order to slake present curiosities, whether through the repository of cultural artifacts or through the transient resource of older yet overlapping generations.[45]

A shared past is a powerful force for uniting individuals. Memory plays an important social function by providing people with an identity and thereby playing a significant role in subsequent group formation and cohesion.[46] Yet, while members of a group may share a memory, the notion that they actually share experiences is more often than not erroneous. The binding historical experience is often not directly experienced but rather, in a sense, borrowed from predecessors or even simply attributed to them. Like the heir of a distant uncle's fortune who has not labored to acquire the wealth, the scions of both the triumphant and the downtrodden inherit a past that they did not live. Rather than a shared experience, it is the belief in a common past, especially a common origin, that is the true cohesive of the group.

Yet groups are composed of individuals with multiple identities, differing interests, and varying motivations. This means that collective memories are built upon common denominators that conceal real social and political differences symbolically.[47] The community is an imagined entity created and sustained through a collective yet unconscious agreement.[48] At times, these groups can become large enough and powerful enough to become recognized as nations; when nations acquire political power and sovereignty, a nation-state emerges. National histories are special in that they promote a moral and emotional attachment to a given territory, which becomes the motherland or homeland. Furthermore, such histories create a seemingly inevitable, if not destined, linking of a people, a territory, and a polity.[49]

By means of state power asserted though modern compulsory education systems and conscription into the armed forces, outlying groups are brought under the national umbrella through their acceptance of the state's language and version of history or their removal from territorial boundaries or in some cases are allowed to remain as a minority group. The expansion of the nation occurs in two directions: outward to assimilate peripheral and minority groups whose intransigence may cause a reevaluation of the nation's common points and onward to connect new generations to the nation. By binding present generations to past ones, an identity as well as a sense of a place in the world and in world history is perpetuated.[50]

Memory and identity are indelibly linked and often employ pathos to be effective. Because of our inherent sociability, manifested in part through empathy, we can gain a sense of experiencing events that happened to groups long before we joined them as if they were our own personal pasts. As a consequence, we can feel pride, pain, or shame regarding events that were experienced or accomplished or perpetuated by individuals in a given group even prior to our membership in that group.[51] Individuals who profess their belonging to a group are likely to refer to that group's history in the first-person plural "we." That inclusive "we" can extend to dead ancestors or even to dead people of no relation (even to the exclusion of dead ancestors' experiences).

However, collective memory cannot possibly encapsulate the experiences of all the members, past and present, of the group. It is inevitable that the national pantheon will not be all-inclusive. Memory is a process and a very selective one. The selectivity of memory is not helter-skelter; nor is it benign. In the "natural selection" of collective memory, those memories that survive the winnowing are most likely the fittest for the group's coherence and continuity.[52]

Memory can be useful, so it follows that attempts will be made to use it. It should shock no historian to state that the past is often constructed with particular group interests in mind.[53] History is written by someone in his or her present who is inevitably influenced by contemporary circumstances and trends and thus, whether consciously or not, writes a subjective history with an arbitrary selection of facts.[54]

It is important to state that history is more than the mere construction of the past, which would indicate some kind of complete manipulability. History cannot simply be dictated from on high. Such an approach would reduce memory to politics, meaning "who wants whom to remember what?" and thereby relegate the masses to being passive entities void of voice and without choice.[55] We would then be led to believe that the memory of the nation is determined solely by state power and that state power is enhanced through the control of memory. In Orwell's *1984* a totalitarian state is able to dictate memory—and thus forgetting, summarized in the pithy aphorism: "He who controls the present, controls the past. He who controls the past, controls the future."[56]

Power is indeed important in matters of memory; yet no state can be omnipotent in this process. While states can promote certain memories at the expense of others in order "to legitimate their monopoly on administrative control,"[57] no state can dictate forgetting by fiat. Memory is ultimately a negotiation, and individuals will always retain some leverage and autonomy. Furthermore, state and society interact in their various manifestations, and neither entity is monolithic. The diverse and often diverging interests to be found within the state and within society mean that memories are likely to be contested and that multiple, even contradictory, memories can exist simultaneously in the same group. Individuals can have membership in more than one group at the same time, and the state can attempt to appropriate memories into the national metanarrative. Some states will have more openness to multiple identities and as a result more memories than others. Part of making peasants into Frenchmen entails having them adopt not only a language but also an identity and a memory at the expense of another identity and memory.

The fact that multiple cleavages exist within any society means that memory is a battleground for various subgroups, each of which seeks to promote a set of events or version of events that legitimates the status quo (such as the continuation of the state) or advances grievances, thereby calling for an alteration of current arrangements. For example, despite its internal cleavages, the state clearly will seek to gird its legitimacy and hence its continuation through the promotion of a memory that points to the necessity of the state and the inevitability of the nation of which it is a manifestation.

I have sought to underscore that history is not the pure invention of power, for ultimately the public, through subtle and often inscrutable psychological and sociological processes, will decide which memories are received and which are rejected. On the other hand, I do not wish to diminish the important point that memory requires sponsorship: that is to say, in this battlefield in which memories will be promoted and received the mobilization of resources is required. Powerful interests will try to promote those notions that are beneficial to them and in this way attempt to become society's spokesperson.[58] The resources, both human and material, that go into memory sponsorship and promotion are impressive. Archaeologists, historians and journalists, professors, and school board members work on multiple layers in constructing memories. Documents and documentation, archives, and libraries are the raw materials and storage depots, while publishing houses, conferences, Internet sites, and museum exhibitions all serve to spread the news. All of these require financing, and most of them require a great deal of organization. Yet it is worth emphasizing that financing can come not only through state and local governments but through nongovernmental organizations such as diaspora groups and other civil society and corporate entities whose objective is to promote certain versions of the past, or sets of events from the past, for the public's present attention as well. Not every participant in this negotiation is conscious of his or her role, which means that the notion of an active coordination of memory making should not be overestimated (read "memory is not a conspiracy"). At the same time, it should be more or less obvious that, without some form of sponsorship that supplies the organization and resources, certain memories are less likely to come to the public fore than others.

The political setting will also influence the negotiation over memory. While the state will always weigh in heavily in all bargaining over the past, it will never weigh in alone. If the public sphere is open and associational life is thriving, there will be considerably more participants—and therefore competition—in history's determination. Subaltern memories vying for official recognition will be as common as the multiplicity of identities allowed to exist within any given society. Conversely, when the public sphere is shrunken due to a less open political situation, associational activity will decrease, and as a consequence the state will have a more dominant role in memory's debate.

Ample thought, interaction, and discussion must occur for a memory to be broadly accepted and maintained. The memories that will have the greatest chance of being accepted by the group need to make an emotional connection with the people at a particular moment and have some motivating force to change thoughts and behaviors.[59] This will be the case most of all when the memory is relevant in the present, for the present context will affect how memories are recalled and received. Memory is apt to evolve over time as group interests change and as world happenings affect outlooks and provoke questions. This means that social memory can be, and often is, triggered or altered by current events that raise new questions and require new answers. History changes: just when matters seem to be settled, then enters the historian, who, "uninvited, disturbs and reverses" the commonly accepted beliefs about the past.[60]

MUHACIRS AND MEMORY

In analyzing the memory of the 1877–1878 Muhacirs and their associated traumas, here I use the preceding framework to clarify why a more salient memory of their experience did not develop. How, for example, did the political environment of the period affect memory formation? What kind of sponsorship of memory was available for the Muhacirs? What was the role of the state and its ideologies over time in the formation of a receptive or unreceptive public milieu? Through such an approach, we may be able to understand the failure for a memory to develop and furthermore why subsequent and similar events failed to trigger a recollection of the traumas of 1877–1878. We may also understand the prospects for the recovery and utilization of these memories in the future. What comes into view is a series of sociopolitical elements that were largely coincidental rather than deliberate, and which taken together were something of a perfect storm, for these memories to have sunk into collective oblivion.

From the outset I would like to dismiss one possible answer proposed to me by interlocutors both Turkish and non-Turkish: that these events simply took place too long ago for them to serve as an important, moving memory today. Historical remoteness does not preclude an event from having emotional resonance and political significance. For example, slavery in America is still an important and emotional issue and formative memory for African Americans today even though it was officially abolished in 1865 (and the slave trade itself even earlier). Interestingly, the history of slavery has been much less of an issue in Brazil than in the United States, even though it was on a greater scale and lasted until much later.[61] Another example drawn from America is the persecution and suffering of the Mormons up to and during their migration to the American West in the 1840s. This suffering, as well as a sense of persecution, is still evoked in Mormon Sunday schools and in reenactments of their sorrowful trek to America's western deserts. The Trail of Tears is an important memory for Native Americans today, though it happened in the 1830s. Shia Muslims mournfully re-create the suffering of Hussein through self-flagellation, and Christians in a few countries still reenact the crucifixion of Jesus. Does anyone really believe that in sixty years the importance of the Holocaust of the Jews will have significantly receded in the collective Jewish memory? As Halbwachs states, "to the extent that the dead retreat into the past, this is not because the material measure of time that separates them from us lengthens; it is because nothing remains of the group in which they passed their lives."[62] In truth, the passage of time is not important in and of itself: rather, sociological and political factors are far more crucial.

LIMINAL STATES

The first factor to be proposed is that the relatively swift settlement, assimilation, and dispersion of a predominantly illiterate group of refugees forestalled the formation of a trenchant Muhacir identity. Without question, migration had an effect on the identity of refugees. Identity becomes most relevant in such refugee situations, where security and property are at risk and people are forced to question their place in this world.[63] For the refugees, who survived their traumatic ordeals, with origins elsewhere, this was bound to be the case. Identities melded and solidified for these refugee groups. For example, Tatars who had previously been divided into groups such as Nogays, Yaliboys, and Kerish in the Crimea and Dobruca were simply Tatars in the new Anatolia.[64] Similarly, the multiple ethnicities of trans-Caucasia were all to be caught in the wide eponymous net of "Circassian" (Turkish "Çerkez").[65]

The Muslims coming from Bulgaria, also an ethnically diverse group, came to be known as Muhacirs—an appellation that has also been applied to more recent waves of migration from the Balkans. The dethronement of Abdülhamid II put an end to the oppressive climate that hindered the public sphere. As a consequence of the restoration of associational rights, a newspaper entitled *Muhacir* came into circulation in 1909. The newspaper dealt with immigrant issues, defended immigrant rights, offered advice to new immigrants, and related immigrant stories, albeit only for one year.[66] We can see that some identity creation took place based on shared experience and status. Given the right political climate, it would seek to express itself.

In this case, however, the identities that were formed were relatively weak, especially in the case of the Muhacirs. When considering groups whose trauma produced strong identities, we can see why. One relevant contrast would be the Palestinians, who, having fled their homes in a very similar manner to the Muhacirs coming from Bulgaria due to reports of civilians being massacred and fear of what would befall them, ended up as refugees in perpetual refugee camps spread throughout various Arab lands.

Two points stand out. First, the Ottoman Muslims were definitively deprived of the hope of returning to their homelands. The Ottoman state was too weak to enforce a return of the refugees and as a consequence did not encourage them to believe in an eventual return. The concept of a right of return, in Dawn Chatty's words, "mythologizes the homeland and thus creates new imagined communities."[67] Fortunately for them, the Ottoman Muslim refugees from the Balkans harbored no such illusions about a right to return; they thus accepted the need to be permanently settled and assimilated. This belief in a right of return would have "lock[ed the refugees] in purgatory" because the Ottoman state was powerless to enforce their repatriation.[68]

The second point concerns resettlement. Having given up a right to return, both refugees and the state accepted the need for permanent settlement. Knowing that the settlement was permanent in effect ended the liminal state of the refugees. Resettlement is key in shifting attention from return to rebuilding life.[69] Thanks to preexisting dispositions such as their religion, their long affiliation with the Ottoman state, and their Turkish ethnicity in some cases, these refugees were not isolated to nearly

مهاجر

Mouhadjir

Mercredi le 22 Décembre 1909. No 1

Redaction et administration : Rue

Constantinople

Le numéro à Constple 10 Paras

افادۀ مرام

افادۀ خصوصیه

مقالۀ مخصوصه

5.2. *Muhacir* newspaper (1909).

the same extent as members of other diasporas such as the Armenians or Jews. The continuous waves of immigrants from other conflict zones reinforced a sense of rootedness in the Anatolian soil, as those who had previously been refugee immigrants witnessed the lapping of subsequent waves of refugee immigrants and in turn began to view themselves as natives.

These facts coupled with state policies—deliberate and otherwise—served to hasten their assimilation, meaning that the refugees and immigrants developed relatively weak identities as refugees, which became subordinate to other identities. In contrast, the case of the Palestinians went in a very different direction but might easily have gone the way of the Ottoman Muslims of Bulgaria. The Palestinians, as Muslims and Arabs, could potentially have been absorbed by the bordering Arab states and granted full citizenship. While not completely abandoning nostalgia for their lost land, they would have focused on the future. Under such circumstances the Palestinian identity would presumably have existed but in a much weaker form.

Liisa Malkki, in an important study of Hutu refugees in Tanzania in the 1970s, offers very important insights into the way in which the liminal status of refugees affects their identity and awareness of history—in other words, their memory. In her study refugees from the same conflict were interviewed in refugee camps and in cities. Those in refugee camps demonstrated a greater awareness of their history as "a people." The city refugees, in contrast, had less preoccupation with their history and had identities that were "multiple" and "shifting."[70]

For the city-dwelling refugees in Malkki's study, insistence on strong group identity and historical purity was seen negatively in that it would hinder social mobility. Thus "the town refugees, while being knowledgeable about the past, had with history a relationship consisting largely of denial."[71] Whether individuals were isolated or assimilated figured greatly into this equation. Displacement and deterritorialization present two possibilities: a liminal collectivity or fitting in with the national order.

The Ottoman Muslim refugees from Bulgaria were not isolated, but rather assimilated. Their stays in refugee camps, such as old Istanbul's mosques and the tent cities erected on the outskirts of Istanbul, while dramatic and traumatic, were, when compared to a case such as the Palestinians, relatively short. This (as shown in chapter 4) was due to the fear of an epidemic, the potential for political instability following the failed coup attempt of Ali Suavi, and the Berlin Conference's failure to provide for a right of return. With the first refugees arriving in Istanbul in July 1877, and large waves subsequently arriving in January 1878, serious efforts at resettlement commenced as soon as June 1878. The refugees were accepted by the state as full citizens even though natives in the areas where they were resettled harbored resentments.

In the Armenian diaspora in North America, assimilation was not rapid. Linguistic and cultural differences kept Armenians somewhat separate from the larger American society. As such, community leaders developed and maintained a role of speaking for these groups. However, as time has passed, and the features that originally kept them from assimilating (such as religion and language) have disappeared or become less relevant with newer Americanized generations, the existence of a distinct Armenian community has been threatened.[72] This explains to a certain extent the growing importance of the Armenian Genocide in Armenian memory, as it has become an increasingly important glue for the entire community and thus a new foundation of identity.[73] This is true to such an extent that any diaspora Armenian who forgets the massacres suffered at the hands of the Turks risks opting out of being an Armenian.[74]

Rapid assimilation meant that the Muhacirs were not kept aloof from larger society as a separate community. They did not have community leaders who would have sought to preserve their positions by preserving distinctiveness. Assimilation implied the dissolution of memory. At least from an anthropological perspective, we can see why the Muhacirs did not develop a strong group identity and as a consequence why their engagement with their own history was less than it might otherwise have been.

A CRITICAL JUNCTURE FOR MEMORY IN THE HAMIDIAN STATE

Not only were state policies regarding resettlement instrumental in the rapid assimilation of the Muhacirs, but other state policies affected the Muhacir identity and memory too. The political context, which was in large part a function of state ideology and policy, hindered a more complete recording of the Muhacir experience. Abdülhamid II is well known for his paranoia. Indeed, the long Ottoman history of court intrigue and royal fratricide had frayed the nerves of a number of sultans before him. Despite a fondness for many Western imports, Abdülhamid II was not a liberal. The defeat during the Russo-Ottoman War of 1877–1878 only served to increase the sultan's paranoia and ultimately his autocratic tendencies. By 1878 he had already disbanded Parliament and abolished the constitution only two years after it had been proclaimed. The hopes for a more liberal and open society had been dashed, and the state drifted toward increasing autocracy and a shrinking public sphere. The undercurrent of the sultan's policies was the desperate wish to right the ship and forestall further dismemberment of the empire.

The sultan was also motivated by an instinct for self-preservation. Moreover, he equated the continuation of his rule with the preservation of the state and its territorial integrity, which was in fact the primary objective of his tenure.[75] The sultan and many other elites had become aware of the lack of cohesion within the empire, especially when contrasted with the nationalist fervors in the Balkans. It was determined that the preservation of the Ottoman state necessitated a unifying ideology.

Following the influx of such a large number of Muslims from the Balkans and the loss of Balkan Christian subjects, the demographic composition of the state had significantly changed in favor of the Muslims. Whereas, considering the extent of diversity among the sultan's subjects, the state previously had unsuccessfully relied on a sense of loyalty to the sultan as well as on giving a large degree of autonomy to the millets, the sultan now embarked on the expedient promotion of the Muslim character of the state in an appeal to the now heavily Muslim majority population. This was also the easiest way for him to integrate the diverse Muslim population that he ruled.[76] Before this time the state had never sought to politicize Islam, despite being ruled by a Muslim dynasty and governed by means of Islamic law. Earlier for most Muslims, Islam was part of the social life that was reflected in their customs, traditions, and names.[77] After the disaster of defeat at the hand of the Russians and the huge influx of refugees in the capital, the state began to promote Islam as a political identity. Having been targeted in Bulgaria for no other reason than their identity, the empire's Muslims were now endowing that identity with a new salience and immediacy.

Abdülhamid II took advantage of these sentiments to develop his policy of pan-Islamism. The sultan's worldview had been impacted by the stories of massacre and the influx of refugees. Layard, who had never before seen the sultan angry, reports that the sultan fumed: "We are accused in Europe of being savages and fanatics . . . [yet] unlike the czar, I have abstained till now from stirring up a crusade and profiting from the religious fanaticism, but the day may come when I can no longer contain the fits of indignation of my people at seeing their co-religionists butchered in Bulgaria and Armenia."[78]

The Muslim world, according to the pan-Islamist view, was under siege from European imperialism and colonialism, exemplified by the Russians in Central Asia, the Dutch in the East Indies, the French in North Africa, the British in India and Egypt, and so on. Muslim territory was shrinking. A Muslim state under the sultan's guidance was their only hope. For Muslims outside of the Ottoman Empire, the caliph's independence and voice were important for the preservation of Islam, as it was "the last manifestation of the independence of a Muslim world beleaguered by enemies."[79] Henceforth the Muslim identity was remolded into an identity of resistance and was increasingly equated with a specific territory. This politicization of Islam helped give new urgency to the notion of community for Muslims that would extend beyond the boundaries of the empire.

The refugees not only spurred this political development but also facilitated it through their immigration to the empire, where they increased the Muslim proportion of the population. They were also affected by it: as recently displaced and resettled refugees, the Muhacirs' traumatic experiences coincided with the beginnings of a new state-promoted identity based on a newly politicized awareness of Islam. The Ottoman education system played down ethnicity, Turkishness, language, and other fissures in favor of stressing Islam as the fount of identity.

Abdülhamid II was well aware of the power of schools in inculcating identity in the masses. He established a committee to develop an educational package that would emphasize the loyalty of students to the sultan-caliph and develop their bond to each other through Islam, as it was the clearest common denominator for uniting such disparate Muslim groups. Moreover, in the version of history taught in Ottoman schools, the Ottoman dynasty was given a historic role in Islam's promotion and preservation.[80] In addition, understandings of citizenship were transformed: as we saw earlier, for example, the empire's immigration policy changed in favor of Muslims exclusively.

While pan-Islamism worked as a temporary stopgap and the empire temporarily ceased to fragment under Abdülhamid II, the idea of ethnic nationalism continued to make ground until the sultan was finally overthrown and varying ethnicities were celebrated under an Ottoman banner. The massacres and migrations that most violently affected the victims and refugees from Rumelia and the Danube, depriving them of their homes and casting them off to settle foreign Anatolia, should have caused them to reevaluate and redefine their identity. However, this redefinition of identity coincided with a large-scale shift in identity for the rest of the empire's Muslims. Though caught in their own whirlpool, they were to be swept along by a much bigger current.

The second factor pertaining to the political milieu of the Abdülhamid period was the autocratic nature of the state. The paranoia of Abdülhamid II only increased following the disastrous war with Russia. Not only had Russian troops approached the gates of Istanbul but a civilian coup attempt had also been made against the sultan. In order to preserve his position, the sultan became decidedly more domineering. As mentioned earlier, Abdülhamid II was committed to staying on the throne and was concerned with saving face after the debacle of war.

Abdülhamid II came to power during the Balkan crisis with Serbia and Bulgaria, and the great defeat (*büyük bozgun*) ensued in the first years of his reign. While Abdülhamid II himself was very sympathetic to the plight of the refugee masses, he nevertheless was more concerned with perpetuating his rule and legitimating his governance. As a result, the sultan was attentive to the promotion of a form of history writing that served to justify and strengthen his reign. Due to the calamity that defined his first years on the throne and the subsequent failures, he preferred that recent history not be broached. Ottoman losses were largely ignored as a historical subject in school as well as in the tightly controlled press,[81] especially because Ottoman losses might be attributed to the sultan's incompetence or cowardice. As one observer put it, "Not the emigration of their fellow Muslims, nor the serious fact of which it is a consequence have roused the passion of the Turks against either Greeks or foreigners. The effect has been quite different, that is to say to deeply discredit their own government in their own eyes."[82]

The sultan had already seen how refugee emotions had combined with public anger over the Ottoman debacle to threaten his rule. It would follow that keeping a lid on such resentment was imperative for his continuation on the throne. His reign, not by accident, is known for an aggressive state censor and a shrunken public sphere. Meanwhile, because of the debacle in Bulgaria, the state opened up to significant Westernizing reforms in the military and expanded its education system under the Maarif-i Ummumiye Nizamnamesi edict of 1879.[83] But as a rule the state became decidedly more repressive and censorship, which was first initiated into law by the Matbuat Nizamnamesi of 1864, became the norm. As already noted, the Abdülhamid II regime shut down *Basiret* after the Ali Suavi coup attempt. The newspaper had been the primary source in Ottoman Turkish that dealt with the immediate situation of refugees from the Bulgarian provinces. *Basiret* had also sought to highlight the need for reform in the empire because of the defeat in the Balkans, whose most visible consequence was the refugees themselves.[84] Such an editorial line was clearly not going to be sanctioned by the Abdülhamid regime. Even the official gazette *Takvim-i Vekayii* was temporarily closed, and a rigid control of political columnists was generally enforced.

Because of the censor, history textbooks had to be approved by the Ministry of Education, while other books dealing with historical subjects were not permitted, were banned after publication, or were denied entry at customs.[85] In this way, the state became very active in history definition in this formative period for the development of Muhacir memory. During his reign, the state was deeply engaged in the writing of history wherein Ottoman losses were avoided as a subject in both the schools and the press.[86]

The extent to which the Hamidian regime had stifled associational life became all the more clear after the overthrow of Abdülhamid and the proclamation of a new constitution in 1908, when the public sphere opened as never before. With the official lifting of state censorship, intellectual and associational life flourished, although state intervention in history writing continued, but in a lessened form. In fact, the publication of histories increased steeply in this period, and these now mentioned the recent past and aimed to delegitimize the Abdülhamid II era.[87] This was also a period when politics were opened to the masses. The advent of new political and civil organizations, including associations for the refugees, ensued. One such group, the Roumelian Society, even founded a short-lived newspaper devoted to immigrant issues. The Circassian refugees also formed a group called the Society for Circassian Unity and Mutual Aid (Çerkez İtihat ve Teavün Cemiyet).[88] During this period the state, in order to enhance its legitimacy and justify the overthrow of the sultan, benefited from delegitimization of Abdülhamid II. The discussion of recent political events came into vogue, and the former sultan was demonized in new high school history books.[89]

The constitutional period, however, was short lived. Within three years of Abdülhamid II's abdication, the Balkan Wars (1912–1913) broke out. The empire ended up losing more of its European territory, and more Muslims were displaced. Irredentist feelings were on the upswing, invoking an emotional link to the lost Balkan territories, including the Danube and Rumelia. This indicates that the new political climate and the recent war had triggered the memory of the 1877–1878 calamity. In 1914, for example, the president of the Ottoman Parliament, Halil Menteşe, who was also an influential member of the Committee of Union and Progress (CUP), expressed the new mood in a speech:

> I address myself, from this high pulpit, to my nation. I recommend that it does not forget Salonika, the cradle of liberty and the Constitution, green Monastir, Kosova, Scutari of Albania, Janina and the whole of beautiful Rumelia. [At which the assembly shouted, "We shall not forget!"] I ask our teachers, journalists, poets and all our intellectuals to remind continuously our present generation and the future ones, via their lessons, writing and moral influence, that beyond the frontiers there are brethren to be liberated and bits of the Fatherland to be redeemed. This is the only way to avoid repeating the errors which have brought about our defeats and calamities.[90]

Yet before such an approach could be implemented, the empire would once again be plunged into war. The First World War witnessed the alliance of the Ottoman Empire with Bulgaria as well as with the Austrians and Germans. While the Ottomans had irredentist intentions in their entry into the war, these could not be directed toward the lost provinces of Bulgaria. In the end the war proved a deathblow for the empire. With Istanbul under occupation, the fate of Anatolia's Muslims was at the mercy of the Paris Peace Conference, which ultimately decided to shrink Ottoman territory still further in favor of the Christian minorities. In order to prevent this and fight off an invasion of Greeks on the Aegean coast of Anatolia, General Mustafa Kemal (later given the name Atatürk) organized a resistance that was successful in defeating the Greek invasion but also brought an end to the Ottoman dynasty via the creation of the Turkish Republic in 1923.

Three important factors came together at a critical period to hinder the development of a Muhacir memory based on the experiences of massacre, rape, and flight: (1) the rapid and full resettlement and assimilation of refugees, (2) the promotion of a pan-Islamic identity that superseded a Muhacir identity, and (3) the autocratic nature of the state, which stifled associational life and discouraged the publicizing of the recent past. These three factors worked together to severely impede the development of Muhacir identity and memory, with effects that still last today. This is because Abdülhamid II's remaining three decades on the throne were a critical period for the documentation of the experiences of the refugees: the memories needed to be committed to paper while the Muhacirs were still alive in order to become a resource for later generations. This opportunity was for the most part missed.

DOCUMENTING MEMORIES

Memories that are spoken but not recorded are ephemeral because they are at risk to "remain buried in a voiceless past." It is when they are made lapidary by some physical recording that they "gain a foothold on eternity."[91]

Documents and documentation are an important foundation for memory, its re-creation, and its prolongation. Documents are crucial, because "[i]n the modern world people lose an embodied sense of the past, and their access to earlier periods only becomes possible through archived, alienated or dutifully followed histories, rather than orally transmitted memories."[92] Not only do documents serve to prove or at least give credence to the veracity of events, but they can also provide a potent and even emotive link across time to the creator of the document. This is especially true when the writer is not just a witness but also a participant. When the historical subject at hand deals with the trauma of violence and ethnic cleansing, the victim's voice resonates powerfully, and the act of a victim recording testimony in the first person reverberates through time. As a general rule, the more such voices join forces, the greater the effect—the choir is louder than the soloist. This is so because the more first-person accounts that are set forth, the greater range of experience and emotion that will be recorded. This extended range can prove useful in creating new narratives based on current events because it increases the likelihood for finding parallels and that a "relevant" experience having been documented will exist.

The recording of experience can keep alive dead memories even if the organic experiential relationship is lost because the one who could tell it is dead.[93] Though it may lie unused, gathering dust in a box, a document has the potential to be marshaled in the future. In short, documents are resources for memory. While oral histories are important, they are only important as long as they can be repeated. This is obviously problematic once the generation in question is deceased. In the words of Barry Schwartz, "If part of the past is forgotten, it is because of the disappearance of the groups which sponsored the corresponding memories."[94] The dearth of firsthand accounts of refugees from the 1877–1878 Russo-Turkish War is clearly an important reason for the lack of a sharp and poignant memory of the trauma that similar incidents have bequeathed.

One of the common surmises from a Turkish point of view as to why the Muhacir memory did not form is that the Muslim refugees were more stoic and more resilient than their Christian counterparts, who "loudly publicised their plight."[95] However, attributing such behavior to cultural traits alone ignores the frequent attempts by the Muslim refugees who were eager to share their stories with the population of Istanbul as well as with Europeans who would listen. In fact, the Ottoman government made efforts to drag scarred victims before European journalists and even had a number of injured women refugees photographed with their wounds in order to garner European sympathy.[96] As already seen, the government did not have the same attitude about publicizing the experiences of the Muslim victims when it came to the domestic press. Cultural explanations simply fail to take into account some clear structural issues encountered in that particular setting. As has already been underscored, the political inclination of the state during the thirty years following the Ottoman defeat was to discourage talk about the recent

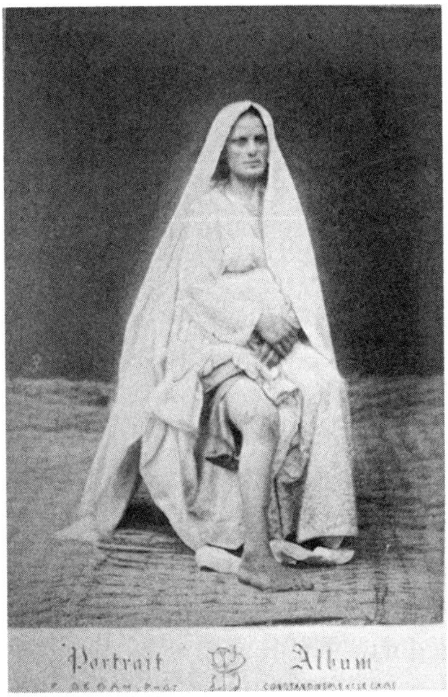

5.3. Wounded refugee woman displaying leg wound. By Pascal Sebah. From the photo series "Russian Atrocities" (Istanbul, 1877), Berlin, Political Archive of the Federal Foreign Office, R 12818.

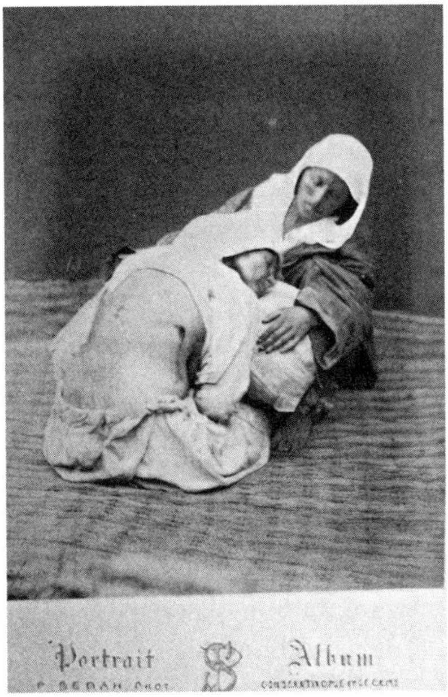

5.4. Wounded refugee woman displaying wound in back. By Pascal Sebah. From the photo series "Russian Atrocities" (Istanbul, 1877), Berlin, Political Archive of the Federal Foreign Office, R 12818.

past. Furthermore, the development of an organization that would sponsor the memory of the Muhacirs by means of some type of association was stifled by the repressive political climate and the sociological factors concerning identity formation in the immediate aftermath of their migration.

If cultural reasons are to explain a supposed reticence, they may have more to do with shame than with stoicism. Women would most likely have preferred silence to speaking up about the outrages inflicted on them. Men may have felt shame in their decision to flee rather than to fight or in their impotence to protect their families and, above all, the honor of their women. It was also seen as a great embarrassment to be defeated by former vassals. Regarding the humiliation caused by losses in the Balkan Wars, for instance, an early Turkish nationalist wrote, "We were driven out by our former shepherds and servants. We must not remove from our hearts . . . the pain of this insulting blow which we have received."[97]

The shame of being a powerless victim is not uncommon in these types of situations. For instance, in the decade after the Holocaust, Jews in Israel preferred to ignore and even look down on the ordinary Holocaust survivors coming from Europe, compared to those European Jews who participated in the resistance. Survival from the concentration camps especially aroused suspicions of collaboration. Given this sense of shame, concentration camp survivors preferred to keep quiet about their ordeals.[98] Sigmund Freud saw forgetting as a commonplace way to repress painful and unpleasant memories.[99] Yet even that sense of shame can be overcome under the right sociopolitical conditions. Those same survivors of the Nazi-committed genocide, while reticent in Israel, were quite involved in recording their testimonies in postwar Europe prior to their migration to Israel.

It should not be assumed that the documentation of collective suffering is entirely spontaneous. For example, upon being seized by the Nazis, Jewish historian Simon Dubnow is said to have encouraged record keeping of the experiences: "Brothers, write down everything you see and hear. Keep a record of it all."[100] Moreover, following World War II, Jewish historical commissions in postwar Europe organized the collection of personal accounts. They actively encouraged the writing of personal narratives in an emotional "spirit of Martyrology" with the intention of creating a historical monument and memorializing the catastrophe.[101] These documents later became valuable resources of memory after the Adolf Eichmann trial, which detailed the true conditions of the camps and resulted in a newfound sympathy for the survivors.

In the Ottoman Empire no such efforts to document firsthand accounts of refugees were organized. The refugees themselves were being resettled and assimilated and were probably too busy building homes and villages, making fields farmable and life livable. The state's attitude did not encourage the retelling of the recent past, as doing so could call into question the sultan's leadership during and after the war. Only one book is known to be a firsthand account of a refugee's experience during the war, which was written by the mufti of Stara Zagora.[102] His account is relatively free of the graphic, "nauseating profusion of detail" that can be found in similar victim accounts from other tragedies, and it remains a lone voice lacking in the "heart-rending repetitiveness" that would have been accrued had other refugees documented their experiences.[103]

An unavoidable explanation for this is that documentation and recording of testimony require literacy. Oral histories dissolve as quickly as sound waves dissipate through space unless they are put to paper. The Ottoman Muslims of the late nineteenth century were overwhelmingly illiterate; therefore the likelihood of the recording of history by the refugees was severely diminished. According to one estimate, Ottoman literacy rates in the generation following 1877–1878 were under 10 percent.[104] Those most likely to be literate were wealthy men who were also able in many cases to be the first to flee, thereby avoiding the worst suffering, the direct attacks from Bulgarian bandits and roaming Cossacks, and the perilous winter journey. Most of the refugees were women, children, and elderly men—categories of the population that can safely be assumed to have had the least access to education. In this largely illiterate Ottoman Muslim society in the nineteenth-century Balkans, oral rather than written histories were significantly more prominent, leaving only an ephemeral testimony. The Christian inhabitants of the Ottoman Empire, in contrast, often benefited from foreign schools set up by foreign missionaries or, in the case of the Bulgarians, Russian pan-Slav societies. For this reason, the Christians were more literate than their Muslim counterparts and subsequently more capable of documenting their experiences. As an illustration of the importance of literacy, consider the contrast between the ways in which Jews, a people known for committing their history to writing, and Gypsies, a people with a historic near-aversion to literacy but a penchant for expressing nostalgia via song, have related their experiences in the Holocaust.[105]

Finally, the Turks have the rare distinction of being one of the few nations to have changed their alphabet in modern times. This they did in 1928 when the newly founded Turkish Republic initiated a language reform, beginning with the adoption of the Latin alphabet to replace the Arabic script. While the new alphabet was conceived in greater concordance with the phonetic structure of Turkish, the misconception that the change to the Latin alphabet was essential because the Arabic script was incapable of rendering Turkish's complex system of agglutination and vowel harmony needs to be corrected.[106] A large number of phonetically and grammatically diverse languages have achieved notable literacy rates using the Arabic alphabet. In these instances sounds that are not found in Arabic are expressed through the use of diacritics and other language-specific innovations. These variations of the Arabic script are witnessed in all of the languages that have made use of the script from Malay to Urdu to Persian and beyond.

The reorientation of the Turkish nation away from its Ottoman-Islamic heritage should not be viewed as an unintended consequence of the Turkish alphabet change but rather as one of the primary purposes of the Turkish language reformers. Indeed, the alphabet change was accompanied by a massive purge of Arabic and Persian loanwords and the search for (and sometimes wholesale invention of) suitable Turkic replacements. The empire was a thing of the past, and Westernization and nationalism were understood to be the ways of the future. Ultimately the reorientation of society, rather than phonetics, necessitated a complete rupture with the writing system of the Turkish dynasties and the holy book. Henceforth Turks would no longer be able to access documents written as late as the 1920s without specialized training. Ottoman archives thus have become the potential quarry of only a small number of researchers. The net effect is to a great extent a compelled forgetting. Partly for this reason, Geoffrey Lewis deemed the Turkish language reform a "catastrophic success."[107] The alphabet reform effectively served to sever the new Turkish generations from their Ottoman ancestors, which was a catastrophe for Turks wishing to find their nation's soul within its past.

The Syrian poet Adonis reflected as much in the following lines:

> Fragments of history in my throat
> and signs of victimhood on my face
> how bitter language is now
> and how helpless the alphabet.[108]

Since ex nihilo invention of writing has been an extremely rare phenomenon in human history, easily numbering fewer than ten instances, writing has spread through borrowing and influence. In premodern times writing systems were often adapted from adjacent states or civilizations. Later alphabet changes typically accompanied major historical reorientations of society. The advent of Islam, for example, triggered the demise of the Pahlavi script in Iran and a movement away from a Zoroastrian society. In only few instances were writing systems successfully abandoned for more phonetically favorable ones. The Korean adoption of the Hangul alphabet in the fifteenth century is perhaps the most salient success story, whereas Kublai Khan's attempt to create an empire-wide script in fourteenth-century China came to naught.

In modern times, though, colonialism has been the primary impetus for alphabet changes. The Malays, Swahili speakers of East Africa, and others were induced to adopt Latin alphabets at the expense of the Arabic scripts that had previously been the means for writing those languages. In French Indochina in the early twentieth century the Vietnamese were compelled to adopt a romanized script, the Quốc Ngữ, which had been devised by the Portuguese for the evangelization of Vietnam. French administrators hoped to weaken Vietnam's cultural connection to China and break the grip of the Confucian literati. In Cambodia they forcefully instituted a romanized version of Khmer in 1943, which was the impetus for massive anti-French protests. The Khmer alphabet was reinstated during Japanese occupation two years later. Such alphabet conversions have especially bedeviled the Turkic peoples under Moscow's yoke. In Soviet Central Asia the Muslims (as well as the Mongols in their Soviet satellite state) were forced to adopt new scripts. Originally the Russian Empire had granted the Muslim khanates of Central Asia a degree of autonomy, and the Arabic script continued to be used; however, when the Bolsheviks came to power they sought, much like the Kemalist state, to reorient the culture of the Muslim people away from the Islamic culture and toward the metropolis. The Arabic script was banned and replaced first by Latin scripts in 1929 and then by Cyrillic in 1940. The Soviet enforced rupture with the past was much more brutal. Citizens in Turkey were still allowed to transcribe Ottoman into the new script, while the state focused on subsidizing the romanization of new materials such as newspapers, whereas the Soviets were rigorous in banning the works of previous generations.[109] Of all the Turkic groups that began adopting the Arabic script in the ninth century with the beginning of Turkic conversions to Islam, the Uyghurs of western China are the only Turkic people still writing in the Arabic script today.

What makes the Turkish language reform with its accompanying conversion of alphabet unique, though, is that it was a self-inflicted wound. In the other cases mentioned above, alphabet change primarily occurred under the auspices of colonial rule. After its war of national independence against the Greek invasion, however, Turkey was ruled by a new, Westernized elite that saw within its Ottoman heritage the causes of its national weakness. These leaders were convinced that a reorientation of society was necessary for the renewal of the nation and that alphabet change, despite the prevailing sentiment of the masses, was essential to the project because it implied the creation of new elites while undermining the old Ottoman and religious officials as well as the liberation of the nation from the dead weight of the past.[110]

The "conversation with an absent author" was no longer a possibility for the descendants of the Ottoman Muslims.[111] Those illiterate generations—or at best literate in a dead language—would suffer from aphasia, the inability to speak. As a consequence of their ancestors' aphasia, Turkish society would develop a grave case of amnesia. The lack of documentation (caused by the factors already outlined, when combined with the language reform that made any extent documentation difficult to access, led to what sociologist John Barnes has deemed "structural amnesia."[112] In the case of the Muhacirs, all of the factors were aligned to hinder rather than promote the writing of histories related to their traumatic experiences.

Although a burst of associational life combined with history writing followed Abdülhamid II's dethronement, the constitutional period was a spring shower too brief for the memories to sprout and take root. The War of '93 was already thirty years in the past, and the ensuing Balkan Wars would create new displacements and traumas that would, on one hand, remind the Ottomans of their stolen Rumelia but, on the other, overshadow those traumas as well. The Balkan Wars of 1912–1913 would again threaten the empire and violently displace the European Turks afresh, refilling Istanbul's mosques with refugees and replaying pitiful scenes. The Balkan Wars would have a more lasting imprint on Turkish memory in part because they had a greater effect on the generation of Muslims who would become the leaders of the incipient Turkish Republic. Literacy had increased, and memoir writing was now a more common feature in society. Indeed, memoirs in the early Republic inevitably mentioned the Balkan Wars and their associated losses.

The memory of the Russo-Turkish War of 1877–1878 lived on indirectly from parents to children. The children of refugees carried their sense of loss more personally. For example, the Turkish writer and intellectual Şevket Süreyya Aydemir, who was born in Edirne in 1897, recalled the environment of his youth: "ours was a refugee neighborhood. The flotsam of torrents of refugees torn by war and massacres from the Crimea, Dobruca and the banks of the Danube . . . the returning remnants of the conquering armies."[113] The settlers from the Balkans are said to have transferred a sense of vengeance against the Christians of Anatolia.[114] Erik Jan Zürcher points out that many individuals associated with the destruction of the Armenian population in Anatolia were children of refugees who must have been raised with the memory of the loss and a sense of bitterness.[115]

Karl Mannheim points to the socialization of generations as a way that memory and culture are perpetuated. Generations invariably overlap, so they are able to transmit memories and knowledge to newer generations. Yet some things from this accumulated cultural heritage will inevitably be lost on the way. Later generations will reevaluate the knowledge in a new social light and discard that which they find irrelevant or useless. Periods of rapid socialization can serve to exacerbate sentiments of discontinuity.[116]

According to James Pennebaker, the experiences of an individual between the ages of twelve and twenty-five are the most important in terms of memory.[117] This is important for the discussion of the memory of the Muhacirs of 1877–1878, who, from that age cohort, would have been between fifty-seven and seventy years old at the beginning of the Turkish Republic. They would not be the founders of the Republic but rather their parents or grandparents or just as likely deceased. Just as they would have reached an age at which they could flex their economic and political clout in terms of memory, promoting their memories through state or civilian mechanisms, the state was again involved in war, which would continue almost unabated for a decade. The historical window for a generation had slammed shut.

RUPTURE AND REPUBLIC

The historical rupture initiated by Atatürk with the establishment of the Turkish Republic was, in effect, more like a palimpsest than a clean sheet

5.5. Turkish refugees from Edirne. Public domain: Wikimedia Commons.

of paper. The Turkish Republic was a new project, not to be associated with the Ottoman Empire, even though it was constructed on top of it.

The Republican ideology rejected continuity between the new state and its Ottoman predecessor.[118] The new state was not just a new polity; it was a new era—not the inheritor of an Ottoman past. Through various means, such as the institution of a new calendar, a new script and language reform, and a new orientation in historical matters, the young Republic was basing itself to a large degree on forgetting.[119]

Ruptures are often initiated through trauma.[120] In Turkey's case the defeat of the Ottoman Empire and the occupation of parts of the empire by European forces were the impetus to search for new beginnings. The victory of Mustafa Kemal against the Greek invasion of Anatolia provided a glorious moment on which to found a new state. The Turkish Republic was shaped by victory rather than by the defeats that characterized the late Ottoman period. Victory was a beginning to be celebrated, thereby imposing discontinuity on the historical narrative. The rupture of Turkish history involved several aspects that were, in effect, to cement the amnesia of the 1877–1878 sufferings.

But, as Paul Connerton notes, "the absolutely new is inconceivable. It is not just that it is very difficult to begin with a wholly new start . . . it is that in all modes of experience we always base our particular experiences on . . . an organized body of expectations based on recollection." Indeed, the Ottoman experience in the Balkans was highly influential on the elites of the young Republic. They saw the force and fury of a nationalist idea. They also saw the weakness of the Ottoman idea based on pluralism and multiculturalism. Heterogeneity was a weakness. Therefore an early aim of the Republic was to unify society around a Turkish identity. This would require a uniform language as well as a unique history of the nation.[121]

The Committee of Union and Progress (CUP) leadership, which tugged the country to defeat in the First World War, was composed of many individuals from the Balkans who had harbored strong irredentist and revanchist feelings toward the Balkan provinces following the humiliation of the Balkan Wars. As noted earlier, this brief period witnessed a sense of victimization and a renewed recollection of the loss and suffering, not only of the territories conceded during the Balkan Wars but also of the Danube and Rumelia.[122]

Yet the geopolitical constraints imposed by a war-ravaged country meant that any irredentist notions had to be entirely disavowed. The traumas of war and suffering had created a legitimate space to acknowledge the sufferings of Muslims in the Balkans, but in order to abandon irredentist claims it was imperative to abandon the memories that were at their root. The need to create a Turkish identity for the nation in the new Republic required the state to become forcefully involved in the manipulation of history.[123] As a result, it promoted above all the Anatolian homeland as the source of Turkishness. Central Asia was also invoked as the cradle of the Turks, their language, and their pre-Islamic customs. The idea of Turanism (pan-Turkism) was tolerated by the Republican state until the late 1930s (although its promoters were often Turkish immigrants from the Russian Empire before World War I).[124]

The state believed that if the people could become aware of their origins and heritage their memories would develop in such a way that the strength of their identification would increase.[125] Islam would be deployed when expedient, but it would not be at the core of the identity.[126] Instead the core was ethnic Turkishness, defined by language and an attachment to Anatolia (and the important civilizations that had inhabited it, such as the Hittites, but not the Greeks). In sum, the Turkish gaze had definitively turned away from the Balkan distraction, and the Balkans were now viewed in Turkey with the same type of Balkanist distaste commonly expressed in Europe, which saw the Balkans as a source of trouble best to be avoided.[127]

Because the Balkans had played such a large role in Ottoman history, forgetting the Balkans was a convenient upshot of forgetting the Ottoman historical roots of the state. The early leadership had become very sensitive to the stigma that Europe had attached to all things Ottoman, and in an effort to be viewed as part of modern and Western civilization the Ottoman past was largely denied.[128] Atatürk considered the creation of a new national history an opportunity to change Western attitudes concerning Turks.[129] Ironically, in order to create a European-style state, the Turks forgot their European past.

In imitation of the Balkan nationalisms, which were seen as representations of European modernity, the new Republic sought to unify the population around an ethnic identity. Although the population consisted of numerous ethnic, linguistic, and sectarian fissures, all Muslims in Turkish society were deemed "Turks," and the state aimed to socialize non-Turkish Muslims into Turks by altering or changing their culture and language. Distinct identities were not allowed to be expressed under this totalizing Turkishness.[130] This was in sharp contrast to the Ottoman "tolerance" of identity exemplified in the constitutional period. Under the treaty that concluded peace between Turkey and the victors of the First World War, Turkey accepted a minority status for Greeks, Armenians, and Jews living in Turkey.[131] By contrast, all Muslims in Turkey, regardless of ethnicity, were forced to become Turks. Kurds, for example, were deemed to be "Mountain Turks" who had simply forgotten their Turkish language. In this political climate there was no space to put forward identities or subidentities with particularistic histories and memories. Muhacir memory could only acquiesce to a larger Turkish narrative.

Political calculations would continue to weigh heavily in issues regarding the Balkans. In 1943 books about the Bulgarian Turks were banned by İsmet İnönü's government, which was at the time trying to improve relations with Bulgaria.[132] While Bulgaria and other Balkan states engaged in the destruction of Muslim heritage sites within their states, the Turkish government would at times make protests that elicited not only denials but charges of neo-Ottomanism. The Turkish leadership, still averse to the Ottoman past, was extremely sensitive to such accusations.[133]

Though the totalizing Turkish identity did not leave much free space for multiple identities and memories in the Turkish Republic, society did not fully swallow the state-sponsored history. Sections of society that contested the state's use of power also contested the memory promoted by the state. More conservative and religious, these elements rejected the rupture imposed on history. They had not forgotten the Ottoman past and were more likely to see the continuity of society rather than its rupture. The glue of Muslim Ottoman society was religion, and the identity of Ottoman Muslims living in the Balkans was first and foremost as Muslims. This identity was rejected by the increasingly secularist Republicans.[134] Opposing the Republic and its ideology entailed retaining nostalgia for the tolerant Ottoman past and thus the Balkans.[135] Remembering the Balkans to a certain degree implied contemplating the loss thereof, and "memories shaped by trauma are the most likely to subvert totalizing varieties of historicism."[136] As Milan Kundera wrote, "The struggle of man against power is the struggle of memory versus forgetting."[137]

The new Turkish state was founded on a victorious moment, the War of Liberation, and it sought to create a nation through homogenizing its various Muslim elements into Turks. Turks were therefore inherently triumphant and magnanimous—they were not victims. Implicit in this endeavor to create an ethnic Turkish identity was the rewriting of history. Having accepted Anatolia as the Turkish homeland, the state also rejected any irredentist claims to lost lands. This reshaping of society implied the further suppression of the memory of the Balkans, which had been briefly rekindled following the Balkan Wars (1912–1913). The totalizing Turkish identity did not allow room for the development of a Muhacir subidentity, so the memory continued to languish.

IN FOREIGN HANDS

In light of the circumstances that coincided to hinder the memory of the Muhacirs, we inevitably might ask how we know anything at all about them and their ordeal. Most of what is known about the sufferings of the Ottoman Muslims from Bulgaria comes to us from third-person sources, most of which are non-Turkish.

Ottoman sources come to us primarily through the *Basiret* newspaper, which was shut down quite suddenly in 1878, and Ottoman state sources. However, the problem with state sources is that, first, they are written in Ottoman and are mostly inaccessible to the masses but, second, the individual experience is subordinated to the need for data and a state response in this type of documentation. Thus a reliance on state documents gives an impression of individuals without agency, a passive herd of subjects in a war between larger political entities.

As has been demonstrated, the refugees were far from monolithic and were in fact active participants in their own drama. Circumstances necessitated difficult choices, and the responses were not uniform. In short, the Ottoman state archives often rob the victims of their human essence. If, as already discussed, the memories that are most likely to resonate with the public have an emotional element, then we should not harbor lofty expectations for the development of memory via the Ottoman bureaucratic documents.

The greater part of documentation concerning the events of 1877–1878 comes from foreign sources—journalists, diplomats, doctors, military men, and tourists. The Russo-Turkish War of 1877–1878 was the biggest European war since the Crimean War. Many of the children of the Crimean generation were eager to make a name for themselves or seek adventure as journalists or as attachments to the marching armies in the theater of war that was likely to settle the Eastern Question. For the most part, their interest in the plight of the Muslim civilians was only tangential. The main event was clearly the war itself, the attacks and defenses, the maneuvers, chases, and sieges. These writers were far from fluent in the languages in question; hence we possess numerous accounts from such individuals who were able to see the Muslim refugees and their suffering but were unable to converse with them. The Muslim victims were thus rendered voiceless corpses and silent sufferers marching from danger to peril. As S. Anski lamented, "Woe to the nation whose history is written by foreign hands and whose own writers are left to later compose only songs of lament, penitential prayers and threnodies."[138]

Even so, the foreign witnesses were capable writers evoking tragedy with elegance—albeit not in Turkish.

The sources that have proven to be most important in the few Turkish studies, writings, and websites dealing with these events are the diplomatic cables—primarily from England, although sometimes from France. The British government, represented in Istanbul by ambassador Austen Henry Layard, who in his younger years had acquired fame as an amateur archaeologist and the discoverer of the library of Nineveh, took a great interest in the civilian Muslim victims of this period. While for the most part sincere, this interest was not bereft of geopolitical implications. He was knighted in 1878, in part for his efforts in Constantinople on behalf of the British Empire. Just as the news of atrocities in Bulgaria had a domestic political effect on Britain's ability to intervene in favor of the Ottomans, news of Russian and Bulgarian barbarity could, if necessary, tip public opinion back in favor of Britain's involvement.

The British cables are the most important source of information because British consulates were the most strategically placed to witness the effects of the war in Bulgaria. The other European powers generally had the majority of their consuls placed in the western Balkans and out of the conflict zone during this period. Ambassador Layard's personal connection with the sultan as well as his attention to the droves of refugees in Istanbul, culminating in extraordinary efforts to solicit donations for their relief, meant that a sympathetic and powerful advocate for the Ottoman sufferings left a lengthy paper trail.

It is largely from such records that the 1970 work of Bilal Şimşir, *Rumeli'den Türk Göçmenler* (Turkish Migrants from Rumelia), was compiled. Şimşir was born in Osmanpazarı, Bulgaria, in 1933 but migrated to Turkey. He became a diplomat and eventually an ambassador for the Turkish Republic. In his various diplomatic posts he also worked as a historian to bring to light the past of his forefathers in Bulgaria.

Şimşir's three-tome collection of diplomatic cables regarding the massacres and flight of Ottoman Muslims from Bulgaria is a foundational element in a gradual resurgence of interest on this subject in Turkey, much as al-Maqqarī's work rekindled interest in Muslim Spain in the nineteenth century. With precious little scholarship on this subject preceding it, Şimşir's compilation has become the primary, if not sole,

5.6. British ambassador Austen Henry Layard. By London Stereoscopic & Pictographic Company. Credit Wellcome Collection CC BY.

source of information for Turkish authors and researchers wishing to know more about this chapter of Ottoman history. Turkish websites that reference these events invariably use Şimşir's compilation as a source if not, as seems to be the case in nearly all of them, the only source—and this more often than not entails a correspondence with Ambassador

Layard. While Great Britain chose to sit out the war, thus paving the way for a Russian advance to Constantinople, it is largely through British efforts that documents, albeit ones that would collect dust for nearly a century, were created.

The problem with these diplomatic cables is the same as the problem with the Ottoman documents: the victims and refugees are referred to, not spoken with; viewed but not heard. There are, however, two documents of seminal importance that have been almost entirely neglected. In fact, the fate of the two documents will also sheds light on some geopolitical reasons for the refugees' disappearance from public consciousness. These two documents are (1) *Report by Consul Blunt on the Effects of the Russian Invasion of Roumelia*, dated December 30, 1877, and (2) the verbal process of *Correspondence Respecting the Proceedings of the International Commission Sent to the Mount Rhodope District*, dated 1878. Both of these documents are governmental investigations: the first a lone British undertaking, while the second was international, and both of these documents—in sharp contrast to the other Ottoman state and foreign sources—let the victims speak.

Consul Blunt's report is a collection of testimonies from Muslim victims in the Tundja valley region of Bulgaria. He was commissioned by Ambassador Layard to investigate the rumors of atrocities against the Muslim population that had reached him at Constantinople. With the help of a few other Englishmen, translators, and doctors, Blunt made a meticulous sketch of the events through first-person testimonies. In the document, in contrast, with Ottoman state documents, the victims have names, hometowns, ages, and, most importantly, a voice—an "I."

The Rhodope Commission Report was commissioned following the Berlin Conference. The commission had one representative each from Great Britain, France, Austria, Germany, Italy, Turkey, and Russia. Its mandate was to investigate the conditions of the Muslims in the Rhodope region of Bulgaria. The commissioners set up their work in various buildings throughout the region and invited Muslims to appear before them and testify. The verbal process of this report also presents riveting first-person, detailed accounts of the painful experiences resulting from Russia's occupation of Bulgaria. More importantly, it directly implicates Russian soldiers in the massacre and rape of Muslims. These two documents, however, ingloriously vanished from the public discourse.

An interesting side note is to consider the role of state-sponsored trials and investigations in documenting and thus memorializing humankind's most sinister moments. The Eichmann trial, for example, gave a meticulous account of Nazi crimes, forming a narrative of memory of the Holocaust of Europe's Jewry in the world psyche. The effort of bringing Nazis to trial necessitated the compilation and collation of numerous documents and testimonies, thereby facilitating future research on the subject. The Eichmann trial, by producing an authoritative account of events as well as a clear declaration of culpability, released Holocaust survivors from the purgatory of stigma that they endured inside of Israel. Similarly, when the Ottoman state had capitulated after the First World War and the capital was occupied, the Western powers instigated criminal proceedings against those responsible for the massacres of Armenians. The documentation collected and produced as a result of these trials, which were permanently interrupted by the insurgency led by Mustafa Kemal, have been the foundation of legalistic Armenian claims of genocide,[139] although they are not the heart of emotive Armenian protestations. Given the role that state-sponsored investigations and trials can play in documenting crimes against humanity as well as defining culpability, it is interesting to consider what happened to these reports.

Consul Blunt's report was well received by ambassador Layard, but in a letter to Blunt dated January 4, 1878, he informs his consul, "Unluckily the 'Times' has got hold of the fact that you were preparing the report and has been doing his [*sic*] best by *influencing* public opinion on the subject to prevent the government from publishing it" (underlined by Blunt in the original). Layard hoped that he might be influential in making sure that the report was presented to Parliament but assured Blunt that sooner or later his report would be published. However, he later informed Blunt that "for reasons of state it was not produced as it was feared the revelations it contained would raise a storm of public feeling" (underlined in the original).[140] While the report was submitted to the Foreign Office and to Parliament, it was never published and remained stamped "confidential." Moreover, in the version submitted to Parliament, at Blunt's request, the names of the victims were crossed out in order to spare them from possible recrimination, thereby condemning the victims to eternal anonymity. Fortunately, these names were not blotted out in the copy given to the Foreign Office. The report has remained undistributed, and no part of it was included in Şimşir's compilation.

Blunt, it appears, lent his copy out when he found someone curious enough to read it. In 1909, after Blunt had retired to Malta, he received a letter from the governor there, Sir Henry Grant, who wrote a note penned at the "Auberge d'Aragon" with the following words:

> Many thanks for sending me your report to see. It is too horrible a tale and I've often heard Turks say in general terms that those sort of horrors did take place but I've never before heard of them from any one in so good a position as yourself to bear testimony to them. The mere recollection of what you were almost an eye witness yourself must be a continual night mare to you.[141]

The Rhodope Commission report also was destined for desuetude. The commission's work was continuously interrupted by objections from the Russian representative, a Mr. Basily. He specifically objected to the recording of the verbal process as well as to questions pertaining to the motive for the Muslims to abandon their homes. He and the German representative attacked the testimony of the witnesses as being biased and therefore untrustworthy since they were, after all, the victims. In the end the Russian and German delegates refused to sign the report; the Austrian delegate, who presided over the commission, regretfully informed the commission that he was too ill to make the journey to add his signature. In essence, the League of Three Emperors proved to be a fruitful alliance, but the lack of those three signatures was seen as invalidating the entire document, and the signatory countries did not press the matter.

Layard regretted that "no notice should have been taken of the Commissioners' report." Francis Charteris, Lord Elcho, implored him: "Surely this Report ought not to be allowed to remain any longer a dead letter, thus ignoring the misdeeds of the Russians and the sufferings of the Mussulmans."[142] Thus two of the most important documents, though written by foreign sources, have preserved the Muslim victims' firsthand perspective. Even though they have been neglected for more than a century, they can still have the emotive force and first-person immediacy to resurrect the Muslim voice and the victims' memory.

NEO-OTTOMAN: A RETURN TO MEMORY

As has been suggested, the history of the Muhacirs of 1877–1878 has been gradually making a return to public memory for several reasons.

First, the end of the Cold War has had a major impact on the Turkish state's reassessment of its place in the world. As a staunch ally of the West through most of the Cold War, Turkey was heavily engaged in its role as a North Atlantic Treaty Organization (NATO) member bordering states of the Eastern Bloc, but the alliances and hostilities that were based on the Communist-capitalist divide of the world no longer made sense, and the funds that subsidized the geostrategic positioning tended to dry up.

Internally, the fissures that were worrisome had also been seen more in a leftist versus rightist context. Military coups d'état had recurred almost every decade in Turkey based on leftist and Islamist worries. In the stifling conditions of the postcoup years, many union and other leftist political entrepreneurs set their sights on heading ethnic-based associations. Yet the demise of the Soviet Union, the end of the Cold War, and receding fears of leftist threats also ushered in an opening of the public sphere, initiated under Turkish prime minister Turgat Özal, who introduced a series of economic reforms opening up the Turkish economy to more neo-liberal market influences. As a result, a class of Turkish entrepreneurs dubbed the Anatolian tigers benefited economically from a more open economy. They tended to be from a previously excluded class of Turkish society that harbored memories contesting the Republican dogmas. In addition to the opening of the economy, the same period brought a relaxing of the state's grip on the media and the appearance of new private television stations and newspapers. The state's monopoly on the education system, too, was broken, and the growth of private education outside of rigid state control was expanded. Such private schools tended to view Islam, the Republic, and the Ottoman Empire differently from state schools.[143]

Externally Turkey was poised to benefit from its strategic location in a post–Cold War era. New markets were open to exploit in neighboring countries that had been part of the Eastern Bloc. At the same time, Turkey's role as the easternmost member of NATO had lost its importance. The Turkish Republic needed to find a new role. In doing so, it looked to its past Ottoman history as a model.

The end of the Cold War also entailed the end of Communist regimes throughout the Balkans, which could no longer count on Soviet funding. The demise of these regimes was followed by much ethnic conflict in the former Eastern Bloc countries, especially Azerbaijan/Armenia and the Balkans. In the waning years of the Balkan regimes the Communist regimes tried to gain new legitimacy by promoting their nationalist credentials. In Bulgaria this resulted in the policy to rename Muslim Bulgarians with Slavic names, forbid circumcision, and other measures that forcibly tried to wash away Muslim identity in Bulgaria. As a result, a huge number of Bulgarian Turks and Pomaks headed for the Turkish border, reaching a crescendo in 1989. This event was dramatically broadcast and reported throughout Turkey. A few years later after the death of Josip Broz Tito, Yugoslavia was plunged into fractious war as Serbian nationalist Slobodan Milošević evoked the humiliation of the Kosovo Fields battle in order to declare war on the country's Muslims—primarily Bosnians and Kosovars. The atrocities that ensued throughout a large swath of the 1990s included mass murder, rape, and torture as well as Western indifference and inaction. The horrible violence in the former Yugoslavia was also highly publicized throughout Turkey.

Yet in Turkey the resemblances to 1877–1878 were not evoked, and contemporary journalists were not declaiming that history was repeating itself. Simply put, the experiences of the refugees of the War of '93 were not widely known. However, the violence and intimidation suffered by Muslims in the Balkans in the waning years of the Cold War were sure to renew an interest in the Ottoman experience in this region.

Former prime minister and current president Recep Tayyip Erdoğan's success is in large part a result of this economic and political opening created by Özal. In many ways, Erdoğan embodies the contested past subdued during the Kemalist era. Both internally and externally he has promoted what has come to be called neo-Ottomanism.[144] Under Erdoğan, Turkey's foreign policy has been much more engaged in both the Balkans and the Middle East (the former Ottoman sphere) than at any time since the demise of the Ottoman Empire. Internally, the vogue for the Ottoman past has been manifested visibly in architecture (see the newly constructed presidential palace) as well as in less visible ways. The opened economy and a rehabilitated Ottoman history have had a large effect on identity within Turkey.

However, given the duration of Ottoman rule, neo-Ottomanism is naturally loaded with internal contradictions. Periods of relative tolerance alternated with fits of intolerance. Both reformists and reactionaries played roles in the Ottoman centuries. These contradictions are visible within the AKP (Adalet ve Kalkınma Partisi) itself. Ali Suavi, whose failed coup was described in chapter 4, was revered by swaths of the AKP for being something of an early Ottoman thinker of Muslim democracy. AKP spokesman Hüseyin Çilek even wrote a mostly laudatory biography of the man who tried to overthrow the sultan.[145] Erdoğan, on the other hand, has preferred to find in Abdülhamid II an Ottoman ideal for power wielding and leadership in the Muslim world. Increasingly, Erdoğan's vision has become dominant, and today Abdülhamid II's portrait is found hanging in various establishments in Turkey, much as photos of Atatürk have been for decades.

Tolerans has become a buzzword in Turkey, evoking the way in which Turks see the Ottoman Empire, but this tolerance in a Turkish-Ottoman context is loaded with meaning. It is a challenge to what is seen as the totalitarian Republic in the realms of religion and identity—not the tolerance that overly optimistic liberals were hoping for.

The tolerance of the millet system with regard to the empire's multiple religions and identities was demanded by more religious-minded Turks. Once they were empowered, however, the appeals for tolerance proved cynical. Yet Turkish *tolerans*, which is a term borrowed from French, is an opening in terms of changing notions of identity within Turkey itself. It is now very common for Turks to readily identify—in addition to being Turks—as Crimeans, Circassians, Kurds, Laz, Albanians, Bulgarians, Pomaks, Bosnians, Afro-Turks, Mubadils (people whose ancestors arrived to Turkey as part of the population exchange between Turkey and Greece), and so on in such a way as to present a subtle, if not direct, challenge to the very notion of Turkishness.[146] This is an important novelty in Turkish society, as the state was previously hostile to separate identities because of fears of regionalism and separatism and threats to national unity.[147] Turkey still struggles with the emerging multiplicity of identity as well as the long-recognized non-Muslim minorities. Erdoğan, for example, has viewed minority rights as a question of reciprocity rather than one of principle—a bargaining chip for bilateral relations. This has been evident in the issue of the Greek patriarch and the Halki Seminary.[148]

Naturally, with a growing number of identities comes a growing number of histories. These histories and identities are being increasingly explored. Associations for ethnicities, regional groups, and migrant hometowns increased dramatically in Turkey in the 1990s.[149] One such group concerned with Turks of Balkan ancestry is the Balkan Göçmenleri Kültür ve Dayanışma Derneği (Balkan Immigrant Culture and Solidarity Association), shortened to Bal-Göç. This association, in addition to other activities, sponsors conferences about Turkish history in the Balkans as well creating a forum for Turkish descendants of the various waves of Muhacirs to meet, discuss, and develop an identity based on this shared origin.

Another place to look for the Muhacir is in Turkish literature. One Turk laments how the difficult experiences of the refugees coming from the Balkans have not been remembered in Turkish literature: "If this tragedy experienced by hundred thousands of hungry and miserable people escaping from terrible chetas and towards Anatolia had happened to some other nation, it would have constituted a theme for thousands of novels, motion pictures, dramas and TV serials until today." The author of this statement continues by pointing out that migration played a formative role in the social atmosphere of Anatolia at the end of the nineteenth and beginning of the twentieth centuries, yet the suffering that was part and parcel of these migrations has never been reflected in Turkey's social-scientific research or literature: "an important deficiency."[150]

Indeed, Turkish literature makes little mention of the Muhacirs. Not only were the Ottoman generals no match for their Russian counterparts on the battlefield at the time of the Russo-Turkish War of 1877–1878, but Turkish literature was also well behind that of Dostoevskii and Tolstoi. The Turkish novel was in its infancy, and Turkish literature of the period consisted primarily of poetry and theater. At the end of the mufti of Zagora's firsthand account he wrote a long poem recounting his experience in verse. Only a few other poems composed in the period and passed down orally are known to us today. One of them includes the following lines:

> My friends, in the Morning Prayer
> I visited you
> The troubles in my heart
> I wish to tell you

Come my friends, come my brothers
I am going
away from my home and hearth
forced to part from my flower.[151]

The Muhacir also scarcely makes a cameo appearance in Ottoman and Turkish novels. Ottoman literature did deal with war in its European provinces. Namık Kemal, for example, wrote a play that took place during the Crimean War and exalted the Danube as an indelible part of Turkish life. Yet later works only tangentially mentioned refugees, while having to face the Hamidian censor. From the beginning of the Balkan Wars in 1912, followed by ten consecutive years of war, Turkish productivity in literature came to a standstill. And with the new Republic came a new alphabet and new themes. I have been able to only find one novel written in the earlier years of the Republic that refers to the refugee experience. It is considered a classic of modern Turkish literature and was later adapted to an eleven-part made-for-TV movie in 1983. The protagonist of *Üç İstanbul* (The Three Istanbuls, 1938) by Mithat Cemal Kuntay is a refugee who came from Bulgaria as a child during the War of '93. Between taking care of his sick mother and writing a novel, which he hopes to give the title "A Refugee Child," he broods on his hatred of the despotic sultan Abdülhamid II. In a fragment of the novel being written within the novel, he describes autobiographically a refugee child sheltered in a Bosphorus palace:

> After resting in bed, he [Adnan] felt the need for some literary excitement. He got up and started to write the chapter that he would call "A Refugee Child":
>
> > Every child is part poet, part novelist. He conjures made-up monsters in his mind's eye and he plays with his own fears as if they were a game. There are children who for sheer pleasure's sake wake up their mothers begging for a little fright. Just like the well-off who spend big sums of money to go tiger hunting in pursuit of a thrill, these children are wealthy in vitality and imagination. But in addition to these lucky kids are to be found children stricken with grief; refugee children! A scrawny child hounded by an army, nay even an entire state. Those bronze bullet eyes peering through their

5.7. *Cemetery at Scutari* by Abdullah Frères (ca. 1880). Public domain.

> chests, those black bayonet teeth reaching for their shoulders. The stream of children holding onto a mother's hand to escape from the monsters of war fully understand that these are not figments of the imagination. No, these are history's demons.
>
> Adnan authored these lines with the delight of someone recounting his own sorrows. There was pride to be found in pain, and a proud man would appreciate Adnan's words.[152]

Yet, following Kuntay's work, there is a nearly complete caesura in Turkish literature regarding refugees from 1877–1878 and refugees in general for the next fifty years. This only began to change in the late 1980s, coinciding with the aforementioned changes in the Turkish political climate.[153] The events that took place in the Balkans in the 1990s are today finding a literary echo. Literary works dealing with the refugee experience in the Caucasus and the Balkans have begun to make more frequent appearances, adding a new dimension to the way Turkey perceives itself and its past.

CONCLUSION: FORGOTTEN BUT NOT LOST

This chapter has sought to offer explanations for the nonformation of memory regarding the large-scale tragic events relating to the Muslim exodus from Bulgaria. A virtual perfect storm prevented the full development of a memory similar to other traumatic memories that in other times and other places under other conditions not only developed but have also endured. Ebru Boyar claims that Turkish identity is in part based on a victim mentality, but this victim mentality is construed in relation to the state, not the people.[154] Even so, graphic depictions of violence from the wars that plagued the state from 1912 to 1923 were ephemeral and had disappeared by the 1930s.[155] The fact that graphic renderings and emotive narratives of the Ottoman fate in the Balkans were not developed means that this victimhood is not based on the suffering of people, at least with respect to the Balkans and Bulgaria in particular.

Rather, where there is a sense of victimhood in a Turk, that victimhood is related to the state, which was vivisected by a grasping West. Indeed, as mentioned earlier, most Turks view what happened in the Balkans as a mere redrawing of the borders and thus an attack on the state's sovereignty—not an episode of mass violence against the Muslim population. Therefore the common feeling is one of betrayal against a state that had treated the non-Muslims with *tolerans*. The loss of territory rankles, but this is very different from reliving a graphic trauma that can be seen in other communities. The sense of betrayal that Turks feel toward former subjects of the empire is compounded by a sense of injustice vis-à-vis the West, which they see as hypocritical.[156] However, a victim mentality requires a memory of victimhood, which has been largely absent in Turkey—at least until now.

Turkish society has preferred to focus on victory by commemorating its War of Independence and the founding of the Republic, but new developments suggest harbingers for the future. A widening public sphere indicates that the state is ceding power to society in Turkey, which, according to Pierre Nora, means that the nation as the foundation of identity has eroded.[157] Turkish identity is becoming more complex, varied, and accepting of "other" identities. This has been seen at times with a new approach to the Kurdish part of society, which has benefited from increased linguistic and cultural rights. This new approach to identity might be viewed as a domestic form of neo-Ottomanism based on the much-hyped value of tolerance. Such tolerance was desired not only by Kurds but also by Muslims who wished to be more open about expressing their religion in Turkish society. AKP politics seemed to grasp these transformations in the culture of Turkey and momentarily ride the wave of a new Turkish identity increasingly open to various subidentities. The ethnic mosaic of Turkey is being rediscovered, not unlike the glittering mosaics of Hagia Sophia after centuries of preservation under plaster and whitewash. Circassians, Mubadils, Laz, Kurds, and Muhacirs now find a space to develop, but identity and memory are companions; memory is the return of the repressed.[158]

Muhacir memory lay suppressed, unexplored, underdeveloped, and underdocumented, which meant that the collective memory lacked the resources to see subsequent events as horrible reminders rather than as horrible novelties. In 1912–1913, when the shadow of Gladstone loomed and the phrase "bag and baggage" was being uttered again, Istanbul's mosques once again filled up with miserable refugees. As late as 1989 caravans of Bulgarian Muslims rushed to the safety of Turkey, and in 1993 Muslim women of Serbia were locked up in rape camps while their menfolk were executed. Usually memory allows us to locate events in a narrative context, but here a nonextant memory could offer no such guidance. Past tense and portents were neglected, while in the Balkans the pretense for violence had endured and was reinforced. Yet the victims of the ensuing Balkan calamities prefigured by the events of 1877–1878 can lend a voice to the illiterate, the mute, and the dead.

The Canadian-American poet Mark Strand evoked as much in the lines:

> And to sit there,
> In the sunken silence of the place and speak,
> Of what he had lost, what he still possessed of his loss
> . . .
> It came in a language
> Untouched by pity, in lines lavish and dark,
> Where death is reborn and sent into the world as a gift,
> So the future, with no voice of its own, nor hope
> Of ever becoming more than it will be, might mourn.[159]

5.8. *Clearing Out of Europe Bag and Baggage* by Fred Leist. *Graphic* (December 7, 1912).

THE "BAG AND BAGGAGE" LINE.
BLACK SEA
MIDIA
SEA OF MARMORA
ASIA
THE SHADE OF MR. GLADSTONE: And that is all that is left of Turkey in Europe? It is very nearly the "bag and baggage" point

5.9. *The Shade of Gladstone. Westminster Gazette* (November 23, 1912).

Jorge Luis Borges tells us that all knowledge is but remembrance and "all novelty is but oblivion," because the past redounds if we care to recognize it—if we care to reexperience it. In such a vein we can understand Borges's words about the universality of experience and the cyclic nature of time: "I shall be all men—I shall be dead."[160]

If, as has been said, "[t]he past is a foreign country,"[161] then Vladimir Nabokov's command *Speak, Memory* can be seen as an exhortation to undertake a voyage.[162] The Ottoman-Turkish poet Mehmet Akif Ersoy invited Turks to go on a voyage of memory in a land of the past:

> Do you know what the Balkans were, compatriot?
> Your beloved forefathers' resting place
> How long you've yearned for home
> Off you go, now's just the time![163]

Or perhaps it is better to forget, for there are risks in remembering. Emotions can expel nuance, and in turn "[n]ostalgia is the enemy of historical understanding."[164] Moreover, the recollection of the past has not always proven to be the catharsis promised by the promoters of reconciliation committees and truth councils. The resurrection of the past brings with it new fissures, and closure may prove elusive. Remembering may lead neither to reconciliation nor to justice. Maybe it is best to leave the dead in their slumber.

The suffering that Muslims endured in the Balkans is not unique in world history. How many refugees throughout the annals of time have abandoned their homes, key in pocket, harboring a hope to return in the heart? Stories are told of Spanish Jews who to this day still have the key to their forefathers' homes in Andalusia. The same goes for Palestinian refugees who now hold onto keys for homes left on the other side of the wall in Israel. The key to an abandoned home, whether it truly exists or not, is a poetic as well as a potent symbol. It is a metaphor of dispossession but also a symbol of hope. That same key, though, is also a potentially ominous opening for irredentism. What happens when the refugee goes back to the abandoned home, uses the key to unlock the door, and finds a stranger living there? Some have lived that very experience: Pied-Noir French going to see what became of their now Arab-inhabited homes in Algiers; Sudetenland Germans visiting their parents' home in Prague. Inevitably that awkward moment occurs when a stranger opens the door, eyes meet, and past and present collide. Some exiled nations have been permitted to return after long forced sojourns. The Kalmyks under Nikita Khrushchev and the Crimean Tatars under Mikhail Gorbachev were granted a reprieve from the repercussions of Joseph Stalin's paranoia. That friction upon return has been unresolvable. Possession has both spatial and temporal aspects—one owner at a time. Memory, though, is another dimension. It can transcend.

EPILOGUE

> In order to determine . . . the borderline at which the past must be forgotten if it is not to become the gravedigger of the present, we would have to know . . . [the force] of a person, a people, or a culture . . . [for] growing . . . reshaping and incorporating the past and . . . [for] healing wounds, compensating for what has been lost, rebuilding shattered forms out of one's self.
>
> Friedrich Nietzsche, "The Uses and Abuses of History for Life"

The traumas suffered by Ottoman Muslims in the provinces of the Danube and Rumelia are unfortunately not unique in history, but they are indicative of a relatively new development in history: the ethnonation state. The fury unleashed on mixed populations by the idea that territories must be populated by homogeneous populations and ruled by someone of that same ethnicity has terrorized many individuals who were not part of the right group and who did not fit the national paradigm. For many, the horror of those experiences continues to haunt their memories even now. It should not necessarily be seen as a negative that the sufferings of the nightmarish events experienced by the Ottoman Muslims of Bulgaria have not become a basis of identity for Turkey.

There is still so much hatred against Turks today for what happened generations if not centuries ago. This is something that has troubled me since I first became aware of it. In casual conversations with Armenians in Yerevan and Beirut, over dinner with a Cypriot woman (a friend of a friend) in Paris, or talking to a taxi driver in Plovdiv or a woman in a

Sofia bar, I encountered a generalized vitriol that could only accurately be defined as racism. Victimhood can be used to unite a group, but that does not mean that it is the ideal way to do so. Perpetual victims can become obsessed with perpetrators perpetually, and they can also become engaged in a "competition of victims."[1] Since victimhood can nurture vengeance, it is an unhealthy undertaking, especially when coupled with power, and in the context of nationalism, when amorphous groups can be held accountable for the sins of previous generations: "the sins of the fathers." But victimhood is in vogue, probably because it can create a sense of self-righteousness and a justification for bad behavior. As the Polish historian Witold Kula stated, "In the past Jews were envied because of their money, qualifications, positions, and international contacts—today they are envied because of the crematoria in which they were burned."[2]

The aim of this book is not to contribute to a similar feeling of victimization among Turks. Rather, I hope that these horrific experiences can be viewed with a sorrow bereft of bitterness. Each nation has its villains as well as its victims. It is important to remember that we all belong to the same human race, for good and bad. I hope that this work can serve in countering the anti-Turk racism that I have encountered in the surrounding countries. As Atatürk magnanimously stated, "If this history has painful memories, then all the Balkan people share them. The Turkish part is no less bitter."[3] Is there not room to seek for fraternity in remembering that Arabs and Jews were evicted from Spain together and that Turks and Jews fled the Balkans together? Gypsies shared in the suffering of the concentration camps of the Holocaust. Unfortunately, it seems that societies choose to remember their sufferings alone. Any ethnoracial nationalism or religiously based view of history that deprives us of sympathy for the sufferings of another group is not an ideology worth having and should be shunned. History, as Paul Valéry observed, is the human intellect's most dangerous product. "It sets people dreaming, it intoxicates them, spawns in them false memories, exaggerates their reflexes, keeps old wounds open, torments them in their repose, prompts them to delusions of grandeur or deliriums of persecution, and makes nations bitter, arrogant, unbearable and vain."[4] But, as both Georg Hegel and Sigmund Freud believed, memory can be used to overcome traumas and emancipate individuals by transcending history and acknowledging its scars. The best way to retain memory and avoid victimhood is to acknowledge the sufferings of others.

CHRONOLOGY AND RELEVANT PLACE NAMES

END OF OTTOMAN RULE IN EUROPEAN TERRITORIES

Croatia, 1698
Montenegro, 1699
Hungary, 1717
Moldova, 1812 (ceded to Russia)
Greece, 1830
Serbia, 1867
Romania, 1878
Bulgaria, 1878 (limited sovereignty: creation of Bulgarian Principality)
Bessarabia, 1878 (ceded to Russia)
Bosnia, 1878 (annexed by Austria)
Cyprus, 1878 (administration assumed by Great Britain)
Rumelia, 1885 (joined to Bulgaria)
Crete, 1898 (joined to Greece in 1908)
Bulgaria, 1908 (full independence)
Macedonia, 1912 (divided between Greece and Serbia)
Albania, 1912

RUSSO-OTTOMAN WARS

1568–1570
1676–1681
1686–1700 (under Peter the Great, Russians briefly win a port in the Sea of Azov)
1710–1711
1735–1739

1768–1774 (under Catherine the Great, Russia gains access to Black Sea and is granted privileges concerning Ottoman Orthodox Christians in the Treaty of Küçük Kaynarca; Crimea becomes a Russian protectorate)
1787–1792 (with Austria, ending with Treaty of Jassy; Crimea is confirmed as Russian)
1806–1812 (Treaty of Bucharest)
1828–1829
1853–1856 (Crimean War)
1877–1878
1914–1918 (First World War)

CHRONOLOGY OF EVENTS

681–1018: First Bulgarian Empire
1186–1396: Second Bulgarian Empire
1762: Father Paisi publishes Slavonic-Bulgarian history
1814: Filiki Eterya founded in Odessa
1839: Tanzimat begins
1853–1856: Crimean War
1858: Moscow Benevolent Society begins financing Bulgarian students in Russia
1870: Bulgarian Exarchate formed
July 1875: Serbian revolt in Bosnia begins
May 2, 1876: April Uprising
August 31, 1876: Abdülhamid II ascends to the throne
September 1876: Gladstone's pamphlet on the Bulgarian Horrors published
April 24, 1877: Russians declare war against Ottoman Empire
June 22, 1877: Russians cross the Danube
July 20, 1877: Siege of Pleven begins
October 22, 1877: Russians occupy Edirne
December 11, 1877: Siege of Pleven ends
February 23, 1878: Russians reach outskirts of Istanbul
March 3, 1878: San Stefano Treaty signed
May 20, 1878: Ali Suavi coup attempt
June 13, 1878: Congress of Berlin convenes
July 13, 1878: Treaty of Berlin signed

1912–1913: Balkan Wars
1914–1918: First World War
1923: Turkish Republic proclaimed
1970: Bilal Şimşir's *Rumeli'den Türk Göçmenler* published

RELEVANT PLACE-NAMES

Turkish	**Bulgarian**	**Greek**	**Other**
Dobruca	Dobrich		
Edirne	Odrin	Adrianople	
Eski Zağra	Stara Zagora	Beroe, Irenopolis	
Filibe	Plovdiv	Phillopolis	Philippopoli
İstanbul	Istanbul	Constantinople	Byzance, Tsargrad, Stamboul, Islambol
Kalas	Galatz		Galaţi
Lofça	Lovech		
Plevna	Pleven		
Silistre	Silistra		
Sofya	Sofia	Sardica (ancient)	Triaditsa, Sredets
Şumnu	Shumen	Soumen	
Tatarpazarcik	Pazarzhik		
Tırnova	Veliko Tarnovo		Tirnova
Yeni Zağra	Nova Zagora		
Yeşilköy	San Stefano	Ayos Stefanos	
Ziştovi	Shvishtov		Sistova

NOTES

INTRODUCTION

1. Kerwin Lee Klein, "On the Emergence of Memory in Historical Discourse," 131.
2. Robert Musil, "Essay on Monuments," quoted in Klaus Kreiser, "Public Monuments in Turkey and Egypt, 1840–1916" (1995), 103: http://archnet.org/system/publications/contents/3417/original/DPC1306.pdf?1384775050.
3. The name "Byzantine Empire" is a relatively new invention. For those who lived in it, it was none other than the Roman Empire itself and as such its citizens were Romans. "Istanbul" is most likely derived from the Greek phrase εἰς τὴν Πόλιν (eis ten polin) meaning "to the city," which demonstrated its centrality in the Greek world. The name "Islambol" was used in Ottoman times (and still might reappear in Islamist circles) but is not the origin of the city's current name. Following the foundation of the Turkish Republic and the language reform, Istanbul became the official name of the city and was promoted as its sole name internationally.
4. In 2016 the Russian Federation and the Turkish Republic, as part of an effort at rapprochement in bilateral relations, concluded an agreement that provided for the reconstruction of the San Stefano Russian monument to the Russian dead in exchange for the construction of several monuments to Turkish soldiers killed and taken prisoner in Russian-Ottoman conflicts (*Hürriyet Daily News*, April 1, 2016: http://www.hurriyetdailynews.com/turkey-moves-to-rebuild-san-stefano-russian-monument-in-istanbul-.aspx?pageID=238&nID=97191&NewsCatID=341).
5. The "Tsar-Liberator" earned his nickname twice over. He emancipated the serfs of Russia in 1861 and the Bulgarians in 1878. Like his American counterpart, the "Great Emancipator" Abraham Lincoln, he was killed by an assassin.
6. Faik Gur, "Sculpting the Nation in the Early Republic."
7. Kreiser, "Monuments in Turkey and Egypt, 1840–1916," 112.
8. There are Napoleonic statues in his birthplace of Corsica and other European cities. Napoleon remains a divisive figure in France today, however, and the French still struggle with how to see his legacy. See Brian Eads, "Why Napoleon's Still a Problem in France," *Newsweek*, May, 8, 2014.

1. TWILIGHT IN TURKEY-IN-EUROPE

1. Rudyard Kipling, "The Ballad of East and West" (1889).
2. Bram Stoker, *Dracula*, 293.
3. The more "dignified" lyrics cited are from Franz von Gernerth and replaced earlier satirical words written by Joseph Weyl. See "The Story Behind the Blue Danube,"

https://www.classicfm.com/composers/strauss-ii/guides/story-behind-blue-danube/. Lyrics cited here from https://en.wikipedia.org/wiki/The_Blue_Danube#cite_note-:0-1 (accessed December 16, 2018).

4. Rossitsa Gradeva, *War and Peace in Rumeli: 15th to Beginning of 19th Century*, 9.
5. The linguistic interchange took place through many political configurations: the Roman, Byzantine, Bulgarian, and Serbian Empires preceded the Ottoman Empire. However, Balkan Turkish dialects also conformed to a number of aspects of the Balkansprachbund. This indicates that, while this linguistic phenomenon may have predated the Turks, the intermingling necessary for it continued long after their arrival. For a very concise introduction to Balkansprachbund, see Olga Mišeska Tomić, *Balkan Sprachbund Morpho-syntactic Features*; Maria Todorova, *Imagining the Balkans*, 162.
6. See, for example, the Bulgarian documentary *Chiya e Tazi Pesen*? (Whose Song Is This?). The film's synopsis begins as follows: "In a small nice restaurant in Istanbul I was having dinner with friends from various Balkan countries—a Greek, a Macedonian, a Turk, a Serb, and me the Bulgarian. There I heard the song. As soon as it sounded we all started singing it, everyone in his own language. Everyone claimed that the song came from his own country. Then we found ourselves caught in a fierce fight—Whose is this song?"
7. The five holy cities of Christendom—Rome, Constantinople, Jerusalem, Antioch, and Alexandria—were deemed to be so due to the existence of a patriarchate seated in each of them.
8. Bernard Lory, *Le sort de l'héritage ottoman en Bulgarie: L'Exemple des villes bulgares*, 107.
9. Ibid.
10. It should be mentioned that some churches, too, were victims to the vogue of wide and straight boulevards.
11. Nazim Hikmet, "Davet." Nazim Hikmet might not approve of using his poem to refer to minarets. Staunchly Communist and atheist, one of Turkey's greatest poets fled persecution in Turkey one night in a boat up the Bosphorus, finding refuge in Communist Bulgaria. For more about the life and poetry of Nazim Hikmet, see Saime Göksu, *Romantic Communist.*
12. Maria Todorova, "The Ottoman Legacy in the Balkans," 66.
13. See also the Turkish toponym for the city and province of "Erzerum," which also hints at previous inhabitants, the Romans (Greeks).
14. The Turks have another word for Greeks "Yunanlı," derived from the Greek "Ion" (as in "Ionic"), which is primarily used for Greeks living in the independent state of modern Greece. "Rum" would be the more common appellation for ethnically Greek citizens of Turkey.
15. H. T. Norris, *Islam in the Balkans: Religion and Society between Europe and the Arab World*, 27.
16. David Nicolle, *Cross and Crescent: The Ottoman Conquest of Southeastern Europe*, 3. In fact, the very word "Bulgar" is from a Turkic root. While it was previously thought to derive from "Volga Er," which in Turkish means something to the effect of "Volga Man," the lack of analogous *V* to *B* consonantal changes has proven such an etymology false. It actually comes from the verb *bulgamak*, which means in

essence "to mix," as in the bulgar rice that is a common feature in Turkish cuisine today.

17. Only in Britain were the Germanic tribes successful in making their language the dominant language of the masses. In the rest of Europe outside of their Germanic homelands they assimilated to the languages of the people they conquered. Their linguistic contribution is best seen in the common surnames they bequeathed throughout Europe, which were then adapted locally, such as Wilhelm (William, Guillaume, Guillermo), Ludwig (Louis, Luigi), Robrecht (Robert, Roberto), Karl (Charles, Carlos), and so on.
18. Mercia MacDermott, *A History of Bulgaria: 1393–1885*, 16.
19. Ali Eminov, "Turks and Tatars in Bulgaria and the Balkans," 130.
20. Norris, *Islam in the Balkans*, 37.
21. John K. Cox, *The History of Serbia*, 23.
22. Steven Runciman, *The Great Church in Captivity*, 206.
23. Charles Jelavic and Barbara Jelavic, *The Establishment of the Balkan National States, 1804–1920*, 9.
24. R. J. Crampton, *A Concise History of Bulgaria*, 33.
25. Fatma Müge Göçek, "Ethnic Segmentation, Western Education, and Political Outcomes: Nineteenth-Century Ottoman Society," 517.
26. Cathie Carmichael, "Was Religion Important in the Destruction of Ancient Communities in the Balkans, Anatolia and Black Sea Regions, c. 1870–1923?," 358.
27. Crampton, *A Concise History of Bulgaria*, 33.
28. Dawn Chatty, *Displacement and Dispossession in the Modern Middle East*, 52.
29. Mark Mazower, *The Balkans: From the End of Byzantium to the Present Day*, 74.
30. Ali Eminov, *Turkish and Other Muslim Minorities of Bulgaria*, 47.
31. Karen Barkey and Mark von Hagen, eds., *After Empire: Multiethnic Societies and Nation Building*, 16.
32. Kemal Karpat, *Ottoman Population 1830–1914: Demographic and Social Characteristics*, 20.
33. Maria Todorova, *Imagining the Balkans*, 70.
34. Marco Dogo, *Storie balcaniche: Popole e stati nella transizione alla modernità*, 111; Chatty, *Displacement and Dispossession*, 9.
35. Todorova, *Imagining the Balkans*, 63.
36. Reşat Kasaba, *A Moveable Empire: Ottoman Nomads, Migrants and Refugees*.
37. Kemal Karpat, *The Politicization of Islam: Reconstructing Identity, State, Faith, and Community in the Late Ottoman State*, 341.
38. Ilhan Tekeli, "Involuntary Displacement and the Problem of Resettlement in Turkey from the Ottoman Empire to the Present," 204.
39. Nilgün Kiper, "Resettlement of Immigrants and Planning in Izmir in the Hamidian Period," 21.
40. Ibid., 205.
41. Barkey and von Hagen, *After Empire*, 103.
42. Eminov, "Turks and Tatars in Bulgaria and the Balkans," 131.
43. Such Turkish historiography seems to be a myopic reaction to Bulgarian claims and in my view surrenders certain historical terrain in terms of age-old rights to land that only highlight the injustice of previous expulsions.

44. Crampton, *A Concise History of Bulgaria*, 33.
45. Karpat, *Ottoman Population*, 8.
46. Ibid., 20.
47. Ibid., 24.
48. Justin McCarthy, "Muslims in Ottoman Europe: Population from 1800–1912," 29.
49. Karpat, *Ottoman Population*, 26.
50. Mazower, *The Balkans*, 20.
51. Eminov, *Turkish and Other Muslim Minorities of Bulgaria*, 28.
52. Youssef Courbage, "Demographic Transition among Muslims in Eastern Europe," 162.
53. McCarthy, "Muslims in Ottoman Europe," 31.
54. Eminov, *Turkish and Other Muslim Minorities of Bulgaria*, 37.
55. Karpat, *Ottoman Population*, 26.
56. Cited in ibid., 46.
57. Alexandre Toumarkine, *Les migrations des populations musulmanes balkaniques en Anatolie (1876–1913)*, 11.
58. Alexandre Popovic, "Représentation du passé et transmission de l'identité chez les musulmans: Mythes et réalités," 139, 141.
59. Bernard Lewis, *The Multiple Identities of the Middle East*, 13.
60. MacDermott, *A History of Bulgaria*, 46.
61. Toumarkine, *Les migrations des populations musulmanes balkaniques*, 34; Lory, *Le sort de l'héritage*, 48.
62. Toumarkine, *Les migrations des populations musulmanes balkaniques*, 22.
63. Kemal Karpat, "The *Hijra* from Russia and the Balkans: The Process of Self-Definition in the Late Ottoman State," in Dale F. Eickelman and James Piscatori, eds., *Muslim Travellers: Pilgrimage, Migration and the Religious Imagination*, 135.
64. The English term "Gypsies" is derived from the word "Egypt," because of an incorrect understanding of their origins. David M. Crowe, "Muslim Roma in the Balkans," 93.
65. Elena Marushiakova and Vesselin Popov, *Gypsies in the Ottoman Empire*, 26.
66. Crowe, "Muslim Roma in the Balkans," 99.
67. Marushiakova and Popov, *Gypsies in the Ottoman Empire*, 47.
68. Ilona Tomova, "Roma," in Anna Krasteva, ed., *Communities and Identities in Bulgaria*.
69. Iranians in this context means speakers of Iranian languages, probably descendants of earlier migrations routed north of the Black Sea, such as the Alans. Toumarkine, *Les migrations des populations musulmanes balkaniques*, 15.
70. McCarthy, "Muslims in Ottoman Europe," 33.
71. Popovic, "Les Turcs de Bulgarie," 396; Eminov, *Turkish and Other Muslim Minorities of Bulgaria*, 123.
72. Toumarkine, *Les migrations des populations musulmanes balkaniques*, 17.
73. Karpat, *The Politicization of Islam*, 342.
74. Ibid., 18.
75. Ibid., 19.
76. Eminov, *Turkish and Other Muslim Minorities of Bulgaria*, 30.

77. Crampton, *A Concise History of Bulgaria*, 38.
78. History has a way of repeating itself in the Crimea. Following the Second World War, the Crimean Tatars in the Stalinist Soviet Union were once again accused of being a fifth column and deported to Siberia and Uzbekistan. And more recently Crimea has again been annexed to Russia, this time from Ukraine, under Vladimir Putin in 2014 against the wishes of its Crimean Tatar population.
79. Eminov, "Turks and Tatars in Bulgaria and the Balkans," 132.
80. McCarthy, "Muslims in Ottoman Europe," 33.
81. Walter Richmond, *The Circassian Genocide*, 3.
82. Eickelman and Piscatori, *Muslim Travellers*, 132.
83. Justin McCarthy, *Death and Exile: The Ethnic Cleansing of Ottoman Muslims, 1821–1922*, 36.
84. Ibid., 34.
85. Zvi Keren, *The Jews of Rusçuk: From Periphery to Capital of the Tuna Vilayeti*, 37.
86. Ibid., 207.
87. Mazower, *The Balkans*, 265.
88. Mary Neuburger, "The Russo-Turkish War and the 'Eastern Jewish Question': Encounters between Victims and Victors in Ottoman Bulgaria, 1877–78," 58.
89. Ferdinand Schevill, *The History of the Balkans from the Earliest Times to the Present Day*, 384.
90. Crampton, *A Concise History of Bulgaria*, 37.
91. André Gerolymatos, *The Balkan Wars: Conquest, Revolution and Retribution from the Ottoman Era to the Twentieth Century and Beyond*, 123.
92. Mazower, *The Balkans*, 76.
93. R. J. Crampton, "The Turks in Bulgaria, 1878–1944," in Kemal Karpat, ed., *The Turks of Bulgaria: The History, Culture and Political Fate of a Minority*, 44.
94. Norris, *Islam in the Balkans*, 100.
95. Lory, *Le sort de l'héritage*, 54.
96. Bernard Lewis, *Islam et laïcité: La naissance de la Turquie moderne*, 288.
97. Interview conducted with Rossitsa Gradeva, October 18, 2012, Sofia, Bulgaria.
98. Eminov, *Turkish and Other Muslim Minorities of Bulgaria*, 28.
99. Mark Pinson, "Ottoman Bulgaria in the First Tanzimat Period: The Revolts in Nish (1841) and Vidin (1850)," 117.
100. Popovic, "Les Turcs de Bulgarie," 398.
101. Marco Dogo in Stefano Bianchini and Marco Dogo, eds., *The Balkans: National Identities in Historical Perspective*, 63, 129.
102. Twelve wars were waged between the Russian Empire and the Ottoman Empire. Some of these involved other parties. While some of these wars have come to be known to historians in the West by more particular designations, such as the Crimean War or the First World War, the bulk of them are placed under the rubric of Russo-Turkish or Russo-Ottoman wars followed by the year. Naturally, the parties involved tend to have developed more revealing appellations for these military engagements.
103. Ivo Andrić, *The Bosnian Chronicle*, 10.
104. Micha Glenny, *The Balkans: Nationalism, War and the Great Powers, 1804–1999*, 95.
105. Karpat, *Ottoman Population*, 11.

106. Gerolymatos, *The Balkan Wars*, 119.
107. Pinson, "Ottoman Bulgaria in the First Tanzimat Period," 115.
108. Ibid., 129, 133.
109. Karpat, *The Politicization of Islam*, 5.
110. Karpat, *Ottoman Population*, 24.
111. Crampton, *A Concise History of Bulgaria*, 56.
112. Georges Castellan, *History of the Balkans from Mohammed the Conqueror to Stalin*, 308.
113. L. S. Stavrianos, *The Balkans since 1453*, 368.
114. Göçek, "Ethnic Segmentation, Western Education, and Political Outcomes," 522.
115. Karpat, *The Politicization of Islam*, 12.
116. Ibid., 315.
117. Boris Akunin, *The Turkish Gambit*, 39.
118. Pinson, "Ottoman Bulgaria in the First Tanzimat Period," 117.
119. Göçek, "Ethnic Segmentation, Western Education, and Political Outcomes," 517.
120. Pinson, "Ottoman Bulgaria in the First Tanzimat Period," 105.
121. Karpat, *The Politicization of Islam*, 96.
122. Chatty, *Displacement and Dispossession*, 60.
123. For a more detailed account of the Salonika Incident, see Berke Torunoğlu, *Murder in Salonika, 1876: A Tale of Apostasy and International Crisis*.
124. Steven Runciman, *A History of the First Bulgarian Empire*, 259.
125. Quoted in MacDermott, *A History of Bulgaria*, 93.
126. MacDermott, *A History of Bulgaria*, 89.
127. Boriana Panayotava, "Soi et l'autre dans la perspective de l'antagonisme 'barbarie-civilisation': Le case de la Bulgarie et ces voisins balkaniques," *Canadian Journal of History* 38 (August 2003): 205.
128. Konstantin Jireček, *Geschichte der Bulgaren*.
129. Crampton, *A Concise History of Bulgaria*, 66.
130. Jelavic and Jelavic, *The Establishment of the Balkan National States*, 131.
131. The original church of Saint Stephen, built on the shore of the Golden Horn, was a small wooden structure that burned down. It was replaced in 1898 with the large neo-Gothic church, made from prefabricated cast iron with a steel skeleton. The pieces were produced in Vienna and shipped down the Danube and across the Black Sea to Constantinople. The bells were forged in Yaroslavl, Russia.
132. MacDermott, *A History of Bulgaria*, 137.
133. Crampton, *A Concise History of Bulgaria*, 75.
134. Ibid., 43, 47.
135. Barbara Jelavic, *Russia's Balkan Entanglements, 1806–1914*, 9.
136. On October 11, 2018, the ecumenical patriarch was back in the headlines. Patriarch Bartholomew granted a separate status to the Ukrainian Autocephalous Church, effectively removing it from under the Moscow Patriarchate. This time Russia was incensed, and the Russian Orthodox Church severed its ties with the Ecumenical Patriarchate of Constantinople.
137. Jelavic, *Russia's Balkan Entanglements*, 123, 31.
138. Jelavic and Jelavic, *The Establishment of the Balkan National States*, 158.
139. Jelavic, *Russia's Balkan Entanglements*, 133.

140. Ibid., 153.
141. Lory, *Le sort de l'héritage*, 54.
142. Bozidar Samardziev, "Traits dominants de la politique d'Abdulhamid II relative au problème des nationalités (1876–1885)," *Études Balkaniques* (Sofia) 4 (1972), 60.
143. MacDermott, *A History of Bulgaria*, 195.
144. Castellan, *History of the Balkans*, 313.

2. BAG AND BAGGAGE

1. Leo Tolstoi, *Hadji Murad*, 3. The following quotations from this work are also from this source.
2. Mercia MacDermott, *A History of Bulgaria: 1393–1885*, 233.
3. David Harris, *Britain and the Bulgarian Horrors of 1876*, 17.
4. Elena Marushiakova and Vesselin Popov, *Gypsies in the Ottoman Empire*, 70.
5. Justin McCarthy, *Death and Exile: The Ethnic Cleansing of Ottoman Muslims, 1821–1922*, 95.
6. Tetsuya Sahara, "Two Different Images: Bulgarian and English Sources on the Batak Massacre," in M. Hakan Yavuz, *War & Diplomacy: The Russo-Turkish War of 1877–1878 and the Treaty of Berlin*, 484.
7. Mehmet Hacisalihoğlu, "Muslim and Orthodox Resistance against the Berlin Peace Treaty in the Balkans," in Yavuz, *War & Diplomacy*, 134.
8. Akçam, *From Empire to Republic*, 65.
9. Ann Pottinger Saab, *Reluctant Icon: Gladstone, Bulgaria and the Working Classes, 1856–1878*, 63.
10. MacDermott, *A History of Bulgaria: 1393–1885*, 277.
11. Ibid., 82.
12. Sahara, "Two Different Images," in Yavuz, *War & Diplomacy*, 496.
13. Micha Glenny, *The Balkans: Nationalism, War and the Great Powers, 1804–1999*, 109.
14. Quoted in Taner Akçam, *From Empire to Republic: Turkish Nationalism and the Armenian Genocide*, 100.
15. André Gerolymatos, *The Balkan Wars: Conquest, Revolution and Retribution from the Ottoman Era to the Twentieth Century and Beyond*, 201.
16. Fyodor Dostoyevsky, *The Brothers Karamazov*, 262.
17. Bilal Şimşir, *Rumeli'den Türk Göçmenler*, 2:cxxii (all quotations from this source are in their original languages).
18. Catherine Brown, "Henry James and Ivan Turgenev: Cosmopolitanism, Croquet, and Language," 3–4.
19. Ivan Sergeevich Turgenev, "Croquet at Windsor," originally appeared in English in *Illustrated Weekly*, a New York–based newspaper on June 2, 1877: http://www.katinkahesselink.net/blavatsky/articles/v1/y1877_008.htm.
20. Leo Tolstoy, *Anna Karenina*, 759.
21. Sahara, "Two Different Images," in Yavuz, *War & Diplomacy*, 497.
22. Harris, *Britain and the Bulgarian Horrors of 1876*, 251.
23. These figures, which have no substantiation other than MacGahan's hearsay, have been widely circulated in Bulgarian national histories.

24. Sahara, "Two Different Images," in Yavuz, *War & Diplomacy*, 497.
25. Richard Millman, "The Bulgarian Massacres Reconsidered," 229–31.
26. Saab, *Reluctant Icon*, 24.
27. Harris, *Britain and the Bulgarian Horrors of 1876*, 220.
28. Justin McCarthy, *Death and Exile: The Ethnic Cleansing of Ottoman Muslims, 1821–1922*, 62.
29. Fatma Müge Göçek, "Ethnic Segmentation, Western Education, and Political Outcomes: Nineteenth-Century Ottoman Society," 533.
30. Saab, *Reluctant Icon*, 129.
31. S. A. Nikitin, "Russia and the Liberation of Bulgaria," 89.
32. Robert Crews, *For Prophet and Tsar: Islam and Empire in Russia and Central Asia*, 302.
33. Karel Durman, *Lost Illusions: Russian Policies towards Bulgaria in 1877–1878*, 49.
34. Isabela Fonseca, *Bury Me Standing: The Gypsies and Their Journey*, 271.
35. Slobodan Drakulic, "Anti-Turkish Obsession and the Exodus of Balkan Muslims," 5.
36. Quoted in Elizabeth Siberry, *The New Crusaders: Images of the Crusades in the 19th and Early 20th Centuries*, 84.
37. Adam Knobler, "Holy Wars, Empires, and the Portability of the Past: The Modern Uses of Medieval Crusades," 310, 316.
38. Jacques Semelin, *Purify and Destroy: The Political Uses of Massacre and Genocide*, 17.
39. Ibid., 38.
40. Dogo, *Storie balcaniche*, 43.
41. Quoted in Wolfgang Höpken, "Flucht vor dem Kreuz? Muslimische Emigration aus Südosteuropa nach dem Ende der osmanischen Herrschaft (19./20. Jahrhundert)," 1.
42. Quoted in Cathie Carmichael, *Ethnic Cleansing in the Balkans: Nationalism and the Destruction of Tradition*, 22.
43. Quoted in Harris, *Britain and the Bulgarian Horrors of 1876*, 176.
44. Quoted in Ebru Boyar, *Ottomans, Turks and the Balkans: Empire Lost, Relations Altered*, 100.
45. Quoted in Benjamin Lieberman, *Terrible Fate: Ethnic Cleansing in the Making of Modern Europe*, 18.
46. Other examples of legal doublets include "aid and abet," "intents and purposes," "flotsam and jetsam," and "kith and kin." David Crystal, *The Stories of English* (Woodstock, NY: Overlook Press, 2004), 152.
47. John Mill, *The Ottomans in Europe; or, Turkey in the Present Crisis, with the Secret Societies' Maps*, 12.
48. Harris, *Britain and the Bulgarian Horrors of 1876*, 235.
49. See Ali Fuat Örenç, *Balkanlarda İlk Dram: Unuttuğumuz Mora Türkleri ve Eyaletten Bağımsızlığa Yunanistan*.
50. *The Pall Mall Budget: Being a Weekly Collection of Articles Printed in the Pall Mall Gazette from Day to Day, with a Summary of News* 17 (1877): 28.
51. Dogo, *Storie balcaniche*, 44.
52. Quoted in Harris, *Britain and the Bulgarian Horrors of 1876*, 371, 171.

53. Quoted in ibid., 111.
54. Quoted in Orhan Koloğlu, *Abdülhamid Gerçeği*, 383; English translation in Taner Akçam, *From Empire to Republic: Turkish Nationalism and the Armenian Genocide*, 64.
55. Şimşir, *Rumeli'den Türk Göçmenler*, 2:cxxxi.
56. Edward Said, *Orientalism*.
57. McCarthy, *Death and Exile*, 12.
58. Quoted in ibid.
59. Örenç, *Balkanlarda İlk Dram*, 18.
60. John Henry Newman, *Lectures on the History of the Turks in Their Relation to Europe* (delivered at Catholic University of Liverpool, October 1853), 221: http://newmanreader.org/works/historical/volume1/turks/lecture9.html.
61. Voltaire, *Oeuvres complètes de Voltaire: Correspondance avec le Roi de Prusse*, 167.
62. Nilgün Kiper, "Resettlement of Immigrants and Planning in Izmir in the Hamidian Period."
63. Anna Reid, *Borderland: A Journey through the History of Ukraine*, 9.
64. Charles J. Halperin, *Russia and the Golden Horde: The Mongol Impact on Medieval Russian History*, 63.
65. David Schimmelpink van dere Oye, *Russian Orientalism: Asia in the Russian Mind from Peter the Great to the Emigration*, 21.
66. Steven Runciman, *The Great Church in Captivity*, 321.
67. Adam Knobler, "Holy Wars, Empires, and the Portability of the Past: The Modern Uses of Medieval Crusades."
68. Schimmelpink van dere Oye, *Russian Orientalism*, 124.
69. Hans Kohn, *Pan-Slavism: Its History and Ideology*, 128.
70. Steven Graham, *Peter the Great*, 62.
71. Leon Dominian, "The Site of Constantinople: A Factor of Historical Value," 57.
72. Lindsey Hughes, *Russia in the Age of Peter the Great*, 22.
73. Lindsey Hughes, *Peter the Great: A Biography*, 1.
74. Gwyn Jones, *A History of the Vikings*, 259.
75. Runciman, *The Great Church in Captivity*, 206.
76. John Meyendorff, *Byzantium and the Rise of Russia*, 6.
77. Barbara Jelavic, *Russia's Balkan Entanglements, 1806–1914*, 36.
78. Kohn, *Pan-Slavism*, 127.
79. Philip Mansel, *Constantinople: City of the World's Desire, 1453–1924*, 50.
80. Donald Ostrowski, "'Moscow the Third Rome' as Historical Ghost," 176.
81. Hughes, *Russia in the Age of Peter the Great*, 46.
82. Durman, *Lost Illusions*, 18.
83. Quoted in Hughes, *Peter the Great*, 96.
84. Hughes, *Russia in the Age of Peter the Great*, 352.
85. Hughes, *Peter the Great*, 96.
86. Kalpana Sahni, *Crucifying the Orient: Russian Orientalism and the Colonization of Caucasus and Central Asia*, 17.
87. Ian Grey, *Catherine the Great: Autocrat and Empress of All Russia*, 219, 304, 202.
88. Kohn, *Pan-Slavism*, 197.
89. MacDermott, *A History of Bulgaria*, 16.

90. Kohn, *Pan-Slavism*, 122.
91. "Oleg's Shield," in Jesse Zeldin, *Poems and Political Letters of F. I. Tyutchev*, 124.
92. "Russian Geography," in ibid., 131.
93. "Dawn," in ibid., 132.
94. "A Prophecy," in ibid., 134.
95. Quoted in Sahni, *Crucifying the Orient*, 77.
96. Victor Taki, "Orientalism on the Margins: The Ottoman Empire under Russian Eyes," 323.
97. Karel Durman, *The Time of the Thunderer: Mikhail Katkov: Russian Nationalist Extremism and the Failure of the Bismarckian System, 1871–1887*, 181.
98. Sarah McArthur, "Being European: Russian Travel Writing and the Balkans, 1804–1877," 200.
99. Crews, *For Prophet and Tsar*, 302.
100. Knobler, "Holy Wars, Empires, and the Portability of the Past," 301–303.
101. Quoted in Mary Neuburger, "The Russo-Turkish War and the 'Eastern Jewish Question': Encounters between Victims and Victors in Ottoman Bulgaria, 1877–78," 56.
102. Dogo, *Storie balcaniche*, 43.
103. Kohn, *Pan-Slavism*, 209.
104. Fyodor Dostoevsky, *The Diary of a Writer, Volume 1*, 358.
105. Kohn, *Pan-Slavism*, 209.
106. Quoted in Sahni, *Crucifying the Orient*, 74.
107. Kohn, *Pan-Slavism*, 186.
108. Sahni, *Crucifying the Orient*, 74.
109. Dostoyevsky, *The Diary of a Writer, Volume 2*, 904.
110. Ibid., 364.
111. Quoted in Kohn, *Pan-Slavism*, 220.
112. Ibid., 257.
113. Carmichael, *Ethnic Cleansing in the Balkans*, 22.
114. Maria Todorova, *Imagining the Balkans.*
115. John K. Cox, *The History of Serbia*, 32.
116. Machiel Kiel, *Art and Society of Bulgaria in the Turkish Period*, 33.
117. Anton Donchev, *Time of Parting*, 276.
118. Ivan Elenkov and Daniela Koleva, "Historiography in Bulgaria after the Fall of Communism: Did 'The Change' Happen?," 188.
119. Kiel, *Art and Society of Bulgaria*, 33.
120. See also Dissislava Lilova, "A Canon without Messianic Myth: Narrating How Bulgaria Fell under Ottoman Rule," in Murat Belge and Jale Parla, eds., *Balkan Literatures in the Era of Nationalism*, 167.
121. Franz Fanon, *The Wretched of the Earth*, 249.
122. Alexandre Popovic, "Représentation du passé et transmission de l'identité chez les musulmans: Mythes et réalités," 140.
123. The term "Apostles" used for the leading figures in the Bulgarian independence movement endowed them, as well as the movement itself, with a religious role—not insignificant given that their enemies were of another religion.
124. Quoted in MacDermott, *A History of Bulgaria*, 209.
125. Mark Biondich, *The Balkans: Revolution, War, & Political Violence since 1878*, 28.

126. Bernard Lory, *Le sort de l'héritage ottoman en Bulgarie: L'Exemple des villes bulgares*, 34.
127. The English translation by James W. Wiles (1930) is available in full at http://www.njegos.org/petrovics/wreath.htm. The following quotations from this poem are also from this source.
128. Tim Judah, *The Serbs: History, Myth and the Destruction of Yugoslavia*, 77.
129. Ivan Vazov, "The Dark Hero," in *Selected Short Stories*, 174.
130. Semelin, *Purify and Destroy*, 58.
131. Biondich, *The Balkans*, 245.
132. Semelin, *Purify and Destroy*, 242.
133. Quoted in ibid., 110.
134. Ibid., 143.
135. J. Drew Gay, *Plevna, the Sultan, and the Porte: Reminiscences of the War in Turkey*, 237.

3. MASSACRE AND EXPULSION

1. Sinan Kuneralp, ed., *The Queen's Ambassador to the Sultan: Memoirs of Sir Henry A. Layard's Constantinople Embassy, 1877–78*, 158.
2. John Foster Fraser, *Pictures from the Balkans*, 94.
3. *Report by Consul Blunt on the Effects of the Russian Invasion of Roumelia* (1877), 44.
4. Ibid., 19.
5. Dorothy Anderson, *The Balkan Volunteers*, 175.
6. Vereshchagin, *At Home and in War, 1853–1881*, 384.
7. The Hijra calendar is the Islamic lunar calendar that begins with the Prophet Muhammad's flight from Mecca to Medina in the year AD 622.
8. James Reid, *Crisis of the Ottoman Empire: Prelude to Collapse, 1839–1878*, 318.
9. Charles Jelavic and Barbara Jelavic, *The Establishment of the Balkan National States 1804–1920*, 148.
10. Quoted in Karel Durman, *Lost Illusions: Russian Policies towards Bulgaria in 1877–1878*, 52.
11. McCarthy, *Death and Exile*, 66.
12. Peter Holquist, "The Russian Empire as 'Civilized State': International Law as Principle and Practice in Imperial Russia, 1874–1878," 15.
13. Comité International de la Croix-Rouge, *Bulletin international des sociétés de secours aux militaires blessés*, 41, 43, 45.
14. Camille Farcy, *La guerre sur le Danube (1877–1878)*, 154.
15. Ibid., 150–53.
16. Toumarkine, *Les migrations des populations musulmanes balkaniques*, 41.
17. Semelin, *Purify and Destroy*, 248.
18. Maria Todorova describes this phenomenon in *Imagining the Balkans*.
19. Quoted in Semelin, *Purify and Destroy*, 113.
20. Ibid., 218.
21. Quoted in Semelin, *Purify and Destroy*, 199.
22. Ibid., 15, 166, 196 (quotation).
23. Quoted in Kuneralp, *The Queen's Ambassador*, 141.

24. Quoted in Gary J. Bass, *Freedom's Battle: The Origins of Humanitarian Intervention*, 300.
25. McCarthy, *Death and Exile*, 64–73.
26. N. R. Ovsianyi, *Russkoe Upravlenie v Bolgarii v 1877–78–79 gg.*, 1:185.
27. Ibid., 1:186.
28. Vereshchagin, *At Home and in War*, 251 (quotation), 254.
29. *Report by Consul Blunt*, 70.
30. Aleko Konstantinov, *Bai Ganyo: Incredible Tales of a Modern Bulgarian*, 94.
31. *Report by Consul Blunt*, 70; Kuneralp, *The Queen's Ambassador*, 143.
32. Farcy, *La guerre sur le Danube*, 43.
33. *Report by Consul Blunt*, 28.
34. Ibid., 30.
35. Ibid., 31.
36. Ibid., 23, 122.
37. B. Destani, ed., *Ethnic Minorities in the Balkan States, 1860–1971*, 286.
38. McCarthy, *Death and Exile*, 69.
39. American Board of Commissioners for Foreign Missions, *The Missionary Herald*, 317.
40. Vereshchagin, *At Home and in War*, 329.
41. H. Mainwaring Dunstan, *The Turkish Compassionate Fund: An Account of Its Origin, Working and Results*, 9.
42. Quoted in Edmund Ollier, *Cassel's Illustrated History of the Russo-Turkish War*, 350.
43. Ovsianyi, *Russkoe Upravlenie v Bolgari*, 1:252.
44. Benjamin Lieberman, *Terrible Fate: Ethnic Cleansing in the Making of Modern Europe*, 26.
45. Holquist, "The Russian Empire as 'Civilized State,'" 22.
46. Quoted in Bilal Şimşir, *Rumeli'den Türk Göçmenler*, 1:169.
47. Ibid., 1:301.
48. *Russkaya Starina* 88 (1895): 29.
49. Kuneralp, *The Queen's Ambassador*, 235.
50. Quoted in Ovsianyi, *Russkoe Upravlenie v Bolgarii*, 1:211.
51. Quoted in ibid., 1:274.
52. *Turkey, No 49: Correspondence Respecting the Proceedings of the International Commission Sent to the Mount Rhodope District*, 38.
53. Giuseppe Marcotti, *Tre mesi in Oriente: Ricordi di viaggio e di guerra*, 235.
54. Şimşir, *Rumeli'den Türk Göçmenler*, 1:39.
55. Kuneralp, *The Queen's Ambassador*, 210.
56. Şimşir, *Rumeli'den Türk Göçmenler*, 1:200.
57. Vereshchagin, *At Home and in War*, 330.
58. McCarthy, *Death and Exile*, 71.
59. Reid, *Crisis of the Ottoman Empire*, 354.
60. Lory, *Le sort de l'héritage*, 56.
61. Dogo, *Storie balcaniche*, 37 (quotation), 36.
62. Semelin, *Purify and Destroy*, 165.
63. John Fife-Cookson, *With the Armies of the Balkans and at Gallipoli*, 53.
64. Henry Otis Dwight, *Turkish Life in War Time*, 140.
65. *Report by Consul Blunt*, 96.
66. Fife-Cookson, *With the Armies of the Balkans*, 37.

67. *Report by Consul Blunt*, 105.
68. Dunstan, *The Turkish Compassionate Fund*, 14.
69. Ibid., 13.
70. Ruth Seifert in Alexandra Stiglmayer, *Mass Rape: The War against Women in Bosnia-Herzegovina*, 54 (quotation), 85.
71. *Turkey, No. 49, Correspondence Respecting the Proceedings of the International Commission*, 23.
72. *Turkey, No. 45: Further Correspondence Respecting the Affairs of Turkey*, 55.
73. *Te Aroha News* 6, no. 312 (October 31, 1888): 3.
74. Mary Neuburger, "The Russo-Turkish War and the 'Eastern Jewish Question': Encounters between Victims and Victors in Ottoman Bulgaria, 1877–8," 57, 60. Russian-Yiddish writer S. Ansky wrote a short story called "Mendl Turk," in which a Jewish village in Lithuania is riven between the Jews who support Russia in the war and those who support the Turks. It gives an interesting and humorous picture of how the war was being followed on the outside as well as showing that many Russian Jews did not feel a strong sense of solidarity with their government. "Mendl Turk," in S. Ansky, *The Dyubbuk and Other Writings*.
75. Mary Neuburger, "The Russo-Turkish War and the 'Eastern Jewish Question,'" 54.
76. Quoted in Destani *Ethnic Minorities in the Balkan States*.
77. Semelin, *Purify and Destroy*, 230.
78. J. Drew Gay, *Plevna, the Sultan, and the Porte*, 127.
79. Frederick Boyle, *The Narrative of an Expelled Correspondent*, 199–200.
80. Quoted in Şimşir, *Rumeli'den Türk Göçmenler*, 1:157.
81. Ibid., 474.
82. Lieberman, *Terrible Fate*, 20.
83. Ibid., 28; Fife-Cookson, *With the Armies of the Balkans*, 55.
84. Şimşir, *Rumeli'den Türk Göçmenler*, 1:271.
85. Ibid., 1:371.
86. Lory, *Le sort de l'héritage*, 41.
87. Hüseyin Raci Efendi, *Zağra Müftüsünün Hatıraları: Tarihçe-i Vak'a-i Zağra*, 87.
88. Lory, *Le sort de l'héritage*, 38.
89. Reid, *Crisis of the Ottoman Empire*, 357.
90. McCarthy, *Death and Exile*, 68.
91. Fife-Cookson, *With the Armies of the Balkans*, 151.
92. Wentworth Huyshe, *The Liberation of Bulgaria: War Notes in 1877*, 181.
93. Joyce A. Sharpey-Schafer, *Soldier of Fortune: F. D. Millet, 1846–1912*, 43.
94. Dick de Lonlay, *À travers la Bulgarie: Souvenirs de guerre et voyage par un voluntaire au 26e Régiment de Cosques du Don*, 143.
95. Francis Vinton Greene, *Sketches of Army Life in Russia*, 107.
96. Mahmud Celaleddin Paşa, *Mir'at-i Hakikat: Tarihi Hakikatlarin Aynasi*, 508.
97. de Lonlay, *À travers la Bulgarie*, 261.
98. *Turkey, No. 49: Correspondence Respecting the Proceedings of the International Commission*, 38.
99. Archibald Forbes, *Czar and Sultan: The Adventures of a British Lad in the Russo-Turkish War of 1877–78*, 358; Greene, *Sketches of Army Life*, 108 (quotation).
100. *Turkey, No. 49: Correspondence Respecting the Proceedings of the International Commission*, 55.

101. Robert de Heimann, *À cheval de Varsovie à Constantinople par un capitaine de hussards de la Garde Impériale Russe (1877/78)*, 235.
102. Sharpey-Schafer, *Soldier of Fortune*, 47.
103. Heimann, *À cheval de Varsovie*, 244.
104. Quoted in Linus Pierpont Brockett and Porter Cornelius Bliss, *The Conquest of Turkey; or, The Decline and Fall of the Ottoman Empire, 1877–8: A Complete History of the Late War between Russia and Turkey*, 663.
105. Archibald Forbes, *Czar and Sultan*, 357.
106. Greene, *Sketches of Army Life*, 108.
107. Celaleddin Paşa, *Mir'at-i Hakikat*, 508.
108. Forbes, *Czar and Sultan*, 357.
109. George Washburn, *Fifty Years in Constantinople and Recollections of Robert College*, 128.
110. Boyle, *The Narrative of an Expelled Correspondent*, 196.
111. de Lonlay, *À travers la Bulgarie*, 263.
112. Quoted in Lieberman, *Terrible Fate*, 25.
113. Tarık Özcelik, "Basiret Gazetesi'ne Göre Doksanüç İstanbul'da Rumeli Göçmenleri (1877–1878)," 4.
114. Fife-Cookson, *With the Armies of the Balkans*, 6.
115. C. Martner, *Emploi des chemins de fer pendant la guerre d'Orient, 1876–1878*, 48.
116. Nedim İpek, *Rumeli'den Anadolu'ya Türk Göçleri*, 33.
117. Şimşir, *Rumeli'den Türk Göçmenler*, 1:267.
118. Özcelik, "Basiret Gazetesi'ne Göre," 9.
119. Anderson, *The Balkan Volunteers*, 182.
120. Quoted in Şimşir, *Rumeli'den Türk Göçmenler*, 1:279.
121. *Aberdeen Journal*, January 16, 1878, p. 3.
122. Quoted in Şimşir, *Rümeli'den Türk Göçmenler*, 1:273.
123. Quoted in ibid., 1:288.
124. Quoted in ibid., 1:323.
125. Chatty, *Displacement and Dispossession in the Modern Middle East*, 22.
126. Ömer Turan, *Rodop Türkleri'nin 1878 Direnişi*, 5.
127. Bernard Lory, "Ahmed Aga Tamrashliyata: The Last Derebey of the Rhodopes," *International Journal of Turkish Studies* 4, no. 2 (1989).
128. *Turkey, No. 49: Correspondence Respecting the Proceedings of the International Commission*, 58.
129. Turan, *Rodop Türkleri'nin 1878 Direnişi*, 5.
130. Vemund Aarbakke, Vassilis Koutsoukos, and Niarchos Georgios, "The Tamrash Rebellion (1878–1886)," paper presented at the Keni International Conference "Revolutions in the Balkans," Athens, Greece, October 31, 2013.
131. *Turkey, No. 49: Correspondence Respecting the Proceedings of the International Commission*, 1, 10 (quotation).
132. *Turkey, No. 42: Further Correspondence Respecting the Affairs of Turkey*, 2.
133. Kazantzakis, *Freedom and Death*, 323.
134. Ivan Vazov, "Old Yotso Is Watching," in *Selected Short Stories*, 136.
135. Ibid., 136–138.
136. Kazantzakis, *Freedom and Death*, 323.

137. "Father Nestor," in Ivan Vazov, *Bulgarian Short Stories*, 13.
138. Aylmer Maude, *The Life of Tolstoy: Later Years*, 482.
139. Roosevelt was speaking of Nicaraguan dictator Anastasio Somoza. John Jacob Nutter, *The CIA's Black Ops: Covert Action, Democracy, and Foreign Policy* (New York: Prometheus Books, 1999), 95.
140. Quoted in Lieberman, *Terrible Fate*, 23.
141. Justin McCarthy, "Muslims in Ottoman Europe: Population from 1800–1912," 35.
142. Cited in İpek, *Rumeli'den Anadolu'ya Türk Göçleri*, 40.
143. Cited in Toumarkine, *Les migrations des populations musulmanes balkaniques*, 40.
144. Richard Crampton, *Bulgaria*, 426.
145. Ali Eminov, *Turkish and Other Muslim Minorities of Bulgaria*, 37.
146. Kemal Karpat, ed., *The Turks of Bulgaria: The History, Culture and Political Fate of a Minority*, 47.
147. Dirk Hoerder, *Cultures in Contact: World Migrations in the Second Millennium*, 445.
148. Quoted in Lieberman, *Terrible Fate*, 20.
149. This is very much in the vein of John Milton's unintended rendering of Lucifer as conflicted, imperfect, and somehow worthy of the reader's empathy, in stark contrast to an unsympathetic, unbending, and distant yet perfect God in *Paradise Lost*.
150. Kazantzakis, *Zorba the Greek*, 21–23.

4. REFUGE AND RESETTLEMENT

1. Quoted in J. Drew Gay, *Plevna, the Sultan, and the Porte*, 64.
2. de Lonlay, *À travers la Bulgarie*, 303; Vereshchagin, *At Home and in War*, 404 (quotation).
3. Richard Graf von Pfeil, *Experiences of a Prussian Officer in the Russian Service during the Turkish War of 1877–78*, 285, 298; Greene, *Sketches of Army Life*, 189.
4. Quoted in Alan Palmer, *The Decline and Fall of the Ottoman Empire*, 154.
5. Mansel, *Constantinople*, 306.
6. The term "jingoism" refers to extreme patriotism: ironically, it was coined for a war in which the English took no part to defend territory that was not English.
7. The music and lyrics were composed by Gilbert Hastings MacDermott. The words of the verses are a rather interesting condemnation of Russian imperialism.

    The misdeeds of the Turks have been "spouted" thro' all lands,
    But how about the Russians, can they show spotless hands?
    They slaughtered well at Khiva, in Siberia icy cold,
    How many subjects done to death will never perhaps be told,
    They butchered the Circassians, man, woman, yes and child,
    With cruelties their Generals their murderous hours beguiled,
    And poor unhappy Poland their cruel yoke must bear,
    Whilst prayers for "Freedom and Revenge" go up into the air.

    May he who 'gan the quarrel soon have to bite the dust,
    The Turk should be thrice armed for "he hath his quarrel just,"

'Tis sad that countless thousands should die thro' cruel war,
But let us hope most fervently ere long it will be o'er;
Let them be warned, Old England is brave Old England still,
We've proved our might, we've claimed our right, and ever, ever will,
Should we have to draw the sword our way to victory we'll forge,
With the battle cry of Britons, "Old England and Saint George!"

The lyrics are available online at http://www.victorianweb.org/mt/musichall/macdermott1.html or listen to the song at https://www.youtube.com/watch?v=h1ZFzs7hL5g_last (posted June 11, 2013).

8. Mansel, *Constantinople*, 307.
9. S. P. Polushkin, *Dnevnik Donskogo Kazaka*, 191.
10. Ibid., 199.
11. Ulysses S. Grant, *The Papers of Ulysses S. Grant*, 356.
12. İpek, *Rumeli'den Anadolu'ya Türk Göçleri*, 46–47.
13. Kuneralp, *The Queen's Ambassador*, 210.
14. Erol Haker, *93 Harbi: Tuna'da Son Osmanlı Yahudileri*, 191.
15. Özcelik, "Basiret Gazetesi'ne Göre," 9.
16. İpek, *Rumeli'den Anadolu'ya Türk Göçleri*, 56.
17. Özcelik, "Basiret Gazetesi'ne Göre," 9.
18. Henry Otis Dwight, *Turkish Life in War Time*, 166.
19. Kuneralp, *The Queen's Ambassador*, 142.
20. Mordtmann et al., *Les réfugiés de la Roumelie*, 8.
21. T. Lauder Brunton, *The Practioner: A Journal of Therapeutics and Public Health*, 467.
22. Mordtmann et al., *Les réfugiés de la Roumelie*, 8.
23. Quoted in Boyar, *Ottomans, Turks, and the Balkans*, 131.
24. İpek, *Rumeli'den Anadolu'ya Türk Göçleri*, 56.
25. Quoted in Şimşir, *Rumeli'den Türk Göçmenler*, 1:143.
26. İpek (*Rumeli'den Anadolu'ya Türk Göçleri*, 56) gives the number of refugees as 100,000. Dunstan (*The Turkish Compassionate Fund*, 197), however, based on a report from a railway official at Çorlu, with an admittedly low guess of 50 people to a wagon, puts the number at nearly 55,000. This number would not have included arrivals by boat or on foot.
27. Dwight, *Turkish Life in War Time*, 214.
28. Dunstan, *The Turkish Compassionate Fund*, 192.
29. Dorothy Anderson, *The Balkan Volunteers*, 159.
30. İpek, *Rumeli'den Anadolu'ya Türk Göçleri*, 57.
31. Dunstan, *The Turkish Compassionate Fund*, 205.
32. Özcelik, "Basiret Gazetesi'ne Göre," 10.
33. Stanford Shaw and Ezel Kural Shaw, *History of the Ottoman Empire and Modern Turkey: Volume 2, Reform, Revolution, and Republic: The Rise of Modern Turkey, 1808–1975*, 156.
34. İpek, *Rumeli'den Anadolu'ya Türk Göçleri*, 55.
35. Özcelik, "Basiret Gazetesi'ne Göre," 13.
36. Kuneralp, *The Queen's Ambassador*, 142
37. Dunstan, *The Turkish Compassionate Fund*, 181.

38. Kuneralp, *The Queen's Ambassador*, 184.
39. Dwight, *Turkish Life in War Time*, 214.
40. Tarık Özcelik, "Basiret Gazetesi'ne Göre," 13.
41. Ibid., 15.
42. Quoted in Karpat, *The Politicization of Islam*, 122.
43. Dwight, *Turkish Life in War Time*, 214.
44. İpek, *Rumeli'den Anadolu'ya Türk Göçleri*, 91; Brunton, *The Practitioner*, 468; Mordtmann et al., *Les réfugiés de la Roumelie*, 11.
45. *London Standard*, February 7, 1878.
46. I have supplemented the full list of Istanbul mosques providing shelter for refugees provided by İpek (*Rumeli'den Anadolu'ya Türk Göçleri*, 60) with other mosques sheltering refugees mentioned by Özcelik, "Basiret Gazetesi'ne Göre"; Dwight, *Turkish Life in War Time*; and Mordtmann et al., *Les réfugiés de la Roumelie*: Acı Musluk Mescidi, Ağaçkakan Camii, Ak-Baba Camii, Atik-Ali Paşa Camii, Atik Valide, Ayasma, Aynı Hayat Hatun Camii, Bali Paşa Camii, Bebek Camii, Behruz Ağa Camii, Beşiktaş, Beyazıt Camii, Bostanı Ali Camii, Canbaziyye Mescidi, Cedid Valide, Cerah Paşa, Cezayirli Ahmed Paşa Camii, Cezerı Kasım Paşa Camii, Çezhade Camii, Çıkrıkcı Kemaleddin Mescidi, Çırağ-ı Hüseyin Efendi, Çoban Çavuş Camii, Daud Paşa, Dizdariye Camii, Dülger-zade Mescidi, Elvan Camii, Emir Camii, Fatma Sultan Camii, Fethiye Camii, Gül Camii, Guraba Hastahanesi Camii, Hacı Bekir Ağa Camii, Hafız Ahmed Paşa Camii, Haseki, Hatunniye Camii, Haydar-hane Camii, Haydar Kethüda, Hekimoğlu Ali Paşa Camii, Hoca Hayreddin Camii, Hocapaşa Camii, Hüseyin Ağa Camii, İbrahim Çavuş Mescidi, İshak Paşa Camii, Kapudan İbrahim Paşa, Kapudan Sinan Paşa Camii, Kasap Halil Camii, Kasap İlyas Camii, Kemankeş Ahmed Ağa Camii, Kızıl Minare Camii, Kızıltaş Camii, Küçük Ayasofya Camii, Kürkcü-başı Camii, Kürkçü Paşa Camii, Kuruçeşme, Lala Hayreddin Camii, Laleli Camii, Mahmud Paşa Camii, Mehrime Sultane, Merzifonlu Mustafa Paşa Camii, Mir-i Miran Halil Paşa Camii, Molla Fenari Camii, Murat Paşa, Nahilbent Camii, Nur-ı Osmaniye Camii, Nuri Süleyman Mescidi, Rum-Mehmet Paşa, Rüstem Paşa Camii, Sakine Hatun Mescidi, Sanki-Yedim Mescidi, Sarıgüzel Camii, Şehzade Camii, Sepsa-Latun at Zeyrek Yukusu, Şeyh Süleyman Mescidi, Şeyhü'lharem Mescidi, Şirmert Çavuş Mescidi, Sokullu Mehmed Paşa Camii, Süleyman Ağa Camii, Süleymaniye Camii, Süleyman Subaşı Camii, Sultan Ahmet Camii, Sungurlu-Mehmet Paşa, Ümmü Gülsüm Hatun Mescidi, Yavuz Ersinan Bey Camii, Yeni Camii, Zeynep Sultan Camii.
47. İpek, *Rumeli'den Anadolu'ya Türk Göçleri*, 68.
48. Ibid., 90.
49. Gay, *Plevna, the Sultan, and the Porte*, 39.
50. Şimşir, *Rumeli'den Türk Göçmenler*, 1:363.
51. Özcelik, "Basiret Gazetesi'ne Göre," 14.
52. Ibid., 14.
53. Mordtmann et al., *Les réfugiés de la Roumelie*, 12.
54. Raci Efendi, *Zağra Müftüsünün Hatıraları*, 252.
55. Mordtmann et al., *Les réfugiés de la Roumelie*, 24.
56. Ibid., 25.
57. Ibid., 29.

58. George Washburn, *Fifty Years in Constantinople*, 130.
59. Ibid., 12.
60. Stafford House Committee for the Relief of Sick and Wounded Turkish Soldiers, *Report and Record of the Operations of the Stafford House Committee for the Relief of Sick and Wounded Turkish Soldiers: Russo-Turkish War, 1877–78*, 128.
61. *Lady Layard's Journal*, February 4, 1878: https://pops.baylor.edu/layard/xml.php?fn=18780204.xml.
62. Brunton, *The Practitioner*, 470.
63. M. A. Gazenkampf, *Moi Dnevnik, 1877–78 gg.*, 528.
64. Dunstan, *The Turkish Compassionate Fund*, 210.
65. İpek, *Rumeli'den Anadolu'ya Türk Göçleri*, 90.
66. Özcelik, "Basiret Gazetesi'ne Göre," 45; Ipek, *Rumeli'den Anadolu'ya Türk Göçleri*, 91.
67. Özcelik, "Basiret Gazetesi'ne Göre," 45.
68. Kuneralp, *The Queen's Ambassador*, 261.
69. Josephe Reinach, *Voyage en Orient: Les premières stations, le Danube, le Bosphore*, 189.
70. İpek, *Rumeli'den Anadolu'ya Türk Göçleri*, 90.
71. Paul Bourde, *Russes et turcs: La guerre d'Orient*, 887.
72. İpek, *Rumeli'den Anadolu'ya Türk Göçleri*, 92.
73. Quoted in Şimşir, *Rumeli'den Türk Göçmenler*, 411.
74. İpek, *Rumeli'den Anadolu'ya Türk Göçleri*, 90.
75. Kuneralp, *The Queen's Ambassador*, 358.
76. Özcelik, "Basiret Gazetesi'ne Göre," 14; Grattan Geary, *Through Asiatic Turkey: Narrative of a Journey from Bombay to the Bosphorous*, 330.
77. İpek, *Rumeli'den Anadolu'ya Türk Göçleri*, 92.
78. Dwight, *Turkish Life in War Time*, 282.
79. Şimşir, *Rumeli'den Türk Göçmenler*, 1:407.
80. Mordtman et al., *Les réfugiés de la Roumelie*, 50.
81. Dwight, *Turkish Life in War Time*, 283.
82. Dunstan, *The Turkish Compassionate Fund*, 137.
83. Stafford House Committee, *Report and Record of the Operations of the Stafford House Committee*, 156.
84. *Turkish Life in War Time*, 136.
85. Ibid., 223.
86. Behlül Özkan, *From Abode of Islam to the Turkish Homeland in Turkey*, 43.
87. Palmer, *The Decline and Fall of the Ottoman Empire*, 152.
88. Karpat, *The Politicization of Islam*, 128.
89. Reid, *Crisis of the Ottoman Empire*, 368.
90. Kasım Bolat, "Turkish Migrations from the Balkans to Istanbul: 1877–1890," 93.
91. Karpat, *The Politicization of Islam*, 132.
92. Raci, *Zağra Müftüsünün Hatıraları*, 254, 278.
93. Dwight, *Turkish Life in War Time*, 300.
94. Hakan Yavuz, "The Transformation of 'Empire' through Wars and Reform," in Yavuz, *War & Diplomacy*, 28.
95. Şimsir, *Rumeli'den Türk Göçmenler*, 1:505.

96. *Appel des musulmans opprimés au Congrès de Berlin* (Constantinople: Constantinople Publisher, 1878), 1, 9.
97. Justin McCarthy, "Ignoring the People: The Effects of the Congress of Berlin," in Yavuz, *War & Diplomacy*, 438.
98. Biondich, *The Balkans*, 110.
99. İpek, *Rumeli'den Anadolu'ya Türk Göçleri*, 112, 115.
100. Davide Rodogno, *Against Massacre: Humanitarian Interventions in the Ottoman Empire, 1815–1914, the Emergence of a European Concept and International Practice*, 167.
101. İpek, *Rumeli'den Anadolu'ya Türk Göçleri*, 120.
102. Ovsianyi, *Russkoe Upravlenie*, 2:23.
103. Ibid.
104. Şimşir, *Rumeli'den Türk Göçmenler*, 1:443.
105. McCarthy, *Death and Exile*, 82.
106. Howard Adelman and Elazar Barkan, *No Return, No Refuge: Rites and Rights in Minority Repatriation*, xi.
107. Reinach, *Voyage en Orient*, 164.
108. Lady Annie Brassey, *Sunshine and Storm in the East, or Cruises to Cyprus and Constantinople*, 390.
109. Reinach, *Voyage en Orient*, 252.
110. Toumarkine, *Les migrations des populations musulmanes balkaniques*, 85.
111. Quoted in Isci Onur, "Wartime Propaganda and the Legacies of Defeat: The Russian and Ottoman Popular Presses in the War of 1877–78," 17.
112. Karpat, *The Politicization of Islam*, 330.
113. Reinach, *Voyage en Orient*, 254.
114. Toumarkine, *Les migrations des populations musulmanes balkaniques*, 81.
115. Ibid., 86.
116. Chatty, *Displacement and Dispossession*, 98.
117. Quoted in Toumarkine, *Les migrations des populations musulmanes balkaniques*, 88.
118. Toumarkine, *Les migrations des populations musulmanes balkaniques*, 90.
119. Ibid., 88.
120. Karpat, *The Politicization of Islam*, 113.
121. Kemal Karpat, "The *Hijra* from Russia and the Balkans: The Process of Self-Determination in the Late Ottoman State," in Eickelman and Piscatori, *Muslim Travellers*, 139.
122. Toumarkine, *Les migrations des populations musulmanes balkaniques*, 91.
123. Karpat, *The Politicization of Islam*, 186.
124. İpek, *Rumeli'den Anadolu'ya Türk Göçleri*, 161.
125. Ali Rıza Gönüllü, "Antalya'da Iskan Edilen Muhacirler (1878–1923)," 293.
126. Mustafa Tanrıverdi, "The Treaty of Berlin and the Tragedy of the Settlers from the Three Cities," in Yavuz, *War and & Diplomacy*, 472.
127. Karpat, *The Politicization of Islam*, 179.
128. Nesim Seker, "Identity Formation and the Political Power in the Late Ottoman Empire and Early Republic," 63.
129. Ryan Gingeras, *Sorrowful Shores: Violence, Ethnicity and the End of the Ottoman Empire, 1912–1923*, 28.

130. Reşat Kasaba, *A Moveable Empire: Ottoman Nomads, Migrants and Refugees*, 109.
131. Ibid., 109, 111.
132. Carter Findley, *Bureaucratic Reform in the Ottoman Empire: The Sublime Porte, 1789–1922*, 265.
133. Yavuz, "The Transformation of 'Empire' through Wars and Reforms," in Yavuz, *War & Diplomacy*, 34.
134. Karpat, *The Politicization of Islam*, 55.
135. Ibid., 179; Yavuz, "The Transformation of 'Empire' through Wars and Reforms," in Yavuz, *War & Diplomacy*, 35.
136. In 1911 the commission codified a distinction between the Turkish words *mülteci* and *muhacir*, both which can be translated as "refugee," although *muhacir* can also be translated as "migrant" or "immigrant."
137. Kasaba, *A Moveable Empire*, 115.
138. Karpat, "The *Hijra* from Russia and the Balkans," in Eikelman and Piscatori, *Muslim Travellers*, 137.
139. Quoted in Karpat, *The Politicization of Islam*, 185.
140. Karpat, "The *Hijra* from Russia and the Balkans," in Eickelman and Piscatori, *Muslim Travellers*, 138.
141. Karpat, *The Politicization of Islam*, 97.
142. Ibid., 97.

5. APHASIA AND AMNESIA

1. Interestingly, "Andalusia" is most likely a corrupted form of the word "vandal," recalling that the Ottomans also named their conquered territory in Europe Rumelia, after its previous rulers the Romans (Greeks).
2. The first five lines here are quoted from Syed Tanvir Wasti, "1912–1913 Balkan Wars and the Siege of Edirne," 76. The rest of the poem is my translation.
3. Another reference to Andalusia: Ṭāriq ibn Ziyād led the first Muslim invasion from Africa into Spain in 711. Gibraltar is named after him—Jabal Ṭāriq (the mountain of Ṭāriq).
4. Ahmad Shawqī, *al-Shawqīyāt*: my translation with the assistance of the French translation found in Antoine Boudot-Lamotte, *Ahmad Sawqi: L'homme et l'oeuvre* (Damascus: Institut Français de Damas, 1977), 103.
5. Aḥmad ibn Muḥammad al-Maqqarī, *The History of the Mohammedan Dynasties in Spain* 1:vii.
6. While in exile in Spain, Shawqī asked his family to send him his copy of al-Maqqarī's oeuvre.
7. al-Maqqarī, *The History of the Mohammedan Dynasties in Spain*, 1:17.
8. Ibid., 1:8.
9. Bernard Lewis, *History: Remembered, Recovered, Invented*, 73.
10. Richard Fletcher, *Moorish Spain*, 137.
11. Conversion to Christiantiy was an option for Muslims and Jews in Spain but not for Turks in the Balkans. This is because in the era of nationalism one could not easily convert one's ethnic/national identity. In the Balkan Wars of 1912–13 Pomaks were often "encouraged" (that is, forced) to convert to Orthodox Christianity.

12. Fletcher, *Moorish Spain*, 168.
13. al-Maqqarī, *The History of the Mohammedan Dynasties in Spain*, 2:392.
14. Ami Boué, *Recueil d'itineraires dans la Turquie d'Europe*, 2:331, translated in Mark Mazower, *The Balkans: From the End of Byzantium to the Present Day*, 12.
15. Alexandre Popovic, quoted in Rudolph Peters, ed., *Proceedings of the Ninth Congress of the Union Européene des arabisants et islamisants, Amsterdam, 1st to 7th September 1978*, 245.
16. Stanley Lane-Poole, *The Moors in Spain*, xi.
17. Naturally, the Ottomans were not able to replicate the rediscoveries of the ancients. This had already been accomplished in Andalusia, so there was no further need to rediscover Socrates and Aristotle: the torch had been passed to the North. But the Ottoman Balkans also boasted centers of learning, such as in Bosnia, Albania, Bulgaria, and Greek Macedonia. See Machiel Kiel's *Studies on the Ottoman Architecture of the Balkans*, 43.
18. Quoted in Fletcher, *Moorish Spain*, 130.
19. Quoted in Robert Fisk, *The Great War for Civilisation: The Conquest of the Middle East*, 330; Andrew Bell-Fialkoff, "A Brief History of Ethnic Cleansing," 113.
20. Robert Kaplan, *Balkan Ghosts: A Journey through History*, 27. President Bill Clinton read Kaplan's book, which influenced U.S. policy during the Bosnian genocide. See Michael T. Kaufman, "The Dangers of Letting a President Read," *New York Times*, May 22, 1999.
21. Mazower, *The Balkans*, 159. The remark about balance is absurd, because McCarthy explains in his introduction that his decision to focus on the Muslim suffering is a counterbalance to the tendency to do otherwise. Furthermore, Mazower suggests that Toumarkine takes a more balanced approach. Having read and relied on both works, I frankly cannot see what Mazower is talking about. They are complementary in their findings.
22. Micha Glenny, *The Balkans: Nationalism, War and the Great Powers, 1804–1999*, 109.
23. Semelin, *Purify and Destroy*, 312.
24. Andrew Wheatcroft, *The Ottomans: Dissolving Images*, 233.
25. Quoted in Semelin, *Purify and Destroy*, 138.
26. This sentiment extends even to the Arab countries. Once on a trip to Jordan I overheard a tour guide tell his group, "Look around you, what did the Turks build? They built nothing!"
27. Georgi Georgiev, *The Russo-Turkish War of Liberation (1877–1878) and the World Public*, 82.
28. George Orwell, "Notes on Nationalism," paragraph 13.
29. Available online at http://www.igdir.edu.tr/incoming-students-igdir-province (accessed October 25, 2012). The inscription on the monument states that its erection is a direct response to the publicization of Armenian victimhood: "Resolved, that a monument of martyrs should be erected in Iğdır and a cemetery for martyrs should be established in Oba Village in order to eternalise the memories of more than one million Turks that fell in Eastern Anatolia and to give a similar answer to those declaring 24 April as a genocide day and to the monuments erected in many places of the world for the alleged genocide perpetrated against the Armenians."

30. Norris, *Islam in the Balkans*, 14.
31. Esra Özyürek, ed., *The Politics of Public Memory in Turkey*, 8.
32. Erik Jan Zürcher, *The Young Turk Legacy and Nation Building: From the Ottoman Empire to Atatürk's Turkey*, 196.
33. Ebru Boyar, *Ottomans, Turks and the Balkans: Empire Lost, Relations Altered*, 140.
34. Fazil Bülent Kocamemi, *Urumeli'nin Gözyaşları*, 15.
35. Interview with Nedim İpek, December 20, 2010.
36. Tanil Bora, "Turkish National Identity, Turkish Nationalism, and the Balkan Question," in Günay Göksu Özdoğan and Kemali Saybasili, eds., *Balkans: A Mirror of the New International Order*, 116.
37. Jorge Luis Borges, *Labyrinths*, 63.
38. Friedrich Nietzsche quoted in Miroslav Volf, *The End of Memory: Remembering Rightly in a Violent World*, 160. Cases of individuals who can remember virtually every detail of their lives have recently been recorded. Their condition is called hyperthymesia or superior autobiographical memory. An exposé on this condition was aired on *60 Minutes* on December 16, 2010: https://www.cbsnews.com/news/the-gift-of-endless-memory/.
39. Jamaica Kincaid, "In History," *Callaloo* 20, no. 1 (1997): 1–7.
40. Regarding the distinction between history and memory, we might analogously use the aphorism that the difference between a language and a dialect is that a language has an army.
41. Another distinction put forward is that history is written, whereas memory is oral.
42. Cihan Tuğal, "Memories of Violence, Memoirs of a Nation: The 1915 Massacres and the Construction of Armenian Identity," in Özyurek, *The Politics of Public Memory in Turkey*, 159.
43. Maurice Halbwachs, *On Collective Memory*.
44. Klein, "On the Emergence of Memory," 135.
45. Noa Gedi and Yigil Alam, "Collective Memory—What Is It?, 4.
46. Klein, "On the Emergence of Memory," 135.
47. Alon Confino, "Collective Memory and Cultural History: Problems of Method," 1400.
48. Benedict Anderson, *Imagined Communities*.
49. Liisa H. Malkki, *Purity and Exile: Violence, Memory, and National Cosmology among Hutu Refugees in Tanzania*, 1.
50. Klein, "On the Emergence of Memory," 130.
51. Olick, *States of Memory*, 123.
52. Susan A. Crane, "Writing the Individual Back into Collective Memory," 1380.
53. Confino, "Collective Memory and Cultural History," 1387.
54. Olick, *States of Memory*, 110.
55. Confino, "Collective Memory and Cultural History," 1393.
56. George Orwell, *1984*. 35.
57. Popovic, "Représentation du passé et transmission de l'identité chez les Musulmans," 139.
58. Gedi, "Collective Memory," 4.
59. Confino, "Collective Memory and Cultural History," 1393; James Pennebaker, ed., *Collective Memory of Political Events: Social Psychological Perspectives*, 4.
60. Olick, *States of Memory*, 110.

61. It should be noted that the records matter, whether in the case of the Muslim refugees from Bulgaria or any other case. Brazilian archives relating to slavery were burned when slavery was abolished in Brazil. See Joseph Page, *The Brazilians*, 69.
62. Halbwachs, *On Collective Memory*, 73.
63. Chatty, *Displacement and Dispossession*, 22.
64. Kemal Karpat, "The *Hijra* from Russia and the Balkans: The Process of Self-Determination in the Late Ottoman State," in Eickelman and Piscatori, *Muslim Travellers*, 140.
65. Gingeras, *Sorrowful Shores*, 29.
66. Züriye Çelik, Osmanlının Zor Yıllarında Rumeli Göçmenlerinin Türk Basınındaki Sesi: 'Muhacir' Gazetesi (1909–1910)."
67. Chatty, *Displacement and Dispossession*, 297.
68. Howard Adelman and Elazar Barkan, *No Return, No Refuge: Rites and Rights in Minority Repatriation*, x.
69. Ibid., xvi.
70. Malkki, *Purity and Exile*, 3.
71. Ibid., 233.
72. Lorne Shirinian, *Writing Memory: The Search for Home in Armenian Diaspora Literature as a Cultural Practice*, 34, 41.
73. Jacques Revel and Giovanni Levi, eds., *Political Uses of the Past: The Recent Mediterranean Experience*, 56.
74. Özyürek, *The Politics of Public Memory in Turkey*, 148.
75. Selim Deringil, *The Well-Protected Domains: Ideology and the Legitimation of Power in the Ottoman Empire 1876–1909*, 20.
76. Karpat, *The Politicization of Islam*, 329.
77. Karpat, "The *Hijra* from Russia and the Balkans," 131.
78. Deringil, *The Well-Protected Domains*, 46.
79. Ibid., 47.
80. Karpat, *The Politicization of Islam*, 232, 292.
81. Boyar, *Ottomans, Turks and the Balkans*, 13.
82. Quoted in Karpat, *The Politicization of Islam*, 151.
83. Reid, *Crisis of the Ottoman Empire*, 308.
84. Onur Isci, "Wartime Propaganda and the Legacies of Defeat: The Russian and Ottoman Popular Presses in the War of 1877–78," 5.
85. Ibid., 14.
86. Boyar, *Ottomans, Turks and the Balkans*, 13.
87. Ibid., 23, 15.
88. Gingeras, *Sorrowful Shores*, 27.
89. Boyar, *Ottomans, Turks and the Balkans*, 88.
90. Quoted in Jacob Landau, *Pan-Turkism: From Irredentism to Cooperation*, 35; Akçam, *From Empire to Republic*, 93.
91. Klein, "On the Emergence of Memory," 134.
92. Özyürek, *The Politics of Public Memory in Turkey*, 7.
93. Olick, *States of Memory*, 110.
94. Barry Schwartz, "The Social Context of Commemoration: A study in Social Memory," 375.

95. Sinan Kuneralp, "Book Review: Justin McCarthy's *Death and Exile*," available online at http://sam.gov.tr/wp-content/uploads/2012/02/SinanKuneralp.pdf (accessed December 8, 2018).
96. Martina Baleva, "The Empire Strikes Back: Image Battles and Image Frontlines during the Russo-Turkish War of 1877–1878." More images can be found in this article, although one scholar expressed doubt to me about their authenticity based on a belief that Muslim women would not expose their bodies in such a manner to a stranger.
97. Boyar, *Ottomans, Turks and the Balkans*, 98.
98. Orna Kenan, *Between Memory and History: The Evolution of Israeli Historiography of the Holocaust, 1945–1961*, 12.
99. Patrick H. Hutton, "The Art of Memory Reconceived: From Rhetoric to Psychoanalysis," 387.
100. Quoted in Kenan, *Between Memory and History*, 51.
101. Kenan, *Between Memory and History*, 30.
102. Raci, *Zağra Müftüsünün Hatıraları*.
103. Quoted in Tetsuya Sahara, "Two Different Images: Bulgarian and English Sources on the Batak Massacre," in M. Hakan Yavuz, *War & Diplomacy*, 496.
104. Benjamin C. Fortna, *Learning to Read in the Late Ottoman Empire and the Early Turkish Republic*, 20. By 1910 only 3 percent of Muslim Gypsies in Bulgaria were literate. See Crowe, "Muslim Roma in the Balkans," 100.
105. Fonseca, *Bury Me Standing*, 5. The Franco-Romani Tony Gatlif's film *Latcho Drom* is a beautiful illustration of song as a means for relaying Gypsy memory. One moving scene involves a female Gypsy survivor of the concentration camps.
106. The Arabic script, for example, has only three vowels, which can be expressed in a long or short form, whereas Turkish boasts of eight vowels and a complex system of vowel harmonics and agglutination.
107. Geoffrey Lewis, *The Turkish Language Reform: A Catastrophic Success*.
108. Adonis, "The Time," BBC News, February 15, 2012, http://www.bbc.co.uk/news/entertainment-arts-17039368.
109. Olivier Roy, *The New Central Asia: Geopolitics and the Birth of Nations*, 77.
110. İlker Aytürk, "Script Charisma in Hebrew and Turkish: A Comparative Framework for Explaining Success and Failure of Romanization," 107, 121.
111. Hutton, "The Art of Memory Reconceived," 383.
112. Quoted in Paul Connerton, "Seven Types of Forgetting," 59.
113. Quoted in Carmichael, *Ethnic Cleansing in the Balkans*, 21.
114. Shaw and Shaw, *History of the Ottoman Empire and Modern Turkey*, 116.
115. Zürcher, *The Young Turk Legacy and Nation Building*, 287. It is important to point out that directly attributing the fate of the Armenians to the Muhacirs would be to ignore other important social factors as well as the fact that many of those involved were not the descendants of Muhacirs.
116. Cited in Joseph Demartini, "Change Agents and Generational Relationships: A Reevaluation of Mannheim's Problem of Generations," 2.
117. Pennebaker, *Collective Memory of Political Events*, 16.
118. Todorova, *Imagining the Balkans*, 50.
119. Özyürek, *The Politics of Public Memory in Turkey*, 3.

120. Ibid., 11.
121. Paul Connerton, *How Societies Remember*, 6 (quotation), 13.
122. Akçam, *From Empire to Republic*, 94.
123. Boyar, *Ottomans, Turks and the Balkans*, 10.
124. Landau, *Pan-Turkism*, 75, 35.
125. Hutton, "The Art of Memory Reconceived," 386.
126. Karpat, *The Politicization of Islam*, 354.
127. Bora, "Turkish National Identity," in Özdoğan and Saybasili, *Balkans*, 112.
128. Karpat, *The Politicization of Islam*, 353.
129. Boyar, *Ottomans, Turks and the Balkans*, 20.
130. Nesim Şeker, "Identity Formation and the Political Power in the Late Ottoman Empire and Early Republic," 67.
131. Hugh Poulton, *Top Hat, Grey Wolf, and the Crescent: Turkish Nationalism and the Turkish Republic*. Turkish Jews, however, renounced article 42 of the Lausanne Treaty and thereby have a different status and a distinct notion of loyalty to the Turkish Republic compared with the Turkish Armenian and Turkish Greek communities. See Reyhan Zetler, "Turkish Jews between 1923–1933: What Did the Turkish Policy between 1923 and 1933 Mean for the Turkish Jews?"
132. Boyar, *Ottomans, Turks and the Balkans*, 83.
133. Popovic, "Les turcs de Bulgarie," 387; Landau, *Pan-Turkism*, 195.
134. Bora, "Turkish National Identity," in Özdoğan and Saybasili, *Balkans*, 113.
135. Todorova, *Imagining the Balkans*, 50.
136. Klein, "On the Emergence of Memory," 138.
137. Milan Kundera, *The Book of Laughter and Forgetting*, 3.
138. Quoted in Kenan, *Between Memory and History*, 51.
139. See, as an example, Taner Akçam, *A Shameful Act: The Armenian Genocide and the Question of Turkish Responsibility*.
140. From correspondences in the Blunt Papers in the Cadbury Research Library at Birmingham University, Provisional Catalog Number MS46/A/1/3/1, 3, 7.
141. Ibid., 8.
142. Francis Charteris (Lord Elcho) *Russian Lessons in Massacre*, 20.
143. Hakan Yavuz, *Islamic Political Identity in Turkey*, 122.
144. Hakan Yavuz, "Turkish Identity and Foreign Policy in Flux: The Rise of Neo-Ottomanism," 22.
145. Hüseyin Çilek, *Ali Suavi ve Dönemi*.
146. Yavuz, "Turkish Identity and Foreign Policy in Flux," 24. Some have suggested coining a new term for Turkish citizens, "Türkiyeli," which would imply a citizen of Turkey but not an ethnic Turk. Russia employs a similar kind of distinction between "Russkii" (ethnic Russian) and "Rossiisskii" (a citizen of the Russian Federation). However, in Turkey attempts to introduce this new term have been met with vigorous objections, and "Türkiyeli" has not gained any traction.
147. Jeanne Hearsant and Alexandre Toumarkine. "Hometown Organisations in Turkey: An Overview," paragraph 19.
148. Ali Dayıoğlu and İlksoy Aslım, "Reciprocity Problem between Greece and Turkey: The Case of Muslim-Turkish and Greek Minorities," 45.
149. Hearsant and Toumarkine, "Hometown Organisations in Turkey," paragraph 26.

150. Bora, "Turkish National Identity," in Günay Göksu Özdoğan and Saybasili, *Balkans*, 115. As far as I have been able to ascertain, no Turkish motion picture or novel has dealt with this subject, although recently a Turkish television series, *Elveda Rumeli* (Farewell, Rumelia) has been produced about a Turkish family in Ottoman Macedonia.
151. Hayriye Süleymanoğlu Yenisoy, *Edebiyatımızda Balkan Türklerin Göç Kaderi*, 9.
152. Mithat Cemal Kuntay, *Üç İstanbul* , 30.
153. Levent Bilgi, "Türk Romanında Savaş Sonrası Anadolu'ya Zorunlu Göçler."
154. Consider for example, the Sèvres Syndrome, a term used to characterize a lingering suspicion among Turks about Western intentions in regard to their territory.
155. Boyar, *Ottomans, Turks and the Balkans*, 116.
156. Bora, "Turkish National Identity," in Özdoğan and Saybasili, *Balkans*, 102, 105.
157. Cited in Olick, *States of Memory*, 121.
158. Klein, "On the Emergence of Memory," 138.
159. Mark Strand, "Orpheus Alone," in *The Continuous Life: Poems*, 9.
160. Jorge Luis Borges, *The Aleph and Other Stories*, 3, 18.
161. L. P. Hartley, *The Go-Between*, 1.
162. Nabokov originally intended to call his memoir dealing with his experience as a Russian émigré *Speak, Mnemosyne*, after the Greek goddess of memory and mother of the nine Muses, but his publisher talked him out of an unpronounceable title.
163. Mehmet Akif Ersoy, "Çenk Şarkısı," quoted in Nadir Yaz, *Ağlayan Batı Trakya*, 122. Mehmed Akif Ersoy (1873–1936) was a Turkish poet who is best known for writing the lyrics to the Turkish national anthem, *Istiklal Marşı*. Akif was happy to drum up support for Ottoman claims in the Balkans and wrote a number of poems urging men to sign up for military combat. His words often evoke a journey. Such as "Durma git evlâdım, açıktır yolun" (Don't just stand there, go by, boy, your road is clear) and "Yükselerek kuş gibi Balkanlara" (Fly to the Balkans like a bird). In other places he urges people to stay in place, "Gitme ey yolcu, beraber oturup ağlaşalım" (Don't go, traveler, let's sit down and cry together), quoted in M. Ertuğrul Düzdağ, *Mehmet Akif Ersoy*, 40. While the verse quoted in the text was originally used in a militant and revanchist manner during the Balkan Wars, I choose to reinterpret it here in a new vein.
164. Fletcher, *Moorish Spain*, 171.

EPILOGUE

1. Semelin, *Purify and Destroy*, 315.
2. Quoted in Carolyn J. Dean, *Aversion and Erasure: The Fate of the Victim after the Holocaust*, 1.
3. Quoted in Boyar, *Ottomans, Turks and the Balkans*, 142.
4. Quoted in Semelin, *Purify and Destroy*, 23.

WORKS CITED

Adelman, Howard, and Elazar Barkan. *No Return, No Refuge: Rites and Rights in Minority Repatriation*. New York: Columbia University Press, 2011.

Akçam, Taner. *From Empire to Republic: Turkish Nationalism and the Armenian Genocide*. London: Zed Books, 2004.

———. *A Shameful Act: The Armenian Genocide and the Question of Turkish Responsibility*. New York: Metropolitan Books, 2006.

Akmeşe, Handan Nezar. *The Birth of Modern Turkey: The Ottoman Military and the March to World War I*. London: I. B. Tauris, 2005.

Akunin, Boris. *The Turkish Gambit*. New York: Random House, 2005.

Al-Maqqarī, Aḥmad ibn Muḥammad. *The History of the Mohammedan Dynasties in Spain*. 2 vols. London: Oriental Translation Fund, 1840.

American Board of Commissioners for Foreign Missions. *The Missionary Herald*. Vol. 73. Cambridge, MA: Riverside Press, 1877.

Anderson, Benedict. *Imagined Communities*. London: Verso, 1993.

Anderson, Dorothy. *The Balkan Volunteers*. London: Hutchinson, 1968.

Andrić, Ivo. *The Bosnian Chronicle*. New York: Arcade Publishing, 1963.

Ansky, S. *The Dyubbuk and Other Writings*. New York: Schocken Books, 1992.

Aytürk, İlker. "Script Charisma in Hebrew and Turkish: A Comparative Framework for Explaining Success and Failure of Romanization." *Journal of World History* 21, no. 1 (March 2010).

Baleva, Martina. "The Empire Strikes Back: Image Battles and Image Frontlines during the Russo-Turkish War of 1877–1878." *Ethnologia Balkanica* 16 (2012).

Barkey, Karen, and Mark von Hagen, eds. *After Empire: Multiethnic Societies and Nation Building*. Boulder, CO: Westview Press, 1997.

Bass, Gary J. *Freedom's Battle: The Origins of Humanitarian Intervention*. New York: Knopf, 2008.

Belge, Murat, and Jale Parla, eds. *Balkan Literatures in the Era of Nationalism*. Istanbul: Istanbul Bilgi University Press, 2009.

Bell-Fialkoff, Andrew. "A Brief History of Ethnic Cleansing." *Foreign Affairs* 72, no. 3 (Summer 1993).

Bianchini, Stefano, and Marco Dogo, eds. *The Balkans: National Identities in Historical Perspective*. Ravenna: Longo Editore, 1998.

Bieber, Florian. "Muslim Identity in the Balkans before the Formation of the Nation State." *Nationalities Papers* 28, no. 1 (2000).

Bilgi, Levent. "Türk Romanında Savaş Sonrası Anadolu'ya Zorunlu Göçler." PhD dissertation, Marmara Üniversitesi, 2006.

Biondich, Mark. *The Balkans: Revolution, War, & Political Violence since 1878*. Oxford: Oxford University Press, 2011.

Blunt, J. E. "Notes Preceding Report of Consul Blunt on the Effects of the Russian Invasion of Roumelia 1877." John Blunt Papers, MS46/A/2/3/1, Special Collection, Cadbury Library, University of Birmingham, England.

———. *Report by Consul Blunt on the Effects of the Russian Invasion of Roumelia* (FO 881/3651, British Foreign Office, London. 1877). John Blunt Papers, MS46/A/2/3/1 & 2, Special Collection, Cadbury Library, University of Birmingham, England.

Bolat, Kasım. "Turkish Migrations from the Balkans to Istanbul: 1877–1890." M.A. thesis, Fatih University, 2012.

Borges, Jorge Luis. *The Aleph and Other Stories*. New York: Penguin Classics, 2004.

———. *Labyrinths*. New York: New Directions, 2007.

Boué, Ami. *Recueil d'itineraires dans la Turquie d'Europe*. Vol. 2. Vienna: Braumüller, 1854.

Bourde, Paul. *Russes et turcs: La guerre d'Orient*. Paris: Société Anonyme de Publications Périodiques, 1878.

Boyar, Ebru. *Ottomans, Turks and the Balkans: Empire Lost, Relations Altered*. London: Tauris Academic Studies, 2007.

Boyle, Frederick. *The Narrative of an Expelled Correspondent*. London: Richard Bentley and Son, 1877.

Brassey, Lady Annie. *Sunshine and Storm in the East, or Cruises to Cyprus and Constantinople* (1880). Piscataway, NJ: Gorgias Press, 2005.

Brockett, Linus Pierpont, and Porter Cornelius Bliss. *The Conquest of Turkey; or, The Decline and Fall of the Ottoman Empire, 1877–8: A Complete History of the Late War between Russia and Turkey*. Philadelphia: Hubbard Bros., 1878.

Brooks, Sarah T., ed. *Byzantium: Faith and Power (1261–1557): Perspectives on Late Byzantine Art and Culture*. New York: Metropolitan Museum of Art, 2014.

Brown, Catherine. "Henry James and Ivan Turgenev: Cosmopolitanism, Croquet, and Language," https://catherinebrown.org/wordpress/wp-content/uploads/2014/03/TJ-article.pdf (accessed October 3, 2018).

Brunton, T. Lauder. *The Practitioner: A Journal of Therapeutics and Public Health*. Vol. 22. London: Macmillan and Co., 1879.

Carmichael, Cathie. *Ethnic Cleansing in the Balkans: Nationalism and the Destruction of Tradition*. New York: Routledge, 2002.

———. "Was Religion Important in the Destruction of Ancient Communities in the Balkans, Anatolia and Black Sea Regions, c. 1870–1923?" *Southeast European and Black Sea Studies* 7, no. 3 (September 2007).

Castellan, Georges. *History of the Balkans from Mohammed the Conqueror to Stalin*. Boulder, CO: East European Monographs, 1992.

Celaleddin Paşa, Mahmud. *Mir'at-i Hakikat: Tarihi Hakikatlarin Aynası*. Istanbul: Berekat Yayinevi, 1983.

Çelik, Züriye. "Osmanlının Zor Yıllarında Rumeli Göçmenlerinin Türk Basınındaki Sesi: 'Muhacir' Gazetesi (1909–1910)." *Türkiyat Araştırmaları Dergisi* 28, (Autumn 2010).

Charteris, Francis (Lord Elcho). *Russian Lessons in Massacre*. London: Harrison, 1878.

Chatty, Dawn. *Displacement and Dispossession in the Modern Middle East*. Cambridge: Cambridge University Press, 2010.

Çiçek, Nazan. "The Turkish Response to Bulgarian Horrors: A Study in English Turcophobia." *Middle Eastern Studies* 42, no. 1 (January 2006).
Çilek, Hüseyin. *Ali Suavi ve Dönemi.* Istanbul: İletişim Yayınları, 1994.
Comité International de la Croix-Rouge. *Bulletin international des sociétéss de secours aux militaires blessés.* No. 30B. Geneva: Soullier, 1877.
Confino, Alon. "Collective Memory and Cultural History: Problems of Method." *American Historical Review* 102, no. 5 (December 1997).
Connerton, Paul. *How Societies Remember.* Cambridge: Cambridge University Press, 1989.
———. "Seven Types of Forgetting." *Memory Studies* (2008).
Courbage, Youssef. "Demographic Transition among Muslims in Eastern Europe." *Population: An English Selection* 4 Paris: Institut National d'Etudes Démographiques, 1992.
Cox, John K. *The History of Serbia.* Westport, CT: Greenwood Press, 2002.
Crampton, Richard J. *Bulgaria.* Oxford: Oxford University Press, 2007.
———. *A Concise History of Bulgaria.* Cambridge: Cambridge University Press, 2005.
Crane, Susan A. "Writing the Individual Back into Collective Memory." *American Historical Review* 102, no. 5 (December 1997).
Crews, Robert. *For Prophet and Tsar: Islam and Empire in Russia and Central Asia.* Cambridge, MA: Harvard University Press, 2006.
Crowe, David M. "Muslim Roma in the Balkans." *Nationalities Papers* 28, no. 1 (2000).
Dayıoğlu, Ali, and İlksoy Aslım. "Reciprocity Problem between Greece and Turkey: The Case of Muslim-Turkish and Greek Minorities." *Athens Journal of History* (January 2015).
Dean, Carolyn J. *Aversion and Erasure: The Fate of the Victim after the Holocaust.* Ithaca, NY: Cornell University Press, 2010.
de Heimann, Robert. *À cheval de Varsovie à Constantinople par un capitaine de hussards de la Garde Impériale Russe (1877/78).* Paris: Ollendorff, 1893.
de Lonlay, Dick. *À travers la Bulgarie: Souvenirs de guerre et voyage par un voluntaire au 26e Régiment de Cosaques du Don.* Paris: Garniers Frères, 1888.
Demartini, Joseph. "Change Agents and Generational Relationships: A Reevaluation of Mannheim's Problem of Generations." *Social Forces* 64, no. 1 (September 1985).
Deringil, Selim. *The Well-Protected Domains: Ideology and the Legitimation of Power in the Ottoman Empire, 1876–1909.* London: I. B. Tauris, 1998.
Destani, B., ed. *Ethnic Minorities in the Balkan States, 1860–1971.* Vol. 1. Cambridge: Cambridge Archive Editions, 2003.
Dogo, Marco. *Storie balcaniche: Popole e stati nella transizione alla modernità.* Gorizia, Italy: Libreria Editrice Goriziana, 1999.
Dominian, Leon. "The Site of Constantinople: A Factor of Historical Value." *Journal of the American Oriental Society* 37 (1917).
Donchev, Anton. *Time of Parting.* New York: William Morrow and Co., 1968.
Dostoyevsky, Fyodor. *The Brothers Karamazov* (1880). New York: Lowell Press, 2005.
———[Dostoevsky]. *The Diary of a Writer, Volume One.* New York: C. Scribner's Sons, 1949.
———. *The Diary of a Writer, Volume Two.* London: Octagon Books, 1973.
Drakulic, Slobodan. "Anti-Turkish Obsession and the Exodus of Balkan Muslims." *Patterns of Prejudice* 43, no. 3–4 (2009).

Dunstan, H. Mainwaring. *The Turkish Compassionate Fund: An Account of Its Origin, Working and Results*. London: Remington and Co., 1883.

Durman, Karel. *Lost Illusions: Russian Policies towards Bulgaria in 1877–1878*. Stockholm: Almqvist and Wiksell International, 1988.

———. *The Time of the Thunderer: Mikhail Katkov: Russian Nationalist Extremism and the Failure of the Bismarckian System, 1871–1887*. Boulder, CO: East European Monographs, 1988.

Düzdağ, M. Ertuğrul. *Mehmet Akif Ersoy* . Ankara: Kültür ve Turizm Bakanlığı, 1996.

Dwight, Henry Otis. *Turkish Life in War Time*. New York: C. Scribener's Sons, 1881.

Eickelman, Dale F., and James Piscatori, eds. *Muslim Travellers: Pilgrimage, Migration and the Religious Imagination*. Berkeley: University of California Press, 1990.

Elenkov, Ivan, and Daniela Koleva. "Historiography in Bulgaria after the Fall of Communism: Did 'The Change' Happen?" *Historein* 4 (2003–4).

Emerson, Ralph Waldo. *Essays: The First Series*. New York: Vintage Books, 1990.

Eminov, Ali. *Turkish and Other Muslim Minorities of Bulgaria*. London: Hurst and Co., 1997.

———. "Turks and Tatars in Bulgaria and the Balkans." *Nationalities Papers* 28, no. 1 (2000).

Fanon, Franz. *The Wretched of the Earth*. New York: Grove Press, 2005.

Farcy, Camille. *La guerre sur le Danube (1877–1878)*. Paris: A. Quantin, 1879.

Fife-Cookson, John. *With the Armies of the Balkans and at Gallipoli*. London: Cassel, Petter, Galpin and Co., 1880.

Findley, Carter. *Bureaucratic Reform in the Ottoman Empire: The Sublime Porte, 1789–1922*. Princeton, NJ: Princeton University Press, 1980.

Fisk, Robert. *The Great War for Civilisation: The Conquest of the Middle East*. New York: Vintage Books, 2007.

Fletcher, Richard. *Moorish Spain*. Berkeley: University of California Press, 1992.

Fonseca, Isabela. *Bury Me Standing: The Gypsies and Their Journey*. New York: Random House, 2011.

Forbes, Archibald. *Czar and Sultan: The Adventures of a British Lad in the Russo-Turkish War of 1877–78*. New York: Charles Scribner's Sons, 1894.

Fortna, Benjamin C. *Learning to Read in the Late Ottoman Empire and the Early Turkish Republic*. New York: Palgrave Macmillan, 2011.

Fraser, John Foster. *Pictures from the Balkans*. London: Cassel and Co., 1912.

Gay, J. Drew. *Plevna, the Sultan, and the Porte: Reminiscences of the War in Turkey*. London: Chatto and Windus, 1878.

Gazenkampf, M. A. *Moi Dnevnik, 1877–78*. St. Petersburg: Berezovskii, 1908.

Geary, Grattan. *Through Asiatic Turkey: Narrative of a Journey from Bombay to the Bosphorous*. London: S. Low, Marston, Searle and Rivington, 1878.

Gedi, Noa, and Yigil Alam. "Collective Memory—What Is It?" *History and Memory* 8, no. 1 (1996).

Georgiev, Georgi. *The Russo-Turkish War of Liberation (1877–1878) and the World Public*. Sofia: Sofia Press, 1987.

Gerolymatos, André. *The Balkan Wars: Conquest, Revolution and Retribution from the Ottoman Era to the Twentieth Century and Beyond*. New York: Basic Books, 2002.

Gingeras, Ryan. *Sorrowful Shores: Violence, Ethnicity and the End of the Ottoman Empire, 1912–1923*. Oxford: Oxford University Press, 2011.

Gladstone, William. *Bulgarian Horrors and the Question of the East.* New York: Lovell, Adam, Wesson and Company, 1876.

Glenny, Micha. *The Balkans: Nationalism, War and the Great Powers, 1804–1999.* New York: Viking Press, 1999.

Göçek, Fatma Müge. "Ethnic Segmentation, Western Education, and Political Outcomes: Nineteenth-Century Ottoman Society." *Poetics Today* 14, no. 3, period I (Autumn 1993).

Göksu, Saime. *Romantic Communist.* London: Hurst and Co., 2006.

Gönüllü, Ali Rıza. "Antalya'da Iskan Edilen Muhacirler (1878–1923)." *Türkiyat Araştırmaları Dergesi* 26 (2009).

Gradeva, Rossitsa. *War and Peace in Rumeli: 15th to Beginning of 19th Century.* Istanbul: Isis Press, 2005.

Graf von Pfeil, Richard. *Experiences of a Prussian Officer in the Russian Service during the Turkish War of 1877–78.* London: E. Stanford, 1893.

Graham, Steven. *Peter the Great.* New York: Simon and Schuster, 1929.

Grant, Ulysses S. *The Papers of Ulysses S. Grant.* Edited by John Y. Simon. Vol. 28: *November 1, 1876–September 30, 1878.* Carbondale: University of Southern Illinois Press, 2005.

Greene, Francis Vinton. *Sketches of Army Life in Russia.* New York: C. Scribner's Sons, 1885.

Grey, Ian. *Catherine the Great: Autocrat and Empress of All Russia.* Philadelphia: J. B Lippincott Company, 1962.

Gur, Faik. "Sculpting the Nation in the Early Republic." *Historical Research* 86, no. 232 (May 2013).

Haker, Erol. *93 Harbi: Tuna'da Son Osmanlı Yahudileri.* Istanbul: Timaş Yayınları, 2011.

Halbwachs, Maurice. *On Collective Memory.* Chicago: University of Chicago Press, 1992.

Halperin, Charles J. *Russia and the Golden Horde: The Mongol Impact on Medieval Russian History.* Bloomington: Indiana University Press, 1987.

Harris, David. *Britain and the Bulgarian Horrors of 1876.* Chicago: University of Chicago Press, 1939.

Hartley, L. P. *The Go-Between* (1953). New York: New York Review Books, 2002.

Hearsant, Jeanne, and Alexandre Toumarkine. "Hometown Organisations in Turkey: An Overview." *European Journal of Turkish Studies.* Thematic Issue No. 2. 2005.

Hikmet, Nazim. "Davet." In Nazim Hikmet, *Şiirleri: Bu Memleket Bizim*, 4. Ankara: Bilgi Yayinevi, 1976.

Historical Narrative of the Turko-Russian War. London: Adam and Co., 1886.

Hoerder, Dirk. *Cultures in Contact: World Migrations in the Second Millennium.* Durham, NC: Duke University Press, 2002.

Holquist, Peter. "The Russian Empire as 'Civilized State': International Law as Principle and Practice in Imperial Russia, 1874–1878" (July 14, 2004), http://www.ucis.pitt.edu/nceeer/2004_818-06g_Holquist.pdf.

Höpken, Wolfgang. "Flucht vor dem Kreuz? Muslimische Emigration aus Südosteuropa nach dem Ende der osmanischen Herrschaft (19./20. Jahrhundert)." *Comparativ* 1 (1996).

Horowitz, Donald. *The Deadly Ethnic Riot.* Berkley: University of California Press, 2001.

Hughes, Lindsey. *Peter the Great: A Biography.* New Haven, CT: Yale University Press, 2002.
———. *Russia in the Age of Peter the Great.* New Haven, CT: Yale University Press, 1998.
Hutton, Patrick H. "The Art of Memory Reconceived: From Rhetoric to Psychoanalysis." *Journal of the History of Ideas* 48, no. 3 (July–September 1987).
Huyshe, Wentworth. *The Liberation of Bulgaria: War Notes in 1877.* London: Bliss, Sands and Foster, 1894.
İpek, Nedim. *Rumeli'den Anadolu'ya Türk Göçleri.* Ankara: Türk Tarih Kurumu Basımevi, 1994.
Irving, Montagu. *Camp and Studio.* London: W. H. Allen and Co., 1892.
Isci, Onur. "Wartime Propaganda and the Legacies of Defeat: The Russian and Ottoman Popular Presses in the War of 1877–78." MA thesis, Miami University, Oxford, Ohio, 2007.
Jelavic, Barbara. *Russia's Balkan Entanglements, 1806–1914.* Cambridge: Cambridge University Press, 1991.
Jelavic, Charles, and Barbara Jelavic. *The Establishment of the Balkan National States, 1804–1920.* Seattle: University of Washington Press, 1977.
Jireček, Konstantin. *Geschichte der Bulgaren.* Prague: F. Tempsky, 1876.
Jones, Gwyn. *A History of the Vikings.* New York: Oxford University Press, 1968.
Judah, Tim. *The Serbs: History, Myth and the Destruction of Yugoslavia.* New Haven, CT: Yale University Press, 2010.
Kaplan, Robert. *Balkan Ghosts: A Journey through History.* New York: Vintage Books, 1993.
Karpat, Kemal. *Ottoman Population, 1830–1914: Demographic and Social Characteristics.* Madison: University of Wisconsin Press, 1985.
———. *The Politicization of Islam: Reconstructing Identity, State, Faith, and Community in the Late Ottoman State.* Oxford: Oxford University Press, 2001.
———, ed. *The Turks of Bulgaria: The History, Culture and Political Fate of a Minority.* Istanbul: Isis Press, 1990.
Kasaba, Reşat. *A Moveable Empire: Ottoman Nomads, Migrants and Refugees.* Seattle: University of Washington Press, 2009.
Kazantzakis, Nikos. *Zorba the Greek.* New York: Simon and Schuster, 1952.
———. *Freedom and Death.* New York: Simon and Schuster, 1955.
Kemal, Namık. *Vatan Yahut Silestre.* Ankara: Dün-Bugün Yayın Evi, 1960.
Kenan, Orna. *Between Memory and History: The Evolution of Israeli Historiography of the Holocaust, 1945–1961.* New York: Peter Lang Publishing, 2003.
Keren, Zvi. *The Jews of Rusçuk: From Periphery to Capital of the Tuna Vilayeti.* Istanbul: Isis Press, 2011.
Kiel, Machiel. *Art and Society of Bulgaria in the Turkish Period.* Maastricht, Netherlands: Van Gorcum, 1985.
———. *Studies on the Ottoman Architecture of the Balkans.* Brookfield, VT: Variorum Publishing Group, 1990.
Kiper, Nilgün. "Resettlement of Immigrants and Planning in Izmir in the Hamidian Period." PhD dissertation, Graduate School of Engineering and Sciences of Izmir Institute of Technology, 2006.

Klein, Kerwin Lee. "On the Emergence of Memory in Historical Discourse." *Representations* 69 (Winter 2000). Special Issue: Grounds for Remembering.
Knobler, Adam. "Holy Wars, Empires, and the Portability of the Past: The Modern Uses of Medieval Crusades." *Comparative Studies in Society and History* 48, no. 2 (April 2006).
Kocamemi, Fazil Bülent. *Urumeli'nin Gözyaşları*. Istanbul: İskeneriye Yayınları, 2009.
Kohn, Hans. *Pan-Slavism: Its History and Ideology*. New York: Vintage Books, 1960.
Koloğlu, Orhan. *Abdülhamid Gerçeği*. Istanbul: Gür Yayınları, 1987.
Konstantinov, Aleko. *Bai Ganyo: Incredible Tales of a Modern Bulgarian* (1895). Madison: University of Wisconsin Press, 2010.
Krasteva, Anna, ed. *Communities and Identities in Bulgaria*. Ravenna, Italy: Longo Editore, 1998.
Kundera, Milan. *The Book of Laughter and Forgetting*. Trans. M. H. Heim. Markham, Ontario: Penguin, 1986.
Kuneralp, Sinan, ed. *The Queen's Ambassador to the Sultan: Memoirs of Sir Henry A. Layard's Constantinople Embassy, 1877–78*. Istanbul: Isis Press, 2009.
Kuntay, Mithat Cemal. *Üç İstanbul*. Istanbul: Oğlak Yayıncılık ve Reklamcılık, 2012.
Landau, Jacob. *Pan-Turkism: From Irredentism to Cooperation*. Bloomington: Indiana University Press, 1995.
Lane-Poole, Stanley. *The Moors in Spain*. New York: G. P. Putnam's Sons, 1886.
Layard, Mary. "Lady Layard's Journal." February 4, 1878. https://pops.baylor.edu/layard/xml.php?fn=18780204.xml.
Lewis, Bernard. *History: Remembered, Recovered, Invented*. Princeton, NJ: Princeton University Press, 1975.
———. *Islam et laïcité: la naissance de la Turquie modern*. Paris: Fayard, 1988.
———. *The Multiple Identities of the Middle East*. New York: Schocken Books, 1998.
Lewis, Geoffrey. *The Turkish Language Reform: A Catastrophic Success*. Oxford: Oxford University Press, 2002.
Lieberman, Benjamin. *Terrible Fate: Ethnic Cleansing in the Making of Modern Europe*. Chicago: Ivan R. Dee, 2006.
Lory, Bernard. *Le sort de l'héritage ottoman en Bulgarie: L'Exemple des villes bulgares*. Istanbul: Isis Editions, 1985.
MacDermott, Mercia. *A History of Bulgaria: 1393–1885*. London: George Allen and Unwin, 1962.
Malkki, Liisa H. *Purity and Exile: Violence, Memory, and National Cosmology among Hutu Refugees in Tanzania*. Chicago: University of Chicago Press, 1995.
Mansel, Philip. *Constantinople: City of the World's Desire, 1453–1924*. London: John Murray Publishers, 1995.
Marcotti, Giuseppe. *Tre mesi in Oriente: Ricordi di viaggio e di guerra*. Florence: Tipografia Editrice della Gazzetta d'Italia, 1878.
Martner, C. *Emploi des chemins de fer pendant la guerre d'Orient, 1876–1878*. Paris: Librairie Militaire de J. Dumaine, 1878.
Marushiakova, Elena, and Vesselin Popov. *Gypsies in the Ottoman Empire*. Hatfield, UK: University of Hertfordshire Press, 2001.
Maude, Aylmer. *The Life of Tolstoy: Later Years*. New York: Dodd, Mead and Company, 1911.

Mazower, Mark. *The Balkans: From the End of Byzantium to the Present Day*. London: Phoenix Press, 2000.
———. *Salonica, City of Ghosts: Christians, Muslims and Jews 1430–1950*. New York: Random House, 2006.
McArthur, Sarah. "Being European: Russian Travel Writing and the Balkans, 1804–1877." PhD dissertation, University College London, School of Slavonic and East European Studies, 2010.
McCarthy, Justin. *Death and Exile: The Ethnic Cleansing of Ottoman Muslims, 1821–1922*. Princeton, NJ: Darwin Press, 1995.
———. "Muslims in Ottoman Europe: Population from 1800–1912." *Nationalities Papers* 28, no. 1 (2000).
Meyendorff, John. *Byzantium and the Rise of Russia*. Crestwood, NY: Saint Vladimir's Seminary Press, 1989.
Mill, John. *The Ottomans in Europe; or, Turkey in the Present Crisis, with the Secret Societies' Maps*. London: Weldon and Co., 1876.
Millman, Richard. "The Bulgarian Massacres Reconsidered." *Slavonic and East European Review* 58, no. 2 (April 1980).
Moczar, Diane. *Islam at the Gates: How Christendom Defeated the Ottoman Turks*. Manchester, NH: Sophia Institute Press, 2008.
Mordtmann, Dr., Dr. Gabuzzi, and Dr. Stécouli. *Les réfugiés de la Roumelie en 1878: Rapport présenté au Conseil International de Santé*. Constantinople: Typographie et Lithographie Centrales, 1879.
Nabokov, Vladimir. *Speak, Memory: A Memoir.* London: Gollancz, 1951.
Neuburger, Mary. *The Orient Within: Muslim Minorities and the Negotiation of Nationhood in Modern Bulgaria*. Ithaca, NY: Cornell University Press, 2004.
———. "The Russo-Turkish War and the 'Eastern Jewish Question': Encounters between Victims and Victors in Ottoman Bulgaria, 1877–78." *Eastern European Jewish Affairs* 26, no. 2 (1996).
Nicolle, David. *Cross and Crescent: The Ottoman Conquest of Southeastern Europe*. Barnsley, UK: Sword and Pen, 2010.
Nietzsche, Friedrich. "On the Use and Abuse of History for Life" (1874). Translated by Ian Johnston (2010). http://johnstoniatexts.x10host.com/nietzsche/historyhtml.html.
Nikitin, S. A. "Russia and the Liberation of Bulgaria." *Soviet Studies in History* 20, no. 4 (Spring 1982).
Norris, H. T. *Islam in the Balkans: Religion and Society between Europe and the Arab World*. Columbia: University of South Carolina Press, 1993.
Olick, Jeffrey. *States of Memory: Continuities, Conflicts, and Transformations in National Retrospection*. Durham, NC: Duke University Press, 2003.
Ollier, Edmund. *Cassel's Illustrated History of the Russo-Turkish War*. London: Sell and Company, 1877–1879.
Onur, Isci. "Wartime Propaganda and the Legacies of Defeat: The Russian and Ottoman Popular Presses in the War of 1877–78." MA thesis, Miami University, Department of History, 2007.
Örenç, Ali Fuat. *Balkanlarda İlk Dram: Unuttuğumuz Mora Türkleri ve Eyaletten Bağımsızlığa Yunanistan*. Istanbul: Babıali Kültür Yayıncılığı, 2009.
Orwell, George. "Notes on Nationalism." *Polemic* (October 1945).

———. *1984*. San Diego: Harcourt Brace Jovanovich, 1984.
Ostrowski, Donald. "'Moscow the Third Rome' as Historical Ghost." In *Byzantium: Faith and Power (1261–1557): Perspectives on Late Byzantine Art and Culture*, edited by Sarah T. Brooks. 170–79. New York: Metropolitan Museum of Art, 2014.
Ovsianyi, N. R. *Russkoe Upravlenie v Bolgarii v 1877–78–79 gg*. 3 volumes. St. Petersburg: Voenno-Istoricheskaia Komissiia Glavnago Shtaba, 1906.
Özcelik, Tarık. "Basiret Gazetesi'ne Göre Doksanüç İstanbul'da Rumeli Göçmenleri (1877–1878)." M.A. thesis, Marmara Üniversitesi, Istanbul, 1993.
Özdoğan, Günay Göksu and Kemali Saybasili, eds. *Balkans: A Mirror of the New International Order*. Istanbul: Eren Yaymcilik, 1995.
Özkan, Behlül. *From the Abode of Islam to the Turkish Homeland in Turkey*. New Haven CT: Yale University Press, 2012.
Özyürek, Esra, ed. *The Politics of Public Memory in Turkey*. Syracuse, NY: Syracuse University Press, 2007.
Page, Joseph. *The Brazilians*. Boston: Da Capo Press, 1996.
Palmer, Alan. *The Decline and Fall of the Ottoman Empire*. London: Faber and Faber, 1992.
Pejoska-Bouchereau, Frosa, ed. "L'Image de la période Ottomane dans les littératures balkaniques." *Cahiers Balkaniques* 36–37. Paris: Publications Langues INALCO, 2007–2008.
Pennebaker, James, ed. *Collective Memory of Political Events: Social Psychological Perspectives*. New York: Psychology Press, 1997.
Peters, Rudolph, ed. *Proceedings of the Ninth Congress of the Union Européene des arabisants et islamisants, Amsterdam, 1st to 7th September 1978*. Leiden: E. J. Brill, 1981.
Pinson, Mark. "Ottoman Bulgaria in the First Tanzimat Period: The Revolts in Nish (1841) and Vidin (1850)." *Middle Eastern Studies* 11, no. 2 (May 1975).
Polushkin, S. P. *Dnevnik Donskogo Kazaka*. Saint Petersburg: Tipografiia A. M. Kotomina u Obukhovskago Mosta, 1880.
Popovic, Alexandre. "Les turcs de Bulgarie, 1878–1985: Une experience des nationalités dans le monde communiste." *Cahiers du Monde Russe et Soviétique* 27, no. 3/4 (July–December 1986).
———. "Représentation du passé et transmission de l'identité chez les musulmans: Mythes et réalités." In *Les Balkans à l'époque ottoman*, ed. Danziel Panzac, 139–44. Aix-en-Provence: Éditions Edisud, 1992.
Poulton, Hugh. *Top Hat, Grey Wolf, and the Crescent: Turkish Nationalism and the Turkish Republic*. Washington Square, NY: New York University Press, 1997.
Qureshi, Emran, and Michael A. Sells, eds. *The New Crusades: Constructing the Muslim Enemy*. New York: Columbia University Press, 2003.
Raci, Hüseyin Efendi. *Zağra Müftüsünün Hatıraları: Tarihçe-i Vak'a-i Zağra*. Istanbul: Iz Yayıncılık, 2009.
Reid, Anna. *Borderland: A Journey through the History of Ukraine*. New York: Basic Books, 2000.
Reid, James. *Crisis of the Ottoman Empire: Prelude to Collapse, 1839–1878*. Stuttgart: Franz Steiner Verlag, 2000.
Reinach, Josephe. *Voyage en Orient: Les premières stations, le Danube, le Bosphore*. Paris: G. Charpentier, 1879.

Revel, Jacques, and Giovanni Levi, eds. *Political Uses of the Past: The Recent Mediterranean Experience*. Portland, OR: Frank Cass, 2002.
Richmond, Walter. *The Circassian Genocide*. New Brunswick, NJ: Rutgers University Press, 2013.
Rodogno, Davide. *Against Massacre: Humanitarian Interventions in the Ottoman Empire, 1815–1914, the Emergence of a European Concept and International Practice*. Princeton, NJ: Princeton University Press, 2012.
Roy, Olivier. *The New Central Asia: Geopolitics and the Birth of Nations*. New York: New York University Press, 2007.
Runciman, Steven. *The Great Church in Captivity*. Cambridge: Cambridge University Press, 1968.
———. *A History of the First Bulgarian Empire*. London: G. Bell and Sons, 1930.
Saab, Ann Pottinger. *Reluctant Icon: Gladstone, Bulgaria and the Working Classes, 1856–1878*. Cambridge, MA: Harvard University Press, 1991.
Şahin, Turhan. *Öncesiyle ve Sonrasıyla 93 Harbi*. Ankara: Kültür ve Turizm Bakanlığı Dizisi, 1988.
Sahni, Kalpana. *Crucifying the Orient: Russian Orientalism and the Colonization of Caucasus and Central Asia*. Oslo: White Orchid Press, 1997.
Said, Edward. *Orientalism*. New York: Vintage Books, 1979.
Schem, Alexander Jacob. *The War in the East: An Illustrated History of the Conflict between Russia and Turkey, with a Review of the Eastern Question*. New York: H. S. Goodspeed, 1878.
Schevill, Ferdinand, *The History of the Balkan Peninsula, from the Earliest Times to the Present Day*. New York: Harcourt, Brace and Co. 1922.
Schimmelpink van dere Oye, David. *Russian Orientalism: Asia in the Russian Mind from Peter the Great to the Emigration*. New Haven, CT: Yale University Press, 2010.
Schwartz, Barry, "The Social Context of Commemoration: A Study in Social Memory." *Social Forces* 61, no. 2 (December 1982).
Seegel, Steven J. "Virtual War, Virtual Journalism?: Russian Media Responses to 'Balkan' Entanglements in Historical Perspective, 1877–2001." Kokkalis Workshop Paper, Brown University, February 2002, Center for European Studies/Kennedy School.
Şeker, Nesim. "Identity Formation and the Political Power in the Late Ottoman Empire and Early Republic." *Haol* 8 (Autumn 2005).
Semelin, Jacques. *Purify and Destroy: The Political Uses of Massacre and Genocide*. New York: Columbia University Press, 2007.
Sharpey-Schafer, Joyce A. *Soldier of Fortune: F. D. Millet, 1846–1912*. Utica, NY: n.p., 1984.
Shaw, Stanford, and Ezel Kural Shaw. *History of the Ottoman Empire and Modern Turkey: Volume 2, Reform, Revolution, and Republic: The Rise of Modern Turkey, 1808–1975*. Cambridge: Cambridge University Press, 1977.
Shirinian, Lorne. *Writing Memory: The Search for Home in Armenian Diaspora Literature as a Cultural Practice*. Ontario, Canada: Blue Heron Press, 2000.
Siberry, Elizabeth. *The New Crusaders: Images of the Crusades in the 19th and Early 20th Centuries*. Burlington, VT: Ashgate Publishing, 2000.
Şimşir, Bilal. *Rumeli'den Türk Göçmenler*. 3 vols. Ankara: Türk Kültürünü Araştırma Enstitüsü, 1970.

Stafford House Committee for the Relief of Sick and Wounded Turkish Soldiers. *Report and Record of the Operations of the Stafford House Committee for the Relief of Sick and Wounded Turkish Soldiers: Russo-Turkish War, 1877–78*. London: Spottisoode and Co., 1879.
Stavrianos, L. S. *The Balkans since 1453*. New York: Holt, Rinehart and Winston, 1958.
Stiglmayer, Alexandra. *Mass Rape: The War against Women in Bosnia-Herzegovina*. Lincoln: University of Nebraska Press, 1994.
Stoker, Bram. *Dracula*. New York: Dover Publications, 2000.
Strand, Mark. *The Continuous Life: Poems*. New York: Knopf, 1990.
Taki, Victor. "Orientalism on the Margins: The Ottoman Empire under Russian Eyes." *Kritika: Explorations in Russian and Eurasian History* 12, no. 2 (Spring 2011).
Te Aroha News 6, no. 312 (October 31, 1888).
Tekeli, Ilhan, "Involuntary Displacement and the Problem of Resettlement in Turkey from the Ottoman Empire to the Present." *Special Issue: Population Displacement and Resettlement: Development and Conflict in the Middle East*. New York: Center for Migration Studies, 1994.
Todorova, Maria. "The Balkans from Discovery to Invention." *Slavic Review* 53, no. 2 (Summer 1994).
———. *Imagining the Balkans*. Oxford: Oxford University Press, 1997.
———. "The Ottoman Legacy in the Balkans." In *Imperial Legacy: The Ottoman Imprint on the Balkans and the Middle East*, edited by Carl Brown, 45–77. New York: Columbia University Press, 1996
Tolstoy, Leo. *Hadji Murad*. New York: Modern Library, 2003.
———. *Anna Karenina*. New York: Thomas Y. Crowell Company Publishers, 1886.
Tomić, Olga Mišeska. *Balkan Sprachbund Morpho-syntactic Features*, Studies in Natural Language and Linguistic Theory 67. Dordrecht, Germany: Springer, 2006.
Torunoğlu, Berke. *Murder in Salonika, 1876: A Tale of Apostasy and International Crisis*. Istanbul: Libra Kitapçılık ve Yayıncılık, 2012.
Toumarkine, Alexandre. *Les migrations des populations musulmanes balkaniques en Anatolie (1876–1913)*. Istanbul: Les Éditions Isis, 1995.
Trumpbour, John. "The Clash of Civilizations: Samuel P. Huntington, Bernard Lewis, and the Remaking of the Post-Cold War World Order." In *The New Crusades* edited by Emran Qureshia and Michael A. Sells, 88–130. New York: Columbia University Press, 2003.
Turan, Ömer. "Raporlarda 1878 Türk-Pomak Direnişi ve Rodop Komisyonu Raporu." *Türk Kültürü Araştırmalrı* 34 (1996).
———. *Rodop Türkleri'nin 1878 Direnişi*. Ankara: Mavi Ofset Matbaacılık San, 1998.
Turkey, No. 42: Further Correspondence Respecting the Affairs of Turkey. London: Harrison and Sons, 1878.
Turkey, No. 45: Further Correspondence Respecting the Affairs of Turkey. London: Harrison and Sons, 1878.
Turkey, No. 49: Correspondence Respecting the Proceedings of the International Commission Sent to the Mount Rhodope District. London: Harrison and Sons, 1878.
Valéry, Paul. *Collected Works Volume 10. History and Politics*. New York: Pantheon Books, 1962.
Vazov, Ivan. *Bulgarian Short Stories*. Sofia: Sofia Press, 1950.

———. *Selected Short Stories*. Sofia: Sofia Foreign Language Press, 1967.
———. *Under the Yoke*. New York: Twayne Publishers, 1971.
Vemund, Aarbakke, Vassilis Koutsoukos, and Niarchos Georgios. "The Tamrash Rebellion (1878–1886)." Paper presented at Keni International Conference "Revolutions in the Balkans" Athens, Greece, October 31, 2013.
Vereshchagin, Alexander. *At Home and in War: 1853–1881*. New York: Thomas Y Crowell and Co., 1888.
Volf, Miroslav. *The End of Memory: Remembering Rightly in a Violent World*. Grand Rapids, MI: Eerdmans, 2006.
Voltaire. *Oeuvres complètes de Voltaire: Correspondance avec le Roi de Prusse*. Vol. 4. Brussels: Ode et Wodon, 1828.
Washburn, George. *Fifty Years in Constantinople and Recollections of Robert College*. Boston: Houghton Mifflin Company, 1909.
Wasti, Syed Tanvir. "1912–1913 Balkan Wars and the Siege of Edirne." *Middle Eastern Studies* 40, no. 4 (July 2004).
Wheatcroft, Andrew. *The Ottomans: Dissolving Images*. London: Penguin Books, 1995.
Yavuz, M. Hakan, *Islamic Political Identity in Turkey*. Oxford: Oxford University Press, 2005.
———. "Turkish Identity and Foreign Policy in Flux: The Rise of Neo-Ottomanism." *Critique: Critical Middle Eastern Studies* 7, no. 12 (Spring 1998).
———, ed. *War & Diplomacy: The Russo-Turkish War of 1877–1878 and the Treaty of Berlin*. Salt Lake City: University of Utah Press, 2011.
Yaz, Nadir. *Ağlayan Batı Trakya*. Istanbul: Yeni Batı Trakya Dergisi, 1986.
Yenisoy, Hayriye Süleymanoğlu. *Edebiyatımızda Balkan Türklerin Göç Kaderi*. Ankara: Toplumsal Gelişim Derneği, 2005.
Zeldin, Jesse. *Poems and Political Letters of F. I. Tyutchev*. Knoxville: University of Tennessee Press, 1973.
Zetler, Reyhan. "Turkish Jews between 1923–1933: What Did the Turkish Policy between 1923 and 1933 Mean for the Turkish Jews?" *Bulletin der Schweizerischen Gesellschaft für Judaistische Forschung* 23 (2014).
Zürcher, Erik Jan. *The Young Turk Legacy and Nation Building: From the Ottoman Empire to Atatürk's Turkey*. London: I. B. Tauris, 2010.

INDEX

Page numbers in *italics* refer to images.